extreme journey

get more out of it.

extreme journey

get more out of it.

Unless otherwise indicated, all Scripture quotations are from The Contemporary English Version (CEV), copyright © 1995 by the American Bible Society. Used by Permission.

Verses marked "NKJV" are taken from the New King James Version, copyright © 1982 by Thomas Nelson, Inc.

The Scripture quotations contained herein from the New Revised Standard Version (NRSV) of the Bible are copyright © 1989 by the Division of Christian Education of the National Council of Churches of Christ in the United States of America, and are used by permission. All rights reserved.

Verses marked "RSV" are taken from the Holy Bible: Revised Standard Version, second edition, copyright © 1978 by the New York International Bible Society.

Scripture quotations marked "NLT" are taken from the Holy Bible, New Living Translation, copyright © 1996. Used by permission of Tyndale House Publishers, Inc., Wheaton, Illinois 60189. All rights reserved.

Developed and produced with the assistance of The Livingstone Corporation. Project staff includes: Katie E. Gieser, Christopher D. Hudson, Betsy Schmitt, Joan Woodhead, Tim Baker, Carol Smith, and C.J. Watson.

Brand Manager: Hayley Morgan

Editors: Kate Etue and Gillian Taaffe

Interior design by Mozdren and Associates, St. Charles, IL.

Typesetting by Andrea Reider.

Library of Congress Cataloging-in-Publication Data
    Extreme Journey
        p.   cm.
    ISBN 0-7852-4595-2
    1. Bible-Introductions. I. Thomas Nelson Publishers
BS475.3 .E98   2001   220.6'1—dc21

Printed in the United States of America
1 2 3 4 5 6 — 05 04 03 02 01

Contents

Author's Preface

Welcome to *Extreme Journey*.

When I have a choice, I don't venture into unfamiliar territory without taking some kind of guidebook or map—usually one or more of both. At the moment, my family is about ready to go on a two-week vacation to places we've never been. You'd need a yardstick to measure the pile of travel guides, brochures, maps, and travel articles we've collected in getting ready for the trip.

Why such bother? We want to get the most out of our experience. We want to see everything worth seeing and do everything worth doing—that is, everything within the energy level and bank account of a Ford-driving, middle-aged man.

For the masses of people who've never read the Bible, cracking it open and getting started can be a daunting challenge. It's one huge book. Where do you begin?

How about starting with the big picture? Scan the biggest scenes of the Bible. Introduce yourself to some of the starring characters. Familiarize yourself with the terrain. That done, turn to individual books within the Bible and do the same.

We've created Extreme Journey to help Bible newcomers do just that. For the millions of people still unfamiliar with the world's all-time best-seller, we've provided a guidebook. Actually, it's perhaps more like the printed program you'd get before watching a play. It will help you get your bearings as you sit back and begin to enjoy one of the most wonderful journeys you'll ever take—a journey into the mind and heart of God.

A few friends.

I'd like to express my deep gratitude to the following people:

- Linda Annalisa Miller, my wife, frontline proofreader, articulate critic, persistent encourager.
- Joseph Coleson, gentle spirit, Old Testament professor at Nazarene Theological Seminary, and one of 90 scholars who produced the New Living Translation. He offered me his Old Testament insights. And I gladly, quickly snatched them up and included them in this book.
- Mark E. Roberts, editor, and a doctoral candidate in New Testament studies. He guided this project down its circuitous path to publication, and provided New Testament background that I would have otherwise missed.
- Lee Hollaway, contract editor turned reference editor, who handled the nuts and bolts of making the various elements of this book fit together.

God bless them, every one.

And God bless you as you read this book, and more importantly as you read His Book.

Steve Miller

How To Use This Book

As you turn the pages of this book, here's what you'll find, and why.

- **How We Got Our Bible**. This is a fast-paced article that traces the story of the Bible from the days before it was written—when eyewitnesses told astonished listeners what they saw—to the computer age, when we can again see video recreations of the Bible events. It's astonishing to discover how God has preserved his message throughout the ages.
- **Genesis through Revelation**. From the first Bible book to the last, you'll get a thorough preview preparing you to read each book for all it's worth.
  - **Quotables** from each book—quotes you've probably heard, but never knew where they came from.
  - **Starring Roles**, briefly identifying each of the main characters in the book.
  - **What to Look For**, pointing out insights you might otherwise zoom right past.
  - **Stage Directions**, helping you picture where the book fits into other events going on in the Bible lands and beyond.
  - **Inside Scoop**, intriguing nuggets of information about each book.
  - **Author and Date,** evidence about who wrote the book and when. (Most Bible books were written anonymously, but clues in the text and in other ancient writings often suggest possible writers.)
  - **On Location,** maps of key sites.
  - **Director's Notes,** brief facts that give additional insight into the time and place where the Bible events take place.
  - **Extreme Scenes**—the heart of *Extreme Journey* — quickly acquaints you with the main events and teachings in each book, using illustrations and captions.
  - **Interviews with the Stars,** experience a first-hand interaction with the characters made famous through the Bible. Witness their joys and triumphs, sorrows and disappointments.
  - **Reviews,** a section that lets you listen in on what the critics are saying about the book. You encounter both affirmations and challenging perspectives.
  - **Related Productions**, pointing you to related books in the Bible. If you like the book of Ruth, for example, you'll also enjoy the dramatic story of another heroine: Esther.

Getting Started

You don't have to read this book from cover to cover before opening your Bible. Our hope is that you'll read the two together.

There are dozens of Bible translations you can choose from. Or you might select one of the paraphrases of the Bible, which seek to convey the key ideas in the Scripture without sticking to the Hebrew or Greek words used in the passage. A few versions deliberately choose to use only a limited vocabulary to tell the Bible's story. We especially like the Contemporary English Version because of its readability and accurate translation. In fact, unless we indicate otherwise, it's the version we use throughout *Extreme Journey*.

One tip about looking up Bible references. If you see "John 3:16," for example, John is the name of the book, and 3:16 means chapter 3, verse 16.

One warning—but a happy one. It's a bit like the warning my wife and I got before we started our family. Our parents told us that having children would radically change the way we live, but that we would never regret the changes. They were ever so right. Our daily schedule is nothing like it once was, but our joy is rich beyond expression. There are times when I put my arms around each one of my children and tell them how happy I am that they have become a part of my life.

My warning to you about the Bible is much the same. Reading and learning about what God wants to say to you through the Bible can change your life forever, but you will never regret the changes. After living with them daily for many years, the words of God continue to change my life and fill it with joy. I believe they can do the same for you.

How We Got Our Bible

Here's the short version of how we got the Bible—and why: "All Scripture is inspired by God and is useful to teach us what is true and to make us realize what is wrong in our lives" (2 Timothy 3:16, New Living Translation).

Paul wrote this right before his death. Initially, he was referring to Jewish Scripture (what Christians consider the Old Testament) since the New Testament was not finished yet. But Christians believe that Paul's words apply equally to the 27 books of the New Testament, which revolve around the life and teachings of God's Son.

Exactly how God "inspired" the many biblical writers remains a mystery—as well as a source of hot debate. But all Christians who believe that the Bible is God's revelation to the human race agree on one rock-solid point: God had his hand in the more-than-millennium-long process, from beginning to end. He personally saw to it that humans got the message he wanted to deliver.

In the beginning, stories about God probably were passed on by word of mouth long before they were written onto clay slabs or tanned sheepskin. In ancient times, gifted storytellers preserved and passed along the community's tradition and history. Listeners became familiar with the stories and typically refused to allow storytellers to skip or add material—much like children today carefully supervise the familiar stories that their parents read to them.

The Writing Begins

No one knows when the first Hebrew put pen to parchment, or should we say, stylus to clay. Moses is the first person the Bible identifies as a writer. Perhaps as early as the 1400s BC, Moses wrote down the many laws God gave him—probably those preserved in the books of Exodus, Leviticus, Numbers, and Deuteronomy (Deuteronomy 31:9). But hundreds of years before Moses, Abraham, the father of the Jewish nation, may have written the dramatic stories about his life that are recorded in Genesis. He came from the Persian Gulf region where writing was already at least 1000 years old.

Most of the rest of the Old Testament—stories, poems, songs, genealogies, nuggets of wisdom, prophecies, and all the other genres of Hebrew tradition—was likely passed along orally, then eventually collected and recorded by scribes. The writing probably began in earnest after Israel established itself as a powerful nation, during the reigns of David and Solomon in about 1000 BC. As scrolls began to wear out, scribes carefully duplicated the text onto fresh scrolls.

Exactly who wrote the Old Testament remains a mystery; most books don't say. The first five books of the Bible, for example, are anonymous. But ancient Jewish tradition says Moses wrote them. Some Bible authors, on the other hand, are clearly identified; many prophets wrote the books named after them.

All but a few sections of the Old Testament are written in Hebrew, the language of the Jews. A few passages are written in Aramaic, a similar language that the Jews picked up when they were exiled to Babylon. After twenty-some-year-old Alexander the Great swept through the Middle East in the early 300s BC, Greek became the prevailing language.

Within about a century, an Egyptian king decided to create a new holding for his renowned library in Alexandria. As legend has it, he asked the high priest in Jerusalem to loan him about 70 top scholars who would translate the five revered books of Moses into Greek. The result—the first Bible translation—became known as the Septuagint, meaning 70. Over the next hundred years or so, the rest of the Hebrew Bible was added. When New Testament writers later quoted the Old Testament, they quoted it from this Greek translation.

Rome destroyed Jerusalem in 70 AD, leaving the Jews with no temple for offering animal sacrifices. So the Jews began to offer sacrifices of praise and prayer by reading from their sacred writings. The problem was that the Jews had a wide array of revered books and many versions of some books. No one knows exactly how or when the Jews settled on the books that make up their Bible, which Christians call the Old Testament. The five books of Moses, known as the books of Law, were probably among the first ones widely accepted. The books of the prophets likely came next, followed last by books known as the Writings: Psalms, Proverbs, and others. Eventually eliminated—partly because they were not originally written in Hebrew— were many books published in the popular Greek translation. They were called the Apocrypha, meaning "secondary" or "hidden" works, and would later reappear in Roman Catholic and Eastern Orthodox Bibles.

⇒ The Late-Breaking Good News

The story of how we got the New Testament is quite similar, though the time line is fast-tracked. Instead of taking a thousand years or so for spoken stories to become writings and then widely revered, the process

OLD TESTAMENT

Law
Genesis
Exodus
Leviticus
Numbers
Deuteronomy

History
Joshua
Judges
Ruth
1 Samuel
2 Samuel
1 Kings
2 Kings
1 Chronicles
2 Chronicles
Ezra
Nehemiah
Esther

Poetry
Job
Psalms
Proverbs
Ecclesiastes
Song of Songs

Major Prophets
Isaiah
Jeremiah
Lamentations
Ezekiel
Daniel

Minor Prophets
Hosea
Joel
Amos
Obadiah
Jonah
Micah
Nahum

Habakkuk
Zephaniah
Haggai
Zechariah
Malachi

NEW TESTAMENT
Gospels
Matthew
Mark
Luke
John

History
Acts

Letters by Paul to Churches
Romans
1 Corinthians
2 Corinthians
Galatians
Ephesians

Philippians
Colossians
1 Thessalonians
2 Thessalonians

Letters by Paul to Individuals
1 Timothy
2 Timothy
Titus
Philemon

General Letters
Hebrews
James
1 Peter
2 Peter
1 John
2 John
3 John
Jude

Prophecy
Revelation

takes about a century for Christians. The earliest followers of Jesus didn't immediately write their stories, apparently because they expected Jesus to return soon. They urgently spread his teachings in person.

The first New Testament books were probably not written by Jesus' disciples, but by missionary-minded, circuit-preaching Paul. Scholars estimate that Paul's earliest letters of encouragement to young churches he had founded were written about 20 years after the death of Jesus. The rest of the New Testament was written throughout the remainder of the first century, roughly 50 to 100 AD.

Christians had long respected the Jewish Scriptures as God's Word. But they also recognized that the message of Jesus, contained in the Gospels and other writings, was an essential part of God's revelation to human beings. Christians, though, didn't formally agree on which books to include in the New Testament until after Marcion, a Christian leader in the early 100s AD, proposed a short list. His list included Paul's letters and Luke's gospel—all of which he had edited to reflect his belief that Jesus was not human and could not really suffer.

Over the next two centuries, Christians debated which books should be included. Many had been written, including about 60 of questionable content and authorship. By 367 AD, most church leaders agreed to accept as authoritative only the 27 books they believed were written by apostles—ministers who had actually seen Jesus, including the original disciples and Paul. The first known list of these books appears that year in the Easter letter that an Egyptian bishop, Athanasius, sent to his churches. He was the first on record to use the word canon—which originally meant "measure"—to describe the officially recognized books of the Bible. Church leaders decided that no other books should be added to the canon.

The Bible isn't one book, but a library of many books. Most Protestant Bibles have 66 books—39 in the Old Testament and 27 in the New—arranged in the order and categories shown here. Old Testament books by prophets, for example, appear together—starting with the Major Prophets (meaning the longer books), followed by the Minor Prophets.

This arrangement is different for some other Bible-believing faiths.

Roman Catholic and Eastern Orthodox Bibles include the Apocrypha, a collection of books that appeared in the Septuagint, a Greek translation made from the Hebrew Bible about 200 years before Christ. Jews, however, later decided against keeping these books in their Bible.

⋙ The Dangerous Art of Translation

Latin, the preferred language of Romans, eventually spread throughout the empire. Christian scholars began producing several Latin translations of the Jewish and Christian Scriptures. By 382, however, Pope Damasus decided the church needed a single, authoritative Latin translation. He assigned this arduous task to Jerome, a leading Bible scholar of the time.

Jerome knew Latin and Greek, but not very much Hebrew. He was determined to translate the Old Testament from the original Hebrew language, not from the Greek Septuagint. So he moved to a monastery in Bethlehem and learned Hebrew from Jewish scholars. More than 20 years after he began, his monumental translation was complete. It became known as the Vulgate, meaning "common," since he wrote it in the common language of the day.

BIBLE EVENTS

| Moses writes God's laws 1440 B.C. | David writes songs 1000 B.C. | Solomon writes wise sayings 950 B.C. | Jeremiah writes prophecy 600 B.C. | Old Testament translated into Greek 200 B.C. | New Testament written A.D. 100 | New Testament accepted as Scripture 367 |

1500 B.C. — **1000 B.C.** — **500 B.C.** — **A.D. 100**

WORLD EVENTS

| Canaanites create first alphabet (pictures used before) 1500 B.C. | Trojan War ends in sacking of Troy 1190 B.C. | David becomes king of Israel 1010 B.C. | Solomon dedicates first Jewish temple 960 B.C. | Confucius born 551 B.C. | Jews win independence 164 B.C. | Paper invented in China A.D.103 | Pagan temples closed in Roman Empire 354 |

At first, his translation met stiff resistance. After one congregation heard his version of Jonah read to them, instead of worshiping, they rioted. They preferred the earlier version they were used to hearing and memorizing.

Because language changes, updated versions can sometimes sound radically different from previous versions. To further complicate the process, it's not always clear how to interpret the ancient text. For example, ancient Hebrew had no vowels and no lowercase letters. If we wrote English that way, "once upon a time" would look like this: NC PN TM. But those same letters could also read "Nice pun, Tom." Ancient readers familiar with the story seemed to have little trouble reading it. Others had to look for context clues, which were plentiful. Solving the puzzle of one word gives you a clue about what the next word should be. When you put a lot of words together it's easier to figure out what the story is about.

At about the time Jerome was translating the Bible into Latin, a missionary named Ulfilas was inventing an alphabet for German tribes so he could translate the Bible into their Gothic language. This scene has been repeated throughout the world, throughout the ages.

ENGLISH BIBLES
A Sampler from Psalm 23

Readers today can choose from many Bible translations in modern English. To give you an idea of how they compare—and how they have changed over the centuries—here are excerpts from the most famous psalm in Scripture, a psalm often quoted in times of difficulty or read at funerals.

Wycliffe Bible, 1380s (first English Bible)   The Lord gouerneth [governs] me, and no thing shal faile to me; in the place of pasture there he hath set me.

King James Version, 1611   The Lord is my shepheard, I shall not want. He maketh me to lie down in greene pastures.

Jerome translates Bible into Latin 405	Caedmon, a monk puts parts of Bible to music 670		Wycliffe produces first English Bible 1384	Tyndale executed for translating Bible into English 1536	King James Version of Bible 1611	English Revised Version 1885	Dead Sea Scrolls discovered 1947	Revised Standard Version 1952

500   1000   1500   1900

Muhammad has vision, recorded in Koran 610	Crusades begin 1095	Eyeglasses invented 1300	Bubonic plague kills one-third of Europe 1348	Columbus sails for new world 1492	Shakespeare becomes a London playwright 1592	Puritans land on Plymouth Rock 1620	Mark Twain writes Huckleberry Finn 1884

As Christianity grew, so did the number of Bible translations. Most Bibles were too expensive for common people, because it took months of work to copy them. In the 1300s a Bible could easily cost a priest a year's salary. This changed dramatically in about 1456, when the Bible was first printed with movable type. By the end of that century, printers were busy in more than 250 European towns, publishing a wide variety of Bible editions.

Surprisingly, Christian church leaders resisted the notion of translating God's Word into everyday language. The prevailing opinion was that people should get their teaching from ministers, not the Bible—because it was thought most people were not capable of traveling through God's Word without a spiritual guide. Oxford scholar John Wycliffe became viewed as a heretic for creating the first English Bible—which was banned in England. He died before anyone killed him, but 43 years later church leaders dug up his remains, burned them, and threw the ashes into a river. William Tyndale produced an improved English translation in the early 1500s. For this, he was publicly strangled with a rope and his body burned. His dying words were, "Lord, open the King of England's eyes." Within two years the king ordered English Bibles placed in every church.

New International Version, 1973	The Lord is my shepherd, I shall not be in want. He makes me lie down in green pastures.
New King James Version, 1982	The Lord is my shepherd; I shall not want. He makes me to lie down in green pastures.
Contemporary English Version, 1995	You, Lord, are my shepherd. I will never be in need. You let me rest in fields of green grass.
New Living Translation, 1996	The Lord is my shepherd; I have everything I need. He lets me rest in green meadows.

The most famous English Bible of all time is the King James Version, known in England as the Authorized Version. It remained the principal Bible of English-speaking Protestants for some 300 years, beginning with the time of Shakespeare. In 1611 the translation was presented to King James of England, who had commissioned about 50 of England's foremost scholars to produce it. Working at Oxford, Cambridge, and Westminster, they completed the task in about seven years.

Then, as now, people resisted change. It took 40 years for the public to warm up to this new version and accept it as a replacement for the Geneva Bible, which was translated 50 years earlier and was used by the American Puritans.

⇒ Bibles Today

Since King James commissioned his masterpiece translation, archaeologists have unearthed Bible manuscripts much older than the ones that his translators used—up to a thousand years older. For example,

some Old Testament texts from the renowned Dead Sea Scrolls, a library cache preserved in dry caves near Israel's Dead Sea, date as far back as about 200 years before Christ. Variation in the Scripture is surprisingly minor—a tribute to the care taken by copyists.

So far, none of the original Bible manuscripts have surfaced. But translators today make good use of the ever-emerging ancient texts, linking them with cutting-edge technology. To piece together brittle and broken fragments of leather scrolls, for example, some scientists are using DNA testing to determine what sections belong together.

Today there are countless millions, perhaps a billion or more, Bibles in homes throughout the world. At the moment, at least parts of the Bible have been translated into about 2,200 languages from Abau in Papua, New Guinea to Zulgo in the Cameroon. Surveys report that in the United States nine out of ten homes have at least one Bible—and the average home has about six. These are just the printed Bibles. People can now choose from a staggering array of ancient and new Bible translations on computer, via electronic disks, online services, and the Internet. People can also listen to narrated tapes of Scripture.

For children, there are Bible stories in comic book style and other age-tailored editions. And for kids who would never consider curling up with the Good Book, there are Bible story cartoons and dramas, and even interactive Bible video games.

Adults, too, can choose Bibles targeting their interests. There are storybook Bibles for parents to read to their children, and devotional Bibles with inspiring articles for singles. Readers interested in studying the cultural background of each Bible passage can buy thick volumes such as the Nelson Study Bible, with 15,000 expository study notes based on the latest scholarship. The less scholarly, yet equally inquiring, can turn to the Word In Life Study Bible, designed for today's media-smart reader. In addition to in-text maps and charts, this edition contains hundreds of articles and features, including information on occupations in the Bible, geography and culture, and personality profiles.

The Bible has been the world's best-selling book since Johannes Gutenberg invented the printing press 550 years ago. With modern publishers producing niche editions that meet the spiritual needs of even the narrowest segments of the market, the Bible is likely one of the best-read as well.

➢ Using the Bible at swearing-in ceremonies grew out of the ancient Jewish practice of making a promise and reminding each other that "God is watching" (Genesis 31:50). In the Middle Ages, Christians swore by kissing or touching a cross, a Bible, or a sacred object they believed once belonged to a holy person.

➢ The oldest Bible text is a Dead Sea Scroll fragment written in about 225 BC. It's from one of the Old Testament books of Samuel.

➢ The oldest surviving New Testament text is a fragment of John 18:31-33, which includes Pilate's question to Jesus: "Are you the king of the Jews?" The fragment dates to about 125 AD, roughly one generation after the original was written.

➢ Bible typos produced dubious nicknames for some editions. "The Adulterer's Bible," also called "the Wicked Bible," dropped an all-important "not" and commands "Thou shalt commit adultery." The printer was fined a hefty sum.

➢ Bizarre translations of key words spawned Bible nicknames. "The Bug Bible" (more respectfully known as Coverdale's Bible, 1535) encouraged its readers not to be afraid of "bugs by night." The King James Version later replaced "bugs" with "terror."

➢ The word "Bible" comes from a Greek word for papyrus (biblos), a plant used to make paper.

➢ "Gospel" comes from the old English word godspell. English scholars used it to translate the Greek word euangelion, which means "good news" and from which we get the word evangelist.

➢ The most widely translated Bible book is the Gospel of Mark—the shortest of the four Gospels about Jesus. It's available in about 900 languages.

➢ Christians were among the first people to discard the 3,000-year-old tradition of using scrolls. They adopted the codex, or book format. Every surviving fragment of Christian writing from the second century comes from books. But only 14 of 870 non-Christian works of that time are from books. Books, printed on front and back, were cheaper and easier to use.

➢ After Johannes Gutenberg of Germany invented the printing press in the mid-1400s, the first book printed was the Bible. The first press run, of about 180 copies, sold out before the presses started. Forty-eight copies of this masterpiece survive.

➢ The Bible didn't originally have chapters and verses. Scholars added chapters in 1231 and verses in 1551.

Genesis

SCHEDULE OF SCENES

Adam	Abraham	Joseph dies	Moses	David	Ezra	Jesus is Born
4000+ B.C.	2100 B.C.	2100 B.C.	1500 B.C.	1000 B.C.	450 B.C.	7/6 B.C.

Where it all began...

Ever spend an all-night gabfest with your buds tackling the really *BIG* questions: Who am I? Where did I come from? Why am I here? Looking for *real* answers? Looking for the Truth with a capital T? It's simple, really. Just start at the very beginning, Genesis. That's what this word means in ancient Greek: beginning, the start of it all, the source, the origin, Creation. That's what Genesis is all about—the beginning of the universe, the world, the human race, sin, the Jewish nation. Here we watch God breathe life into man and woman; sail with Noah during the Flood; stand with mouths open at the incredible faith of Abraham, and travel with Jacob's family as they leave Israel to find food and security in Egypt. (Years later they'll wind up as slaves, making bricks for Pharaoh.)

Without Genesis, the rest of the Bible makes no sense. The Bible is really about one thing: God's plan of salvation—his strategy for reaching out to us and saving us from sin and the destruction it causes. Genesis shows us why salvation is necessary: God created the perfect place and created the perfect companions (us) to inhabit that place. But it all fell apart when sin invaded and ruined God's creation. Now, only the Creator can fix his creation.

QUOTABLES

In the beginning God created the heavens and the earth (1:1).

"Am I my brother's keeper?" (4:9, KJV). Cain's reply to God, when asked where Abel was, whom Cain had murdered.

Noah found grace in the eyes of the Lord (6:8, KJV). The reason Noah and his family weren't killed in the Flood.

"I will bless you and give you such a large family, that someday your descendants will be more numerous than the stars in the sky or the grains of sand along the beach" (22:17). God's promise to Abraham, father of the Jewish nation.

SNEAK PREVIEW

Proverbs
Bite-size wisdom from the heart of philosophers.

BEHIND the SCENES
of Genesis

STARRING ROLES

Adam and Eve, the world's first human couple (3:20)
Noah, builder of the ark and survivor of the Flood (5:29)
Abraham, the man God chooses to become father of the Jews (17:4)
Isaac, the son God promises to Abraham; born when Abraham is 100 (17:19)
Jacob, father of the men whose descendants become the 12 tribes of Israel (25:26)
Joseph, Jacob's favorite son, who becomes a leader in Egypt (30:24)

PLOT

Scene One: God makes a beautiful, sinless world, and human beings to take care of it. These first humans, Adam and Eve, enjoy a tight relationship with God and with each other. They are told to watch over their new world and take care of all the totally cool things God created. Enter Satan and sin. Things come to a screeching halt when Adam and Eve decide to eat fruit (with a little sales pitch from Satan) that God had warned would kill them. God kicks the couple out of Eden and lays down the consequences: As promised, they now will die. But first, woman will now "suffer terribly" when giving birth. And man will have to "sweat to earn a living" (3:19).

Scene Two: Humanity and God drift apart. God's world becomes a real downer. Evil is everywhere, so God decides to clean house by sending a flood, saving only Noah and his family. Afterward, God launches a plan to set humanity free from sin's grip.

Scene Three: God begins his plan by creating a new nation, Israel, through his faithful servant, Abraham. This nation is to learn how to obey him and "do what is right and fair" (18:19). Later, God promises, he will enlarge the scope of his salvation, making the Jews "a blessing to all other nations on earth" (18:18).

STAGE DIRECTIONS

	God creates the universe before 2500 B.C.	Flood destroys the world before 2500 B.C.	God promises Abraham a nation 2100 B.C.	Joseph goes to Egypt, Hebrews follow 1800 B.C.

BIBLE EVENTS

4500 B.C.	○ ○	2500 B.C.	○	2000 B.C.	1000 B.C.

Dates are approximate

WORLD EVENTS

First known Egyptian calendar 4230 B.C.	Floods devastate river basin of Iraq 3400 B.C.	Chinese develop acupuncture 2700 B.C.	Most pyramids completed 2200 B.C.	Stonehenge built in England 2000 B.C.

AUTHOR AND DATE

Jewish tradition says Moses wrote the first five books of the Bible. Jesus agreed (John 7:19). Moses probably received some info directly from God as he did the Ten Commandments. Other material may have come from stories passed on orally and in writing. (Abraham was from the region where writing was invented, so he may have recorded part of his story.) No one knows for sure when Genesis was written, either. Some scholars think it was written as late as the 500s B.C. But if Moses wrote the book, he probably did it during the 40 years he and the Israelites were wandering in the Sinai after leaving Egypt. That would put the writing at either the 1400s B.C. or 1200s B.C.

ON LOCATION

The events in Genesis cover a lot of ground. More than 1,000 miles stretch between Abraham's hometown of Ur (in current Iraq), to Canaan (Israel), and then to Egypt. It's uncertain exactly where the Garden of Eden was located. Most experts think it was located somewhere in the Middle East, especially in the fertile strip of land between the Tigris and Euphrates rivers in Iraq, or along the Nile river in Egypt.

WHAT TO LOOK FOR

- **Truth in creation.** Don't read the Creation story expecting it to be like a science class lab report. Genesis gives you the truth about how the world was created, but not in technical, hyper-precise sciencespeak. It focuses on the *who* of Creation more than the *hows* and *whats*.
- **God's Rescue Plan.** Notice how quickly sin infects and corrupts God's perfect world. It doesn't take long. By Chapter 3, we witness the first sin. By Chapter 4, brother kills brother, and two chapters later, the world is so bad off that God purges the world with a flood. That's the bad news. The good news is that God has a plan to rescue the world from itself, beginning with one righteous man, Abraham.
- **Loving the underdog.** God's love doesn't include just the holier-than-thou types. Throughout Genesis, and the rest of the Bible, see how God extends his love to the unlovely (childless women like Sarah and Rebekah) and those society tends to look down on (like younger sons Isaac, Jacob and Joseph).

EXTREME SCENES
from Genesis

⇥ The finishing touch (1:26–31; 2:7)

After God creates the heavens and the earth, he completes his work with his crowning touch: human beings. *"The Lord God took a handful of soil and made a man. God breathed life into the man, and the man started breathing."* God makes Eve from one of Adam's ribs. Unlike any other creature on the face of the earth, humans are made in God's own image, that is *"to be like himself."* Humans further are given the job of running the show and taking care of the earth.

DIRECTOR'S NOTES

Ever wonder what causes rainbows? It's sunlight being reflected into different colors by droplets of water in the air. The angle at which we see the colors makes it appear as though they form an arch. Even today the rainbow is a reminder of God's promise to Noah. Never again will we have to worry about the world being destroyed by a flood. Genesis 9:12, 13

⇥ Forbidden fruit (3:1–5)

God gives Adam and Eve a totally awesome place to live. He talks with them on a daily basis; they have all they need to eat. It is, in a word, paradise. And there is only one rule in paradise: they are not to eat fruit from one particular tree because it will kill them. Eve goes ahead and eats it anyway. Then to make matters worse, she convinces Adam to eat some, too. God kicks both of them out of paradise. Now, he promises them, they *will* die after living a harsher life unlike anything they had experienced before. Eve will have great pain in childbirth. Adam will have to work—and work hard—for a living. Sin radically changes creation, for the worse.

⇥ The first murder (4:1–16)

It's a case of sibling rivalry gone too far. Cain, a farmer, is the older son of Adam and Eve. Abel, a shepherd, is the younger brother. Each man makes an offering to God; Cain gives crops and Abel selects the best of his flock. God is pleased with Abel's offering but he rejects Cain's. Maybe it's because Cain did not sacrifice the first or best of his crop. Whatever the reason, Cain is insanely jealousy and he kills his brother. As punishment, Cain can never again grow crops; if he tries, the ground will produce zilch. He is also doomed to become a fugitive, "wandering from place to place." But God protects him with an undescribed mark that somehow alerts others not to kill him.

A clean sweep (6–9)

Things progress from bad to worse. "Cruelty and violence have spread everywhere," God tells Noah, the only righteous man left. "Now I'm going to destroy the whole earth and all its people." God instructs Noah to build a massive, three-deck houseboat about 150 yards long, 15 yards wide, and 25 yards high. In this boat, God will preserve Noah and his family, along with pairs of "every kind of animal, wild and tame." And then the rain begins—40 days and 40 nights, covering even the mountains. After five months, the waters finally recede enough that the boat comes to rest in the Ararat mountain range of Armenia, some 500 miles north of where many scholars believe civilization began.

It's all talk (11:1–9)

Noah's descendants speak the same language and work together. But then they get an attitude because of their accomplishments. They decide to build a huge tower (some say it was supposed to be a staircase to heaven; others say it was a tribute to some pagan gods) to show just how good they are. "This is just the beginning," God says. God puts the kibosh on the building project and puts human pride on hold by suddenly making the people speak different languages. As a result, they scatter all over the earth, apparently clustering by language groups.

Plan B (12:1–9)

God initiates his plan to restore his creation to its original goodness through one man, Abraham. Abraham is 75 years old when he gets the call from God to leave his homeland and go to what is now Israel. Further, God tells Abraham not only will he give this land to him, but he will "make your descendants into a great nation." Even though Abraham is childless at the time and probably wonders how this is going to happen, he wastes no time in obeying God and sets out for Canaan.

The contract (15:1–21)

God makes a formal contract, also called a covenant, with Abraham. God's promise: "Look at the sky and see if you can count the stars. That's how many descendants you will have." To seal the contract, Abraham offers a sacrifice of a cow, a goat, a ram, a dove, and a pigeon.

No laughing matter (18:1–2)

A trio of divine messengers, on their way to check out what's going on in Sodom and Gomorrah, visit Abraham. They deliver some pretty amazing news: God promises that he and Sarah will have a son. Sarah, listening from inside the tent, FOFL (falls on the floor laughing). After all, Abraham is 99 and she is 90. Who's kidding who here? But within a year a star is born: Isaac. And the Jewish nation is begun.

Final destruction (19:1–29)

After delivering the good news, the divine messengers move on to Sodom and Gomorrah, twin cities in a plain somewhere in Canaan, to deliver some not-so-good news. On checking out the scene, they find the twin cities are so far gone with depravity that God decides to destroy them. In fact, the men of Sodom go so far as to try to gang rape the angelic messengers that God sends to warn Lot and his family to leave. The angels blind the would-be rapists and help Lot and his family escape. "The Lord sent burning sulphur down like rain on Sodom and Gomorrah" (19:24). Lot's wife can't resist one final look back. When she looks, she turns into an instant salt lick.

The test (22:1–19)

God gives Abraham the ultimate faith test. He tells Abraham to kill his son, Isaac, as a sacrifice—the son through whom God promised to produce the Jewish nation. Yet Abraham doesn't question the plan; he obeys. Before they reach the site where Abraham will build the sacrificial altar, Isaac looks around and asks where the lamb is for the sacrifice. Abraham calmly replies, "God will provide the lamb." As Abraham is about to plunge his knife into Isaac, an angel suddenly appears and tells him to stop. "Now I know that you truly obey God," the angel says, "because you were willing to offer him your only son."

This extreme scene is really a foreshadowing of Jesus. What Abraham was *willing* to do, God *actually* did, offering His only son as a sacrifice for the world (see John 3:16; Romans 3:21–25). John the Baptist introduced Jesus to the world, saying: "Here is the Lamb of God who takes away the sin of the world!" (John 1:29).

DIRECTOR'S NOTES

Names were a very big deal in ancient times. The meaning of a person's name often revealed a very important characteristic about him. In many cases, it was a symbol of what he stood for. In Hebrew, *Ab* means "father" and *raham* means "many." Genesis 17:4, 5

Wrestling mania (32: 22–32)

Isaac grows up, marries, and has two twin boys: Esau and Jacob. A split occurs between the brothers after the younger twin, Jacob, tricks his father into giving him the deathbed blessing traditionally due the eldest son. The night before Jacob's tense reunion with his older brother, who has vowed to kill him, Jacob meets a mysterious man. Maybe Jacob knows this man is a divine messenger because Jacob grabs him and says, "You can't go until you bless me." They wrestle until dawn, when the mysterious man throws Jacob's hip out of joint. This man then blesses Jacob by giving him the new name of Israel. Jacob has 12 sons, whose descendants will become the tribes of Israel. The most famous son is Joseph.

Favorite son (37:12–28)

Joseph is Jacob's favorite son—and everybody knows it, including Joseph. He does little to help his case by flaunting his "favorite son" status in front of his 10 older brothers. His brothers have had it with Joseph so they decide to get rid of their bratty brother. They get their opportunity when Joseph comes out to the fields one day to check on them. Faster than you can name all the colors in Joseph's coat, the brothers grab him and throw him in a pit. As they argue over whether to kill him, a caravan of slave traders en route to Egypt happens by. Joseph's brothers quickly make a deal: Joseph for 20 pieces of silver. (It's a scene that appears to foreshadow Judas betraying Jesus for 30 pieces of silver in Matthew 26:15). In Egypt, Joseph's troubles continue. He lands in prison after he is falsely charged with trying to rape his master's wife. He remains in prison until—incredibly—the ruler of Egypt summons him.

The dream team (41:1–40)

Pharaoh, the king of Egypt, has been having some pretty weird dreams. He dreams of seven hungry, scrawny cows devouring seven fat cows, yet not getting any fatter. This dream is followed by one of seven rotten ears of corn consuming seven good ears. Since many people then believed that the gods communicated through dreams, Pharaoh asks his wise men to interpret the dream. When they fail, someone recommends Joseph, who has earned a reputation for correctly interpreting dreams while in jail. Joseph tells Pharaoh that God is warning Egypt that the nation will enjoy seven good years of harvest, followed by seven years of drought. Pharaoh, relived to finally know what the dreams mean, makes Joseph his number two man, in charge of managing the grain reserves.

Family reunion (45:1–15)

Famine sweeps across Egypt and Israel as well. With no food, Joseph's brothers decide to head to Egypt where they hear food is available. When they go begging for food from Pharaoh's No. 2 man, they don't recognize it's Joseph. But he recognizes them. At first, he keeps his identity secret. But eventually he can't keep it to himself. "I am Joseph," he says and breaks down crying. When he is able to speak again, he asks if his father is still alive. Jacob is alive, but still depressed over losing Joseph. To his frightened brothers, Joseph offers assurance that he has forgiven them. "Don't worry or blame yourselves," he explains. "God is the one who sent me ahead of you to save lives" (45:5). At Joseph's request and with Pharaoh's approval, Jacob and his entire extended family move to Egypt to weather out the famine. Ironically, they are destined to suffer the same fate of young Joseph; they will become an entire nation of slaves. And freeing them will take an act of God, working through a reluctant shepherd called Moses.

INTERVIEW
with the Stars

The right attitude

Welcome to **Behind the Bible**, the only heavenly news magazine that delivers the hard-hitting, spare-no-punches, in-your-face interviews with the men and women who played supporting, but key roles, in the unfolding drama we now call the Bible. Today's subject is Abel, whose young life was tragically cut short at the hand of his older brother. Before we get into that, Abel, tell us a little about yourself. You have a number of "firsts" to put by your name.

⇒ Abel

Well, I was a member of the first family on earth. I was the first little brother and the first shepherd, among other things. I guess you could say I was also part of the first sibling rivalry.

You also were the first victim of a violent crime. Talk about that. Did you have any idea that your brother Cain was so insanely jealous of you?

⇒ Abel

To be honest with you, I didn't see it coming. We had talked about different ways to approach God, and we both decided it would be cool to offer God a sacrifice—you know, to give up something that meant something to us and that we had worked hard for. I decided to offer God the best thing I had—the first-born of my flock. I killed it and offered God a fat sacrifice.

INTERVIEW
with the Stars

And Cain?

⇒ Abel

Well, he offered God some plants. I guess God liked my sacrifice better. In fact, I know he did. And Cain couldn't handle that. A couple of days after the sacrifices, Cain asked me to go out to the fields with him. I thought we were going to discuss plans for developing the land. Instead, he picked up a rock, well, you know the rest of the story.

Very tragic. Although your life ended so unfairly, what would you say was your contribution to believers today?

⇒ Abel

Well that's the totally awesome thing about this whole deal. I basically invented worship; but more importantly, I had the right attitude in worshipping God. It's not OK just to be there and go through the motions; you really have to be *all there*. And because I was *all there,* I'm the first inductee listed in the Hall of Faith in Hebrews 11.

Wow, that's quite a story. Thanks Abel. For those of you with brothers and sisters, remember, the question is not how you can make a difference by competing with them. Rather, think like Abel: What can *I* do to approach God?

INTERVIEW
with the Stars

An angry young man

Behind the Bible takes you for a rare interview with one of the original bad boys of the Bible, Cain, who not only was the first to commit homicide, but also the first to commit fratricide. Cain, now that you have had several thousands of years to contemplate your actions, how do you view that terrible day when you did in your brother?

⋟ Cain

After all these years, it's still difficult for me to talk about what happened that day. Sometimes I wish it never made it into the Bible, but I know that God can teach others through the bad times and the terrible mistakes we make as well as from the good things we do. I was an angry young man with a low boiling point and I *had* to be the best. I couldn't stand to have second billing under anyone, let alone my younger brother!

From your point of view, how did things get started?

⋟ Cain

We had both decided to bring God a sacrifice. I thought, well, whatever, I'll bring God a couple plants. So I went out to my garden—I had a totally awesome garden—and pulled a few things out. How was I to know that my goody-goody little bro was going to take his *best* sheep? If I had known that I would have at least brought God my best beefsteak tomato.

INTERVIEW
with the Stars

But that wasn't your only mistake, was it?

⋟ Cain

No, I guess not. I mean I was really bummed out about the whole thing because God obviously liked Abel's sacrifice a lot better than mine. And I was hot. I mean how would you like being upstaged by your younger brother or sister in front of God himself? It was a total downer. But God warned me. He told me if I didn't control my temper, things would get out of hand really fast. And that's exactly what happened.

So basically, God gave you a second chance and you blew it. Isn't that right?

⋟ Cain

Yeah, you could say that. Instead of following God, I let my emotions get the better of me. When I saw Abel standing in that field, holding one of his dumb lambs in his arms, I just lost it big time. Then I told God to get off my case when He asked me about Abel. I really made a mess out of my life.

Well, that's all we have for now. Before we go, let Cain's life be a lesson to those of you with short fuses. What you do with your anger could affect the rest of your life, like Cain's. Let God control your anger; don't let your anger control you!

INTERVIEW
with the Stars

The promised child

Today **Behind the Bible** will talk with Isaac, the "promised child," the child that Sarah and Abraham waited for nearly their entire lives and the child that was the promised link from God to create a nation. Isaac, was it tough growing up with such expectations?

⩾ Isaac

Well, being an only child has its plusses and minuses. Since I didn't have any sibs, I never had to share my space in the tent or let anyone else use my things. I also got lots of attention—but that wasn't always a good thing! I don't think it was easy for my parents, either, to have a young, energetic boy around the house when they were in their nineties!

What about being God's promise for an *entire* nation? That had to be a pretty tough billing to live up to!

⩾ Isaac

It was something I just learned to live with. As I was growing up I wasn't sure exactly what it all meant, but I got a pretty good idea early on that this faith stuff was pretty serious.

INTERVIEW
with the Stars

Tell us what happened.

⇒ Isaac

Dad and I were going out on a camping trip—or so I thought. We hiked up this mountain and all of a sudden, Dad announced he's going to make a sacrifice to the Lord. Cool, I thought, but when I looked around I didn't see any lambs or rams or animals of any kind. I asked Dad about it and he just said not to worry, God would provide one. Next thing I knew I was tied up on the altar about to be sacrificed!

You must have been scared out of your mind!

⇒ Isaac

Tell me about it! I knew, though, that my dad trusted God and that if he was obedient, God would take care of things, and God did! You could say that I was saved by the ram!

What about the rest of your life? Was it filled with other challenging experiences?

⇒ Isaac

To be truthful, the rest of my life was pretty quiet. I married the woman of my dreams. I had twin sons and made many of the typical mistakes parents make. I guess if I had to name my greatest accomplishment, it was that I kept the faith and I passed it along.

Well, thanks, Isaac. Your story is an encouragement to many of us. Making a difference for God does not necessarily lead to greatness. God can take the little things—like being a faithful follower of Jesus—and make them into big things.

INTERVIEW
with the Stars

Stepping out in faith

Behind the Bible has the privilege today of talking with a woman who, when faced with an opportunity to make a difference, took a risk and stepped out in faith. Let's welcome Rebekah, the wife of Isaac and mother to the future nation of Israel. Rebekah, tell us a little bit about your background.

⋙ Rebekah

I grew up in the little town of Nahor, the daughter of Bethuel. Isaac's mom was Milcah and her husband was Abraham's brother, Nahor. We had never actually met my great-Uncle Abraham, but I certainly heard stories of his famous journey that brought his family to this land.

You had an unusual marriage proposal, didn't you?

⋙ Rebekah

You could say that! In my culture, men and women didn't decide who they were going to marry. The power to marry was not in my hands, but in the hands of my father and brother. In my case, though, their authority was eclipsed by a higher authority—God himself!

How did that happen?

⋙ Rebekah

The short version is that I turned out to be the answer to the prayer of Abraham's servant Eliezer. You see, Abraham had sent his servant to Nahor to find a wife for Isaac. Eliezer had prayed to God, asking him for guidance in finding a wife. I had no idea who the old man was who I met at the city well. All I did was offer him and his camels some water! Next thing I knew he gave me some beautiful jewelry and asked if he could spend the night with my family. I

INTERVIEW
with the Stars

I bet you had no idea what was coming next.

⋟ Rebekah

Not a clue. That night before dinner, he told my brother and father all about his mission and his prayer. I think you could have knocked my father and brother over with a feather after they heard the whole story. When Eliezer asked them whether I would return with him, I held my breath! It was so clear to me that the Lord was working out all these details and his hand was in this marriage—I just had to go. Thankfully, my father and brother saw it the same way. The next day, I packed up my camel and never looked back.

Looking back on your life, did you make the right decision?

⋟ Rebekah

Absolutely. Later in my life, I made some big-time mistakes. I didn't always make the right choice, and I took matters into my own hands. But God never forgot that I took that first step. Because of that, God was able to bless our family and through our son, the future nation of Israel.

That's a good reminder to our readers that if we want to be major players in God's plans and allow him to work through us, it will hinge on what we do with our nows—the decisions and opportunities right before us. Thanks, Rebekah!

INTERVIEW
with the Stars

The dreamer

Our next subject most likely is a familiar name to our readers. *Behind the Bible* is pleased to talk with Joseph, who probably experienced the greatest turn of events in history—from slave to second-in-command to Pharaoh. Joseph, how did you keep on going and never give up?

⤷ Joseph

In a word, faith. I never gave up believing in the dream God had given me as a boy growing up in Caanan. I didn't know exactly what it meant at the time; I didn't know exactly how God would bring it about; but I never doubted God's power and his ability to make a difference through my life.

Let's talk about that dream. It actually caused you a lot of grief, didn't it?

⤷ Joseph

Yes, it did. I probably was showing off when I bragged about it to my brothers. I guess they didn't exactly go for hearing that I had dreamed that one day I was going to rule over them. But I never thought they would do what they did—throw me in a pit and then sell me as a slave. You could say my life hit rock bottom.

INTERVIEW
with the Stars

Yet, things actually got worse from there didn't they?

⇒ Joseph

You're right, they did. I worked hard for my master, and I was doing well, when his wife came along. Trust me, never mess with the boss's wife. I didn't *and* I still got nailed. That's when I ended up in jail. Things looked really grim. I mean, how could God use me in prison? Yet, somehow, I never gave up hope that God had something better in mind for me.

And he did, didn't he?

⇒ Joseph

I'll say! It didn't happen overnight, but eventually, God gave me an opportunity to use my gifts and abilities even in jail. One thing led to another and boom, there I was helping Pharaoh plan for a major famine. Me, a sheepherder from Caanan, the manager of Egypt!

What an incredible turn of events! And your dream came true?

⇒ Joseph

It sure did. I'll never forget the day they came in—all eleven of my brothers, bowing to me and begging for food. And they didn't even know who I was! What a hoot!

That is an amazing story, Joseph. It helps us remember that even if we don't have as clear a vision as you did, we still can have faith in the same God who worked these things out in your life. Trust in God, and He can make a difference through you!

REVIEWS

In the beginning...of the Bible is the book of Genesis. Genesis packs in more action than all three Star Wars movies combined with the complete works of Shakespeare and a years worth of "Murder She Wrote" re-runs thrown in for good measure. For starters we've got...hmmm, let's see... THE ENTIRE EARTH BEING CREATED IN SIX DAYS. Even God took a day off after that!

The cast ? How 'bout God, Adam, Eve, the serpent, Noah...I could go on, but you get the picture. Even better, all the people are *real people*. No scripts, the action is all live and unplanned and more exciting than "Cops," "Survivor" or "MTV's Real World." This is the REAL real world.

The people in Genesis aren't perfect. They are just guys (and women!) trying to figure out how to connect with a God they can't see, and how to live together the way God wants them to live. Sound familiar? Seems like some of the conflicts and problems from those days are still with us. We can learn a lot from watching people face these situations for the first time...ever.

And the special effects! You've got the whole earth spoken into existence (I bet God ROCKS at Scrabble). Men made from mud and women made from ribs (mmm...ribs). You've got fire burning up whole towns (smoked ribs) and women turning to salt pillars (salt is good on ribs). You've got animals of every kind coming of their own free will into a big boat (delicious animals like cows and pigs. Pork ribs, beef ribs, spare ribs, baby back ribs, rib ribs ribs). Twin brothers struggling to be first before they were even born (Let me OUT...I want to be the first to get some ribs).

(Author pauses for lunch break.)

Not to mention the intrigue. Sibling rivalry that leads to murder. A kid brother who's sold into slavery and rises to be the vice-president of a foreign country. A father who almost sacrifices his only son. A mother who is so desperate to have a child she offers her handmaiden as a surrogate wife.

ENCORE

> For more on the story of Abraham's ever-growing family, read Exodus. It starts where Genesis leaves off, with the Israelites in Egypt. Exodus tells of Moses leading the enslaved nation home to what is now Israel.

> For more about God's work in creation, read his reply to Job, who felt he had the intellectual savvy to argue with God (Job 38:4–40:2). Or try the prophet Isaiah's masterful poem about learning to trust in the God of creation (Isaiah 40:10–31).

> To learn more about why Abraham is so important to Jews and Christians, and how the New Testament presents him as a person who was saved through faith in God, read Romans 4:1–25 and James 2:14–26.

REVIEWS

Genesis really does have it all, the roots of it all, the beginnings of it all.

As many answers as Genesis gives, it still leaves us with a lot of questions. It's a history book about a time when there were no historians. There are no corroborating accounts of Creation. Who would have written them? Genesis is the explanation of where we come from and who we come from, but there's no FAQ section in the back. Let's just trust God on this one, OK?

Did Creation really happen in six 24-hour days? No telling. God is the One who decides how long days are in the first place. A day is as long as He says it is. The sun wasn't even created until the fourth day (well, if God can make a planet out of a word, seeing in the dark is probably easy. Oh, wait a minute, He IS the light, duh!) What Genesis sets out to give us aren't facts to pick apart. It's truth to live by. There is a God who created this world and the people living in it. He gets involved in our lives and draws us to Himself. That's a story worth reading.

Jenny Sisse

Exodus

SCHEDULE OF SCENES

Adam	Abraham	Moses	Exodus	David	Ezra	Jesus is Born
4000+ B.C.	2100 B.C.	1500 B.C.	1440 B.C.	1000 B.C.	450 B.C.	7/6 B.C.

The Great Escape

Quick—what's the single greatest event in the 4,000-year history of the Jewish people? Ask a Jewish friend, and he/she will not hesitate: It's the Great Escape, an epic adventure that begins in the shadows of the Egyptian pyramids and ends at the border of the Promised Land. Freeze-frame this moment in history, and you will capture the moment of Israel's birth as a nation, as a country, and as a people belonging to God. It was just this moment that God had promised to Abraham, hundreds of years earlier.

Into Egypt had come one Hebrew family, led by Jacob, seeking relief from a famine. Out of Egypt came one Hebrew nation, led by Moses, seeking freedom from slavery. During their long journey home, to what is now Israel, they accepted their role as descendants of Abraham, and they vowed to obey God. So God, through Moses, set up the rules that would govern the people. At the heart of these rules are the Ten Commandments. The story is a classic tale—not so much because of what it reveals about the Jewish people, but because of what it reveals about God. We witness God in His greatest role—one He repeats throughout history—as the great deliverer, who can and will invade our world to save all who call on Him for help.

QUOTABLES

"I Am" (3:14). God's name, as revealed to Moses at the burning bush.

"Let my people go" (5:1). God's demand of Pharaoh, the Egyptian king.

"Do not worship any god except me" (20:3). The first of the Ten Commandments.

The payment will be . . . eye for eye, tooth for tooth (21:23–24).

SNEAK PREVIEW

Ruth
A story of devotion.
A romance with a legacy.

BEHIND the SCENES
of Exodus

STARRING ROLES

Moses, who leads the Israelites out of Egypt (2:10)
Egyptian king, known as Pharaoh, who uses the Israelites for slave labor (1:11)
Aaron, older brother of Moses and builder of the golden calf (4:14)

PLOT

To escape a famine in their homeland (what is now Israel), Jacob moves his family to Egypt. They stay about 400 years. Sometime during this extended visit, Jacob's descendants grow so numerous that the Egyptians begin to fear a Hebrew uprising. So an Egyptian king decides there is only one thing to do—make them his slaves. He forces them to make bricks for his massive building projects—including entire cities. The people cry out to God, asking him to send a deliverer. And God sends Moses to be just that.

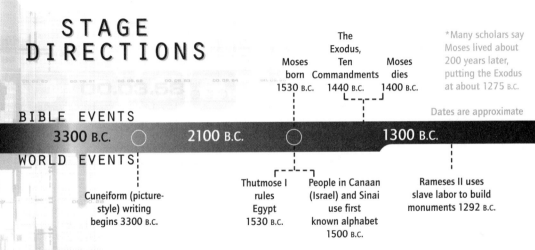

STAGE DIRECTIONS

	Moses born 1530 B.C.	The Exodus, Ten Commandments 1440 B.C.	Moses dies 1400 B.C.	*Many scholars say Moses lived about 200 years later, putting the Exodus at about 1275 B.C.

Dates are approximate

BIBLE EVENTS

3300 B.C.   2100 B.C.   1300 B.C.

WORLD EVENTS

Cuneiform (picture-style) writing begins 3300 B.C.	Thutmose I rules Egypt 1530 B.C.	People in Canaan (Israel) and Sinai use first known alphabet 1500 B.C.	Rameses II uses slave labor to build monuments 1292 B.C.

AUTHOR AND DATE

Although the book doesn't identify its writer, other Bible books credit Moses as the author (Joshua 8:31; Mark 12:26). And Exodus 17:14 says Moses wrote at least part of the book. Critics once said Moses couldn't have written it because the alphabet had not been invented. But archaeologists have since uncovered many alphabetic writings from about 1500 BC in what is now Israel as well as the Sinai Peninsula, where the Israelites spent 40 years. Like the others first five books of the Bible, Moses probably wrote Exodus during the Exodus, probably in the 1400s BC. He wrote the book to remind the Jews about how God delivered them from slavery.

ON LOCATION

The epic confrontation between Pharaoh and Moses takes place in the Nile Delta of northern Egypt. The Exodus—the 40 years of wandering in the wilderness—takes place in the Sinai Peninsula, a barren expanse between Egypt and Canaan, just north of the Red Sea.

WHAT TO LOOK FOR

- **God getting involved.** Notice that God doesn't relax in the comfort of heaven, while expecting us humans to work out our own problems. He's a hands-on God. He produces a leader out of a man who wants to stay with the sheep. He gets Pharaoh's attention with a series of absolutely mind-bending miracles. And he blows a dry path through a standing body of water when the escaping Israelites are trapped between a charging army and the deep blue sea.
- ***Two sections***. The first half of the book is the heroic story about the Israelites escaping from Egypt. The last half, beginning with chapter 19, is made up of laws and worship instructions for the Israelites, now a new nation.

EXTREME SCENES
from Exodus

⇒ The bottom-dwellers (1:1–12)

The Israelites move to Egypt during the days of Joseph to escape a famine in Israel. Life is good, so they stay and produce a lot of children there. But when a new pharaoh takes office, he sees the growing population of Israelites as a threat to national security. So he makes them all slaves and gives them the dirtiest job of all—making mud bricks for massive projects such as the cities of Pithom and Rameses. (An early Egyptian record written on a tomb wall describes the slave brickmaker: "He is dirtier than vines or pigs from the treading under his mud. . . . He is simply wretched through and through.") They probably didn't build pyramids, though, since most of them were finished before 2200 B.C., nearly 1,000 years earlier.

DIRECTOR'S NOTES

Don't overlook numbers in Scripture. Sometimes they can tell us quite a bit. Seventy was a significant number for Israel because it was a multiple of seven, the sacred number. To the Israelites, seven symbolized completion, abundance, and rest. (Consider the seven days of creation in Genesis 1.) Exodus 1:1-5

⇒ Baby in a basket (2:1–10)

To control the rapidly multiplying Israelite population, Pharaoh orders that all their newborn sons be killed at birth. But one Hebrew mother skirts the new law by putting her son into a watertight basket and setting him afloat near where the princess of Egypt bathes. Big sister watches from among the reeds. When the princess finds the child and takes pity on him, big sister walks over and asks if the princess needs someone to nurse him. When Pharaoh's daughter says yes, the child gets the mother, who serves as nurse—and receives a salary as well. Moses, the future deliverer of his people, is now alive and well and living in Pharaoh's very own palace!

⇒ Moses on the run (2:11–22)

Moses grows up in the king's palace with all the privileges and perks that go with being the king's son. Still, Moses knows his roots and he feels a kinship with his people. When he sees an Egyptian foreman beating a Hebrew slave, Moses kills the Egyptian and quickly hides his body in the sand. When Pharaoh finds out, he orders Moses' execution. So Moses runs away, east to Midian, which extends from the Sinai Peninsula to northern Arabia. There he marries into the family of a sheepherder.

The burning bush (3:1–10)

While grazing his flock near Mt. Sinai, Moses witnesses something you don't see every day—a bush on fire that is not burned. Then he hears something you don't hear every day—the voice of God, calling Moses to come close. "Take off your sandals," God says. "The ground where you are standing is holy." God then gives Moses a *real* challenge: return to Egypt and demand that the great pharaoh free the slaves. Understandably, Egypt is the last place Moses wants to go back to, and he says so. But God promises, "I will be with you." So Moses goes to Egypt.

DIRECTOR'S NOTES

Frogs were considered sacred in ancient Egypt, as signs of fertility. You can imagine how confused and alarmed the people became when they saw their land covered with the amphibians. Exodus 8:1-5

"Let my people go" (12:1–32)

It's a simple message. Four words. "Let my people go." But it takes plague after horrible plague to finally get Pharaoh to listen and understand that this message is from none other than God himself. The Nile River turns to blood. Frogs invade the land, followed by gnats, flies, then locusts. The livestock get sick. Lightning and hail destroy the crops. Darkness shrouds Egypt for three days. The people suffer from boils. At which point would you cry uncle?

It's only the last plague that finally breaks Pharaoh. God kills the oldest child in each family, Pharaoh's included. But he passes over the homes of Israelites who have obeyed his directions to splash their front doorposts with the blood of a sacrificial lamb they have eaten. Since that fateful day, Jews annually remember their deliverance from Egypt by eating the Passover meal.

Crossing the sea (14:1–31)

"Get your people out of my country and leave us alone!" Pharaoh tells Moses that night. The Israelites don't need a second invitation. They're gone by daybreak, rushing east toward the Sinai Peninsula. Left with his grief (and no one to make his bricks any more), Pharaoh gets really mad. He orders his massive chariot force to the chase and traps the fleeing Israelites on the banks of the Red Sea. Things don't look good for the escaping slaves.

But God blocks the advancing Egyptian forces with a pillar of smoke and fire. Then he sends a strong east wind to blow-dry a path across the sea. The Israelites walk across the sea floor. When the Israelites safely reach the other side, the Egyptians boldly—but foolishly—follow. The sea walls come splashing down, killing every Egyptian that enters the water.

Free at last! (15:1–21)

In the moment it takes two massive, opposing waves to crash together, the Egyptian threat is gone and the Israelites are free. Totally free! Exhilarated, the entire nation joins Moses in a song of praise to God. Miriam, the sister of Moses, takes out a tambourine and leads the women in dancing.

God's top ten rules (20:1–17; 31:18–32:35; 34:1)

Moses returns to Mt. Sinai, where he earlier met God in the burning bush. Here God gives him the Ten Commandments, written on two stone tablets. And here, God outlines other laws that will govern Israel and make it clear to other nations that Israel is devoted to God. The meeting takes 40 days—long enough for the Israelites to begin wondering whether Moses is taking a permanent vacation. So they talk his brother, Aaron, into building a golden calf, "an image of a god who will lead and protect us."

When Moses finally returns and sees the people dancing around the calf, he is so angry that he breaks the stone tablets into hundreds of pebbles. He hasn't been back five minutes and already the people have broken the first and most important commandment: Do not worship any god except me. Moses returns to the mountain where God replaces the inscribed Commandments.

The portable church (26:1–37)

On God's instruction, the Israelites build a portable worship center called the tabernacle. Wherever they go, they erect it in the center of their camp. The tabernacle courtyard—where people offer sacrifices to God for their sins or to give thanks—measures 50 yards long by 25 yards wide. It is surrounded by a wall of curtains seven feet high. Inside the tent, 15 yards long and 5 yards wide, the Israelites keep the Ten Commandments, secured in a chest called the ark of the covenant. Only priests are allowed inside the sacred tent. The presence of God, in the form of a cloud, settles on the tabernacle. Whenever the cloud moves from the tent, the people break camp and follow.

INTERVIEW
with the Stars

Making a creative difference

It's not every day that *Behind the Scenes* has an opportunity to talk with an artist the caliber of a Michaelangelo, but today we have the privilege of talking with a man who not only was extremely talented, but also was able to use those talents to create one of the most magnificent places to worship God. Welcome Bazalel. Why don't you tell us a little bit about yourself?

⇒ Bazalel

No problem. You might not know too much about me. I'm one of those behind-the-scenes kind of guys. I was part of the group of Israelites who had left Egypt and who had been following Moses in the desert. We had set up camp at the foot of Mt. Sinai, and Moses had a *ton* of instructions for us—you know, how to live, what to eat, how to treat our neighbors, and how to worship. And that's where I came in.

Tell us what you mean about that? What does being an artist have to do with worshipping God?

⇒ Bazalel

Well, in my particular case, everything! You see, I was the one chosen to make the portable worship center we Israelites called the tabernacle. God had given Moses very detailed instructions for building the tabernacle. But guess what? Moses didn't have an artistic bone in his entire body! So he called me.

INTERVIEW
with the Stars

And what exactly were your credentials?

⋙ Bazalel

Well, basically, you could say that I was an artist's artist. I could cast, cut, shape, build, paint, mold, design, sew and weave just about anything. God had given me some incredible talents and gifts! So when Moses needed a pure gold lampstand crafted or a woven tapestry made of blue, purple and scarlet thread, I was da man!

Very impressive. But you couldn't have done all that work yourself. Building the tabernacle and all that went in it was a massive project.

⋙ Bazalel

It certainly was. No, I didn't do it all by myself. I had plenty of help. Because in addition to the skills God had given me as an artist, He also gave me the ability to teach others to do what I did. Together with all the artisans that God had called, we made *everything* that God had ordered. It was an awesome place to worship our Creator and Deliverer.

What an inspiring testimony! Makes you want to get right out there and *do* something for God, doesn't it? The good news is that God has given each one of us special skills and abilities. The only thing we have to do is make ourselves available, like Bazalel. Thanks, Bazalel, for dropping by and sharing your story with us.

REVIEWS

Exodus is the story of several power struggles. First it is the struggle between the Egyptian king and God himself in freeing his people, the Hebrews. (Guess who wins?) Then, it is the struggle between God and the people he has freed (Gee, do you think God might win *again?*).

Exodus is also the story of a family growing into a nation. (Eat all your broccoli, Bobby. Don't you want to be Ethiopia when you grow up?) Genesis ends with a family of less than 100 people coming to Egypt for food (big line at the Matzoh Bell drive-thru THAT day). By the time of Exodus, there are so many Hebrews running around that the king of Egypt is afraid they'll take over. (It seems that the ONE thing God said that EVERYBODY remembers is "be fruitful and multiply," which means to have kids. I used to think it meant go bananas and do lots of math. Go figure.)

Exodus is also about the same basic struggles in life that we face every day. How far do we really need to trust God? Will he come through? What about when life is hard? What about when we think we've done the right thing, but it feels wrong? Once God rescued the Hebrews from Egypt, Exodus follows their journey. They had such a hard time believing that God was going to care for them.

They wanted to trust themselves or their leaders or their fake idols or their lucky charms (think rabbit's foot, not breakfast cereal). God kept saying to them, "Trust only me. Worship only me. I will take care of you." He still keeps that promise. God is rescuing us from lives outside of his love, just as he did the Hebrews, but the journey can be really difficult. Will we want to give up and turn back? Will we trust our

> For the rest of the story, read about the end of the Exodus, when the Israelites finally reach the Promised Land. It's found in Joshua, a book named for the man who led the nation after Moses died.

> To see how Israel later celebrates the Exodus in song, read lyrics from their songbook: Psalm 78, 105—106, 136.

> To discover how the New Testament portrays Jesus as the Passover lamb whose blood saves us from spiritual death, read John 1:29 and 1 Corinthians 5:1–8.

lucky charms (green clovers!), our bad habits (nose picking will NOT get you to heaven), our illegal sub-stances (sorry, I'm brain dead enough without *that* stuff) to get us through? Or will we stand face-to-face with God and trust only him and worship only him? Our path isn't so different from the plotline of the Hebrews story. Truthfully, they didn't do too well. (That's why we have the book of Numbers.) They ended up wandering through the desert for forty extra years because they couldn't get it together enough to have faith. We can't read their story without asking ourselves, is our faith strong enough to get us to the end of the journey?

Xavier Oldham "X.O." Dusse

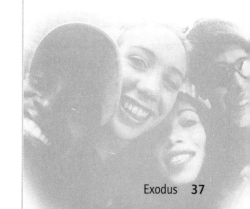

Leviticus

SCHEDULE OF SCENES

Adam — Abraham — Moses — Exodus — Wandering Ends — David — Ezra — Jesus is Born

4000+ B.C.   2100 B.C.   1500 B.C.   1440 B.C.   1400 B.C.   1000 B.C.   450 B.C.   7/6 B.C.

Israel's Spiritual How-To Manual

This book is not exactly what you would call easy reading. But it's essential reading. It was essential reading for the Jews who were serious about honoring their commitment to obey God. And it's essential today for an undistorted view of God's take on sin and how he showed the people how to get rid of it.

Long ago, Jews called this book the Priest's Manual. The name Leviticus came later; it means "about the Levites." The book earned this tag because the Levites were the worship leaders in Israel, and this book is full of detailed instructions about worship. Both titles are misleading, though, because the instructions—about sacrifices, religious holidays, and ritual cleanness—aren't just for priests. They're for everyone.

In many ancient nations, only priests were uniquely set apart to serve the gods and to live by a special code. But the Lord set apart an entire country. He told Israel, "You will be my holy nation and serve me as priests" (Exodus 19:6). The book of Leviticus is their spiritual how-to manual. In a way, it's the volume preceding the new manual coming from Jesus, "the author and finisher of our faith" (Hebrews 12:2, KJV). To understand what Jesus did for us, we need to understand the Jewish faith on which he built.

QUOTABLES

You must become holy, because I am holy (11:45).

Love others as much as you love yourself (19:18). A command later popularized by Jesus.

I will be your God, and you will be my people (26:12).

SNEAK PREVIEW

> **Psalms**
> The stuff of life seen through the heart of a poet.

BEHIND the SCENES
of Leviticus

STARRING ROLES

Moses, who receives detailed worship instructions from God (1:1)
Aaron, older brother of Moses and the chief priest in charge of implementing the instructions (6:8)

PLOT

There isn't much of a story line in Leviticus. After leaving Egypt, the Israelites camp at Mt. Sinai for a year. This is where they receive the Ten Commandments, build a tent worship center, and receive some 600 laws that will govern them—many laws of which are preserved in Leviticus.

STAGE DIRECTIONS

Jewish laws, sacrificial system begin 1440 B.C.

BIBLE EVENTS

Dates are approximate

1500 B.C.   1200 B.C.   1000 B.C.

WORLD EVENTS

Hindu scriptures (Verdas) begin 1500 B.C.

People in Canaan (Israel) and Sinai use first known alphabet 1500 B.C.

Sacrificial altar used in northern Israel 1000 B.C.

AUTHOR AND DATE

Again, the writer is not named, but traditionally considered to be Moses. Much of the book reports on the worship instructions that God gives Moses at Mt. Sinai. In fact, nearly all of Leviticus is from the speeches of God; Moses likely provides the quotes. Like the other books attributed to Moses (the first five in the Bible), Leviticus is probably written during the 40 years it takes Israel to reach the promised land. Perhaps some of Leviticus is written early in the trip, just after Moses receives the worship instructions from God. Moses would have wanted to implement the rules as quickly as possible, which means he had to teach the priests, who would in turn teach the masses.

    The book is written to give Israel directions on how to live in peace with God and with each other. Leviticus is not only a book of religious law, but civil law as well. That's because God presents himself as more than just the Lord at worship time. He's our Lord for all time.

ON LOCATION

Israel is camped for a year at the foot of Mt. Sinai while God gives Moses the laws preserved in Leviticus. One mountain long associated with this event is Jebel Musa ("mountain of Moses"), a 7,500-foot-high peak near the southern tip of the Sinai Peninsula. In the fourth century A.D., Christians built a monastery there to commemorate the meeting between God and Moses.

INSIDE SCOOP

> The Liberty Bell is engraved with words that describe the trumpet blast signaling the release of slaves at the start of Jubilee, a celebration every half-century: "*Proclaim liberty throughout all the land unto all the inhabitants thereof*" (25:10, KJV).

> The idea of a scapegoat—a person who takes the blame for others—is found in Leviticus. On Israel's national day of repentance, known as Yom Kippur, or the Day of Atonement, the high priest puts his hands on the head of a goat, symbolically transferring the nation's sins to the animal. Then he has the goat led into the desert to die. As the goat departs, so does Israel's sins.

WHAT TO LOOK FOR

- **Plan of salvation.** It's easy to get sidetracked by all the details of the law, and by trying to figure out exactly why God orders the Israelites to perform all these rituals and obey these rules—some of which may seem pretty bizarre and even unfair. Instead, read the book as God's first step in his plan of salvation—a step that dramatizes the seriousness of sin and the importance of obeying God.
- **Israel is unique.** The bottom line in laying out these rituals and rules is that God wants Israel to be holy—a nation separated from sinful practices and devoted to him. In this way Israel becomes a witness and an example to the world, testifying that God is holy and deserves our obedience.

EXTREME SCENES
from Leviticus

⇾ Sacrificial lamb (4:27–35)

God creates a complex system of animal sacrifice, which helps serve as a dramatic object lesson and visual aid for the people. One, it gives the people a visible, tangible way of expressing their sorrow for sin and of being assured of God's forgiveness. And two, with the death of the animal, it reminds the people about the seriousness of sin. Sin causes spiritual death.

The ritual calls for the worshiper to lay a hand on the head of the animal, perhaps as a gesture recognizing that the animal is about to lose its life because of his sin. "Life is in the blood," God explains. "I have given you the blood of animals to sacrifice in place of your own" (17:11).

⇾ Thoughts on food

God also gives the Jews elaborate rules about what they can eat and what they can't eat. They may eat animals that chew the cud and have a split hoof (such as cattle), fish that have fins and scales, and certain insects (such as locusts, crickets, and grasshoppers). But God bans a wide variety of animals, including pigs, camels, shellfish, lizards, and many birds. God doesn't give any explanation for these rules. Some think God was protecting the Jews from health problems, or from idolatry, since some forbidden animals were used in pagan rituals—especially the pig. But it may be that God was simply providing a visible way of showing Israel and other nations that the Jews were set apart for special service to God. People who eat nonkosher food become ritually unclean and have to follow certain cleansing rituals before they can worship God.

DIRECTOR'S NOTES

The best and purest olive oil came from green olives. Not only was olive oil used to anoint kings and priests; it was also used to treat wounds. Leviticus 24:2

⇾ Holy days

The Day of Atonement, known also as Yom Kippur, becomes the holiest day on the Jewish calendar. On this day, each autumn, the high priest offers sacrifices for the sins of the entire nation. First, he sacrifices a bull to atone for the sins of his own family. Then he sacrifices a goat for the sins of the nation. Afterward, he lays his hands on the head of a second goat—called a "scapegoat"—and confesses the sins of Israel. This goat is led into the desert and released to die "so that it can take away their sins." In the New Testament, this image of the scapegoat becomes associated with Jesus "who died to take away the sins of many" (Hebrews 9:28).

INTERVIEW
with the Stars

Hero-in-training

Behind the Bible has the totally incredible opportunity to speak with one of the greatest, most beloved and well-known heroes from the Bible. He's an author of several books in the Bible; he's a scholar; and later in his life, he was a key leader of God's people. He was a man who as a youth had all the luxuries and wealth Egypt had to offer. Yet, he never forgot his background and his people. He's a man who needs no introduction. *BB* welcomes Moses.

What an honor, Moses. Your accomplishments speak for themselves. What we would like to focus on today is your upbringing. What part did your background and heritage as a Hebrew play later in your life?

⮞ Moses

Everything, really. As you probably know, even though the Pharaoh's daughter found me that day in the bulrushes, my mother actually raised me. She instilled in me, even as a child, the importance of knowing who my people really were.

Yet, you also were brought up in the Egyptian palace and educated there, too, isn't that right?

⮞ Moses

That's right. I was given the best education and training Egypt had to offer. But I never really considered myself "one of them." When push came to shove much later, I chose to be with my people, the Hebrews.

INTERVIEW
with the Stars

What was the point of no return for you?

⇒ Moses

Actually, it came when I was a young man. I was out walking around, checking out how the building of the pyramids was going, when I came across an Egyptian beating up on one of those poor Hebrew slaves. I totally lost it. I'm not proud of it, but I killed that Egyptian guard. That's when I fled to the desert—and, well, you know the rest of the story. Those years prepared me for later on when I led my people out into the wilderness. Those were tough times, but it never crossed my mind to turn my back on my people.

What else in your youth helped prepare you for the great role you were to fulfill?

⇒ Moses

There were two things that really stand out in my mind. One was my faith in the God of the Hebrews, which my mom and dad had given to me. I never wavered in that. The second was my ability to write. My tutors had taught me well, and I never forgot the basics of writing. Much later, out in the wilderness, I was able to remember those lessons I learned in Egypt and write the first five books of the Bible.

Thanks for stopping by, Moses. We can all learn an important truth from your early years—and that's to make the most of what's available to us while we're young. Youth is not just a place to mark time until you become an adult. You don't know what God will use from your youth when you get older. Pay attention! Make the most of the opportunities to learn about God and your education now. God will take care of the rest when the time is right.

REVIEWS

ENCORE

To discover how New Testament writers build the Christian faith on Jewish traditions, read Hebrews. There, Jesus is shown replacing the sacrificial system, since he offers himself as the ultimate and final sacrifice for sin, "once for all" (Hebrews 7:27).

Leviticus is a survival guide. It's a how-to. It's a documentary, not a drama.

In our world we have compartments. We put certain kinds of information in certain groupings. Some things, like voting or going to court, are "government things." Some things, like praying or church, are "religious things." Other things, like belching the alphabet and seeing how many jellybeans will fit into one nostril are "little brother things."

That's not how it was for the ancient Hebrews. God was their leader so there was no separation between the church and the government. Church *was* the state and visa versa. They didn't have doctors' offices or permanent church structures. All they had was Moses, a portable structure to bring their sacrifices to, and priests to help them figure it all out. That's where Leviticus comes in.

If you could watch Leviticus, instead of reading it, you'd see some wobbly camera work. That's OK, this book isn't meant to be a special effects blockbuster. It was actually just meant to be helpful. This is how you do sacrifices. (Ready class? guts in the bucket and now we throw the carcass onto the altar fire. Feel the burn.) This is how you decide if a skin disease is contagious. (Hey Bob, see those festering boils . . .) This is how you should worship. This is how the priests should honor God's presence in the tabernacle. (I thought a tabernacle was one of these things that grows on the side of a boat. Guess not.)

The bottom line of Leviticus was the difference between clean and unclean. It's like God took the people down to the basics in order to teach them about himself. He told them which animals were clean to eat and which weren't (rules which make a lot of sense in terms of what we know now about bacteria and stuff). He told them which kinds of houses were clean and which weren't (if it has *legs*, it's NOT a raisin).

In the midst of this he was teaching them about holiness —spiritual cleanliness. It was all about how to talk to God, how to make Him happy, how to bring our sins to Him, and how to receive forgiveness for them.

Instead of "Leviticus," what do you think of the alternate title, "Basic Living For Dummies"? Never mind.

Jesse Jehubba

Numbers

SCHEDULE OF SCENES

Adam	Abraham	Moses	Exodus	Wandering Ends	David	Ezra	Jesus is Born
4000+ B.C.	2100 B.C.	1500 B.C.	1440 B.C.	1400 B.C.	1000 B.C.	450 B.C.	7/6 B.C.

The desert years

Don't be fooled by the title. Numbers is not just a series of boring reports from the number-crunchers. Yes, the book does include two census reports (that's how the book got its name): one at the beginning of the book, as the Israelites get ready to leave Mt. Sinai; and the second at the end, as they camp near the border of the Promised Land (now Israel). Sandwiched in between these reports, though, are a number of incredible stories that reveal a lot about what God is like and how He deals with a bunch of rebels (that's us).

Jews in ancient times knew the book by the name "In the Wilderness." That's a more descriptive title, for that's what most of the book is about: what went on during the 40 years it took the Israelites to reach Israel, some 400 miles away—and why it took them so long. The reason it took so long is simple: sin. In fact, one of the main points of the book and a message for all generations is that God punishes sin. He gives help when asked. He shows mercy unrequested. He offers love without strings attached. But when faced with sin, He knows it won't go away if he ignores it. So He doesn't.

Yet even when punishing individuals, leaders, and even nations, God gives encouragement and hope. As the apostle Paul noted: "The Scriptures were written to teach and encourage us by giving us hope" (Romans 15:4).

QUOTABLES

The Lord ... by no means clears the guilty, visiting the iniquity of the fathers on the children to the third and fourth generation (14:8, NKJV). Sin can have long-lasting and painful consequences. The sin of parents can scar children for life.

SNEAK PREVIEW

Esther
An ancient beauty pageant, a queen incognito, an aborted holocaust.

BEHIND the SCENES
of Numbers

STARRING ROLES

Moses, leader of Israel's 40-year trek toward the Promised Land (1:1)
Aaron, high priest and older brother of Moses (1:2)
Miriam, sister of Moses (12:1)
Balaam, sorcerer hired to put a hex on Israel (22:5)
Eleazar, son of Aaron and successor as high priest (19:6)
Joshua, scout who explored Promised Land, successor of Moses (11:28)

PLOT

After about a year camped at the foot of Mt. Sinai, the Israelites finally set out for the Promised Land. The journey is not easy. The Israelites suffer big time. They experience hunger, thirst, sickness, and threats of war along the way. They are not happy campers. They're quick to complain, but too stubborn to ask God for help. Despite being eye-witnesses to God's awesome miracles in Egypt, the Israelites don't seem to trust Him for their future. The final straw comes when they reach the boundary of the Promised Land. They absolutely balk at crossing the boundary when they hear scouting reports that there is no way the ragtag band of Israelites can defeat the fortified cities and giants "so big that we felt as small as grasshoppers" (13:33). They seem to forget that God, who saved them from the powerful Egyptians, is still with them and has *promised* this land to them! Because of their lack of trust, God condemns them to wander in the desert until their generation dies.

STAGE DIRECTIONS

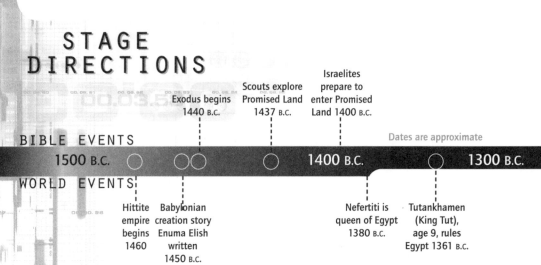

Exodus begins
1440 B.C.

Scouts explore
Promised Land
1437 B.C.

Israelites
prepare to
enter Promised
Land 1400 B.C.

BIBLE EVENTS

Dates are approximate

1500 B.C.   1400 B.C.   1300 B.C.

WORLD EVENTS

Hittite
empire
begins
1460

Babylonian
creation story
Enuma Elish
written
1450 B.C.

Nefertiti is
queen of Egypt
1380 B.C.

Tutankhamen
(King Tut),
age 9, rules
Egypt 1361 B.C.

AUTHOR AND DATE

Moses is assumed to be the main writer. Numbers 33:2 says he wrote at least part of it. Others may have added to it. For example, it seems unlikely that Moses would write this:"Now the man Moses was very humble, more than all men who were on the face of the earth" (12:3, NKJV). (That wouldn't be particularly humble, would it?) Moses probably wrote most of Numbers during the nation's desert travels in the 1400s B.C. Other knowledgeable writers, such as priests, may have added

material and compiled the work into final form after the Israelites settled in the land. Most likely, the main reason Moses wrote the book is to show that God punishes sin.

ON LOCATION

Numbers is set in the Sinai Peninsula, east of Egypt and south of what is now Israel. This is the sun-parched, rugged land where God condemns the Israelites to spend 40 years before entering the Promised Land.

WHAT TO LOOK FOR

- **Punishment for sin.** Notice how quickly God punishes sin. But notice, too, how quickly he forgives this nation of repeat offenders. Time after time they gripe, criticize, and outright rebel. But each time they repent, he forgives. The people suffer the consequences of their actions, but they don't suffer alone. God is with them.

EXTREME SCENES
from Numbers

The first count (1:1–54)

After God gives Israel their governing laws during the year they camp at the foot of Mt. Sinai, he tells Moses to break camp and head for the Promised Land. Since they will be invading land already occupied, God instructs Moses to count the people and find out how many eligible fighting men he has. Among the 12 families descended from the sons of Jacob, there are 603,550 men of fighting age, 20 and older.

Travel by ark (10:11–36)

It's an interesting procession to watch. First, a pillar of cloud representing God's presence begins to move. That's the signal for people to break camp and follow. Next comes the priests carrying the ark of the covenant, the chest containing the Ten Commandments. As the ark sets out each day, followed by the long mass of people, Moses says this short prayer: "Our Lord, defeat your enemies and make them run!" When the people travel by night, the pillar of cloud changes into a pillar of fire.

DIRECTOR'S NOTES

Don't underestimate the size of the Israelite nation. The 603,550 people counted in the census were all men. Throw in the women and children, and you probably had a total population of two million or more! That's quite a population growth from the seventy people who first settled in Egypt. Numbers 1:20-46

No more manna! (11:4–32)

Since leaving Egypt the Israelites have survived by eating manna, an unknown substance "like small whitish seeds" that tastes "like something baked with sweet olive oil" that covers the ground each morning like the dew. The Israelites eventually are bored with eating the same thing every day. So they begin to complain: "In Egypt we could eat all the fish we wanted, and there were cucumbers, melons, onions, and garlic. But we're starving out here, and the only food we have is this manna." So, God sends a wind that pushes quail in from the seacoast. The birds cover the ground "three feet high for miles in every direction." Each person gathers at least 50 bushels; then they begin a feast. What they can't eat right away, they dry in the sun for use later.

Scouting reports (13:1–14:44)

With the Israelites camping on the southern boundary of Canaan, Moses sends 12 men—one from each family tribe—to check out the lay of the land. He wants to know if the towns are fortified with walls, if the soil is good, and if there are trees. The scouts return 40 days later. Two men, Joshua and Caleb, show off the grapes, pomegranates, and figs they bring, urging the people to take the land.

But the other 10 scouts argue, "We won't be able to grow anything in that soil. And the people are like giants." The Israelites believe the majority report and refuse to go any farther. For their lack of faith, God condemns the nation to wander in the desert for 40 years—until most of the adults who left Egypt are dead.

DIRECTOR'S NOTES

If you would like to mark Passover on your calendar, check late March or early April. If you have a Hebrew calendar, check Abib (or Nisan), the first month of the sacred year. Jewish people still celebrate Passover today because God commanded them to remember how He led them out of Egypt. Numbers 28:16

Between a rock and a hard place (20:1–13)

The Israelites retreat south to Kadesh, an oasis where they apparently spend most of the 40 years. The water dries up, and the people have had it. They actually begin to regret leaving Egypt! (They obviously forgot about all those bricks!) Moses and Aaron are tearing their hair out and ask God for help. "Moses," God says, "you and Aaron call the people together and command that rock to give you water."

The two men call the people; Moses is not happy with them. He angrily shouts, "Look, you rebellious people, and you will see water flow from this rock!" Then he strikes the rock twice with his staff and water gushes from the rock. But God gets angry with Moses and Aaron because they don't follow God's instructions exactly so that God gets credit for the miracle. As punishment for their disobedience, He tells Moses that he and Aaron will not lead the Israelites into the Promised Land.

Snakes! (21:4–9)

The nation of Edom, in what is now western Jordan, refuses to allow the people to pass through safely. This would have given the Israelites a shortcut to the Jordan River crossing into Canaan. So Israel turns south, deeper into the desert, to go around Edom. Again, the people begin to moan and complain, criticizing God for making them suffer. God sends poisonous snakes into the camp, which kill many people. The Israelites realize their mistake, repent, and ask for forgiveness. God tells Moses to erect a pole with a bronze snake at the top. Anyone who gets bitten and looks at the pole will not die. Centuries later, Jesus will compare this event to His crucifixion, which provides eternal salvation (John 3:14–15).

⇾ The talking donkey (22:1–24:25)

Now Israel turns north and approaches the eastern border of the Promised Land. First, though, they have to pass through Moab in what is now the Dead Sea area of Jordan. The king of Moab is not thrilled at the prospect of having hordes of foreigners tramp through his country. He hires Balaam, an internationally known prophet and seer, to put a hex on Israel.

Balaam loads up his donkey and begins the journey. Along the way he encounters an angel with a sword. At first only the donkey can see the divine messenger, so the beast sits down and refuses to go further. (The contrast is powerful and wonderfully ironic: a lowly donkey can see what an acclaimed seer can't.) When Balaam beats the donkey, the Lord allows the beast to talk. "What have I done to you that made you beat me?" the animal asks.

Suddenly, Balaam is able to see the angel. This divine being permits Balaam to go to Moab on the condition that he speak only the word of God. Instead of cursing the Israelites, Balaam blesses them and curses their enemies. Furthermore, he predicts that "someday, a king of Israel will appear like a star. He will wipe out you Moabites and destroy those tribes who live in the desert." King David accomplished this in about 1000 BC (2 Samuel 8:2, 11–14).

⇾ A new leader (27:12–23)

Before Moses dies, God tells him to name Joshua as his successor. Moses takes Joshua before a massive assembly of the people, puts his hands on him, and appoints him Israel's leader. Though Moses is not allowed to enter the Promised Land, God does let him see it. Moses climbs a mountain east of the Jordan River. There below him, just across the river, stretches the land "flowing with milk and honey." There on the mountain, with this marvelous and moving vista before him, Moses dies (Deuteronomy 34:5–6).

INTERVIEW
with the Stars

Best supporting sister

It's probably not the easiest thing in the world to grow up in the limelight of a famous sibling, but that's exactly what our next featured interviewee did. **Behind the Bible** welcomes Miriam, who is probably best known as Moses' quick-thinking sister. For starters, Miriam, does it bother you to be introduced as Moses' older sister?

≫ Miriam

It's something I've lived with all my life. And, yes, I guess there were times in my life when it really bugged me being second banana. But you know, hindsight is 20-20, and I realized that I really had an important role to fulfill in God's grand plan for his people then and now.

Can you explain what you mean by that?

≫ Miriam

Sure. You see, I didn't exactly have a terrific childhood. I was the daughter of slaves, which meant that my future wasn't exactly rosy! And to make matters worse, the Egyptian government decided that all male children had to be killed at birth. And that's exactly when my little brother, Moses, was born! My mother was devastated!

So what happened?

≫ Miriam

My mother was determined that her son would live. So we hatched up this plan to keep Moses alive. My mom made a floating basket and when I went to do the laundry in the Nile, I set the basket afloat and gave it a push so it would float down toward where the wealthy Egyptian women bathed. I hid in the bulrushes and watched.

INTERVIEW
with the Stars

Weren't you afraid? I mean, if you were discovered, wouldn't it probably have meant certain death?

⇒ Miriam

I remember being scared to death, but more if no one picked up Moses than for my own safety.

What happened next?

⇒ Miriam

It was unbelievable. Out of all the women to discover Moses, guess who did? The princess of Egypt! I held my breath as she picked him up and looked him over. When I realized she wanted to keep him, I make a quick decision. I rushed out and offered to go find a nanny. Of course, I ran and got my mom. And that's how Moses was able to get Hebrew *and* Egyptian training.

So your quick thinking, Miriam, not only saved the life of your baby brother, but also the future deliverer of an entire nation from slavery. Amazing! I guess your story proves that no matter how small your job may seem, God can use it for *really* important work! In fact, God tells us that those who can be trusted with the small stuff will be trusted with the big stuff. All we need to do is get the job done—no matter what the size.

INTERVIEW
with the Stars

Standing alone

Heroics doesn't always come in the form of great deeds and works. Sometimes it can come in the form of being willing to take a stand, no matter what the opposition. Our next interviewee with *Behind the Bible* is such a hero. Caleb stood against the majority despite overwhelming opposition. Tell us what happened, Caleb.

⇒ Caleb

After years of dragging around the wilderness, we finally had made it to the edge of the Promised Land. Moses called a dozen of us to make a reconassiance of the land. We all paired up, and I went with Joshua. What we saw was unbelievable! After months in the dry, dusty desert, we saw a land that was incredibly beautiful and filled with lots to eat. It was totally amazing. Yeah, there was some opposition, and yeah, they were big people. But hey, who's bigger—them or our God? I'll go with God any day!

That's not what the others saw, was it?

⇒ Caleb

No. Joshua and I were saying go for it, and these guys had the people shaking in their sandals, telling them the people were as big as giants and stuff like that. I mean, where had these guys been? We just walked out on the most powerful nation in the world and nothing happened to us! Where was their faith?

INTERVIEW
with the Stars

Were you able to convince them to go along with you?

≽ Caleb

Sadly, no. Moses, Joshua, and I pleaded with them. We did everything we could to get the people to come along with us, but you know how it goes, majority rules. And the majority said no way. I can tell you, though, God was not pleased.

What happened?

≽ Caleb

Well, at first, God wanted to strike down every single one of them, but Moses pleaded for them. So God relented, *but* He sent us back out into the desert for another 40 years! Joshua and I were devastated. But we never gave up hope, and we never gave up our belief that God would honor us for what we did—to stand alone *with* Him.

And did He?

≽ Caleb

Yep, He did. When the 40 years was up, Joshua and I were the only two to make it into the Promised Land from that generation. I was 85 years old, but I received my portion of the land.

Congratulations, Caleb! And thank you for sharing your story. It demonstrates the importance of being *willing* to stand alone *with* God. Taking God seriously will show where you stand—mostly with the minority! But don't be afraid that your words are falling on deaf ears. God hears—just as he heard Caleb.

REVIEWS

ENCORE

 To find out what happens once the Israelites finally enter Canaan, read the book of Joshua.

 To see the fulfillment of God's promise to reward Joshua and Caleb for being the only two scouts to urge Israel to invade Canaan, read Joshua 14:6–15; 19:49–51. The other 10 scouts died from a "deadly disease" (14:37).

Numbers opens with a census. Ooh, I tremble with excitement. NOT ! Counting people one by one. Fast paced docudrama? No. Necessary? Yes.

Remember that the people of Israel were like a *huge* band of travelling gypsies. It was a forty-year road trip. Way too easy to get separated. "Have you seen Bob, Miriam?" "Not since that restroom break in the Engedi." " Rats, I thought I told everyone to go BEFORE we left Egypt."

They also were going to receive plots of land according to which tribe they were. Because of that it was important to always keep the people organized by tribes. The census did that.

That's before even mentioning the fact that the Israelites were about to walk into a fight. The Promised Land that they were about to enter was the land that God had promised them, but they had been away for hundreds of years. What do you think happened during those hundreds of years? Other people settled there. That meant Israel had to fight to win back their claim. The census was as much about counting the fighting men as anything else. Who wants to go into a battle and not even know how big your army is? "Let's see, there's ten thousand of them and on our side there's me and Bob and . . . me . . . right. Got your running sandals on, Bob?"

The end product of the census was a number that seemed impossibly large for the time that had passed. That might have been because they counted differently in those days. Having to figure out how ancient ways of record keeping translate into the modern world can be a challenge. The fact is that there may have been many fewer Israelites than reported. The Hebrew word for "thousand" can also mean "group," "unit," or "family." They must have been very careful about inviting another "family" over for dinner. "OK, four large pizzas times ten pieces divided by a thousand is . . ."

REVIEWS

After all the counting and lining up and recounting, Numbers is about a dark time in the history of Israel. The people got to the border of the land God had promised them, but they were afraid to go in. Who can blame 'em for not wanting to fight people much larger than they? Who can blame them for being unsure?

God, that's who. He had brought them through so much. He had worked miracles and proved himself to them over and over again. Yet, they didn't believe Him enough to take the last step. The story of Numbers is the story of God's people wandering around in their own doubt and confusion because they weren't brave enough to trust God with the biggest challenge of their lives.

The message here is about trusting God. It might start with standing up and being counted, but it comes down to crossing the line. It would be some time before God's people regained their census. (Get it? "Senses." Ow, that even hurt *me.*)

Noah Kownt

Deuteronomy

Moses' final say

What do you say to the people you love when you're about to die? How do you encourage them when you know they'll be facing the greatest challenge of their lives? Here's the scene: the entire nation of Israel is camped at the border of Canaan, now called Israel. God has promised to give them the land, but they'll have to fight for it. And it won't be an easy fight, either.

The people know Moses won't be there to help anymore. He won't part the waters of the sea when they need to escape. He won't draw water from solid rock when they're thirsty. He won't call down quail when they need meat.

He'll be gone. But God won't. "Stop worrying!" says Moses. "Just remember what the Lord your God did to Egypt and its king. . . . He will again work miracles for you" (7:18–19). To bolster the people's faith, Moses gently reminds them of where they came from, where on the earth they stand, and how they got there.

QUOTABLES

Hear, O Israel: The Lord is our God, the Lord alone (6:4). The creedal statement of the Jewish religion.

Love the Lord your God with all your heart, soul, and strength (6:5). The words Jesus quoted when asked to identify the most important commandment.

Apple of his eye (32:10, KJV). This is the first of several times that the familiar phrase shows up in the Bible. Here, it describes the love God has for Israel.

SNEAK PREVIEW

Matthew
Ancient prophecies in flesh and blood.

BEHIND the SCENES
of Deuteronomy

STARRING ROLES

Moses, who gives his farewell after leading Israel 40 years (1:1)
Joshua, appointed by God to succeed Moses (1:38)

PLOT

After 40 long, hard years, the Israelites are ready to cross the Jordan River and invade Canaan, the Promised Land. Most adults who escaped Egypt 40 years earlier have died. Moses, too, is about to die. The new generation assembled before him is one that grew up during the wilderness trek. They didn't witness the glorious escape. Nor did they stand at the foot of Mt. Sinai when their parents promised to obey God in return for guidance, protection, and blessing.

For this new generation, Moses prepares a series of sermons—history lessons that retell the feats of God and the laws that Israel has vowed to obey. Israel's future, he warns, depends on how the people respond to God. "Today I am giving you a choice," Moses tells the people. "You can choose life and success or death and disaster.... Choose life! Be completely faithful to the Lord your God, love him, and do whatever he tells you ... and he will let you live a long time in the land that he promised to your ancestors Abraham, Isaac, and Jacob" (30:15, 19–20).

What will this generation choose—life or death, as their parents had done?

STAGE DIRECTIONS

Israelites leave
Egypt 1440 B.C.

Moses dies, Israel ready to
invade Canaan 1400 B.C.

Dates are approximate

BIBLE EVENTS

1500 B.C.   1350 B.C.   1200 B.C.

WORLD EVENTS

Hittite
empire
begins
1460

Canaanite
civilization ends
1200 B.C.

AUTHOR AND DATE

Deuteronomy repeatedly says Moses wrote it. So do other Old Testament books and Jesus. Joshua or a priest probably added the closing chapter about Moses' death. Moses probably wrote the sermons that make up Deuteronomy shortly before he died, about 1400 B.C. He delivered these messages to remind the Israelites that they owed their very existence to God and to urge them to remain faithful to him.

ON LOCATION

The Israelites move out of the wilderness and are camped in what is now Jordan, near where the Jordan River empties into the Dead Sea. Soon they will march west and cross the river into Canaan, the land God has promised them. From Mt. Nebo, Moses gets his one and only view of the land.

WHAT TO LOOK FOR

The book reads like a contract with God. Bible experts say the outline of Deuteronomy follows the format of ancient treaties between kings and their people. In these treaties, such as those of the Hittites in the time of Moses, the king outlines what he expects of the people and what he will give them in return. The treaty also warns the people what will happen if they break their part of the bargain.

Here's the basic outline of ancient treaties, compared to the sections of Deuteronomy that seem to fit the pattern.

- Preamble, which identifies the ruler (1:1–5).
- Prologue, describing history of the relationship between ruler and servant (1:6–3:29).
- Rules of the treaty (chapters 4–26).
- Oath of allegiance, with benefits of keeping the treaty and consequences for breaking it (chapters 27–30).
- Instructions for observing the treaty, such as periodically reading it in public (chapters 31–34).

The core of Israel's treaty with the King of kings is summed up in the Ten Commandments. Deuteronomy 28:1–14 explains the benefits of obeying God's law: fertile crops, big families, prosperity, protection against enemies, national fame. Deuteronomy 28:15–68 explains the warnings about disobedience: famines, plagues, and invasions, ending with the people being uprooted and "scattered to every nation on earth." Some will even be loaded on boats and shipped back to Egypt.

INSIDE SCOOP

➢ The concept of safe haven for the fugitive starts in Deuteronomy, among a nation of former fugitives! Moses orders that once the Israelites settle in Canaan, they are to establish six "cities of refuge." These cities are places where people can go after accidentally killing someone. Here, they can get a fair trial and protection from the victim's avenging relatives. Other law codes from this time order the fugitive returned.

➢ The idea of a father/child relationship between God and Israel begins here: "The Lord has taken care of us the whole time we've been in this desert, just as you might carry one of your children" (1:31).

➢ Jesus quotes from this book more than any of the other five books Moses wrote. There are nearly 100 quotes or references to Deuteronomy in the New Testament.

EXTREME SCENES
from Deuteronomy

⋙ Pass it on! (6:1–9)

In one of several farewell speeches before he dies, Moses reminds the Israelites of their rich heritage and of the laws that set them apart from other nations. "The Lord told me to give you these laws and teachings," Moses says, "so you can obey them in the land he is giving you." At the center of the law is this: Israel is to worship God alone. "Memorize his laws," Moses says, "and tell them to your children over and over again. Talk about them all the time, whether you're at home or walking along the road or going to bed at night, or getting up in the morning."

DIRECTOR'S NOTES

While they were traveling, most Israelites made their living as farmers and shepherds—skills that were necessary for their mobile lifestyle. After settling in Canaan they were free to learn new skills and pursue other careers, such as carpentry, metalworking, weaving, masonry, and making pottery.
Deuteronomy 28:12

⋙ Contract renewal (29:1–29)

Some 40 years after God made a covenant with the Israelites at Mt. Sinai, Moses reminds the people about it. "The Lord has made an agreement with you," he says, "and if you keep your part, you will be successful in everything you do." Moses reminds the people that their part of the bargain is to obey the laws of God. And this contract isn't just for them, any more than the contract at Mt. Sinai was for the previous generation. It is, Moses reminds them, for all generations to come.

⋙ The final stop (34:1–12)

Moses is 120 years old. He has spent more than half his lifetime serving God and his people. His sister and brother, Miriam and Aaron, have died. So has most of the generation that he led out of slavery in Egypt. Now it is time for Moses to die. He climbs Mt. Nebo, which rises high above the rich Jordan River valley and Jericho, the oasis "City of Palms." At the summit, Moses sees the land of promise. And then he dies He is buried nearby in an unmarked grave. For a month the people grieve their loss of the one prophet in the Bible who spoke "face to face" with God.

REVIEWS

Deuteronomy is a book about the stuff that matters in life. It's Moses' last words before leaving his people. When you know what Deuteronomy is really about, it's at least a three-hankie flick.

Think about it this way, there were only three people even still alive that had left Egypt and traveled through the desert. Everyone except Moses, Joshua, and Caleb only knew the story second hand, so a lot of Deuteronomy is a big, long flashback. The people were about to finally get their inheritance (the Promised Land), but were risking their lives to win it back. Moses had one last shot to get 'em pumped up and prepared for the tough days ahead without him.

But Deuteronomy isn't just a walk down memory lane, it's a major how-to on living a life of faith and passing that faith down. In the old days, God was into object lessons. He helped his followers see how to follow him by showing them again and again. Deuteronomy is about a rite of passage. The Hebrews were "growing up" a little as a people and God didn't expect to keep having to personally remind them of everything all the time. It was time for people to start building unforgettable faith. They were instructed to pass on the stories of their faith to their children, to write them on their foreheads and doorposts. To remember.

They were also given the great Shema, the code for living: Love the Lord your God with all your heart and with all your soul and with all your strength. Jesus referred to this as the greatest commandment even before loving other people. It's one of the most basic foundations of the Jewish and Christian faith (right up there with the big 10) and it came out of Moses' good-bye speech.

Good-bye? You mean after all of Moses' time and trouble he didn't even enter the Promised Land? That's right. He looked over the hill and saw it, but he didn't go in. (There's the three-hankie part, sniff.) So there were only two of the original cast that actual saw the third act of the show. But thanks to Moses' pregame pep talk, recorded in Deuteronomy, they all knew where they had come from and where they were going. Go team! G'bye Moses! Anybody got a hankie (sniff, sniff)?

Beth Gamul

ENCORE

> To see an elderly Joshua follow Moses' example of a farewell address and a covenant renewal ceremony, read Joshua 24.

> To follow Israel on its conquest of the Promised Land, read the book of Joshua.

> To discover how Israel repeatedly breaks its contract with God, read the book of Judges.

Joshua

Adam	Abraham	Moses	Exodus	Conquest Begins	David	Ezra	Jesus is Born
4000+ B.C.	2100 B.C.	1500 B.C.	1440 B.C.	1400 B.C.	1000 B.C.	450 B.C.	7/6 B.C.

Fight for a homeland

This is the final chapter of a promise God made 700 years ago to an old man with no kids. "Go to the land that I will show you," God told 75-year-old Abraham, "I will bless you and make your descendants into a great nation" (Genesis 12:1–2). When Abraham obeyed and arrived near the center of Canaan—now Israel—God said, "Look around to the north, south, east, and west. I will give you and your family all the land you can see. It will be theirs forever!" (Genesis 12:14–15).

There was a slight detour in the grand plan. Abraham's grandson, Jacob, led the family to Egypt to escape a famine. There they thrived and grew so much that the Egyptians feared a Hebrew takeover, so they made them slaves. But under God's order, Moses freed them. And now, under God's order, Joshua was taking them home.

Many scenes in this story are as show-stopping as those of the great Exodus. The water of the Jordan River stops flowing so the Israelites can enter the Promised Land. The walls of Jericho spontaneously collapse before Joshua's army. The sun and moon stand still, so Joshua's soldiers can finish an important battle.

Throughout the many battles that take place in the story, it is clear that the conquest of Canaan had little to do with Joshua's military savvy or the Israelite's bravery. It had everything to do, however, with a promise God made to an old man with no kids 700 years earlier. God delivers on His promises.

QUOTABLES

The priests blew their trumpets, . . . the soldiers shouted as loud as they could. The walls of Jericho fell flat (6:20).

"Choose for yourselves this day whom you will serve. . . . As for me and my house, we will serve the Lord" (24:15, NKJV). Part of the elderly Joshua's farewell to Israel.

SNEAK PREVIEW

> **Galatians**
> How can grace be free when it cost so much?

BEHIND the SCENES
of Joshua

STARRING ROLES

Joshua, leader and military commander of the Israelites (1:1)
Rahab, a Jericho prostitute who hid two Israelite spies (2:1)
Achan, Israelite whose greed cost his nation a battle (7:1)

PLOT

After escaping from about 400 years in Egypt—much of that in slavery—
and wandering 40 years through the Sinai Desert east of Egypt, the
Israelites finally arrive on the border of the land God has promised them.
Their mission: take the land using any necessary force and purge it of the
idol-worshiping people who live there.

STAGE DIRECTIONS

Israelites invade the
Promised Land
1400 B.C.

Joshua dies
1357 B.C.

Dates are approximate

BIBLE EVENTS

1400 B.C.   **1350** B.C.   **1250** B.C.

WORLD EVENTS

Nefertiti is
queen of Egypt
1380 B.C.

Tutankhamen
(King Tut), age 9,
rules Egypt
1361 B.C.

Seafaring Philistines
settle in Canaan,
along the coast
1300 B.C.

AUTHOR AND DATE

The book doesn't identify its author. But because of Joshua's starring role in the book named after him, he has tradition-ally been considered the main writer. The report of his death may have been added by priests Eleazar (Aaron's son) or Phinehas (Aaron's grandson). Joshua likely wrote the book dur-ing the final years of his life, about 1375 B.C., and reported on the 25 years it took Israel to conquer and begin to settle much of the land God promised them. He primarily wrote this book to remind the Israelites, the book's first audience, that they didn't win their homeland through military genius and courage. The land was a gift from God.

ON LOCATION

Most of the story takes place in what is now Israel. But the Israelites also con-quered and claimed surrounding territory in what is now parts of Jordan, Syria, and Lebanon. After Jericho, they moved west, then south. Only then did they attack the northern area, pressing past the Sea of Galilee (Chinnereth).

WHAT TO LOOK FOR

- **The land is God's gift, not spoils of war.** Just before the invasion, when Joshua must have been plotting his war strategy, God assures His chosen leader that the victories are there for the taking *if* the Israelites continue to trust Him. "Wherever you go," God says, "I'll give you that land" (Joshua 1:2). And before the first trumpet is sounded at the battle of Jericho, God tells Joshua, "I have given Jericho into your hand" (Joshua 6:2, NKJV). The battle is won before it starts.
- **God rewards obedience, punishes disobedience.** When they obey, the results are totally amazing: the walls of Jericho collapse; hailstones rain from the skies, killing enemy soldiers; the sun stands still, giving Israel all the time it needs to win the battle. But disobedience has its prices. When one man takes some war booty from the dead enemies, against God's order, the Israelites lose their next battle. And when they make a peace treaty without consulting God, they get tricked (see Joshua 9).

Joshua and Jesus share the same name. The name Jesus is a Greek form of the Hebrew name for Joshua, much like Jacques is the French equivalent of James. Both Joshua and Jesus mean "God saves."

EXTREME SCENES
from Joshua

Scoping out the enemy (2:1–24)

Before leading the Israelites into Canaan, Joshua sends two spies to scope out Jericho. A prostitute named Rahab informs them that the people of Jericho are shaking in their boots (or sandals) at the thought of an Israeli invasion. They've heard all about Israel's great escape from Egypt and they know how this nation of former slaves has defeated every army that has tried to stop them. The spies return and give Joshua and the people the green light: "We're sure the Lord has given us the whole country," they say. "The people there shake with fear every time they think of us."

Crossing in style (3:1–17)

When it finally comes time for the Israelites to enter the Promised Land, after 40 long years of waiting, they do it in style! Leading the invasion are priests carrying the ark of the covenant, a sacred chest containing the Ten Commandments. As soon as they step into the Jordan River (which borders the eastern boundary of Canaan), the river comes to a complete stop! Water piles up at the town of Adam, some 20 miles to the north, and stays there until the entire nation has safely crossed the Jordan.

The Israelites enter the Promised Land much as they had left Egypt—with God clearing the way for them, sweeping aside a river, just as he earlier swept back the waters of the Red Sea.

Breakthrough at Jericho (6:1–27)

The Israelites encounter their first enemies about five miles across the river. The people of Jericho, protected by the city's massive walls, believe they are safe from the invaders. It may appear laughable at first when, for six days, the "mighty" Israelite army does nothing but march around the city, led by seven priests who continually blow on ram-horn trumpets. On the seventh day, however, no one in Jericho is laughing when the trumpets sound a final blast and the walls collapse. The Israelites charge in to a total rout.

The Israelites lose the next battle, however. One of their soldiers, Achan, decides to help himself to some spoils of war—about five pounds of silver, a pound of gold, and a beautiful robe imported from what is now Iraq. Doesn't sound like a lot, but unfortunately for Achan, this is direct disobedience of God's orders. The Israelites lose the battle; Achan loses his life. Afterward, the Israelites resume a successful campaign, sweeping south, then turning north.

⇒ All the time (literally) in the world (10:1–28)

Joshua discovers that a coalition army from five cities, including Jerusalem and Hebron, is camped in the hills of Gibeon, 15 miles to the west. Immediately, he orders an all-night march uphill. As the battle is waged hour after hour, Joshua asks God to extend the day, maybe to give Israel time to finish off the enemy. As a result, "The sun stood still and didn't go down for about a whole day."

Eventually, the enemy turns and runs. But when they reach a mountain pass about five miles away, God seals the victory for his people by sending a storm of huge hailstones. "More of the enemy soldiers died from the hail than from the Israelite weapons."

⇒ Dividing the land (13–22)

After Joshua's army conquers 31 cities in the highlands of Canaan, he divides the land among the 12 tribes of Israel. Each tribe must finish the job and secure the boundaries to its own territory. Still to be captured are the powerful cities in the coastal plains, particularly those being settled by the Philistines, the new kids on the block.

⇒ Joshua's farewell (23–24)

After leading the fledgling nation into battle and helping the tribes get settled, it's time for the now elderly Joshua to say his good-byes. He calls the leaders together, and like Moses, he reminds them of their agreement—to worship God instead of the idols that had been so popular throughout Canaan. Elderly Joshua calls together the leaders of Israel to bid them farewell. At age 110, Joshua dies and is buried in the rugged hills north of Jerusalem.

INTERVIEW
with the Stars

Stepping up

What happens when a great leader steps down and leaves some mighty big shoes—or in this case, sandals—to fill? Sometimes the person next in line is not prepared or lacks the necessary leadership skills. Fortunately for the people of Israel, our next interviewee was more than capable of stepping up to the task of leading them into the Promised Land. **Behind the Bible** welcomes Joshua.

Joshua, why don't you tell our readers exactly whose shoes, um, sandals you filled?

⋙ Joshua

For years, I was second in command to none other than Moses, the man who as God's representative, led the people of Israel out of Egypt and a life of slavery. As you can imagine, that was a pretty big act to follow.

I'm sure it was. How did you manage to pull it off?

⋙ Joshua

Fortunately for me, I had lots of time to grow into the job. Moses trained and mentored me for more than 40 years. I literally worked in Moses' shadow, learning how to lead the people and make good decisions. Eventually I became Moses' personal assistant *and* his military commander.

What would you say was the most important thing you learned while serving under Moses' command that helped you when you became the new leader?

⋙ Joshua

The thing that struck me the most about Moses was his relationship with God. He had an incredibly close relationship with the Lord. In fact, God spoke to Moses face-to-face, as you would talk to a friend. I knew if I wanted to be successful like Moses, I needed to form my own close relationship with God. So as a youth, I spent as much time alone with God at the tabernacle as possible. You could say I learned everything I needed to know at the feet of my mentor, Moses, and at the feet of God.

INTERVIEW
with the Stars

After Moses had died and you were named successor, weren't you at all nervous or scared about stepping into that leadership position?

⇝ Joshua

You bet I was! But I had something even more amazing than 40 years of training under the best leader the people of Israel ever had. I had God's promise: "As I was with Moses, so I will be with you" (Joshua 1:5). What more does any leader need to know than that? Because I had spent all that time with God as a youth, I knew that God would be with me any time throughout my life. With confidence like that, I could face any battle that came my way.

And you certainly did have your share of battles—and more importantly, victories. I guess the secret to your success is your relationship with God. It's apparent from your life, no time spent with God is wasted time. No relationship in your life will be more significant than a relationship with God.

⇝ Joshua

That's right. What God does in you will impact and improve every other relationship that you have. Trust me on this one! When you choose God, everyone in your life is a winner!

REVIEWS

I know most people think of the Old Testament as kids stuff: the Creation, Noah's ark. It's all happy endings and angels with harps and nobody ever gets hurt, right? *Cha*! As *if*! Read again, my friends. The Old Testament is filled with stories of murder (when God is on the case, the bad guys ALWAYS get caught), deceit (like the coat of many colors story), sex crimes (blush, mumble, giggle) and war, war, and more war. If the Old Testament was a movie, you'd have to be 17 to see it.

These days, war is a bad thing, something to be avoided. Back in Joshua's time, war was a daily reality. Not many people believed in God back then, and the ones who did were homeless in the worst way. They didn't even have a country to be homeless in, somebody else had moved in.

Under God's command, the Hebrews fought to regain their homeland. It was a tough time, they had to walk *from another country* before they could even *start* fighting to get their land back. The next time your parents start griping about how tough things were when they were your age and how they had to walk to school, ask them if they had to walk to *another country*. How will they react to that? How fast can you duck? It took a lot of courage for the Hebrews to walk back into their homeland and take control again. But that's what God commanded them to do. While it might be hard to understand God's ordering his children to start a war, remember that people were pretty primitive back then, the human race was just past infancy. God had simple rules for simple people just like a parent has simple rules for a toddler. (Do not, I repeat, DO NOT picture a bunch of Caananites walking around with swords, long beards, and loaded diapers. STOP IT! It's not funny... not unless you add in baby bonnets and pacifiers.)

ENCORE

> The book of Judges continues where Joshua leaves off, with the Israelites getting settled in the land.

> If you enjoy the book of Joshua, read Deuteronomy. It, too, calls God's people to devote themselves to the Lord and to trust him for their needs. Among the last words of Moses are these: "The eternal God is our hiding place; he carries us in his arms" (Deuteronomy 33:27). Joshua's final speech, a generation later, offers evidence of that promise: "You have seen how the Lord your God fought for you. . . . Always love the Lord your God. Don't ever turn your backs on him" (Joshua 23:3, 11–12). That's good advice for us today, too.

REVIEWS

The big lesson in Joshua is that when the Hebrews followed God's orders, they kicked some serious rear (which is why it's good that nobody was *really* wearing diapers), But when they got ahead of the game plan or tried to do things on their own, without God's direction, they got clobbered. I think of it like a basketball team. You gotta have a coach, somebody who knows the game better than the players, to have a chance at winning. Of course, God is not only the coach, He's the one who came up with the game, built the arena and invented air so we'd have something to put in the ball. The message: fight under God's direction and in His strength and you'll prosper. Fight in your own strength and you'll fail. Eventually, the Hebrews listened to God enough times to win back most of their homeland, but not enough to get rid of all the squatters (I SAID STOP IT!!!).

Jeri Cho

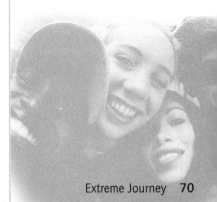

Judges

Abraham	Moses	Exodus	Death of Joshua	Coronation of Saul	David	Ezra	Jesus is Born
2100 B.C.	1500 B.C.	1440 B.C.	1375 B.C.	1050 B.C.	1000 B.C.	450 B.C.	7/6 B.C.

Heroes to the rescue

Looking for that blockbuster book that has it all—sexual intrigue, violence, and larger than life heroes? Look no further. The book of Judges has it all. Consider just two of the stories found in Judges:

- The wife of a religious leader is gang-raped to death by Israelite men from the tribe of Benjamin. A bloody civil war follows that nearly wipes out the tribe of Benjamin.
- Or there's Samson, Israel's famed strongman with a weakness for beautiful, immoral women. He winds up with an unwanted haircut, his strength gone, and his eyes gouged out. His life ends in a final act of strength, which literally brings down the house.

They are not exactly the type of stories you want to point to with pride. These are the skeletons-in-the-closet type stories. And they all happened as a result of sin. God calls His people to Himself. His people run after other gods and get in trouble. God sends in a hero to rescue them. God calls his people to obedience. His people run after...over and over again. It's like bad summer TV with rerun after rerun.

At some point in the book, you feel like grabbing Israel by the collective throat and screaming, "Don't you get it? Don't you remember everything that God has done for you? Don't you remember what you promised—and what would happen if you didn't? Duh?" That's the point, though. The people *didn't* remember. But God did. He punished them for their sins. But He never stopped loving them. And when they got themselves in major trouble and cried out for help, God was there.

QUOTABLES

"I shall put [out] a fleece" (6:37, NKJV). What Gideon did to prove that God would help him.

Delilah had lulled Samson to sleep with his head resting in her lap. She signaled to one of the Philistine men as she began cutting off Samson's seven braids (16:19).

SNEAK PREVIEW

Jeremiah
A broken-hearted prophet with the inside scoop on a nation about to fall.

BEHIND the SCENES
of Judges

STARRING ROLES

Samson, strongman and last of Israel's 12 judges (13:24)
Delilah, Samson's fatal attraction (16:4)
Gideon, a farmer turned commander of 300 militiamen (6:11)
Deborah, the only female judge (4:4)

PLOT

The Israelites have captured and secured most of the highlands in Canaan, now Israel. Joshua has died, leaving them with the charge to A. continue serving God; B. finish conquering the land; and C. get rid of all the idol-worshiping Canaanites.

 The Israelites do none of the above. They settle into the highlands, learn to live with their neighbors, the Canaanites, and begin adopting their religion and way of life. Before long, the lines of distinction between Canaanite and Israelite start to blur. God punishes the Israelites by sending invaders. Israel endures the suffering for a while, then asks God for deliverance. God sends a leader—called a judge—who saves the people. This plot is rerun over and over twelve times.

STAGE DIRECTIONS

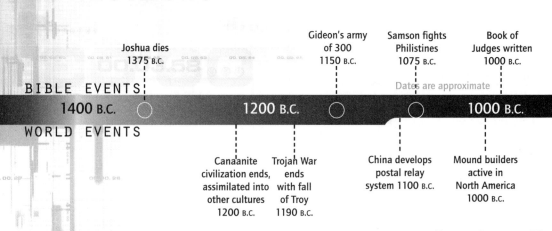

BIBLE EVENTS

Joshua dies
1375 B.C.

Gideon's army
of 300
1150 B.C.

Samson fights
Philistines
1075 B.C.

Book of
Judges written
1000 B.C.

Dates are approximate

1400 B.C.   1200 B.C.   1000 B.C.

WORLD EVENTS

Canaanite
civilization ends,
assimilated into
other cultures
1200 B.C.

Trojan War
ends
with fall
of Troy
1190 B.C.

China develops
postal relay
system 1100 B.C.

Mound builders
active in
North America
1000 B.C.

AUTHOR AND DATE

The writer is unknown, although the prophet Samuel traditionally has been credited as the author. He was Israel's religious leader a few decades after the judges, when many believe that the stories were compiled into a book. The book covers roughly 300 years, just after Joshua dies in about 1375 BC until just before Saul is crowned the first king of Israel in about 1050 BC. The stories spanning these centuries were probably compiled and preserved in writing sometime after Israel had a king. One strong clue is that the writer repeatedly says the stories take place "before kings ruled Israel" (17:6). The book may have been compiled during the reign of Saul or David, the first two kings. The book

was written to preserve an important— though horribly unflattering—slice of Israel's history. The stories vividly show the consequences of disobedience, as well as the never-ending love of God.

ON LOCATION

The stories take place in what is now Israel.

WHAT TO LOOK FOR

- **Repetition.** Judges has one basic pattern or plot repeated throughout the book. The Israelites prosper, then they stop worshiping God, face the consequences of punishment, cry out for God's help, and get that help in the form of a leader chosen by God. Notice that by the end of the book, Israel sinks to a new, all-time low.
- **God's mercy and unrelenting love.** Israel breaks its contract, or covenant, with God. For this, they suffer consequences that Moses warned about, particularly this one: "Your enemies will eat the crops you plant, and I will turn from you and let you be destroyed by your attackers" (Leviticus 26:16–17). For repeated breach of contract, God has every right to do more: "You shall perish among the nations, and the land of your enemies shall eat you up" (Leviticus 26:38, NKJV). But God stops short of allowing this. For as He had explained through Moses, "No matter what you have done, I am still the Lord your God, and I will never completely reject you" (Leviticus 26:44).

> The phrase *missed it by a hair* could have come from Judges. The tribe of Benjamin had 700 left-handed warriors "who could sling a rock at a target the size of a hair and hit it every time" (20:16).

> Most of the 12 judges of Israel were not the legal experts who settled disputes, like our judges today. The Hebrew word that best describes these judges is the word for "savior" or "deliverer." Most Israelite judges were military leaders. God chose them to lead regional campaigns against enemies. Samson was the one exception; he was a one-man army who led no one. The 12 judges, in order, are Othniel, Ehud, Shamgar, Deborah, Gideon, Tola, Jair, Jephthah, Ibzan, Elon, Abdon, and Samson.

EXTREME SCENES
from Judges

Idol worship (2:6–23)

The people of Joshua's generation completely drop the ball in passing along the faith to their kids: "The next generation did not know the Lord or any of the things he had done for Israel." So the people stop worshiping the Lord and begin worshiping the gods of Canaan. God is so angry at the Israelites that he allows other countries to raid Israel and steal their crops and other stuff. When the people can't stand it anymore, they finally turn to the God of their parents. He answers them by sending them a leader, or judge, to rescue them. As long as that judge is around, things go well. But later the Israelites become even more sinful than the previous generations.

DIRECTOR'S NOTES

Carrying the ark of the covenant was no small task. It was about the size of a small desk. The ark had rings on its sides so that the priests could put poles through them and carry the sacred container without actually touching it. The Israelites carried it into battle because they believed it gave them the power of God. Judges 3:3, 4

The battle of Mount Tabor (4:1–24)

For 25 years the people in northern Israel are harassed by a nearby hostile king. Finally, the people have had enough, and they ask God for help. He sends them Deborah, a prophet and judge. She tells the people to assemble an army. The odds seem to favor the enemy, for they have a corp of 900 chariots, manned by seasoned professionals. Israel has untrained militia, hastily called to defend themselves, zero chariots, zero weapons.

The Israelites gather at Mount Tabor, a steep hill on which no charioteer would willingly choose to fight a battle. But the mountain quickly becomes the least of their worries. Rain suddenly pours from the sky, transforming the valley into a huge mud puddle that traps the iron wheels of the chariots. The enemies dart from their chariots and run for their lives, but none escape.

Gideon's rout (7:1–25)

The cycle continues, and the Israelites return to their sinful ways. So at harvesttime each year, God allows desert raiders on camelback to invade Israel. When the people ask God for help, He calls on Gideon who instantly whines: "How can I rescue Israel? My clan is the weakest one in Manasseh, and everyone else in my family is more important than I am." Reluctantly, Gideon raises an army of about 32,000. God then downsizes his forces to only 300 men! In the dark of night Gideon's men secretly surround the enemy camp filled with tens of thousands of invaders. Each Israelite carries a burning torch hidden inside a clay jar. On Gideon's signal they smash the jars, raise the torches, and blow trumpets. The horrified marauders turn for home and run.

⇒ Fatal attraction (16:4–31)

Samson is unlike any of the other judges. He doesn't settle disputes. He leads no army. Instead, he's a one-man army fueled by a deep hatred of the Philistines who have killed his new bride and burned her body. In revenge, he burns their crops, then slaughters a thousand of their soldiers by using nothing but the jaw-bone of a donkey.

Samson has incredible strength given by God. He also has a vow to keep—he is never to cut his hair. When Samson falls in love with Delilah, the Philistines offer her nearly 30 pounds of silver to find his weakness. After two failed attempts, she succeeds. While he is sleeping, she clips the hair she had earlier woven into seven braids. Then she calls in the waiting Philistines. Soldiers rush in, capture Samson, gouge out his eyes, then put him to work at a grinding mill.

By the time they decide to parade him as a war trophy in front of crowds gathered for a religious festival, Samson's hair has grown. Standing between two pillars, probably made of wooden or stone blocks, Samson prays for strength once more, so he can kill more Philistines and die with them. In a powerful surge of strength he breaks the pillars. The roof collapses, killing at least 3,000 Philistines. Samson dies, too, the last of Israel's 12 judges.

⇒ Dark days

As the book of Judges ends, it appears that life in Israel can't get much worse. In one instance, an Israelite man hires a silversmith to craft him an idol. Then he hires a priest to live with him, thinking he's covered all his bases. Apparently, he forgot the first of the Ten Commandments: "Do not worship any god except me" (Exodus 20:3).

Even more disturbing—and sickening—is the story of an Israelite religious leader who is traveling with his wife to the nation's worship center in Shiloh. A mob attacks the couple while they are spending the night at a home in territory owned by the tribe of Benjamin. The mob demands that the man come out so they can have sex with him. Instead, the man pushes his wife outside. She is gang-raped all night and is dead by morning. The husband cuts her into pieces and sends the body parts to the 12 tribes of Israel, with a plea for revenge. The result is a civil war in which 11 of the tribes nearly exterminate the tribe of Benjamin.

The book ends with this unsettling portrait of anarchy: "In those days there was no king in Israel; everyone did what was right in his own eyes" (NKJV).

INTERVIEW
with the Stars

Blinding truth

Behind the Bible has an opportunity to talk with a man who not only had incredible gift of strength, but who also had all the qualifications to be a true champion for his people. Yet, this man made some critical errors in his life that made him achieve far less than his potential. Samson, tell us about your unusual gifts.

⋙ Samson

To be honest, I probably could have qualified as the first Superman. I had incredible strength that left my enemies and friends speechless. Unfortunately, I literally let it all go to my head.

Tell us what you mean by that.

⋙ Samson

God gave me this amazing strength, and in exchange, I was to devote myself to Him as a Nazarite. That meant I wasn't supposed to cut my hair or drink wine. My hair was supposed to be a reminder of the source of my strength—God. Instead I began associating my hair as my strength. As long as I had my hair, I figured I was invincible.

And what led to your downfall?

⋙ Samson

It would be easy for me to blame Delilah. She was the one who tricked me into telling her my secret, or so I thought. But really I was revealing to her my weakness—I didn't realize until too late that the true source of my strength was God.

INTERVIEW
with the Stars

And as a result of that you lost your strength. What happened then?

⋝ Samson

It was total humiliation. Not only did the woman who I thought loved me, betray me, but I also was bound and chained and finally blinded and put on display for all to mock and laugh at. Yet, ironically, when I lost my eyesight, I finally could see clearly my mistakes.

And those were?

⋝ Samson

I finally understood that I had never learned to control the connection between my eyes and my heart. I fell hard for Delilah and never really saw her betrayal coming. And I never took God seriously as the source of my strength. I figured He, along with my ability, would always be with me no matter what.

Do you think ultimately you learned from your mistakes?

⋝ Samson

Yes, in the end, I turned to God for my final strength. But I could have made a bigger difference for God. My weaknesses and my mistakes caused me to fall short. We all make mistakes, especially when we are young. The real test comes in learning from those mistakes and not repeating them. When bad things happen to others because of what they do, don't think that those results can't happen to you. Learn from your own mistakes and from other's mistakes as well. The more you do that, the more you will be able to make a difference with your life.

INTERVIEW
with the Stars

Living with other's mistakes

Our next interviewee is a little known young woman whose life was dramatically changed by her father's tragic mistake. Yet, this young woman accepted her fate with such dignity and courage that she has been forever honored for her grace in the face of great personal tragedy. Her full name is never given. She's known only as the daughter of Jephthah. *Behind the Bible* is pleased to have Jephthah's daughter with us to share her story. Why don't you tell us what exactly happened that fateful day?

≥ Jepthah's daughter

Thank you. You see, my dad was a superhero. He had won many great victories for the people of Israel. And he loved me dearly. But he made one big mistake.

What was that?

≥ Jepthah's daughter

It still hurts to talk about it. But he announced, in public, that he would sacrifice the first thing that came out of his house if he returned home from war victorious. Well, you can guess the rest. He did win—a great victory against our enemies. And the news had traveled back home to us. So when I saw my father coming home in his victory parade, I ran out to greet him. And so it turned out that I was the first one he saw coming out of his house.

INTERVIEW
with the Stars

What did your father do when he saw you?

⋟ Jepthah's daughter

I had no idea what he had promised. But when he saw me, his face went white, he tore his clothes, and then he told me what he had promised to the Lord. And I knew, without any doubt or bitterness, that my father had to keep his promise. No matter how foolish or how much suffering it caused me, I knew I had to honor my father and his vow to God.

It appears that the sacrifice your father made was to commit you, his only daughter, to lifelong virginity. Because of your father's rash promise, you were never to marry or have children.

⋟ Jepthah's daughter

That's right. It was a bitter pill for me to swallow, but also for my father. Not only would I never marry, but he also would never have grandchildren. As you know, children were considered a great blessing from God. My father may have achieved great military successes, but he failed in this one important area of his life.

So, your father made a terrible mistake that cost you *your* happiness and *your* future. Yet, you are remembered and honored today because of the way you handled this very difficult situation. You have given all of us a great example of how honoring others and forgiving them, no matter how difficult, can lead to true freedom. Thank you for your time today.

REVIEWS

ENCORE

➤ To continue the flow of Israel's story, read 1 Samuel. It picks up where Judges leaves off.

➤ Hebrews 11 names several of the judges, calling them models of faith.

Sometimes in a book or movie you can find one line that sums up the whole thing. ("My momma says life's like a box of chocolates.") For Judges the line is "everyone did as he saw fit" (17:6; 21:25). In the time of Judges, people were pretty confused. There weren't any living prophets like Moses or great warriors like Joshua to interpret God's will and keep everybody on the right track, so everybody just kind of wandered around, spiritually, and got further and further from God.

About the only leaders the people had were Judges (hey, maybe that's why they call the book Judges...duh). Judges didn't have as much power over the people as the kings who came later, but they *were* spiritual *and* political leaders. Sometimes they even led the people into battle. Remember Samson, the long-haired muscleman with the two-faced girlfriend? He was a judge. Deborah, the woman who led Israel to a great victory (you go, Girl!) was a judge way before Judge Judy.

All through this book, the Israelites kept making the same goof. When times were good, they forgot who brought them the good times in the first place. (C'mon, Israelites, you *know* this one. Three letters, starts with a REALLY big G.) And when times got bad, they suddenly got over their "amnesia" and came running back to God, begging for help. You'd think they woulda figured it out sooner or later. Unfortunately, when they went from Judges to Kings, it just got worse. There's a good lesson to be learned form this book. I'd give it two thumbs up, if I had any (Judges 1:6).

A. Don Ibezek

Ruth

SCHEDULE OF SCENES

Abraham	Moses	Exodus	Death of Joshua	Saul	David	Ezra	Jesus is Born
2100 B.C.	1500 B.C.	1440 B.C.	1375 B.C.	1050 B.C.	1000 B.C.	450 B.C.	7/6 B.C.

Love story

The story hooks you from the start. Famine drives a family from its homeland. The sons fall in love and marry two native girls. Within 10 years, the father and the sons die. The three grief-stricken women are left destitute. Yet, from these tragic beginnings, God spins a story of devotion, faithfulness, and love, and gives it a jaw-dropping twist at the end: Ruth—a foreigner—gives birth to Israel's most famous family of kings. Not only is she related to King David, born in Bethlehem, but she also is an ancestor of the future King of kings born in that same hamlet hundreds of years later (Matthew 1:5).

Until the very end of the story, though, things don't look good for Ruth. In those days, a woman's greatest accomplishment was to have children. Ruth had none. And nearly all of a woman's legal rights depended on her husband—including the right to own property. Ruth had no husband. Also, in the tiny village of Bethlehem, people found acceptance and support in being part of the close-knit Israelite family, the chosen people of God. Ruth was no Israelite.

From the very beginning, Ruth was an outsider, but she chose God. And He brought her inside, to the very heart of Israel's faith, transforming her into a model of love and the matriarch of Israel's most respected kings.

QUOTABLES

"I will go where you go, I will live where you live; your people will be my people, your God will be my God" (1:16). What Ruth told Naomi after both became widowed.

SNEAK PREVIEW

Genesis
Which came first, the chicken or the egg?

BEHIND the SCENES
of Ruth

STARRING ROLES

Ruth, young widow from Moab and great-grandmother of David (1:4)
Naomi, Ruth's mother-in-law, an elderly widow from Bethlehem (1:2)
Boaz, second husband of Ruth (2:1)

PLOT

To escape a famine in Israel, a Bethlehem man moves with his wife and two sons to a neighboring country. There, his sons marry local women. Then all three men die, leaving their widows destitute. The matron, Naomi, decides to return to her extended family in Bethlehem. She urges her daughters-in-law to go back to their families as well. One does, but Ruth refuses to abandon the elderly Naomi.

The two widows arrive in Bethlehem in time for the spring harvest of barley and wheat. A kind farmer lets Ruth pick some leftover grain for her and Naomi. Ruth later discovers this man is related to Naomi. Ruth proposes marriage to him, he accepts, and they have a son: Obed, the grandfather of King David.

STAGE DIRECTIONS

BIBLE EVENTS			
Judges lead Israel in Ruth's era 1375 B.C.	Saul becomes first king of Israel 1050 B.C.	David crowned king of Israel 1000 B.C.	Dates are approximate
1400 B.C.	1100 B.C.		0900 B.C.

WORLD EVENTS

Nefertiti is queen of Egypt 1380 B.C.	Iron tools, weapons used in Israel 1200 B.C.	China develops refrigeration, using winter ice 1000 B.C.	

AUTHOR AND DATE

The writer is unknown, but Jewish tradition says Samuel wrote it. This seems unlikely since the climax of the book identifies Ruth as the great-grandmother of David, who is crowned king only after the death of Samuel. (Before the people accepted David as king, however, Samuel anointed him as God's choice to succeed King Saul.) The story takes place in the time of the judges, "before Israel was ruled by kings" (1:1). The story was then likely passed on by word of mouth for several generations before being written down sometime during or after the time of David, who began his reign about 1000 BC.

It's unclear why someone decided to preserve this story. One theory is that it was written to trace the family tree of David, Israel's most popular king. But perhaps there were other reasons as well: to encourage the Israelites to embrace God-loving foreigners (as God embraces Ruth),

and to allow future generations to learn from Ruth's example of love for Naomi.

ON LOCATION

The story begins in Bethlehem, then briefly shifts to Moab, Israel's neighbor east of the Dead Sea in what is now Jordan. Within a few paragraphs, the scene switches back to Bethlehem where the rest of the story unfolds. More than a thousand years later, Luke calls this Bethlehem "the city of David" (Luke 2:4) because of family ties going back to Boaz and Ruth.

WHAT TO LOOK FOR

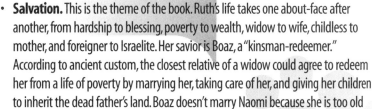

- **Salvation.** This is the theme of the book. Ruth's life takes one about-face after another, from hardship to blessing, poverty to wealth, widow to wife, childless to mother, and foreigner to Israelite. Her savior is Boaz, a "kinsman-redeemer." According to ancient custom, the closest relative of a widow could agree to redeem her from a life of poverty by marrying her, taking care of her, and giving her children to inherit the dead father's land. Boaz doesn't marry Naomi because she is too old to have children. So he agrees to marry Ruth and take care of both women. Many Bible scholars see in Boaz an example of God redeeming Israel from slavery and of Jesus later redeeming the world from sin.
- **Spoken blessings.** In every chapter you'll find one person speaking a word of blessing to another. Naomi blesses her widowed daughters-in-law with a prayer that God will treat them kindly and give them new husbands and homes. And when Boaz greets the workers harvesting his grain he says, "The Lord bless you" (2:4). To which the workers reply, "And may the Lord bless you." The frequency of these blessings suggests that people who believe in God have a right to speak blessings in God's name— and that God hears and responds to those prayers.

Television and film personality Oprah Winfrey was named after Orpah, the daughter-in-law who chose not to stay with Naomi and Ruth. The letters "r" and "p" were switched in Oprah's name.

The mother of Boaz was Rahab, probably the prostitute who helped the Israelite spies in Jericho. That would make Rahab the great, great-grand-mother of King David, as well as an ancestor of Jesus (Matthew 1:5).

Jews today honor Ruth by reading her story during an annual religious festival at the end of the grain harvest.

EXTREME SCENES from Ruth

⋗ Tough love (1:1–22)

A famine in Bethlehem drives an Israelite man out of his country. He takes his wife and two sons east of the Jordan River into Moab, part of what is now Jordan. There his sons marry Moabite women. But within 10 years, all three men die. Naomi, matron of the family, decides to go back home, maybe hoping that some family members will take her in. But she urges her two daughters-in-law not to follow. If they go back to their families, they might be able to remarry. But it's too late for the elderly Naomi. In a time and culture where women depend on a husband or a son to take care of them, Naomi has neither. One daughter-in-law leaves, but Ruth absolutely refuses to abandon Naomi. "Please don't tell me to leave you," Ruth begs, "I will go where you go, I will live where you live; your people will be my people, your God will be my God. I will die where you die and be buried beside you."

DIRECTOR'S NOTES

When God gave His laws to the Israelites, He made sure that everyone was taken care of. For example, a farmer was not allowed to go back to get grain he might have missed during harvesting. The remaining grain was left in the field for the poor people in the area to take. Ruth 2:1-3

⋗ Taking the leftovers (2:1–23)

Naomi and Ruth arrive at Bethlehem in the spring during the harvest season. Fortunately for them, the Israelite system of welfare requires farmers to leave some of their crop for the poor, "including foreigners, orphans, and widows" (Deuteronomy 24:19). (The process of picking up the leftover grain is called gleaning.) Ruth goes to the field of a man named Boaz and gets permission from the harvesting foreman to glean behind the harvesters. Ruth's hard work and her kindness to Naomi make a big impression on Boaz. He tells his worker to leave extra grain for her. He also invites Ruth to eat with the workers.

The proposal (3:1–18)

When Naomi finds out that Boaz is a distant relative of hers, she comes up with a plan to make him their "kinsman-redeemer"—a relative who volunteers to take responsibility for the extended family. If Boaz will marry Ruth, he could take care of both of them and rescue them from a life of poverty. So Naomi tells Ruth to clean up, put on some perfume and her best clothes. Then she is to slip under the covers while Boaz is asleep and lie at his feet. (No, this isn't an attempt by Ruth to seduce Boaz! It was an Israelite custom for a servant to lie at his master's feet. By doing this, Ruth was letting Boaz know that he could be their family redeemer if he wanted.)

DIRECTOR'S NOTES

If you've never threshed grain, you may not know that it involves separating the grain itself from the stalk. In ancient times, this was done by beating the stalks or having animals walk over them. Afterward, the whole smashed mess was thrown into the air. The leaves and stalks were blown away by the wind, and the grain fell back to the ground. Threshing was hard work, but there was usually something special to look forward to when the work was done. Traditionally, the harvest and threshing season was a time of celebration and fun. Ruth 3:2

When Boaz wakes up, he is surprised to find a woman sleeping at his feet! When he asks who's there, Ruth says, "Sir, I am Ruth, and you are the relative who is supposed to take care of me. So spread the edge of your cover over me." Boaz is wowed by her loyalty to her family and to the Jewish traditions. He promises to check it out, and if no one else in the family steps forward to marry her, then he will.

The legacy (4:13–22)

This is one story that has a happy ending. Boaz marries Ruth and also agrees to take care of Naomi. The couple has a son, to the delight of parents and grandmother. He's called Obed, and according to God's great plan, this child will become father to Jesse, grandfather of King David, great-grandfather of King Solomon, and an ancestor of Jesus.

INTERVIEW
with the Stars

Family ties

This next woman gives new meaning to the word loyalty. She gave up her country, her culture and her upbringing, left everything familiar, to accompany her mother-in-law back to her homeland. Her words resonate with love and faithfulness, "For wherever you go, I will go; and wherever you lodge, I will lodge; your people shall be my people, and your God, my God" (Ruth 1:16b). Ruth, tell **Behind the Bible** in your own words about the event leading to your decision.

⊰ Ruth

Naomi and her family, including my future husband, had come to Moab to seek relief from a famine in their homeland. Later, though, both her sons and her husband died. She decided to return to Bethlehem with her grief. My other sister-in-law wanted to go back with her. But she told us she wanted us both to stay. My sister-in-law decided to stay. But I couldn't let her go. I had to return with her and take care of her.

What happened then?

⊰ Ruth

When Naomi saw I was determined to return with her, she stopped arguing with me. And we made the long journey back to Bethlehem. It wasn't easy at first. Even though this was her homeland, there was no one exactly throwing out the welcome mat. To get food, I began gathering the leftover grain in the fields. It turned out that the fields belonged to a relative of Naomi's, named Boaz.

INTERVIEW
with the Stars

And that relationship turned out to be very beneficial, didn't it?

⋝ Ruth

You could say that! It turned out that Boaz had been watching me in the fields and had asked about me. And Naomi knew just what to do! I followed her advice, and one thing led to another, and Boaz and I married! Out of our grief and our poverty, God brought such goodness and richness. And that's not the best part—the best part is that God allowed me to be an ancestor to His very son, Jesus Christ! Isn't that amazing?

We certainly see from your story a beautiful picture of how we can make a difference in the relationships God gives us if we trust in Him. You stood by Naomi, adopted her homeland, her people, but most important, her God.

⋝ Ruth

Despite our differences in culture and in age, we became more than family. We became sisters in our shared relationship with God. I think God wants the same thing for you, too. Every relationship in life offers God an opportunity to work. Where is He working in your relationships? That's the question we all need to ask ourselves.

Thank you for taking time to share your story. It's an inspiration for all of us!

REVIEWS

If there ever was a chick flick in the Bible it's gotta be Ruth. Even though the book of Ruth is set in the rough-and-tumble time of Judges, it has a big ol' mushy story line that begins and ends with a family of four. Only one person appears in both families—the widow Naomi, Ruth's mother-in-law. Kinda like a mini-series or somethin'. Oh, one other cool thing. When Ruth does nab her sweetie, a wealthy landowner named Boaz, they get married and have a kid who is a direct ancestor of King David and Jesus. Yeah, I said Jesus. Top that! Can't you just see Naomi, zipping around town with a "MY GREAT, GREAT (etc.) GRANDSON IS THE MESSIAH!" bumper sticker on her donkey?

The only thing that keeps me from going for the tissues on this one is how absolutely weird the dating rituals of the time were. What did Ruth do to catch her man? Well, first she went and gathered wheat in his fields and caught his eye. (They didn't have malls or dance clubs, so if you wanted to catch a guy's eye, you gathered wheat. Can't you just hear ol' Boaz talking to his buddies: "Hey Bob, check out the way that chick gathers wheat, she is soooo hot!") Then at the right moment she sprinkled on the perfume, slipped into her prettiest robe, and quietly crawled into the barn where Boaz, was sleeping with his men (why does a rich dude sleep in a barn? I better go read this again) and slept at the foot of his bed (which, by the absolutely whacky dating regulations of the time, was some sort of way for a girl to propose marriage?). All night sleeping by someone's feet. She musta really liked this guy. Eventually, they call a town meeting and Boaz has to give up one of his sandals (why is everyone obsessed with this guy's feet?) before he and Ruth can progress further into the freakish dating rituals of the time. I imagine the first date went something like this:

Boaz: So, Ruth. You wanna go gather some wheat?

Ruth: Why Boaz, you naughty boy. I'd never gather wheat with a man on the first date.

Ruth: Now, let me see your toes.

Hosea Downe

ENCORE

For stories of other women who win their way into Israel through their own initiative, read about the Canaanite woman Tamar (Genesis 38) and the Jericho prostitute Rahab (Joshua 2; 5:13—6:25).

Esther is the only other Bible book named after a woman. Like Ruth, she is portrayed as a brave heroine, loyal to her family.

The New Testament story of Mary and Joseph has similarities to the story of Ruth and Boaz. Ruth was an outsider, and that's how Mary would have been treated once her neighbors discovered she had an early baby. Boaz showed compassion for Ruth by agreeing to marry her. Joseph did the same for Mary, though he knew he was not the father of the divine child. Ruth and Boaz raised a family of kings. Mary and Joseph raised the King of kings. You can read the story of Mary and Joseph in Matthew 1—2 and Luke 1—2.

1 Samuel

Abraham	Moses	Exodus	Death of Joshua	Birth of Samuel	Death of Saul	David	Ezra	Jesus is Born
2100 B.C.	1500 B.C.	1440 B.C.	1375 B.C.	1150 B.C.	1010 B.C.	1000 B.C.	450 B.C.	7/6 B.C.

Faulty characters

OK, everyone you know—practically the entire civilized world—has his or her own set of wheels. So what is it that you want more than anything? Your own car, right? Israel was suffering the same they've-got-it-we-want-it syndrome; only what they wanted was a king. Every country around them had a king. Why didn't they? The book of 1 Samuel tracks the history of how Israel made the switch from a loosely connected group of tribes to a united nation led by a king. But the plot goes deeper than that. It's the story of how God continues to accomplish His plan despite a cast of men and women who keep messing up—big time.

Consider some of the starring characters and their major personality flaws (as well as many of the supporting cast). Priest Eli came up way short in the parenting skills department. His two sons grew up crooked and gave a bad name to the priesthood. Samuel didn't do much better with his boys. When he tried to pass on Israel's spiritual leadership to his sons, the people said, "No thanks, we'd rather have a king."

Then there's Saul, Israel's first king. The man was nearly a no-show at his own coronation and then seemed clinically depressed much of the time. When David tried to calm him down with soothing music, Saul threw a spear at him. Twice. Even David, who later would become Israel's most beloved and respected king, had his own particular set of problems. He had a life-sized *idol* in his house! His wife used it once to trick Saul's soldiers, who were coming to kill David. How's that for a major character flaw?

Through this colorful cast of characters, though, we learn, as they did, the depth of God's love for His people and the scope of His resources for proving it. And that's good news for us, who have a few flaws of our own.

QUOTABLES

"Long live the king!" (10:24). An Israelite crowd's response to Samuel introducing Saul as the nation's first king.

"To obey is better than sacrifice" (15:22, NKJV). Samuel's criticism of Saul after Saul disobeys God by keeping livestock as spoils of war, so he can use them as sacrifices.

SNEAK PREVIEW

Luke
God walks way more than a mile in our shoes.

BEHIND the SCENES
of 1 Samuel

STARRING ROLES

Samuel, prophet and spiritual leader of Israel (1:20)
Saul, Israel's first king (9:2)
David, Saul's successor (16:1)

PLOT

The prophet Samuel becomes the spiritual leader of the nation, serving primarily as a prophet who delivers God's messages to the people and as a judge who settles disputes. When he grows old, the people take one look at his sons and decide they want no part of that. What they want is a king "just like all the other nations."

But they are not like other nations. And that's the point. They are *God's* people, and *he* is their king. Yet God gives them what they want. He chooses Saul as their fist king. But after Saul repeatedly disobeys, God gives him the boot. God's next choice is a young shepherd boy named David.

STAGE DIRECTIONS

Samuel is born 1105 B.C.	Saul becomes first king of Israel 1050 B.C.	David anointed to succeed Saul 1025 B.C.	Saul dies 1010 B.C.

Dates are approximate

BIBLE EVENTS

1100 B.C. — **1050 B.C.** — **1000 B.C.**

WORLD EVENTS

Philistines protect their secret of making iron 1100 B.C.			People in eastern North America grow crops 1000 B.C.
China develops mouth organ 1100 B.C.			Lyre players painted on Philistine jar 1000 B.C.

AUTHOR AND DATE

No one knows who wrote the two books of Samuel, originally written as one book. But the author appeared to have access to historical records because the books contain so much detailed and personal information about Samuel, Saul, and David. That's entirely possible because the Bible says such records did exist: "Everything David did while he was king is included in the history written by the prophets Samuel, Nathan, and Gad" (1 Chronicles 29:29).

The book was written sometime after Solomon died and Israel split into two nations, in about 930 BC because the writer refers to the two nations, Israel in the north and Judah in the south (17:52). The reason the book exists is to preserve the history of the Israelite nation as they grew from a ragtag group of 12 tribes to a united nation led by a king.

INSIDE SCOOP

> Ichabod Crane, the vain and cowardly man who is terrorized by a man dressed as a headless horseman in *The Legend of Sleepy Hollow*, gets his name from one of Eli's grandsons. When Eli's daughter-in-law gives birth shortly after the Philistines attack Israel, steal the ark of the covenant, and kill her husband, she calls her son Ichabod, which means *the glory is gone.*

ON LOCATION

The stories take place in Israel. When Saul becomes king, he establishes his capital in Gibeah, the village where he was born, a few miles north of Jerusalem. At this time Jerusalem was still occupied by the Jebusites; this mountain stronghold had not yet been conquered (see Judges 1:21).

> The old saying *stay by the stuff* comes from 30:24, "tarried by the stuff" (KJV). David was arguing that the soldiers who stay behind to guard the camp deserve a share of the booty taken in battle.

WHAT TO LOOK FOR

- **Samuel's birth.** Notice that the book tells the story of Samuel's birth, but not the birth of Israel's first king, or even of Israel's most revered king of all time. This is a clue about how important Samuel is to the story. He plays the key role in Israel's shift from a loose coalition of families to a nation ruled by a king. Not since Moses, whose birth story is reported in Exodus, has Israel had such a charismatic and dynamic leader.
- **Traits that God admires.** You'll find plenty of imperfect characters in this book. But there's also many character traits that God admires and rewards—Hannah's heartfelt prayer; Eli's trust in God even when faced with painful news; David's life-on-the-line total confidence that God will help him cut down a giant.

EXTREME SCENES
from 1 Samuel

The promised child (1:21–28)

Hannah is a desperate woman. She has no children, so she pleads with God to let her have a son. In exchange, she promises that she will let the boy serve God all of his life. Within a year, Samuel is born. True to her word, as soon as the boy is old enough to feed himself (probably about age three), Hannah takes him to the worship center at Shiloh. She hands Samuel over to Eli, saying, "The Lord gave me just what I asked for. Now I am giving him to the Lord, and he will be the Lord's servant for as long as he lives." Hannah later has other children, but she never forgets her firstborn son. Each time she comes to Shiloh to worship with the family, she brings Samuel a new robe.

DIRECTOR'S NOTES

The ark of the covenant was about the size of a small desk. It had rings on its sides so that priests could run poles through them and carry the ark more easily. Once a year, the high priest would stand in front of the ark to offer a special sacrifice to the Lord. To the Israelites, the ark symbolized God's presence and power. 1 Samuel 4:3

A voice in the night (3:1–21)

Young Samuel is a quick study and promising student under Eli. One night, while he is sleeping, Samuel hears his name being called. Thinking Eli must need something, he goes to the old priest and asks what he wants. But it's not Eli calling him. After the third time this happens, Eli finally gets what's going on— it's the *Lord* calling Samuel. He tells the boy to listen to the Lord. The next time God calls, Samuel is ready. He tells Samuel that he, not Eli's corrupt sons, is to be the next spiritual leader for the country. It's not exactly the type of news Eli wants to hear, but he accepts the Lord's decision.

Stolen goods (4:1–10)

The Israelites are fighting a losing battle against their archenemies, the Philistines. They decide to send a patrol 20 miles back to Shiloh to get their secret weapon (or so they think)—the ark of the covenant. This gold-covered chest holds the Ten Commandments and is considered Israel's MVO (most valuable object).

The soldiers believe having the ark on the battlefield will give them magical powers to defeat the enemy. They are dead wrong. Not only do they lose the battle, but Eli's sons are also killed in the fight and the ark is stolen! When Eli gets the bad news, he is so traumatized that he falls off his chair backwards, breaks his neck, and dies.

The Philistines, in the meantime, display their war trophy at the feet of the statue of their god. Seven months later, after discovering that the ark seems to cause diseases, they want no part of the ark and return it to Israel.

DIRECTOR'S NOTES

Priests received answers from God in three different ways: through prayer, through visions and dreams, and through the use of objects called "Urim" and "Thummin." The Urim and Thummin were small gems or stones carried by the high priest. Many Bible experts believe the stones were engraved with symbols and thrown like dice to determine God's will. 1 Samuel 14:1-3

The first king (9:1–10:26)

Samuel is now approaching retirement age, and he plans to turn over the family business of being a spiritual leader and judge to his sons. But they are just as corrupt as Eli's sons, and the people soon begin to complain about them. When they demand a king instead of his sons, Samuel is crushed. But Samuel agrees to take up the matter with God. God tells him not to take it so personally; the one the Israelites really are rejecting is God. God chooses Saul, who is an instant winner with the crowds.

The giant-killer (17:1–52)

For more than a month, the armies of Israel and Philistia have been at a stalemate. To make matters worse, every morning and evening, the biggest, baddest dude in Philistia comes out, draws a line in the dirt, and dares the Israelites to cross it and fight him. No one wants to mess with Goliath. After all, the guy is nine feet tall and wears more than 150 pounds of armor! No one, that is, until a young Israelite shepherd boy comes to the battlefield, bringing food to his brothers. When he hears Goliath mocking God, David goes ballistic. He can't understand why no one has gone out there to shut this guy up. So he volunteers. He takes his slingshot, five rocks, and an unshakable faith in God into battle. When Goliath sees his opponent is only a young boy, he practically FOFL. That doesn't stop David. He lets loose and hits Goliath square in the forehead. The giant falls facedown in the dirt; David finishes off the job, takes Goliath's sword and cuts his head off. The rout begins, and the Israelites chase the Philistines from the battlefield.

Over the edge (18:1–11)

Understandably, David is an instant hero. He is the darling of the country, and there are even a couple of songs written about him. One song in particular really fries King Saul. Its lyrics go something like this: "Saul has killed 1,000; David has killed 10,000." If Saul hears it one more time, he will go completely nuts—and he does. Saul begins acting like a crazy man. When David tries to calm him down by playing his lyre—a technique that worked before—Saul completely loses it. He grabs a spear and hurls it at David—twice!

The chase is on (24:1–22)

As quickly as David's popularity skyrockets, he just as quickly rises to the top spot on Saul's enemy list. Saul orders his men to kill David on sight, and David's next role is as the fugitive. The chase begins with Saul's man tracking down David and his growing band of followers in the hill country of Israel. Once, Saul tracks down David and his men into an area honeycombed with caves. Unfortunately for Saul, he chooses to relieve himself in the very cave where David and his men are hiding. It's as if God has given David the perfect opportunity to do in his enemy. But David knows better.

He sneaks up behind Saul and cuts off a piece of his robe. When Saul leaves, David bursts out, waving the piece of his robe in one hand. David shouts, "I will not harm the Lord's chosen king. Yet you keep trying to ambush and kill me." It's total humiliation for Saul. He calls off his soldiers and goes home. But Saul can't leave it alone and soon renews his senseless mission to kill David.

Hitting rock bottom (28:1–25)

The Philistine army is on the move again and advancing deep into Israelite territory. Saul rushes to engage the enemy, but is paralyzed with terror. He wants to know what God wants him to do, but there is no one to tell him. Samuel has died. The other prophets have no news, and Saul's own prayers to God go unanswered because of his previous disobedience. Saul is caught between a rock and a hard place. So what does he do? He hits rock bottom. Saul consults a *medium* and asks her to contact Samuel's spirit. To everyone's horror, including the medium's, Samuel actually appears! It's not good news, though, for Saul. When he begs Samuel to tell him what to do, Samuel answers, "If the Lord has turned from you and is your enemy, why are you bothering to ask me?" Then he tells Saul that the Israelites are going to lose big time tomorrow.

The final battle (31:1–13)

It's not exactly the confidence-booster that Saul needs. But he goes into battle, and as predicted, the Philistines break through the Israeli line. One by one, Saul's three sons are killed in battle: Jonathan, Abinadab, and Malchishua. Saul himself is critically wounded. The king asks his weapons-bearer to finish him off before the Philistines capture him and torture him. But the soldier can't bring himself to do it. Saul props the handle of his sword into the ground and falls on the blade. The first king of Israel is dead.

INTERVIEW
with the Stars

Learning to listen

Behind the Bible welcomes a man who was instrumental in helping Israel move from the dark days of the judges to the brief, but shining moments as Israel emerged as a united nation. Samuel, *BB* is certainly glad to share this time with you. Can you share with us the secret to your success as Israel's final judge and renown prophet?

⇒ Samuel

It's not that difficult, really. At a very young age, I learned to listen.

Listen to whom? Eli, the priest, who raised you at the temple since you were a toddler?

⇒ Samuel

Well, certainly to Eli. He was the one who steered me in the right direction. But more importantly, I learned to listen to God's voice and to what He had to say to me.

So God actually spoke to you? Can you tell us about it?

⇒ Samuel

I was only a young boy at the time. I was sleeping, and I heard a voice calling my name. At first, I thought it was Eli calling me to get him something. But when I went into Eli's room, he told me he hadn't called me at all. I was very confused. The next time I heard my name I again went in to Eli. By the third time, Eli knew that it was God calling me. He told me to stay in my bed and *listen* because God had something to say to me.

INTERVIEW
with the Stars

And you did?

⋟ Samuel

Absolutely! When God speaks...well, I guess there are people who don't listen when God speaks. But I learned even as a child that I needed to listen to God.

How did that make a difference in your life?

⋟ Samuel

I was able to be God's chief spokesman for the people at the time. When the people were crying for a king, I conveyed God's message to them that they were only asking for trouble. And then when they insisted, with God's leading, I anointed the first two kings of Israel, Saul and David. Because I *listened* to God, I was able to *speak* for God.

And that was a role that continued throughout your adult life as well, wasn't it?

⋟ Samuel

That's right. I continued to hold the king accountable in God's name for his behavior—and believe me, at times, that was a full-time job! But without that habit of listening to God that I began as a boy, I never would have been able to make a difference at all. And for your readers, today, well, they have God's entire word available to them! I only had Moses' writings—five books out of 66! Eli's advice still stands after all these centuries—when God talks, listen!

INTERVIEW
with the Stars

The right loyalties

What kind of price tag do you put on a friendship? Does your friendship come with hidden costs—like I'll-be-your-friend-if-you-do-something-for-me? Where do your loyalties lie? **Behind the Bible's** next interview is with a man who made a difference because he had his loyalties—especially his ultimate loyalty—straight. **Behind the Bible** is pleased to introduce Prince Jonathan and the future king David's loyal friend. Let's begin with your friendship with David.

⇒ Jonathan

We were friends from the start. I admired his courage on the battlefield; he admired mine. We were like brothers. I loved him as much as anyone can love a friend.

It couldn't have been easy, though, being David's friend.

⇒ Jonathan

No, it wasn't. It cost me big time. I lost my father's trust because of it. I never betrayed my father. I never prevented his plans. But I also wasn't going to help him do something that was wrong. My father never understood why I didn't join him in trying to kill David so I could have the throne.

INTERVIEW
with the Stars

That's understandable from his perspective, though. The throne, according to lineage, rightfully belonged to you. Why didn't you fight for it?

⋟ Jonathan

It's simple really. There's a difference between blind and open-eyed loyalty. I remained loyal to my father my entire life. In fact, I died with him on the battlefield. But I also knew that God's hand was on David—he, not me, was the one anointed to be the next king of Israel. My ultimate loyalty was to God and His plans. And I wasn't going to do *anything* that would prevent that from happening. So when I had an opportunity to warn David about my father, I took it.

That had to be a difficult choice to make.

⋟ Jonathan

It's always going to be difficult when you have to choose between friends and family. Those are the kinds of decisions that break your heart. But the one thing I can tell you is that the *only* way to make those decisions is when your human loyalties are controlled by your ultimate loyalty to God. That's when you can make a difference.

Thanks for stopping by, Jonathan, and sharing this important lesson on getting your loyalties straight.

REVIEWS

ENCORE

The first book of Samuel is full of people and things showing up in unexpected places.

When the Philistines captured the ark of the covenant (a sacred chest containing the Ten Commandments) they brought it to "the temple of their god Dagon and put it next to the statue of Dagon" (5:2). Archaeologists have found the name of this mysterious deity at several places in the region. One document from the 1300s B.C. says Dagon is the father of Baal, the Canaanite god of rain and fertility. Was that any place for a sacred Hebrew chest?

David, who eventually became the greatest king of Israel, spent much of his younger days as a fugitive. (Imagine, if you will, some *Mission Impossible* type music). David and his men hid from Saul in a cave "in the desert around Engedi" (24:1). Engedi had an oasis and was a perfect place to hide because it was concealed in a narrow ravine. Rocky ledges and mounds – with lots of convenient caves – surround the oasis on three sides. The fourth side opened onto the shore of the Dead Sea. This was David's favorite secret hideout until he took over his kingdom.

Before David took the throne, Saul was king. God chose a shy and humble man to become Israel's first king. Saul was actually out looking for some of his father's donkeys that had run off when he first came upon Samuel, the prophet who anointed him king. As Saul was donkey hunting Samuel broke the news to him about his coming inauguration. Saul was dumbfounded. "I'm from Benjamin, the smallest tribe in Israel," Saul said, "and my clan is the least important in the tribe" (9:21).

Later, when Samuel was about to introduce Saul to the people, no one could find the reluctant monarch. He was hiding among the pack animals. Just goes to show you, the most significant things can often turn up in the most unexpected places.

Saul E. Mann

To read the rest of the story, turn to 2 Samuel. The two books were originally one, but were separated when they were translated from Hebrew into Greek, in about 300 BC. This apparently made the size more manageable, allowing each volume to fit onto a single scroll.

For the story of another infertile woman who has a son and who promises to let him serve the Lord, read about the mother of Samson. It's in Judges 13.

For a song in the spirit of Hannah's in 2:1–10, read Mary's song in Luke 1:46–56.

2 Samuel

SCHEDULE OF SCENES

Abraham	Moses	Exodus	Death of Joshua	Death of Saul	Death of David	Ezra	Jesus is Born
2100 B.C.	1500 B.C.	1440 B.C.	1375 B.C.	1010 B.C.	970 B.C.	450 B.C.	7/6 B.C.

David: super king, sorry father

It's the stuff tailor-made for the soaps. One son falls madly in love with his half-sister. He seduces her, rapes her, then hates her. Enter son two, the sister's full brother. He kills his half-brother, then flees the country and remains the black sheep of the family for five years. Whose kids are these, anyway? King David's.

It's really not such a big surprise when you consider the father's behavior. David, when he gets an eye full of his hot next-door neighbor (who also happens to be married), invites her over to the palace, gets her pregnant, *kills* her husband, and then marries her. Like father, like son.

The stories grab at our hearts, but confuse us as well. What was God thinking about when he described David as "a man after His own heart" (1 Samuel 13:14, NKJV)? This guy, who messes up his own life *and* his kids' lives, this king is the one God loves? But that's good news for us. Because there is a message here for all who have ever made a total mess of their life and wondered if God can forgive them. (Sound like someone you might know?) Throughout this book, God forgives David—whenever David asked, no matter how badly David messed up.

And that same mercy, that same irrational love for a rebellious child, is available to us today. As David put it in a song, "Give thanks to the Lord, for He is good! For His mercy endures forever" (1 Chronicles 16:34, NKJV).

QUOTABLES

"I have sinned" (12:13, NKJV). David's response when Nathan accuses him of committing adultery with Bathsheba and killing her husband.

"My son, my son . . . I wish I could have died instead of you!" (18:33). David's reaction to hearing that his son Absalom has been killed while trying to overthrow him.

SNEAK PREVIEW

Song of Songs
Passion and love.
An unbeatable pair.

BEHIND the SCENES
of 2 Samuel

STARRING ROLES

David, king of Israel (1:1)
Absalom, crown prince who leads a rebellion (3:3)
Nathan, prophet and David's chief advisor (5:14)

PLOT

David becomes the new king, replacing Saul. During the 40 years of David's reign, he expands the borders of Israel as far north as the Euphrates River into what is now Iraq, and eastward into Jordan. The taxes he gets from these conquered neighbors help lower taxes for the Israelites. The nation of Israel hits an all-time high in achieving land, status, and peace. On the political front, David's reign is a complete success. But closer to home, his family life is a total bust. A big chunk of the book includes stories you would expect to see bannering the supermarket tabloids: king having affair with married neighbor; king's son rapes half-sister; king's son leads attempted takeover.

STAGE DIRECTIONS

End of David's
reign 970 B.C.

David secretly   David
anointed king   becomes   Absalom's revolt
1025 B.C.   king 1010 B.C.   975 B.C.

BIBLE EVENTS   Dates are approximate
1040 B.C.   1000 B.C.   900 B.C.
WORLD EVENTS

Calendar of farming
cycles, oldest example
of Hebrew writing
1000 B.C.

Wigs worn
by Egyptian
aristocrats
950 B.C.

Greeks worship Zeus,
Aphrodite, and other
gods 1000 B.C.

AUTHOR AND DATE

The same unknown author who wrote 1 Samuel also wrote this book because both books were originally one volume. The book was separated into two books when the Hebrew text was translated for Greek-speaking Jews in about 300 BC. The two books could fit onto a single scroll written in Hebrew because the ancient Hebrew language used no vowels. But Greek used vowels and required about twice as much space.

Like 1 Samuel, the story was written sometime after Solomon died and Israel split into two nations, in about 930 BC. The book was written to preserve the history of David's 40-year rule over Israel.

ON LOCATION

Most of the stories take place in Israel. But some, such as battles, occur in surrounding nations that include Jordan and Syria. After he made Jerusalem his capital, it became known as the city of David.

WHAT TO LOOK FOR

- **No sugarcoating.** The writer tells it like it is. He doesn't try to make super-heroes of imperfect human beings. In all of Israel's history, the king most revered is David. And for good reason. He is a godly man who never becomes so brain-damaged by power and prestige that he refuses to acknowledge his sins and repent. And he does sin—big time!. His most famous is his affair with his married neighbor, Bathsheba, which he tries to cover up by having her husband killed. But David repents. And God forgives.
- **David's everlasting dynasty.** God promises David that one of his descendants will always be king (7:16). David's dynasty continues in Jerusalem for nearly half a millennium, until Israel is defeated in 586 BC and much of the population is taken away in exile. God ultimately fulfills his promise to David through the anticipated Jewish messiah—a new king from the dynasty of kings. In the New Testament, Jesus is presented as that messiah. When he rides into Jerusalem on the day that becomes known as Palm Sunday, the people acknowledge this by shouting, "God bless the coming kingdom of our ancestor David" (Mark 11:10).

EXTREME SCENES
from 2 Samuel

≥ The crowning touch (5:1–5)

With the disastrous defeat of King Saul and his army and the Philistines on the move, the tribal leaders move fast to fill the empty throne. They unite behind David, a proven warrior, and name him king. Finally, years after Samuel has secretly anointed him as king, David takes the throne. For the first seven years, David rules out of Hebron, part of his family's territory in southern Israel. But then he apparently decides he needs a neutral capital to fully unite the 12 tribes and eliminate any favoritism. Jerusalem is the natural choice because it lies on the border of two tribes, near the center of the nation. The only drawback is that the Jebusites still live there. In a daring attack, David's men capture the city by going through an underground water shaft. The village becomes known as the city of David, later called Jerusalem.

DIRECTOR'S NOTES

What made the ark of the covenant so sacred? It contained the two flat stones on which the Ten Commandments were written. The ark was the centerpiece of Israel's worship of God. It had been captured once before in a war against the Philistines. The result was disaster for both the Philistines and the Israelites. David did not want to risk losing it again. 2 Samuel 15:24

≥ Return of the ark (6:1–23)

After being captured by the Philistines and then later returned, the ark of the covenant has been kept on a back shelf, neglected and nearly forgotten. David, though, recognizes that the ark, which holds the Ten Commandments, is a national treasure—a symbol of God's presence among His people. He decides it's time to bring the ark back to center stage in Jerusalem. It's a bold move that will unite in one location the king's throne and the symbolic throne of God.

The entire city comes out for the celebration as the ark is returned to Jerusalem. David leads the parade, dancing and shouting joyfully. David's wife, the daughter of King Saul, though, criticizes her husband for making a fool of himself in public. David could care less what she thinks. He is celebrating in honor of the Lord. The ark gets a temporary house in a tent, but David isn't satisfied. He wants to build a temple for the ark. God, though, plans to give that job to one of David's son. God tells David through the prophet Nathan that a tent was good enough for the ark when the people came out of Egypt; it's good enough for now.

Forbidden fruit (11:1–26)

It's a balmy spring night when David apparently is having trouble sleeping. He gets out of bed and takes a stroll on the palace rooftop. Suddenly, he stops. He can't believe his eyes. There on the next-door rooftop is a beautiful woman, bathing. David knows he should turn away, but he can't help himself. The next day he asks about her. Her name is Bathsheba, and her husband is conveniently away fighting in King David's army. The timing couldn't be better. He invites Bathsheba to the palace, has sex with her, and she leaves. Things get considerably more complicated, though, when Bathsheba discovers she's pregnant.

David comes up with a desperate plan. He calls her husband home, hoping the soldier will sleep with Bathsheba and think the child is his. The soldier unknowingly messes up the whole plan when he refuses to sleep with his wife while his comrades suffer on the battlefield. David's back is up against a wall. He then gives orders to put the soldier on the front line, while the troops are pulled back. It's a sure death sentence. The soldier dies, and David ends up marrying Bathsheba. Later, the prophet Nathan confronts David about this sin. Though David repents, Bathsheba's firstborn son dies. She later gives birth to Solomon.

The rebel son (18:1–33)

David's troubles on the home front continue. His son Absalom is furious when David fails to punish Absalom's half-brother for raping his sister. Absalom takes his own revenge and kills his half brother, then flees the country. Three years later David calls his estranged son home, but refuses to meet with him for another two years.

By then, it's too late. Absalom already has decided to overthrow his father. He travels around the country stirring up resentment, then declares himself king. His following is strong enough that David is forced to leave the capital. The armies of father and son clash in a dense forest. There, Absalom gets yanked off his mule when his long hair becomes tangled in tree branches. The mule runs off, leaving Absalom dangling. Some of David's soldiers surround him and, against the king's order, kill him.

The altar (24:18–25)

Under David's leadership, Israel has become a powerhouse. He has expanded the country into an empire that stretches from the Mediterranean coast eastward into what is now Jordan and northward into Iraq. In the process, though, David commits an unspecified sin that God must punish. Perhaps David trusts too much on his military might and too little on God. Whatever the sin, David has to choose the punishment: three years of famine, three months of being chased by enemies, or three days of plague. David opts for the plague. Thousands die. When the plague ends, God tells David to buy the threshing floor on the hilltop overlooking his capital. There, David builds an altar. Later, his son Solomon will build Israel's first temple on that site.

INTERVIEW
with the Stars

Extra effort

It was a boyhood promise made when times were good. But years later, David, now king of Israel, remembered that promise he made with his boyhood friend Jonathan. It was a pledge to care for the other's family members as long as either Jonathan or David was alive. Jonathan was long dead. But David was not only able, he was willing to keep that vow. ***Behind the Bible*** has an opportunity to interview the recipient of that pact made between two close friends. Mephibosheth, tell us a little bit about yourself.

⇒ Mephibosheth

Jonathan was my father, but I don't really remember too much about him. I was only five years old when my father died on the battlefield along with my grandfather, King Saul. When my nurse got news about my father's death, she took me and ran. I guess she was afraid that our enemies might come looking for me , too. But in the hurry to get away, I was dropped and became crippled.

What happened to your other family members?

⇒ Mephibosheth

I was the only surviving member of our family. Of course, I had lost all claim to any property or to the throne when David became king. Some servants of my father's took me in and cared for me.

It must have come as quite a surprise when David called for you.

⇒ Mephibosheth

Surprise doesn't even begin to describe what I felt. I was terrified! I thought for sure that he was going to kill me and finish off Saul's line for good.

INTERVIEW
with the Stars

So what did happen?

⋙ Mephibosheth

It was the most amazing thing. I was prepared to literally beg for my life, and here was the king of Israel, inviting me to come and sit at his table. Not only that, but David also restored to me all the property and everything else that had belonged to my family. It was incredible! And he did it out of respect for my father!

That's quite a story. But I understand that later you had some further difficulties.

⋙ Mephibosheth

Yes, that's right. You see when you have limitations like mine, being disabled, you have to depend on others. Some, like David, respect you in spite of your limitations. Others try to take advantage of you. And that's what happened. My servant Ziba tried to convince David, who was fleeing from his own son Absalom, that I stayed behind in Jerusalem because I wanted to reclaim the throne. It was an outright lie! He knew I couldn't leave because I was lame!

How did you manage to convince David?

⋙ Mephibosheth

When David confronted me, I told him the truth. And I told him to do with me whatever he pleased because really all my grandfather's descendants deserved nothing but death from him. I knew that. I was more than grateful for all David already had given me. And I wasn't going to make excuses or let my limitations become, well, a crutch to get what I wanted.

From all accounts, you handled yourself with dignity and grace. And your persistence paid off as well. Anyone who is frustrated by their limitations—whether it's social, physical, emotional or educational—can take a lesson from you, Mephibosheth, to not use those limitations to demand their own way. Thank you for sharing your story.

REVIEWS

ENCORE

⮞ The story of Israel's history continues in 1 Kings. There, the dying David names his surprise successor: passing over his oldest surviving son, David appoints Solomon, his son with Bathsheba.

⮞ To get a feel for the kind of intimate relationship David has with God, read some of the psalms he wrote. Psalm 51 seems to express the kind of sorrow he felt after committing adultery with Bathsheba.

⮞ Psalm 18 conveys the kind of feelings David may have experienced when his son led a coup against him.

First and Second Samuel are really like home movies, reel #1 and #2. (Did you know that the reason the book of Samuel was divided into two books was simply because it wouldn't all fit on one scroll? Anyway…) If you had planted video-cams all over King David's castle, you'd have seen something similar to 2 Samuel.

David's kingdom was a gritty, brave one. David was a king who grew up as a shepherd and musician (hey, cool). He was not voted "most likely to become king of Israel" by his graduating class, but he became a warrior so dreaded that God wouldn't let him build the temple because of the blood on his hands (figuratively) and eventually he was king (so *there*, classmates).

Second Samuel is David's story: the good, the bad and the ugly (did you hear someone whistle?). He was famous for preparing for the new temple. He was also famous for his affair with Bathsheba, the wife of one of his soldiers and later the mom of Solomon, David's heir to the throne.

David was also famous for returning the ark of the covenant to Jerusalem (you know, that box with the ten commandments inside). At first moving the ark was a major setback for David. The ark was a sacred chest that embodied God's presence among the people. There were strict, strict, STRICT rules for handling it. (Like, rule #1 DON'T *handle* it at all. it was totally forbidden to even *touch* the ark. This made moving it really hard to do.) While transporting it by oxcart, one of the oxen stumbled and the ark began to fall. Uzzah, son of the man who had been taking care of the ark for the past 20 years, reached out and stopped the ark from falling. Know what happened? Uzzah died right there on the spot (ouch !). David put off the ark-moving for a while, but eventually he got it done. This was a huge deal for the people. It was a symbol that God was among them.

Even with David's mistakes, and even some failure, he was the greatest king Israel ever had. He was a man after God's own heart. His story is a good one.

Solomon "Harley" Davidson

1 Kings

SCHEDULE OF SCENES

Abraham — Moses — Conquest of Canaan — David — Solomon — Kingdom Divides — Elijah — Ezra — Jesus is Born

2100 B.C. 1500 B.C. 1400 B.C. 1010 B.C. 970 B.C. 931 B.C. 853 B.C. 450 B.C. 7/6 B.C.

Rise and fall of a nation

Looking for a good read? How about a king who dispenses justice by ordering a baby to be cut in half before two women who both claim to be its mother? Or a battle of prophets—God's prophet vs. 450 prophets of Baal—with the true deity the one who sends fire from heaven to light the sacrifice.(Guess who wins.) Or maybe you'd like a story about the notorious Queen Jezebel, who executes a farmer so her husband can have a vegetable garden for his summer palace.

There's more to this book than just a collection of page-turning stories. The message underlying these stories is unmistakable: You reap what you sow. You get what you deserve. Kings who obey God's law reap the benefits: rain for the crops, peace in the land, power over invaders. Kings who disobey reap disaster: disease, famine, overpowering enemies.

Over and over, the writer lists the godly kings and their blessings. He lists the ungodly kings and the disasters they deservedly get. God is consistent in his discipline. But the Israelites, like stubborn and self-willed children, are persistent in their rebellion. Despite it all, one thing remains certain. No matter what the people have done, God will never completely reject them (Leviticus 26:44).

QUOTABLES

"Cut the baby in half" (3:25). King Solomon's decision when two women each claim a baby boy belongs to her.

"The Lord, He is God!" (18:39, New King James Version). The response of the Israelites after fire from heaven burns up the sacrifice Elijah offers on Mount Carmel.

SNEAK PREVIEW

Titus
Wanna' change the world? Step one....

BEHIND the SCENES
of 1 Kings

STARRING ROLES

David, elderly and dying king of Israel (1:1)
Solomon, David's son and successor, builder of the temple (1:10)
Elijah, prophet who challenges prophets of Baal on Mount Carmel (17:1)
Ahab and Jezebel, Baal-worshiping king and queen of the northern kingdom (16:28, 31)

PLOT

Solomon takes the throne after David dies of old age. Solomon expands the wealth and boundaries of Israel to levels never before attained. With the wars of David's reign behind them, the Israelites enjoy peace and prosperity as they enter into business deals with surrounding nations. But when Solomon grows old, he begins yielding to pressure from his foreign wives to worship the gods of their homeland. The peace begins to collapse as enemies rise up. When Solomon dies, the nation splits in two and the troubles escalate.

STAGE DIRECTIONS

The temple is finished 960 B.C.

Israel splits into two nations 930 B.C.

Solomon becomes king 970 B.C.

Ahab begins his reign 874 B.C.

BIBLE EVENTS

Dates are approximate

1100 B.C.   950 B.C.   800 B.C.

WORLD EVENTS

Egypt splits in two 1085 B.C.

Celts of central Europe migrate to France 900 B.C.

Homer writes the *Iliad* and the *Odyssey* 800 B.C.

The city of Canton, China is founded 887 B.C.

Assyrian empire begins expanding 883 B.C.

AUTHOR AND DATE

Like the two books of Samuel and Chronicles, the two books of Kings were originally one book, written by an unknown writer. They were separated into two books when the Hebrew text was translated for Greek-speaking Jews in about 300 BC. This allowed each book to fit on one scroll. The writer probably drew from a variety of ancient sources, including three that are named: a book about Solomon (11:41); and two books about the many other kings (14:19, 29). The writer also may have had access to records kept by court historians or the prophets: "Everything David did while he was king is included in the history written by the prophets Samuel, Nathan, and Gad" (1 Chronicles 29:29).

It's uncertain exactly when the stories were compiled into a single book. Many scholars believe it was in the mid-500s BC, after the Babylonians had destroyed Jerusalem and dragged off much of the Jewish population into exile. The history recorded in 1, 2 Kings—which spans the 400 years from the final days of David's reign through the fall of Jerusalem—seems targeted to Jewish readers in exile. The history vividly explains that the Jews got where they are because generation after generation disobeyed God. So the Jews suffered the consequences God had been warning them about since the time of Moses.

ON LOCATION

Israel is the center of the action. But other areas in the Middle East add to the setting. To build the temple in Jerusalem, Solomon sends loggers to cut cedar from the forests of Lebanon. The Queen of Sheba makes a visit, probably from southern Arabia, to Jerusalem to check out Solomon's rumored wisdom. Trade and transportation routes through the kingdom added to Solomon's influence.

WHAT TO LOOK FOR

- **The lesson behind the history**. This isn't your typical history lesson. The writer doesn't focus on the kings who *did* the most, like King Omri, one of the most powerful rulers of the northern nation of Israel. He only gets a mere six verses. Instead, the focus is on the kings who were the most obedient or least obedient. The writer is more interested in showing what happens when rulers honor God, and what happens when they don't.

EXTREME SCENES
from 1 Kings

That wise guy (3:16–28)

Before he dies, David names his successor. To the shock of the palace court, he does not name his eldest surviving son, Adonijah. Instead, he names Solomon, the son he had with Bathsheba. At first, Solomon turns out to be a good selection. When God appears to him in a dream and tells Solomon to ask him for anything, Solomon chooses wisdom. God is so pleased with Solomon's request that he also grants Solomon wealth and a long life.

Solomon quickly demonstrates that God has granted his request. Two women appear before him, both claiming to be the mother of a newborn son. There are no other witnesses, so Solomon gives a shocking order—"Cut the baby in two. That way each of you can have part of him." One woman quickly agrees. The other pleads for Solomon to spare the child. Solomon points to the pleading woman, "She is the real mother. Give the baby to her."

DIRECTOR'S NOTES

If the floor plan of Solomon's temple seems familiar to you, it's because it's the same floor plan that was used for the tabernacle for meeting that Moses had built. The only difference was that the temple was twice the size of the tabernacle. Notice that the Most Holy Place was designed to be a perfect cube, equal in length, width, and height. 1 Kings 6:16

God's house (6:1–38)

On a hilltop overlooking Jerusalem, Solomon builds the first of only three temples the Jews have ever had. It is a massive building project. Stonecutters quarry enormous limestone blocks. Craftsmen from throughout the Middle East design furnishings of gold and ivory. Lumberjacks travel to Lebanon to harvest the finest wood available: bug-proof, rot-resistant cedar.

Seven years later, the job is done. Israel now is home to one of the most beautiful and expensive temples in the ancient world—a worship center with golden ceilings, walls, and floors. This white limestone temple is 30 yards long, 10 yards wide, and 15 yards high, shimmering on the Jerusalem hilltop. Here Jews will offer sacrifices to God for 400 years—until Babylonian soldiers invade the city, strip away the gold, then destroy the building.

The visiting queen (10:1–13)

The queen of Sheba, from an Arabian trade nation probably 1,000 miles away, hears about the wisdom and wealth of Solomon. So she assembles a large caravan and goes to check it out. She is amazed. "Solomon," she says, "I had heard about your wisdom and all you've done. But I didn't believe it until I saw it with my own eyes." She showers him with expensive gifts: nearly five tons of gold, along with jewels and rare spices. He returns the favor, giving her anything she wants.

Too many wives

Solomon makes one big mistake. He maintains a harem of 700 wives of royal birth and 300 concubines, or secondary wives. These are mainly political marriages, to secure peace and trade agreements with neighboring kingdoms. But these marriages break a rule that Moses gave several hundred years earlier: a ruler "must not have a lot of wives—they might tempt him to be unfaithful to the Lord" (Deuteronomy 17:17).

That's exactly what happens to King Solomon. "As Solomon grew old, his wives turned his heart after other gods, and his heart was not fully devoted to the Lord his God, as the heart of David his father had been" (11:4, NIV). To punish the king, God raises up enemies who shatter the decades of peace that Israel has enjoyed.

Divided kingdom (12:1–33)

By the time Solomon dies, the people of Israel are fed up. They are tired of paying heavy taxes to support the king's enormous household and administration. They're tired, too, of being drafted to build cities, forts, and palaces. They approach King Rehoboam, Solomon's son and successor, and ask for relief. The rookie monarch responds harshly and foolishly: "My father made you work hard, but I'll make you work even harder."

The northern tribes secede, start their own nation, and appoint their own king. Only the tribe of Judah, in the south, remains loyal to the descendant of David.

The stories that follow in 1 and 2 Kings reveal that all the kings of the northern nation of Israel "disobeyed the Lord" (15:26). Most kings in the southern nation of Judah, however, are good—with notable exceptions.

Battle of Baal (18:1–46)

If you're making up the list of Top Ten Bad Boys of the Bible, Ahab is right up there. He probably is one of the most ungodly kings to rule in the northern nation of Israel. Then he marries the wicked Jezebel and the two make up one of the most evil combos to come along. She kills most of the prophets of God and imports her own prophets of Baal, god of rain. God punishes Israel with a three-year drought. Then he orders the prophet Elijah to challenge Jezebel's 450 prophets to a contest, while crowds of Israelites watch. Baal's prophets and Elijah are each to offer a sacrificed bull, laid on a pile of wood. The catch? The deity that starts the fire on the altar will become the god of Israel. Baal's prophets pray for hours, but nothing happens. Elijah prays one short prayer, and fire falls from heaven. The Israelites kill the prophets of Baal, and the drought ends that day.

INTERVIEW
with the Stars

Making each day count

Behind the Bible is extremely honored to interview our next guest. He's a man that truly needs no intro-duction, a man who once was described as a "man after God's own heart." He's a shepherd, a musician, a writer, a warrior, and a king. King David, welcome. What we would like to focus on today is how your early years prepared you to become one of Israel's most well known and beloved kings.

⋟ David

Wow—for someone who needs no introduction that was quite an introduction! But seriously, you talk about your bottom-dwellers. I was the youngest of seven brothers—think of all those hand-me-downs—and got all the jobs no else wanted. While my brothers got to be soldiers and fight the Philistines, I got to be the shepherd and fight the battle of the sheep! But I learned a lot from my sheep.

What could you possibly learn from sheep?

⋟ David

Well, for one thing, I learned that sheep can make a difference in people's lives. You see, I had two ways of looking at being a shepherd. I could moan and whine about not being able to do the things my brothers did—or I could use the time I had and make it an adventure.

Tell us, how did you make tending sheep an adventure?

⋟ David

For one thing, I used the time I spent out in the fields to practice my marksmanship with my sling. I later made a *big* impression with that giant, Goliath, using that same sling. You could say Goliath didn't see the truth of what God could do through someone as insignificant as me until it hit him right between the eyes!

INTERVIEW
with the Stars

You definitely have a point there. What else did you learn?

⋟ David

I also used that time to practice my singing and playing the harp. I used to lull the sheep to sleep with my music. Later, I used my music as a powerful comfort to King Saul.

So you used that time spent in the fields practicing your abilities to sing and sling. Were they the most important lessons?

⋟ David

No, the most important lesson was understanding that God can make a difference in your life, even in the small, boring things you *have* to do right now. Growing up is not just passing the years and waiting until you're old enough to do something; it's the time when your character is built. Because I was able to handle my father's flock so well, my heavenly Father gave me a kingdom to tend.

So your advice to young people today is to look for God's part in the small things of their lives and allow God to make a difference each day.

⋟ David

Exactly. Until you understand how God can make a difference in the little things of your life—the homework, music lessons, and day-to-day stuff—you'll never understand God's part in the big things of life.

REVIEWS

ENCORE

Reading 1 Kings is like watching a pop fly in baseball. You know how the ball goes up and up and up, then hits it's very highest peak and starts to fall? That's the history that you watch in 1 Kings.

As 1 Kings opens, David's son Solomon takes the plate...I mean throne. (THWACK...*the ball goes up...up...*) David was the greatest king of Israel, but Solomon was almost as famous, maybe more in some circles. Why? Because he was rich, I mean filthy, stinkin', Bill Gates rich. When it came to earthly things, he had it all: women, money, real estate, women, fancy clothes, pretty wives, expensives wines, women, concubines, fine works of art, more women. Not only that, but he also had lots and lots of WOMEN. (*The ball is going long... looks like it may be out of here.*)

Solomon was so famous for being prosperous that even Jesus used him as an illustration. Jesus points out how God clothes the lilies of the field. In order to compare them to the most ritzy, fancy thing imaginable he said, "Even Solomon in all his glory was not arrayed like one of them."

Here's the problem though (*it's gonna be close, the left fielder backs up to the fence. And...it's...*). When Solomon's reign was over the nation had lots of resources in terms of wealth, but not much going on in the faith department. Solomon had mixed his religion with the religions of his foreign wives and neighboring countries. He had watered down the faith of the nation until it was hardly recognizable. He had built a big temple that everybody ooh-ed and aah-ed about (*going...going...it's...*), but what good did it do if nobody was sure who they were worshiping and why? "Our father, who art in heaven" sounds a whole lot better than "to whom it may concern". Don'cha think?

> To read the rest of the story, turn to 2 Kings. The two books were originally one.

> Ecclesiastes, a book that says it was written by a son of David—perhaps Solomon—may reflect the despair Solomon felt after abandoning God. If so, it spotlights the wise conclusion he reached after suffering the consequences of his disobedience: "Respect and obey God! This is what life is all about" (Ecclesiastes 12:13).

> To read about the return of an Elijah-like prophet who will come just before the Messiah, turn to Malachi 4:5–6 and to the words of Jesus in Matthew 11:7–14, where he identifies John the Baptist as that prophet.

REVIEWS

So after Solomon, everything fell apart (*caught by the center fielder*). Civil war broke out. The kingdom divided into two kingdoms, the north and the south (is every civil war always the North and the South? You never hear about an East/West thing. I wonder why. Maybe it's the time difference). Now, instead of one king to mess everything up there were two kings at a time swinging pendulums back and forth between following God and spitting in his face. (Kids, never EVER try spitting in God's face at home. Not unless you want a plague of locusts in your underwear.)

This is the beginning of the end for the nation that used to be called Israel. If you think reading about it is confusing, think about living in it. The cliff notes go like this:

1. The Southern kingdom was basically the tribe of Judah with a couple of others thrown in. For that reason the Southern Kingdom was called Judah.
2. The Northern Kingdom was called Israel for a while, then called Samaria. The Northern Kingdom mingled with all the cultures around them (Bad move. This watered down the faith even further than Solomon's reign.) and so they weren't really a Jewish nation anymore. For this reason the people of Judah looked down their noses at the people of Samaria for a long, long time.

It's a wonder they didn't all end up cross-eyed.

Judy B. South

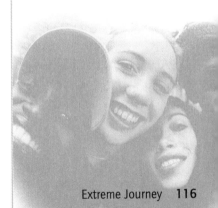

2 Kings

SCHEDULE OF SCENES

Abraham   Moses   Conquest of Canaan   David   Kingdom Divides   Elijah/Elisha   Fall of Israel   Fall of Judah   Ezra   Jesus is Born

2100 B.C. 1500 B.C. 1400 B.C. 1010 B.C. 931 B.C. 850 B.C. 722 B.C. 586 B.C. 450 B.C. 7/6 B.C.

Death of a nation

The rules couldn't have been any clearer: I take care of you and give you everything you need; you obey me. A no-brainer, right? But the Israelites simply didn't get it. God told them repeatedly what would happen if they kept breaking their end of the bargain. But either they A) didn't understand what God was saying; B) didn't care what God was saying; C) didn't want to hear what God was saying; or D) all of the above. Whatever the reason, in 2 Kings, God has had it. The game is over. By the end of the book, Israel is no more. The Jews of Israel now become the Jews of the Diaspora (or dispersion), a people and a nation in exile.

Second Kings is not all bad news (although there *is* plenty of that!). On the bright side, there is also obedience and reward. There are some godly prophets doing totally awesome miracles. And there are a few righteous kings, whose prayers and lives make life-and-death differences for them and the people they rule.

Bottom line: Second Kings clearly shows that religion is not just a personal matter of the heart. It impacts history, for better or worse.

QUOTABLES

"You baldhead!" (2:23, NKJV). How some young people taunt the prophet Elisha. Two bears immediately charge out of the woods and maul the youths.

"He drives like a madman" (9:20, NIV). A watchman on a city wall identifies charioteer Jehu by his driving style.

"Is your heart right? . . . If it is, give me your hand" (10:15, NKJV). Jehu asking a man if he is on Jehu's side. When the man replies he is, Jehu gives him a hand up into the chariot he is driving. Apparently the pedestrian doesn't know what the watchman knows about Jehu's driving.

SNEAK PREVIEW

Joel
A little bit of hope in a whole lot of reality.

BEHIND the SCENES
of 2 Kings

STARRING ROLES

Elijah, prophet who rides to heaven in a fiery chariot (1:3)
Elisha, Elijah's successor (2:1)
Naaman, Syrian commander cured of leprosy (5:1)
Jezebel, an evil queen who is murdered (9:7)

PLOT

The story of the two Jewish nations—Israel and Judah—picks up where 1 Kings leaves off. Elisha now becomes Israel's MVP (most valuable prophet) after his mentor, Elijah, grabs a whirlwind to heaven. Elisha is credited with lots of miracles, including raising a child from the dead and curing an enemy soldier of leprosy. But his efforts to turn the nation's heart back to God go nowhere. Assyria destroys Israel in 722 BC. The southern nation, Judah, gets a 150-year reprieve because it has more godly leadership. But in 586 BC, years of evil kings catch up with it, and it too is destroyed. The nation of Israelites hits rock bottom when Jerusalem and the temple are wiped out.

STAGE DIRECTIONS

Elijah's ministry ends, Elisha's begins 850 B.C.

Northern nation of Israel destroyed 722 B.C.

Southern nation of Judah falls, with Jerusalem 586 B.C.

BIBLE EVENTS

Dates are approximate

850 B.C. 700 B.C. 550 B.C.

WORLD EVENTS

Ohio River people build earth burial mounds 800 B.C.

Rome founded by King Romulus 753 B.C.

Chinese philosopher Confucius born 551 B.C.

First recorded Olympic games in Greece 776 B.C.

AUTHOR AND DATE

We don't know who wrote the two books of Kings, but we do know that they originally were one book. Like the books of Samuel, they were split into two books when the Hebrew text was translated for Greek-speaking Jews in about 300 BC. This allowed each book to fit on a scroll. The author probably drew from several sources to write the books: a book about Solomon, a book about the kings of Israel, and a book about the kings of Judah. The writer also may have had access to the records of royal historians and prophets.

Again, we don't know when the two books were written, but the experts believe that is was sometime in the mid-500s BC, after Israel and Judah were conquered. The books seem to target exiled Jewish readers who were trying to understand what crime they committed to deserve such an awful punishment.

ON LOCATION

The main events take place in the Jewish nations of Israel, in the north, and Judah, in the south. Neighboring empires play important roles. Egypt allies itself with the Jews, but the Assyrians and Babylonians invade and defeat the Jewish nations in spite of this alliance. By 650 BC, Assyria has overrun Israel and dominates the entire Fertile Crescent. Less than 100 years later, Babylon is the major power in the area and defeats Judah.

WHAT TO LOOK FOR

- **The connection between sin and punishment.** The Jews have seen it before: men and women suffering because of the consequences of sin. They've even seen the entire nation suffer because they disobeyed God. But nothing prepared them for the total destruction of their nation—first Israel in the north, and then Judah in the south.

EXTREME SCENES
from 2 Kings

A whirlwind trip (2:1–18)

It's nearing the end of Elijah's 25-year ministry as head prophet for Israel. He and his young associate, Elisha, are walking along the Jordan. At one point, Elijah strikes the river with his cloak, and the river opens a path for them to cross. Elijah tells Elisha that his time is almost up and asks what last-minute request does he have. Elisha wants to be named the next chief prophet. Elijah replies that can only happen if Elisha sees him going to heaven. The very next moment, swoosh! Elijah is taken up to heaven in a fiery chariot. Elisha picks up his mentor's cloak, which has fallen on the ground. Like Elijah just did, Elisha touches the river and BOOM! The river parts and a path opens—a sure sign that God has granted his request.

Raised from the dead (4:8–37)

While traveling through Israel, Elisha gets some free room and board from a couple in the town of Shunem. In exchange for their hospitality, Elisha promises to give them the one thing they don't have—a child. Sure enough, the following year, a son is born. Tragedy strikes years later. The young boy complains of a terrible headache. By noon he's dead. The woman doesn't hesitate. She gets on a donkey and rides to Mount Carmel to find Elisha. She tells him her son has died and convinces him to return with her. When Elisha arrives, he walks into the boy's room, shuts the door, and prays. The boy sneezes seven times and opens his eyes.

A sure cure (5:1–27)

Naaman is a war hero of the mighty Syrian army, which God is using to hammer Israel for its sin. But Naaman has one major problem that even all the war medals can't cover up—leprosy. A young Israeli servant girl in his house (captured during a raid) suggests to Naaman's wife that her husband could be cured if only he would ask Elisha the prophet for help. Naaman, desperate for a cure, goes into enemy territory and visits Elisha. The prophet tells him all he has to do for a complete cure is to wash seven times in the Jordan River. Naaman goes nuts. He was expecting a long-involved ritual, not a bath! He refuses and goes home. With a little encouragement from his servants, Naaman finally gives in and obeys. He is completely cured and tells Elisha, "from now on I will offer sacrifices only to the Lord."

Curtains for Jezebel (9:30–37)

King Ahab is dead and his son now is king. But old Jezebel still has a lot of power and orders everyone to continue worshiping idols. Elisha has a plan, though. He tells Jehu, an Israelite soldier, that he will be the next king, but Ahab's family must die. So Jehu gets some men and rides to the king's summer palace in the hills of Jezreel. Outside the city he meets the king and kills him. Jehu continues toward the city, where Jezebel is waiting for him. "Why did you come here, you murderer," Jezebel screams from the palace window as Jehu approaches. Jehu looks up and yells, "Is anyone up there on my side?" Some palace workers catch his eye. "Throw her out the window!" Jehu orders. They do, and Jezebel falls to her death.

A bad influence (12:1–21)

Ahab's evil influence and Baal-worship creeps southward into Judah. When the two countries sign a peace treaty, Ahab seals the deal by giving one of his daughters in marriage to the crown prince of Judah. When the prince becomes king, Ahab's Baal-worshiping daughter is queen. When her husband dies, the queen makes a grab for power. (Sound familiar? Like mother, like daughter?) She orders the execution of all of David's dynasty and then declares herself queen. What she doesn't know is that one heir survives, her infant son Joash. He claims the throne at age 7 (with a little help from a temple priest!), and the queen is executed. Later, Joash launches a massive renovation project for the 150-year-old temple, which is badly run-down.

Crime & punishment (17:1–41)

Assyria, in what is now Iraq, emerges as one of the most powerful forces in the Middle East. Many nations, including Israel, pay taxes to stay on the good side of the Assyrian rulers. Hoshea, king of Israel, decides to stop payment. It's not long before Shalmaneser, king of Assyria, marches into Israel. He surrounds the capital of Samaria for three years and starves the people into submission. The citizens are deported as slaves to several cities in Assyria. Israel is then resettled with Assyrian homesteaders. The 10 Israelite tribes that once made up the nation eventually lose track of their tribal identity forever. "All of this happened," the Bible says, "because the people of Israel had sinned against the Lord their God."

Spared—for now (18:1–19:37)

Judah also has been paying taxes to Assyria. But when the Assyrian king dies, Judah decides enough is enough. King Hezekiah enters into a treaty of mutual support with Egypt, Assyria's rival power. The army of Sennacherib, the new Assyrian king, marches through Judah, capturing one city after another, until they reach the walls of Jerusalem. The Assyrian commander approaches the walls and taunts the city: "Hezekiah claims the Lord will save you. Were any other gods able to defend their land against the king of Assyria? . . . Do you think the Lord your God can do any better?" The answer comes quickly. God sends an angel to the camp of the Assyrians, and the next morning the camp is filled with dead bodies. Jerusalem is spared—for now.

Bad to the bone (21:1–18)

Hezekiah was one of Judah's most godly kings. His son, Manasseh, goes down in history as one of the baddest. Talk about in-your-face evil. When Manasseh takes over the throne at age 12, he immediately rebuilds all the pagan shrines his father had torn down. Then he reintroduces the worship of Baal, Asherah, as well as the sun, moon, and stars. Plus, he practices witchcraft, consults fortune-tellers, and even sacrifices his own son—all in blatant defiance of God's law.

The final chapter (25:1–26)

Judah was spared once. But time's up. This time it's the Babylonians who invade. Jerusalem is under siege for a year and a half. Large numbers of its citizens starve to death. When the soldiers of Babylonian King Nebuchadnezzar finally break through the city walls, they tear down Jerusalem and totally wipe out Solomon's temple. The people that survive are deported to Babylon as captive. The great nation that God promised to make of Abraham's descendants is no more.

INTERVIEW
with the Stars

Answering God's call

Picture this: You're working in the backyard, raking leaves. Suddenly, you get THE CALL—the call from God to go and do something for him. Do you go? Do you stop to tell your mom bye, see ya later? Do you wait until you get your high school diploma? What do you do? **Behind the Bible** is talking with a man who got THE CALL and finding out what *he* did. Welcome to **BB,** Elisha. Tell us about that particular day.

⋙ Elisha

It started out just like any other day. It was my day to take my father's 12 oxen and plow the family fields. I was busy. And then he came along, and believe me, life was never the same.

Who's he?

⋙ Elisha

It was the old prophet Elijah. Of course, I knew about him. Everyone in the northern kingdom had. But for him to come over to me and toss his mantle over my shoulders—well, I never expected anything like that.

And so you immediately dropped the reins to the ox and followed him, right?

⋙ Elisha

Well, not exactly. I didn't know what to think. He kept on walking, so I had to run after him and ask if I had time to tell my folks a proper good-bye. They probably would wonder what happened to me if they saw the oxen wandering around the field.

INTERVIEW
with the Stars

And what did Elijah say?

⇒ Elisha

He made it real clear to me that this wasn't about following an old prophet; this was about following God's call. So I did the only sensible thing I could do. I took my oxen and sacrificed them, using the yoke for firewood. I shared my barbecue with the other field hands to celebrate . Then I took upon myself the invisible yoke of service to God.

What happened then?

⇒ Elisha

I learned as much as I could before Elijah was taken up to heaven. Right before he went to heaven, I asked God for a double helping of the Spirit, which had been in Elijah. I wasn't asking for that because I wanted to be just like Elijah; I just wanted to be as available to God as Elijah had been. He was my role model, and I wanted my life to be motivated and filled by the Spirit of God so I could make a difference in others' lives.

Which you did for more than 50 years as God's prophet to the northern kingdom. And when God called you to walk away from all that was familiar to you, you did.

⇒ Elisha

That's right. It wasn't easy, and I struggled with it at first. But it's all about being open to what God wants you to do. God's call may not mean you have to pick up and move somewhere else. But it definitely will change your life's focus. It may not change what you do, but it definitely will affect *why* you do it. Just keep an eye out for falling mantles and be ready!

INTERVIEW
with the Stars

A good and faithful servant

Our next subject for **Behind the Bible** has an unusual distinction—we don't know her name! In fact, we don't know much about her at all. All we know about her is that as a young girl she was kidnapped from her home in Israel and taken to Syria. Yet, like so many other anonymous servants of God, she made a real difference in the lives of others around her. Young lady, why don't you give us a bit of your background?

⋙ Naaman's wife's servant girl

Certainly. As you mentioned, I was kidnapped from my home in Israel during a Syrian raid. It was a terrifying experience. But it became even more bewildering when I ended up working in the home of Naaman—the commander of the Syrian army!

You mean the man who most likely *led* the raid against your homeland?! That had to be pretty weird.

⋙ Naaman's wife's servant girl

It was at first. But I was working as a servant for Naaman's wife. And you know, after a while, I really began to feel sorry for the man.

Why is that?

⋙ Naaman's wife's servant girl

Well, it turned out that Naaman had leprosy. I would overhear him talking with his wife about trying this treatment and that treatment. The man was desperate for a cure. And nothing was working! I could hear the fear in his voice. The frustrating thing was I knew someone who could help him back in Israel—God's prophet, Elisha.

INTERVIEW
with the Stars

So what did you do? I mean weren't you at all resentful toward this man because of what he had done to you—tearing you apart from your family and friends and making you a slave in his house?

⋙ Naaman's wife's servant girl

I suppose that's probably how a lot of people would feel. But you didn't see him struggle to live with this terrible disease day in and day out. My heart cried out for him. Finally, one day I went to his wife and told her about Elisha and how he was the only one who could help Naaman because he had God's spirit upon him.

And how did they take your suggestion? I mean you basically were telling Naaman to go and ask the enemy to heal him. I would imagine that wouldn't have gone over very well.

⋙ Naaman's wife's servant girl

I guess the timing was right. Naaman was at the point where he was desperate enough to try anything—including asking the enemy to help him. And his wife was so thankful, especially when Naaman was healed, after finally deciding to follow *all* of Elisha's instructions.

What an inspiring story. And the amazing thing is that's all we know about this young girl and her story. Yet her story just goes to show you that God always has a lot more going on in this world than any one of us is aware of. But God sees it all. Every kind word. Every gesture of faith. Every time a believer gives another person a reason to consider God. In the end, even the nameless, unknown, seemingly insignificant person can make a bigger difference than we ever expected.

REVIEWS

One of the most amazing players in the whole 2 Kings scenario was Hezekiah. Here's a man who lived during a time before toilets or even sinks, and listen to what he did. Hezekiah was the king, so he lived in Jerusalem, the capital. Like a lot of places back then, Jerusalem had a wall around it to protect it during war. Even though the city was protected with an amazing wall (and some of them had walls as thick as your average bedroom) the enemy would often just cut off the water and food supply to the city and starve the people out (although, why anyone would want to take over a place with that many people and no toilets is beyond me).

Hezekiah took care of that. He dug a tunnel from inside the city to a spring outside (he should have dug one for an outhouse while he was at it). Then he camouflaged the spring on the outside. That way fresh water came into the city even during a seige (20:20). (Yeah, but like where did people GO? I guess, if you were surrounded and had no toilets, a catapult could be doubly useful.)

If you visit Israel you can see the remains of this tunnel, cut through nearly 600 yards of solid rock. There's an inscription describing construction: miners started at each end and met in the middle (good thing they did the math right, huh?). The inscription was written shortly before 701 BC, when Assyria invaded Judah and surrounded Jerusalem. Speaking of Assyria. The Bible says Sennacherib led the Assyrians in a siege against Jerusalem, but that he retreated after an unnamed disaster struck his camp and killed many of his soldiers (catapult, maybe?). Sennacherib, in his own records, writes about conquering numerous cities, but about Hezekiah and Jerusalem he says, "As for Hezekiah... I made him a prisoner in Jerusalem, his royal residence, like a bird in a cage. I surrounded him with earthwork." A nice way of saying "I couldn't beat him."

> The two books of Chronicles cover the same period of history as 1, 2 Kings. Chronicles was apparently written later to Jews who had returned from exile wondering if they were still God's people, or if the covenant was irreparably broken.

> To read a detailed, eyewitness account of the fall of Jerusalem, turn to Jeremiah 52. And for more background on this era in history, read the story sections throughout Jeremiah. You can skip the prophecy sections, which in many Bible translations are easily recognizable because they are indented like poetry.

> For another view of Hezekiah, read Isaiah 36–39; this section parallels 2 Kings 18–20.

REVIEWS

What really happened was this. Hezekiah was sick and about to die and the prophet Isaiah told him so. So Hezekiah turned his face to the wall and prayed, "Don't forget that I have been faithful to you, Lord. I have obeyed you with all my heart." Then he cried hard, the kind of crying you do when it doesn't matter who's looking. Before Isaiah left the castle, God gave him a new message: "I heard you pray, and I saw you cry. I will heal you, so that three days from now you will be able to worship in my temple. I will let you live fifteen years more (which should have been *plenty* of time to invent toilets and sinks), while I protect you and your city from the king of Assyria." Sennacherib was out of luck. You can't outmaneuver God. (Notice how the one thing you never hear in the Bible is "Hey God, look over there...Ha! gotcha!") Sennacherib failed to take Jerusalem because God listened to a heartfelt prayer.

Cheri B. Senna

1 Chronicles

SCHEDULE OF SCENES

Abraham	Moses	Exodus	Era of Judges	David becomes King	Death of David	Ezra	Jesus is Born
2100 B.C.	1500 B.C.	1440 B.C.	1375 B.C.	1010 B.C.	970 B.C.	450 B.C.	7/6 B.C.

The homecoming

First and second Chronicles were written at the time the people of Israel were going through an identity crisis. The chosen ones of Israel needed to know if they were now the unchosen. The nation, born when Abraham promised to serve only God, had been crushed. Abraham's descendant had shattered the agreement by worshiping a whole assortment of other gods. As punishment, God used the Babylonians to obliterate Judah, burn its cities and take its citizens captive to live in a country nearly a thousand miles away. Now it was time to go home. Except, to what? Was there still a Promised Land? Was God's agreement still valid? *Were* they still the chosen people?

The books of 1, 2 Chronicles answer these questions. Yes, this is still the promised land. Yes, the covenant is still in force. And yes, the Jews are still the people chosen by God—though a people who have suffered terribly for their sin. Evidence of God's favor? The Jews are back in Israel. The temple is rebuilt. The legacy of the priesthood remains intact, with priestly leaders clearly identified. And David's family has been preserved. All of this is God's doing. He just doesn't give up. That's the good news back then. It's still the good news for us.

QUOTABLES

"Give thanks to the Lord, for He is good! For His mercy endures forever" (1 Chronicles 16:34, NKJV).

SNEAK PREVIEW

Jonah
An unwilling prophet faces his worst enemy with a message of hope.

BEHIND the SCENES
of 1 Chronicles

STARRING ROLES

David, king of Israel who makes plans for the temple (2:9)

PLOT

The first nine chapters are tough reading, but it's critical to Israel's history. It traces the Israelite family tree from Adam, at Creation, to Zerubbabel and beyond. Then Israel's story picks up with the death of Saul, followed by the crowning of David as king. David secures the nation by defeating Israel's enemies and establishing the capital in Jerusalem. Then he brings Israel's most sacred item, the ark of the covenant, which holds the Ten Commandments, into Jerusalem. Though David is not permitted to build a temple, he receives from God the temple plans, which he passes on to his son, Solomon. David also begins gathering the construction supplies that Solomon will need later.

STAGE DIRECTIONS

Adam
is created
before 2500 B.C.

David
becomes
king
1010 B.C.

David
dies
970 B.C.

Dates are approximate

BIBLE EVENTS

2500 B.C.   1700 B.C.   900 B.C.

WORLD EVENTS

Egypt splits
in two
1085 B.C.

Wigs worn
by Egyptian
aristocrats
950 B.C.

China develops
refrigeration,
using winter ice
1000 B.C.

AUTHOR AND DATE

Jewish tradition says Ezra wrote 1, 2 Chronicles along with the books of Ezra and Nehemiah. Ezra, a priest and teacher of Jewish law, returned to Israel after the exile and led in the rebuilding of the temple. Genealogies listed in 1 Chronicles suggest the book was written about the time Ezra lived. Whoever the writer was, he apparently used a wide variety of sources, like the books from the Bible and outside resources such as history books about the kings and records by various prophets. And like the books of Samuel and Kings, the two volumes of Chronicles were originally one book. It probably was written in the early 400s BC, about100 years after the Jews had returned from exile.

These books have many of the same stories that are found in Samuel and Kings—but with one big difference. The earlier books were written for the Jews in exile, to explain how they got where they were. The Chronicles, on the other hand, were written to the returning Jews, to assure them that God's promise to them was still operable.

ON LOCATION

Most of the story takes place in what is now Israel. David's military victories extend the boundaries of the kingdom.

WHAT TO LOOK FOR

- **What's missing.** Notice what the writer leaves out because this is a clue about the purpose of the book. In telling the story of David, the writer doesn't mention the conflict with Saul, the affair with Bathsheba and the murder of her husband, the troubles in the royal family, or the attempted coup led by the crown prince. It's not that the writer is trying to sugarcoat history. He's drawing from a painful history that is already well known and recorded. He's not trying to write the complete history of Israel, either. Instead, he's trying to preserve Israel's connection to their ancient covenant with God. The focus is on the history where God is at work on Israel's behalf.

Years ago, some scholars thought that this book was mostly fictional until archaeologists began digging up artifacts from towns that were named after many people listed among the tribes of Israel.

Asaph, author of many songs in the book of Psalms, is appointed by David to be, in essence, the worship leader. Check out the kind of songs they sang by reading Psalm 105.

The only time a person is recorded as praying while sitting is when David is thanking God for blessing his family and the nation in 17:22. Typically, people either kneeled or prayed while lying on the ground. Solomon prayed standing with his hands raised to the sky.

EXTREME SCENES
from 1 Chronicles

⇾ The family tree (Chapters 1–9)

How far back can you trace your family history? The writer of Chronicles traces the Israelite family tree back to Adam and tracks it through the Jewish exile in Babylon. It's not the most compelling reading, but for the Jews recently returned to Israel after decades in Babylon, the list conveys a powerful message: God has not given up on them. Because they have a past with God, they also have a future as the newly restored community of faith. The list is important for several other reasons. It identifies who the new leaders are. One listed descendant of David is Zerubbabel. He's the leader who rebuilds the temple so the Jews can reestablish their system of worship. The list also identifies the descendants of Levi, who are the temple priests and assistants.

⇾ Saul's last battle (10:114)

Before launching into King David's reign, the writer records the final moments of King Saul's life. Saul and his three sons—Jonathan, Abinadab, and Malchishua—are involved in a brutal battle with the invading Philistines. The Philistines take out the three sons, one by one. Then an enemy archer critically wounds Saul. Saul begs his weapon-bearer to finish the job before the Philistines can capture and torture him, but the solider can't do it. In his last desperate act, Saul props up the handle of his sword and falls on it.

⇾ Return of the ark (13:1–14; 15:1–16:6)

David finally is king and he makes Jerusalem his capital. One of the first things David does is bring back the ark of the covenant, the chest that holds the Ten Commandments. For decades (since the time of Eli the priest) the ark has been out of sight, out of mind. First, the Philistines captured it; then they returned it. Since then it has been neglected, put on a back shelf in a private shrine. David realizes that the ark is the most sacred object in all of Israel and a symbol of God's presence among his people. By bringing the ark back to Jerusalem, David boldly unites the king's throne with the symbolic throne of God. David leads the celebration as the ark is returned to Jerusalem. He places it in a tent, but it starts to bother him that he lives in a palace and God's ark is in a tent. David decides he should build God a temple, but God has other ideas. He tells David that he has fought too many wars to build God's temple. Instead, God wants David's son Solomon to build the temple.

⇾ Preparing for the future (22, 28–29)

David accepts God's decision and begins laying the groundwork for his son to build God's temple. He continues to secure Israel's boundaries so his son will have peace. He defeats many surrounding enemies, including Israel's archenemies, the Philistines, who have harassed them for several hundred years. Although David can't *build* the temple, God trusts him to *plan* the temple. David passes on to his son instructions for building the temple along with a bunch of supplies—cedar logs from Lebanon; 4,000 tons of gold; 40,000 tons of silver; iron for nails and gateways; and an assortment of precious gems. David even develops a management plan for the temple, assigning jobs for the priests, temple support staff, and others who assist in leading worship.

REVIEWS

ENCORE

➢ Read 2 Chronicles to continue the rest of the story that was originally one book.

➢ Read 2 Samuel to fill in the details of David's story.

The first book of Chronicles is a rare case of people doing what they are supposed to do. Remember, in Numbers, when they did a census and, through Moses, God told the people to remember important things and pass them down? Chronicles is kind of both things in one. It's a list of important events *and* a census of the major people involved.

So while the first half of 1 Chronicles may seem like a snoozer (like watching CNN when they take attendance in the senate), it's important stuff when you need to look something up. Unless I'm looking for something in particular, I sometimes fast forward through the name lists to get to the stories.

The real hairpin turn in 1 Chronicles is that these lists and genealogies cover a time period way after David's reign, then they twist back and start with the story part. The story of 1 Chronicles is the same as 2 Samuel, *but* from a different point of view. The facts don't change, but the writers tell *why* certain things happened. The books of Samuel might say: "This king was good and the people followed God. That king was bad and the people fell away *again*." Chronicles goes a little deeper. It tells where the kings and people went wrong and what happened because of it "The people fell away because they were not whole-hearted about obeying God. God did not bless them until they became whole-hearted again." The following will illustrate the importance of explaining why:

Teacher: Michael, why weren't you in school yesterday?

Michael: I didn't feel like going.

Teacher: OK, that's thirty seven years of detention, smart guy. Now let's add in some *why*.

Teacher: Michael, why weren't you in school yesterday?"

Michael: I didn't feel like going *because* a LARGE METEOR hit my house.

Teacher: Oh, OK. That's two weeks' detention. Sorry about your house.

See? Big difference.

The details of David's reign that you'll read about in Chronicles have more to do with David's spiritual contributions. After all he was the one to bring back the ark of the covenant to Jerusalem. *That* was a really big deal. For the Hebrews, the ark was like an Oscar or an Emmy or, better yet, a People's Choice award, only this was *for* the people to tell them they were *God's* choice. A lot of good stuff is in this book, you just have to *look*. Don't miss the big deals hidden among the details.

Whitney "Baby Whit" Baffwater

2 Chronicles

Abraham	Moses	Era of Judges	David	Kingdom Divides	Fall of Israel	Fall of Judah	Ezra	Jesus is Born
2100 B.C.	1500 B.C.	1375 B.C.	1010 B.C.	931 B.C.	722 B.C.	586 B.C.	450 B.C.	7/6 B.C.

Searching for God in a History Lesson

Imagine it. You've been kicked out of your home and sent away for a really long time—let's say, 50 years. Finally, you get to come home. You're almost there, you make the last turn, and BOOM! You come face-to-face with a wasteland of ash and piles of stone. Not a pretty picture, is it? But that's exactly what happened to the Jews, who after a half-century of exile in what is now Iraq, have come home to find total destruction. There's not a building left standing. The temple is history. All that remained for these people was God's promise handed down through the generations that this was their land, their home. But as they look around them, they have some major second thoughts: Were they still part of God's plan? Had God chosen someone else while they were away? Did they mess up so badly that God didn't want any part of them?

What these people needed, more than the name of a good builder, was hope. The writer of Chronicles knew this. This book is about hope. It is a history lesson mixed liberally with a sermon of assurance.

Throughout the book, the writer recounts Israel's long history with God and implies they will have a long future, too.

The message of Chronicles is a classic—if there is hope for these people, who had repeatedly turned their back on God, then there's hope for people like us.

QUOTABLES

"If my people, who are called by my name, will humble themselves and pray and seek my face and turn from their wicked ways, then will I hear from heaven and will forgive their sin and will heal their land" (7:14, NIV). God's promise to Solomon in the event that God has to punish Israel for sin.

SNEAK PREVIEW

Hosea
When a good man loves a bad woman.

BEHIND the SCENES
of 2 Chronicles

STARRING ROLES

Solomon, Israel's king and builder of the temple (1:1)
Hezekiah, a godly king who helps Judah survive Assyria (28:27)
Josiah, king and religious reformer (33:25)

PLOT

Solomon becomes king after his father, David, dies. Just like God promised, Solomon builds the temple and rules Israel during a golden era of peace and prosperity. After Solomon dies, though, things change for the worse. The northern tribes reject Solomon's son as king when the young ruler threatens to rule harshly. These tribes form a separate nation, called Israel, that is later wiped out by the Assyrians. Survivors are deported, and never return. After about 150 years, the southern nation of Judah is also destroyed, the people deported. These Jews, however, are eventually allowed to return home and rebuild their ruined nation.

STAGE DIRECTIONS

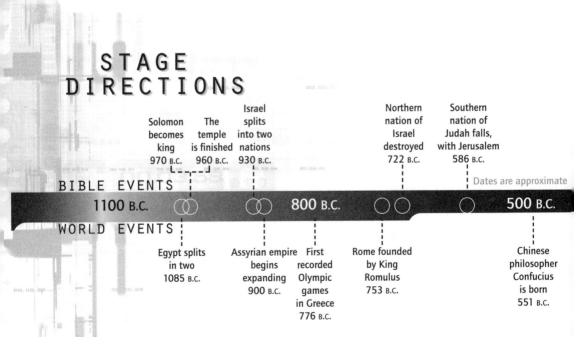

		Israel			Northern	Southern
Solomon	The	splits			nation of	nation of
becomes	temple	into two			Israel	Judah falls,
king	is finished	nations			destroyed	with Jerusalem
970 B.C.	960 B.C.	930 B.C.			722 B.C.	586 B.C.

Dates are approximate

BIBLE EVENTS

1100 B.C.   800 B.C.   500 B.C.

WORLD EVENTS

Egypt splits	Assyrian empire	First	Rome founded	Chinese
in two	begins	recorded	by King	philosopher
1085 B.C.	expanding	Olympic	Romulus	Confucius
	900 B.C.	games	753 B.C.	is born
		in Greece		551 B.C.
		776 B.C.		

AUTHOR AND DATE

The writer is unnamed, but ancient Jewish tradition says Ezra wrote 1, 2 Chronicles along with the books of Ezra and Nehemiah. Like the books of Samuel and Kings, the two books of Chronicles were originally one volume that was later separated so each could fit onto a single scroll. Chronicles was probably written in the early 400s BC, about a hundred years after many of the Jews returned home from exile and rebuilt the temple. The stories are carefully chosen to assure the Jews that they have a godly heritage and that their covenant with God is still in force. But the stories also warn them not to repeat the mistakes of the past.

INSIDE SCOOP

The cedar wood from Lebanon that Solomon used to build the temple was valued above all other trees. Its red-hued wood was slow to decay, free of knots, and was filled with a fragrance that was pleasing to humans but repelled insects. Cedar trees can live for 3,000 years. But because of widespread demand for the wood, only a remnant is left of the once-great cedar forests.

ON LOCATION

Most of the story takes place in what is now Israel. The "golden age" of Solomon's reign ends with his death, and the nation quickly divides in two—Israel in the north and Judah in the south.

WHAT TO LOOK FOR

- **The moral of the story.** As in 1 Chronicles, notice that the book is not just recording history. After all, the history books covering this era have already been written. Chronicles is an attempt to interpret what this history means to Jews who have come back from the exile in Babylon. The moral behind the story is that the Jewish people have a future with God.
- **Lack of material about the northern nation.** The writer almost totally ignores the northern Jewish nation of Israel, except to acknowledge the monumental events: their seceding from the union and their annihilation. As far as the writer of Chronicles is concerned, the Lost Tribes of Israel, as they became known, no longer represent the true Israel. Their connection to the covenant of God has been severed. From the beginning of their secession, they worshiped idols. As a result, their nation is destroyed and their surviving citizens dragged into exile—never to return. Those left behind become assimilated into foreign cultures when they intermarry with Assyrian pioneers.

EXTREME SCENES
from 2 Chronicles

DIRECTOR'S NOTES

Solomon recognized that the best way to strengthen Israel's military force was to invest in chariots, the most important piece of battle machinery available that time. Ancient chariots came in all styles and sizes. Some were pulled by two horses, others by four. Some carried two riders; others carried four. The problem with chariots was the expense. Building, buying, and maintaining a fleet of chariots required more than a few shekels. Only the wealthiest nations could afford to keep a strong chariot force. Later in Israel's history, as the kingdom declined in wealth and power, the use of chariots declined drastically. By the time King Jehoahaz came to power, Israel was down to ten measly chariots in their military. The rest had been destroyed in battle.
2 Chronicles 1:16, 17

A wise guy (1:1–17)

God speaks to Solomon in a dream and tells him to ask for anything and God will give it to him. With all the possibilities before him, Solomon asks for wisdom so he can rule God's people. God likes Solomon's answer. So he decides to give Solomon the whole package—wealth, fame, a long life, and wisdom. Solomon becomes one of the wisest and most famous kings to ever live.

Building the temple (3:1–17)

On a hilltop overlooking Jerusalem, Solomon builds the first of only three temples the Jews have ever had. It takes seven years and a workforce that numbers 150,000 to get the job done. The finished product is one of the ancient world's most beautiful and expensive temples. It is a white limestone worship center with ceilings, walls, and floors made of pure gold. The temple measures 30 yards long, 10 yards wide, and 15 yards high. Only priests are allowed inside. In the back room, where only the high priest is allowed to enter once a year, sits Israel's most sacred object—the ark of the covenant. David's long-held dream is finally realized. The temple will be the focus of Jewish worship and sacrifices to God for 400 years—until the Babylonians invade and destroy the building.

A divided nation (10:1–19)

Solomon also becomes known for his extensive building program. In addition to the temple, Solomon builds himself a lavish palace, along with cities and forts. By the time he dies, the people are tired of paying lots of taxes to support Solomon's habit. They're tired, too, of being forced to do the building. So when Solomon's son, Rehoboam, takes the throne, they ask for relief. The rookie king makes a critical error when, instead of letting up on the people, he promises them even more taxes and harder work than they had ever experienced. Not exactly a winning campaign platform, now or then! The northern tribes bolt and form their own nation, Israel, and name their own king. Only Judah in the south remains loyal to David's descendants.

Defeat at Jerusalem (32:1–23)

The northern kingdom suffers under a series of godless kings for about 200 years. Finally, God delivers on the warnings he has given these people through numerous prophets. In 722 BC, Assyria invades and wipes Israel off the map; the only survivors are taken away as captives. Judah, in the meantime, also pays taxes to Assyria. But when the Assyrian king dies, Judah decides to rebel. The army of Sennacherib, the new Assyrian king, wants to get Judah back in line, so it invades. City after city falls until Sennacherib reaches Jerusalem. He stands outside the city gates and taunts the Jews: "No god of any nation has ever been able to stand up to Assyria. Believe me, your God cannot keep you safe!" Sennacherib soon realizes he has made a serious error. The Lord sends an angel to the camp of the Assyrians, and the next morning the camp is full of dead bodies. Sennacherib returns to Assyria totally disgraced.

Jerusalem falls (36:9–21)

Judah suffers a similar fate as Israel, but it takes 150 years longer. That's because Judah has a few kings who remain obedient to God. But there are other kings who lead the people down the wrong path. God sends prophets to warn the people about their sins, but the people only laugh and mock the prophets. Finally, God decides to punish Judah, too. God sends the Babylonians to invade Judah. Jerusalem is under siege for a year and a half. When the Babylonian army breaks through, they tear the city to the ground. Solomon's temple, the symbol of Jewish national and religious identity, is looted and then destroyed. Survivors are deported to Babylon as captives. The nation of Abraham and David is no more.

Free at last (36:22–23)

What goes around, comes around, and about 50 years later, the Persian empire invades and conquers the Babylonians. The new Persian ruler, Cyrus, is prompted by God to allow the Jews to return to their homeland. In addition, he makes the following decree: "The Lord God of heaven has made me the ruler of every nation on earth. He has also chosen me to build a temple for him in Jerusalem, which is in Judah. The Lord God will watch over any of his people who want to go back to Judah." With this promise, many Jews begin their long trek home.

INTERVIEW
with the Stars

The action reaction

Think back to what you were doing when you were eight years old. Probably going to school, playing soccer with your friends, being a king of a country. Hey, wait! Nobody gets to be king at age eight! Yet, that's exactly what happened to our next subject, Josiah. And despite coming to power at such a young age, Josiah has a special place in God's Word. Look at what's recorded in 2 Kings 23:25 about Josiah: *"Now before him there was no king like him, who turned to the Lord with all his heart, with all his soul, and with all his might, according to all the Law of Moses; nor after him did any arise like him."* Pretty impressive stuff. Welcome to **Behind the Bible,** Josiah. Tell us what you did to earn such rave reviews.

⟫ Josiah

It's certainly not easy being king when your feet barely touch the ground when you're sitting on the throne. I realized right away that I needed help big time. And so when I was about 16 I started seriously seeking God.

That was something new for the kings of Judah at the time, wasn't it?

⟫ Josiah

Unfortunately, you're right about that. It had been some time since any of my family had paid any attention to God. My father was so wicked that the servants ganged up on him and killed him in our house. My grandfather was even worse, but my great-grandfather, Hezekiah, really tried to follow God. If I had any childhood heroes, it would have to be him.

So once you started to learn more about God and His Word, what kind of impact did that make on you?

⟫ Josiah

It really motivated me to want to make a difference in our nation for God.

INTERVIEW
with the Stars

How did you do that?

⇒ Josiah

Well, among other things, I started a renovation of the temple in Jerusalem, which had been neglected for years. Then, while they were digging around in the temple, a scroll containing God's Law was discovered. That was an eye-opener! When I read about all that was expected of God's people to worship and obey God, I tore my clothes in grief! We had fallen so far away from God. That's when I really kicked a reform program into high gear.

Tell us what you mean by that.

⇒ Josiah

I instituted a national revival of true worship. We began an aggressive campaign to get rid of all the idols and pagan worship places. And we began to celebrate the Passover again. What a great time of celebration, remembering all God had done for us. It had been years since we as a nation had done something like that.

That must have been something to see. Your story, Josiah, hopefully will motivate other young people to realize that they don't have to wait until they get older to act on what they learn from God. They can act immediately, as you did.

⇒ Josiah

That's right. Too often, especially when you're young, you think you've got all the time in the world to get to God's agenda. You know, you've got your own plans for now; God can come later. But when you do that, you run the risk of making the wrong kind of difference.

Thank you Josiah for some *timely* advice.

REVIEWS

You know how some movies split the screen in half. Like you'll be watching one story line and someone, let's call him Jerry, will make a phone call to...we'll say, Elaine. Suddenly the screen splits and you can see both of them talking. Well, 2 Chronicles is like that.

The first ten chapters retell the story of Solomon as he builds the temple and gets rich as a skunk (you know, like STINKIN' rich). Then the kingdom divides (the screen splits). Suddenly the story is jumping back and forth between the northern kingdom and the southern kingdom. You've gotta watch close to know if the new king is the king of Judah (South, or Jerry) or Samaria (North, or Elaine). It's almost like watching two movies at once when somebody else has gotten hold of the remote.

Even though 2 Chronicles describes the same time as 1 and 2 Kings, the writers concentrate on different facts. Here's why. The books of the Chronicles were written after the people of Judah had been taken away as exiles to Babylon. Later, when Babylon was conquered by Persia, Cyrus (the Persian king) told the exiles they could go home. So this band of weary, homeless wanderers dragged themselves back to the ruins of their homeland. The Chronicles were written to get them back in touch with their roots. Aaaaahhhhhh. So that's why it's got all those genealogies (which are family trees, not the science of studying genies) and tons of details (do genies have *tails?*). That's also why the writers focus on so many positive and spiritual aspects of their history. This was a beaten down group of people picking themselves up and dusting themselves off. 2 Chronicles is their map back to who they were.

Um...two questions: 1. What happened to Jerry and Elaine? 2. Can I have the remote or the map or whatever? My head hurts.

Jerry and Elaine Cyrus
(and no, Jerry, you can't have the remote back)

ENCORE

> The book of Ezra continues Israel's story, with the Jews returning from exile and starting the job of rebuilding the temple.

> For more details about the era covered in the book, read 1, 2 Kings.

> To catch a glimpse of what Jesus had in mind when he spoke of "Solomon in all his glory" (Matthew 6:29), review chapter nine, about the queen of Sheba's reaction to Solomon.

Ezra

SCHEDULE OF SCENES

Abraham	Moses	Era of Judges	David	Kingdom Divides	Fall of Israel	First Exiles Return	Fall of Judah	Ezra	Jesus is Born
2100 B.C.	1500 B.C.	1375 B.C.	1010 B.C.	931 B.C.	722 B.C.	538 B.C.	586 B.C.	450 B.C.	7/6 B.C.

A Second Great Escape

Maybe once, you'll catch a break when you're down and out. But twice? And with some extra help to boot? That's the kind of stuff found in fairy tales, not reality. But that's exactly what happens to the nation of Israel. From a nation reduced to a pile of ashes and rubble emerges a new nation, a fully restored Israel. It's a miracle that ranks right up there with the first exodus from Egypt. But instead of facing a stubborn pharaoh who refused to let the Jews go, these Jews are encouraged to return home by three Persian kings.

Armed with gifts and tax benefits as added incentives, the Jews begin their second exodus.

Over several decades, wave after wave of exiles pack up their belongings and make the long, nearly thousand-mile walk northward along the fertile Euphrates River valley in what is now Iraq, then south along the Mediterranean coast, through Lebanon and into Israel. The people who had settled into the land during the Jewish exile do not exactly throw out the welcome mat as they see the Jews returning home. But with the help of these pagan kings (whom the Jews believed were instruments of God), the Jews prevail.

This story of restoration, of homecoming, and of a fresh start is an inspiration for anyone who faces the challenge of rebuilding his or her life, home, or faith from the ground up.

QUOTABLES

"Let the temple be rebuilt" (6:3, NIV). The Persian king's declaration about the Jewish temple that the Babylonians had destroyed.

Praise the Lord God of our ancestors! He made sure that the king [of Persia] honored the Lord's temple in Jerusalem (7:27). Priest Ezra's reaction to news that the king was authorizing royal treasurers to contribute silver and other gifts for the rebuilding of the temple. In addition, temple workers would not have to pay taxes.

SNEAK PREVIEW

> Malachi
> Wanted: whole hearts.
> Worship is not about a
> minimum daily requirement.

BEHIND the SCENES
of Ezra

STARRING ROLES

Ezra, priest who preaches against Jews marrying non-Jews (7:1)
Cyrus, Persian king who frees Jewish exiles (1:1)

PLOT

After 50 years of living in exile, the Jews are free to go home. Persia has defeated Babylon, and Persian King Cyrus has ordered that all Jewish captives may return home if they want. The king also encourages the Jews to rebuild their temple. He even returns the temple furnishings that the Babylonians had taken from Solomon's temple before they leveled it. Many Jews return and begin to rebuild the temple in Jerusalem. Opposition quickly surfaces, and the job grinds to a halt. But the work begins again, at the urging of the prophets Haggai and Zechariah who arrive later. Jerusalem's second temple is completed in 516 BC, 70 years after Solomon's temple was destroyed. Ezra the priest later arrives and begins teaching the people from the laws of Moses. His sermons generate nationwide repentance and abruptly end the marriages of many Jewish men to non-Jewish women.

STAGE DIRECTIONS

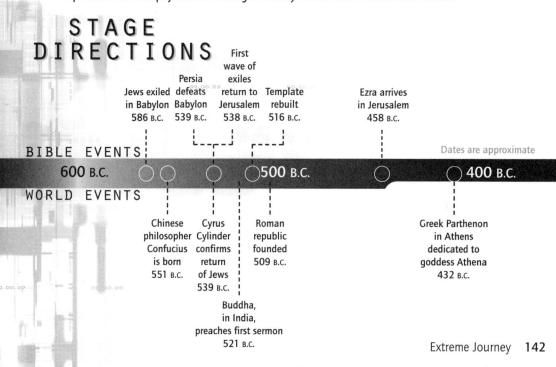

Jews exiled in Babylon 586 B.C.

Persia defeats Babylon 539 B.C.

First wave of exiles return to Jerusalem 538 B.C.

Template rebuilt 516 B.C.

Ezra arrives in Jerusalem 458 B.C.

BIBLE EVENTS

Dates are approximate

600 B.C. — **500 B.C.** — **400 B.C.**

WORLD EVENTS

Chinese philosopher Confucius is born 551 B.C.

Cyrus Cylinder confirms return of Jews 539 B.C.

Roman republic founded 509 B.C.

Greek Parthenon in Athens dedicated to goddess Athena 432 B.C.

Buddha, in India, preaches first sermon 521 B.C.

AUTHOR AND DATE

The writer is not named, but Jewish tradition says the book was written by Ezra, a priest and teacher who returned from exile about 60 years after the temple was rebuilt. Many believe that the author of Ezra also wrote 1, 2 Chronicles as well as Nehemiah. In early Bibles, Ezra and Nehemiah were one book. The first known writer to speak of them as separate was Christian scholar Origen, who lived in the 200s AD. He called them 1, 2 Ezra. Like the two books of Chronicles, Ezra was probably written in the early 400s BC, roughly a hundred years after many of the Jews returned home from exile and rebuilt the temple. The author wrote the book to record how the Jewish exiles began rebuilding their nation by rebuilding their temple. They also made a serious attempt to distance themselves from idol-worshiping foreigners, who could undermine their faith in God.

INSIDE SCOOP

> Though Ezra preached against the Jews marrying non-Jews, King David's great-grandmother was Ruth, a Moabite. (The people from Moab were from a region in what is now Jordan.) While foreigners tended to lead Israel away from God and into idolatry, God accepted non-Jews who worshiped him, as Ruth did.

ON LOCATION

The story takes place in two locations: first in Babylon (modern Iraq), where exiled Jews prepare to return home, then in Jerusalem, where they begin rebuilding the temple. Zerubbabel and the first group of exiles returned to Jerusalem in 538–537 BC. The city walls were not rebuilt until Ezra and Nehemiah led a second wave of Jews back eighty years later.

WHAT TO LOOK FOR

- **God working through people who don't worship him.** Notice that the writer says the temple is rebuilt because of the support of three pagan kings. (1) Persian King Cyrus issues a formal decree inviting the Jews to return to Jerusalem and rebuild the temple. (2) Decades later, Persian King Darius brushes aside non-Jewish opposition to the continued rebuilding project and tells the Jews to finish their work. (3) And a third Persian king, Artaxerxes, encourages Jews who have remained in Babylon to return home. He gives money and supplies to any who wish to go.
- **Copies of official letters.** Most of the book, like most of the Old Testament, is written in Hebrew. But Ezra includes some official Persian messages written in Aramaic, the language used during the exile. One example is the memorandum by King Darius in 6:3-12. These are included to give evidence that the Jews had the king's approval to do what they were doing. Some Bible scholars a few decades ago thought these letters were made up. But recently discovered Persian documents reveal that the letters track with Persian policies, and are written in the language of the region, using the formal tone of royal decrees.

EXTREME SCENES
from Ezra

Going home (Chapters 1–2)

After Babylon falls to Persia, Persian King Cyrus issues a startling decree: any exiled Jews can now return home. Not only that, but Cyrus also encourages the Jews to rebuild their temple and even donates supplies to get the job done. He even returns the sacred furnishings of the temple, stolen by the Babylonians 50 years earlier. Some 42,000 Jews take Cyrus up on his offer, the majority of whom had been born in exile and had never seen the promised land. When they finally arrive in Jerusalem, they take up a collection to begin rebuilding the temple. They collect about a half ton of gold and nearly three tons of silver—a fraction of the nearly 4,000 tons of gold and 40,000 tons of silver that David had set aside for the temple built by his son, Solomon. The Jews begin by rebuilding the altar, so they can quickly renew their practice of worshiping God by offering animal and crop sacrifices.

DIRECTOR'S NOTES

"Peoples of the land" were not necessarily those of another race, but were any who worshiped "foreign" gods–that is, any persons who worshiped a deity or deities other than the Lord God of Israel. Ezra 10:2

The new temple (3:7–13; 6:13–18)

With the altar and sacrificial system back in place, the Jews get down to the tough stuff—clearing away the rubble from the original temple and laying the foundation for a new one. When the foundation is complete, the people gather to sing praise songs to God. But in the middle of the celebration there is a hint of disappointment. Many of the old-timers remember the first temple. They know that this new temple doesn't even come close to the original. But what they don't know is that this smaller, less elaborate temple will last nearly a century longer than its predecessor—about 500 years.

Growing opposition (4:1–24)

While the Jews were in exile, other people have settled in the land. They begin worshiping God, but only as the local god, not as the one and only God of creation. They offer to help the Jews rebuild the temple, but the Jews turn them down. Insulted, the locals begin causing trouble, threatening the workers and trying to undermine their efforts. When a new Persian king takes the throne, the locals escalate their efforts to stop the Jews. They write a letter to the king, telling him that when the Jews finish rebuilding the city, they "won't pay any kind of taxes, and there will be less money in your treasury." They further suggest the king check out the records on these people because they have a past track record of rebelling.

When the king checks it out, he discovers that the Jews do have a history of rebelling. So he stops the work. For nearly 10 years, the work on the temple stops. Then encouraged by newly arrive prophets, the Jews resume building. Again, the locals protest and alert the king. But this time, yet another new king—Darius—has come to power and when he checks the records, he digs out Cyrus' original decree and orders the work to continue. About four years later, in 516 BC, the temple is completed and dedicated.

⇒ Obey God's laws! (9:1—10:17)

Ezra, a Jewish priest, arrives on the scene and discovers that many of the Jewish men have ignored the law against marrying non-Jewish women. Even some of the priests and temple workers have broken this law. Ezra goes to the temple courtyard and begins praying and weeping on behalf of the people. He knows that it's exactly this practice that got Israel into trouble before. And he fears that God will punish the new nation, just as he had punished Judah. One by one, a crowd of worshipers gathers around him. When they hear his prayers, they begin weeping, too. Within three days a vast assembly has gathered there. As rain pours onto the courtyard, Ezra stands to speak: "You have broken God's Law by marrying foreign women. Now you must confess your sins to the Lord God of your ancestors and obey him. Divorce your foreign wives and don't have anything to do with the rest of the foreigners who live around here." The people agree.

REVIEWS

ENCORE

➤ To continue the next stage of the story, read Nehemiah, which was originally the second half of the book of Ezra.

➤ To compare the second and less-magnificent temple of Ezra's day with the first one of Solomon's day, read 1 Chronicles 28—29 and 2 Chronicles 2—7.

➤ To read the words of prophets who inspired the exiles to rebuild the temple and recommit themselves to God, turn to the books of Haggai and Zechariah.

How many movies have you seen that ended with a city in ruins? It might have been a Thunderdome thang, a *Planet of the Apes* movie, a futuristic robot cop flick, or an alien invasion—take your pick. Anyway, get the image of a place that used to be nice, but now it's a burned-out pile of junk.

That's how Ezra *starts*. Ezra's people, the Hebrews, had been forced from their homes and carried off as exiles. Then, years later, King Cyrus sent them back home. Home? The truth was they'd been in exile so long some of them didn't even *remember* home. The other thing is that home was *trashed*. Got the picture? A big group of families finally getting to the city limits and just standing there with their mouths hanging open, staring at the wreckage. Ouch !

The first group of exiles that returned was led by a man named Zerubbabel. (That's zuh-ROO-buh-bul. Sounds like some kind of nuclear powered bubble gum. Maybe that's what trashed the town.) This group worked hard to rebuild. They rebuilt the temple and much of the city. What they couldn't rebuild was the knowledge of why all this mattered to them so much.

That's when Ezra arrived. He looked around to see what had been accomplished and realized that the hearts of the people were in even worse shape than the city was. They had rebuilt the temple but had married into surrounding tribes that worshiped all kinds of weird gods. Their faith got *all kinds* of mixed up with these false faiths. ("Oh mighty Zulububba, whose toes are seven, Howard is to blame! Thy kingdom's dumb. Chew nuclear gum, and blow thy brains to heaven") Not good. It was complete freakville. The people needed the *real* God in a bad way.

REVIEWS

There was only one thing to be done (drum roll, please). Ezra pulled out the scrolls (Ta Da!). When in doubt, read the instructions. They didn't have the whole Bible then, but they did have the law of Moses. So Ezra read and the people listened. For them it was like looking in a mirror and suddenly remembering that you used to be a hottie and seeing that you *could* be again *if* you got yourself together.

A lot of crying followed and some gnashing of the teeth (which people were prone to do in those days when they were freaked out. "Careful, Bob. Don't gnash your teeth on that Zerobubble, you'll blow us all to smithereens"). In the end they cleaned up their act and started all over again, rebuilding themselves and their city at the same time. ("Say, Bob, could you hand me those nails, please. Oh, and some self-respect and sense of purpose while you're at it? Thanks.)

Robertus Villus (host of "This Old City")

Nehemiah

SCHEDULE OF SCENES

Abraham | Moses | Era of Judges | David | Kingdom Divides | Fall of Israel | Fall of Judah | First Exiles Return | Ezra Returns | Jesus Is Born

2100 B.C. | 1500 B.C. | 1375 B.C. | 1010 B.C. | 931 B.C. | 722 B.C. | 586 B.C. | 538 B.C. | 458 B.C. | 7/6 B.C.

Getting the job done

Ever have a huge job on your to-do list—like a monster English paper or organizing a work crew from your youth group to do a service project. Sometimes, big jobs like that call for more than faith and prayer. Sometimes it takes brains, muscle, and courage to get the job done. Nehemiah needed it all.

When we first meet Nehemiah, he's working at the palace in Persia for the king. He gets word that some former Jewish exiles who had returned to Jerusalem were having some major problems. The city walls were a mess, leaving the people there defenseless and dissed by their neighbors. This was more than the people there could handle. After all, Jerusalem, since the days of King David nearly 600 years ago, was the spiritual and political center of their nation. Jews without Jerusalem would be like Americans without America, or a congregation without a church, or a family without a home.

Just thinking about it made Nehemiah depressed. In fact, he was so depressed that even prayer and fasting couldn't help. Finally, he realized the only thing to do was for him to go to Jerusalem and get the job done. Nehemiah, a low-level servant in the king's palace. No building or organizational experience on his resume. Just a cupbearer for the king.

The amazing thing, and what makes the book of Nehemiah a must-read, is that with God's help, Nehemiah did it. He convinced the Persian king into supporting the project, rallied the apathetic Jews to get behind the project, and outmaneuver the local opposition. In getting the job done, Nehemiah wrote himself into history as the model for tackling God's tough assignments.

QUOTABLES

"Come, let us rebuild the wall of Jerusalem" (2:17, NIV). Nehemiah's invitation to Jerusalem-area Jews.

The people had a mind to work (4:6, NKJV).

The people shouted, Amen! Amen! (8:6). How the Jews responded to hearing Ezra reading the laws God had given them through Moses.

The joy of the Lord is your strength (8:10, NKJV).

SNEAK PREVIEW

> **James**
> It's hard to get to where you're going if your faith has no feet.

BEHIND the SCENES
of Nehemiah

STARRING ROLES

Nehemiah, Persian palace servant who oversees repair of Jerusalem's walls (1:1)

Sanballat, leader of opposition and possibly governor of Samaria (2:10)

Artaxerxes, Persian king who gives Nehemiah permission to repair the walls (1:1)

Ezra, priest who reads God's Law to the assembled people (8:1)

PLOT

Nehemiah, a palace servant whose job is to taste-test the Persian king's wine to make sure it's not poisoned, is granted a leave of absence so he can oversee the repair of Jerusalem's walls. Despite opposition and apparent plans to attack the workers and kill Nehemiah, the work is completed in stunningly short order: 52 days. Afterward, the priest Ezra reads from God's Law given through Moses, while the Jews listen. Ezra then leads the people in confessing their sins and pledging their allegiance to God.

STAGE DIRECTIONS

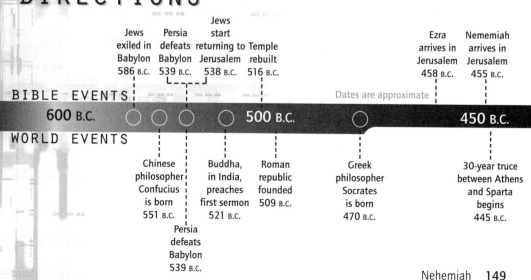

BIBLE EVENTS

Jews exiled in Babylon 586 B.C.

Persia defeats Babylon 539 B.C.

Jews start returning to Jerusalem 538 B.C.

Temple rebuilt 516 B.C.

Dates are approximate

Ezra arrives in Jerusalem 458 B.C.

Nememiah arrives in Jerusalem 455 B.C.

600 B.C. — 500 B.C. — 450 B.C.

WORLD EVENTS

Chinese philosopher Confucius is born 551 B.C.

Persia defeats Babylon 539 B.C.

Buddha, in India, preaches first sermon 521 B.C.

Roman republic founded 509 B.C.

Greek philosopher Socrates is born 470 B.C.

30-year truce between Athens and Sparta begins 445 B.C.

AUTHOR AND DATE

The story is compiled from the memoirs of Nehemiah, a Jewish servant in the palace of the Persian king. The book was originally combined with Ezra, so both books were likely written by the same person. Jewish tradition says the author was Ezra, a priest and teacher who returned from exile after the temple was rebuilt. Many believe that the author, whoever he was, also wrote 1, 2 Chronicles, partly because all these books are set in the time just after the Jewish exile. Like Ezra and the two books of Chronicles, Nehemiah was probably written in the early 400s BC, shortly after the incidents in the book occurred. This was roughly a hundred years after many of the Jews returned home from exile and rebuilt the temple. The author preserved the memoirs of Nehemiah to show how this man of action and hero of the faith turned to God in times of need. The book also reminds the Jews (and us) not to become careless about honoring their commitment to God.

ON LOCATION

The story begins in Susa, winter capital of the Persian Empire, located along the border of Iraq and Iran. Here, the palace servant Nehemiah is granted a leave of absence to go to Jerusalem, where the rest of the story unfolds. By 500 BC the Persians completely dominate the region.

WHAT TO LOOK FOR

- **Faith coupled with action.** Notice that Nehemiah "puts feet to his prayers." When he hears that Jerusalem's walls need repair, he prays and asks the king for a leave of absence and supplies to do the work. Later, when Nehemiah hears of a possible attack against his workers at the walls, he reports "We kept on praying to our God, and we also stationed guards day and night" (4:9).
- **Leadership qualities.** Notice the leadership skills of Nehemiah. He seeks the help of God. Once he realizes what he needs to do, he becomes strong-minded and decisive in pursuing his goal. He uses sound judgment to deal with the sly tactics of his enemies.

Susa, the capital of Persia and where Nehemiah worked in the palace, is the same setting for the story of Esther, the next book in the Bible.

Women helped rebuild the wall (3:12).

Once the walls were repaired, the Jews didn't want to live inside the city. They had to "cast lots," an ancient version of drawing straws, to see who would have to relocate from the villages outside the city into Jerusalem. Maybe one reason they were reluctant to move is that they had seen the walls being destroyed in a recent attack and they feared a repeat attack. Or maybe they feared the neighboring leaders who had opposed the project and threatened the workers.

EXTREME SCENES
from Nehemiah

⋙ Bad news on the homefront (1:1—2:10)

When Nehemiah, a Jew living in Persia and working as a palace servant, gets a visit from his brother Hanani, from Judah, he hears some bad news: the walls surrounding Jerusalem are in shambles. Nehemiah goes into a deep funk that lasts four months. Finally, the king notices that something is up with Nehemiah (who is the chief taste-tester for the king to make sure the wine is not poisoned). He asks Nehemiah what's bugging him, and Nehemiah tells the king that his hometown is disgraced because its walls are in ruins and the gates have been burned down. The king asks how he can help, and Nehemiah is ready. (He's had four months to think about it.) He asks the king for a leave of absence and for supplies from the Persian governors in the west. The king not only grants these requests, but he also gives Nehemiah an armed escort to go back to Jerusalem with him.

DIRECTOR'S NOTES

The Feast of Booths was like a yearly campout for the Israelites. During this harvest celebration, the people made temporary shelters out of leafy tree branches and then lived in those shelters for a short time. The Feast was intended to remind the Israelites of the time their ancestors wandered in the desert, with no homes of their own, after Moses led them out of Egypt. Nehemiah 8:14

⋙ The fast-track building project (Chapters 3—4; 6:15—16)

As soon as Nehemiah gets the Jews organized to begin rebuilding, opposition from non-Jewish leaders surfaces. They mock the Jews' efforts, saying that "even a fox could knock over this pile of stones." Nehemiah even gets wind of a possible attack, so he posts armed guards around the wall and instructs the haulers to keep one hand free to grab a weapon. Nehemiah's opposition even tries to trick him by asking to schedule a so-called meeting with him. Four times. Each time Nehemiah refuses, telling them that his work is too important to stop now. Despite these harassment tactics, the work continues and the walls are rebuilt in an amazing 52 days. Jerusalem's neighbors are astounded! They're also afraid because they know that the only way the work got done this quickly is because God is on the Jews' side.

Ezra reads the Law (8:1–18)

After the walls are repaired, the Jews gather at one of the city gates and listen to Ezra read some of the laws God gave through Moses. From dawn until noon, Ezra reads. Most likely, he reads selections from the first five books in the Bible, or perhaps Deuteronomy, which is a summary of the Law. During or after Ezra reads, teachers of the Law walk among the crowd explaining all that Ezra has read. Maybe they're translating the Law from Hebrew, in which it is written, to Aramaic, the language the Jews learned in exile. Or maybe the teachers are explaining how the people can apply the Law in their daily lives, like pastors and Bible teachers do today.

DIRECTOR'S NOTES

The Levites didn't have their own land or means of income. The rest of the Israelites supported them by giving them one-tenth of every harvest. The Levites, in turn, supported the priests by giving them one-tenth of everything they received. If this one-tenth stuff sounds familiar, it should. This system, called tithing, was established in the Law of Moses. Nehemiah 10:38

Time for change (13:4–22)

Now that the people have heard the Law, it's time to make some changes. Nehemiah notices that some merchants are selling stuff on the Sabbath, so he orders the city gates closed each Sabbath day—from sundown on Friday until sundown on Saturday. He also notices that the temple is being neglected because temple assistants are working on farms instead. They're at their farms because Jews are not paying the temple tithe to support the temple workers. So Nehemiah tells everyone to start living up to their obligations according to the Law. People from the tribe of Levi are to work in the temple, and Jews throughout the region are to support the Levites by bringing a tenth of their crops to the temple storeroom. Nehemiah also convinces the people to make a solemn vow not to let their sons and daughters marry idol-worshiping foreigners. With these reforms in place, the city walls rebuilt and Jerusalem no longer disgraced, Nehemiah concludes his memoirs with this request: "I pray that God will bless me for the good I have done."

REVIEWS

ENCORE

➤ For the other half of what was originally one book, read Ezra.

➤ For another book that speaks of faith in action, read James. He says, "Faith that doesn't lead us to do good deeds is all alone and dead!" (James 2:17).

If ever two dudes earned the role of bad guys it was Sanballat and Tobiah. They made careers out of making Nehemiah's life miserable when all he was trying to do was build a wall. Here's some background.

The people of Israel had been taken captive to Persia. They were exiled there for so long that it had almost become home. Then one day the king said, "OK, you can go back now." So this little remnant gypsy pack of Hebrews trudge back to the ruins of what was their capital, Jerusalem. They rebuilt the temple (which, compared to the old temple, was like a papier-mâché version).

Meanwhile, back in Persia, Nehemiah was sitting in a cushy job as the king's wine taster. Cushy, but kinda risky. The main reason for the job was to taste the king's wine and food to see if it was poisoned. And there was only one way to know...get it? (King: So, Nehemiah, what do you think of tonight's selection? Nehemiah: Hmmm. a 2,000 B.C. Dom Babylon. Amusing bouquet, but the taste is a little AAACK... thump.). Anyway, Nehemiah took some time off from pro-fessional drinking roulette to go to Jerusalem and help his people rebuild the wall around the city.

He's a good guy right? He's a good organizer. He divides up the job and gives each family a section to rebuild. He's doing a good thing, got it?

Then in step Sanballat and Tobiah. They attack. They weasel. They slander. They gossip. They do whatever they can to get this stand-up guy and his people to take their marbles and go home. But you know how stand-up guys go. Nehemiah wouldn't budge. My favorite scene is when he has the men working construction with a tool in one hand and a weapon in the other. They just weren't stopping for anything.

Everybody's seen a Sanballat type whether they were looking for a coat made of Dalmation skins or trying to trick little Red Riding Hood. But Nehemiah beat them at their own game.

Ernestus Julius Gallio

Esther

SCHEDULE OF SCENES

Abraham   Moses   Era of Judges   David   Kingdom Divides   Fall of Israel   Fall of Judah   First Exiles Return   Ezra Returns   Jesus Is Born

2100 B.C.   1500 B.C.   1375 B.C.   1010 B.C.   931 B.C.   722 B.C.   586 B.C.   538 B.C.   458 B.C.   7/6 B.C.

The queen who saved her people

Esther is one of those stories that just seems too good to be true. First, you've got a queen who refuses to make a command performance before the king. Next thing you know the king has ordered her never to appear before him again. Divorce, Persian style. Then there's a beautiful Jewish maiden who catches the king's eye and becomes the next queen. When a plot is discovered to kill all the Jews in the land, Queen Esther becomes the right person in the right place at the right time.

Mix in the perfect villain, Haman, a high Persian official, who vows revenge against a lower official, Mordecai, when he refuses to bow to him. Haman plans a little hanging party for Mordecai after he carries out a diabolical plan to kill all of Mordecai's entire race, the Jews. Thanks to some fast-thinking on Mordecai's part, some brave and bold moves by Esther, and a lot of intervention from God, Haman winds up honoring Mordecai by leading him through the capital on a horse while shouting, "This is how the king honors a man!" (6:11). If Esther had a laugh track, it would kick in right about now. Later, Haman is hanged from the same gallows he built for Mordecai. Happy ending.

But behind this powerfully moving story is an equally powerful message: God looks after His people.

QUOTABLES

"It could be that you were made queen for a time like this!" (4:14). Mordecai's urging of Esther to take the life-threatening risk of asking the king to show mercy on the Jews.

SNEAK PREVIEW

Micah

People on a certain path to destruction. Can God deliver us from ourselves?

BEHIND the SCENES
of Esther

STARRING ROLES

Esther, Jewish queen of Persia who saves the Jews from slaughter (2:7)
Mordecai, Esther's cousin, Persian official who prods her to risk helping the Jews (2:5)
Haman, Persian high official who plots to kill the Jews (3:1)
Xerxes, king of Persia (1:1)

PLOT

Persian King Xerxes divorces his queen. To replace her, he chooses a young Jewish orphan named Esther, raised by her cousin Mordecai, a palace official. Mordecai refuses to bow in honor of a higher official, Haman. In retaliation, Haman hatches a scheme to kill all the Jews in the empire. Without identifying who the "troublesome" people are, Haman manages to talk the king into signing an irrevocable order permitting the citizens to slaughter the Jews on a set day. Esther appeals to the king, who is surprised to hear that Haman has targeted the Jews and that Esther is a Jew. He executes Haman, then issues a second order allowing the Jews to defend themselves. The Jews unite, and with the help of Persian nobles, defeat their enemies.

STAGE DIRECTIONS

Xerxes begins 21-year reign as Persian king 486 B.C.	Esther becomes queen of Persia 479 B.C.	Slaughter of Jews scheduled to take place 473 B.C.		

BIBLE EVENTS   Dates are approximate

500 B.C. ○ ○ ○ **400 B.C.** **300 B.C.**

WORLD EVENTS

Persian King Darius builds a canal between the Nile and Gulf of Suez 500 B.C.	Hippocrates, the father of medicine, is born 460 B.C.			Persia falls to Alexander the Great, of Greece 332 B.C.
	Greeks defeat Persian fleet 480 B.C.			

AUTHOR AND DATE

The writer is unnamed. But the writer's familiarity with the Jewish festival of Purim and with the fact that the Jews had a sense of national identity suggests he was a Jew. His insight into Persian customs, along with the absence of any reference to the Jewish homeland, suggests he lived in Persia—maybe in the city of Susa, where the story takes place. Among possible authors are Mordecai, Ezra, and Nehemiah. King Xerxes, known also by the Hebrew version of his name, Ahasuerus, ruled Persia from 486 to 465 BC, after his father, Darius. Esther was written sometime during or after this, perhaps near the end of his reign, in the waning years of the Persian Empire.

The book of Esther preserves the marvelous story of how the Jews are delivered from an empire-wide slaughter. It also reveals the reason behind the Jewish celebration of Purim, which Jews still observe.

Each spring, usually a month before Passover, Jews celebrate Esther's story during a holiday called Purim, which takes on a Mardi Gras flavor. Many dress up in costume (especially the children), put on plays, have a big dinner, and give gifts to friends and the poor. Purim is an ancient word meaning lots, or dice, that Haman used to select the day on which he would kill all the Jews.

When the Jews read the story of Esther aloud during Purim, they boo Haman by stomping, jeering, and rattling noisemakers so that his name is completely drowned out.

ON LOCATION

The story takes place in the Persian city of Susa, along today's border of Iraq and Iran, about 100 miles north of the Persian Gulf.

WHAT TO LOOK FOR

- **God.** You'll not find him mentioned by name. But if you look closely, you'll see him standing in the wings directing the action. You'll recognize His work in several places, including in the long string of "coincidences" that end up saving the Jews from mass slaughter.

EXTREME SCENES
from Esther

⇒ A new queen (1:10–2:20)

After a week-long banquet of partying and drinking, Persian King Xerxes (who by this time has had too much wine) sends for his queen. He wants to parade her before his other male guests so they can see how beautiful she is. Queen Vashti, however, is entertaining the women guests at another party, and she refuses. Xerxes is so mad that he strips Vashti of her title and forbids her to ever show her face again in the palace. Exit Queen Vashti. But now Xerxes is queenless. So he launches a kingdom-wide search for a replacement. One of the beautiful young women brought to the palace is a young Jew named Esther. She's an orphan raised by her cousin Mordecai, a Persian official. Like the other candidates, Esther goes through a year-long regimen of beauty treatments to prepare her to meet the king. Four years later, it's Esther's turn to meet the king. He falls in love with her at a dinner party and makes her the next queen.

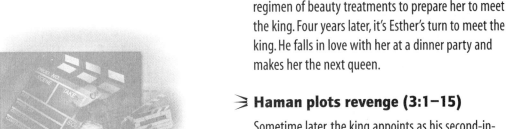

DIRECTOR'S NOTES

Authority figures in the ancient Middle East wore signet rings with their name or their own personal symbol on them. The rings were designed so that the raised name or symbol would make an impression on a seal made of moist clay or wet wax. The seal was used to indicate that a document was official. Putting one's ring on a seal was similar to signing one's name today. By allowing Haman to use his ring, Ahasuerus was giving his approval of the plan. Esther 3:10

⇒ Haman plots revenge (3:1–15)

Sometime later, the king appoints as his second-in-command, Haman, a descendant of the Amalekites, who have long been bitter enemies of the Jews. Though the king orders everyone to bow when Haman walks by, Mordecai refuses. And when Mordecai's colleagues ask why, he responds simply, "Because I am a Jew." This is duly reported to Haman, who totally loses his cool. He decides it's time to wipe out all the Jews in the empire, including Mordecai. He meets with the king and reports: "There are some people who live all over your kingdom and won't have a thing to do with anyone else. They have customs that are different from everyone else's, and they refuse to obey your laws. We would be better off to get rid of them!" To sweeten the deal, Haman reminds the king that property confiscated from the victims will boost the royal treasury.

Apparently without even asking who these people are, the king approves the plan. Haman sets the date for the slaughter—11 months ahead. Meanwhile, he sends couriers throughout the empire to deliver a message translated into every known language. The message says that on the 13th day of Adar (March 7, 473 BC) "all Jewish men, women, and children are to be killed. And their property is to be taken."

⋙ Perfect timing (4:8–5:8; 7:1–10)

When Mordecai hears about the letter, he immediately goes to Esther and asks her to beg the king to have mercy on her people. (At this point, the king doesn't seem to know that his ruling is against the Jews, or that Esther is a Jew.) At first, Esther refuses. After all, according to Persian law, the king can execute anyone who visits him uninvited. Mordecai quickly shoots down his cousin's argument: "Don't think that you will escape being killed with the rest of the Jews, just because you live in the king's palace. If you don't speak up now, we will somehow get help, but you and your family will be killed. It could be that you were made queen for a time like this!" (4:13–14).

Mordecai's argument strikes a chord. Esther agrees to intercede, on the condition that Mordecai have all the Jews in the city fast for three days on her behalf. Afterward, Esther goes to the king. Fortunately, he greets her warmly. She invites him to bring Haman to a dinner that evening. There, building the king's anticipation for what she really wants, she invites the men to dinner the following day. By the second meal, Haman is riding high, thinking that he has become the queen's favorite. Then Esther tells the king that Haman's plot is against the Jews, which means that both she and Mordecai could die in the slaughter. The king is furious. Adding to his anger is that the night before he had been reminded that Mordecai once had warned him of an assassination plot and was never rewarded. The king orders Haman hanged and promotes Mordecai to the No. two spot.

⋙ Time to celebrate (9:1–32)

Although according to Persian law, King Xerxes can't change the decree against the Jews, he writes a new one allowing the Jews to defend themselves. These orders are delivered throughout the empire on swift horses, bred for the king. When the day of fighting arrives, on the thirteenth of the Jewish month of Adar, Persian nobles and governors lend their support to the Jews. The fighting extends into a second day, with the Jewish forces killing 75,000 throughout the empire. On the third day, the fifteenth day of Adar, the Jews celebrate their survival and victory with a feast. Every springtime, Jews memorialize the event in a joyful celebration called Purim.

INTERVIEW
with the Stars

Choosing to make a difference

Do you think the choices you make mean anything to anyone else? Or do you feel you are trapped by the choices others have made for you? In those situations, can you still make a difference? Our next subject's life story will help us sort out some of the answers to those questions. **Behind the Bible** is pleased to talk with Queen Esther. Queen Esther, describe for us your own situation.

⋗ **Esther**

Please, call me Esther. It's been so long since I've worn an earthly crown. Every important decision in my life—where I was going to live, who was going to raise me, who I was going to marry, how I was going to be treated—was made by someone else. I grew up in a foreign country. I was raised by my uncle. I was picked by others to be in a beauty contest and then I found myself being selected as queen!

But as queen, you must have had some decision-making power.

⋗ **Esther**

Obviously, you don't know much about the Persian court. I had little, if any, job security. If the king so desired, I could have been sent back to the harem and never seen again. My life was totally under his control.

But you *were* able to make a tremendous difference in the lives of your people, the Jews. How did that happen?

⋗ **Esther**

The one area where I could still make decisions was how I responded to the opportunities that came my way. And I didn't have to go looking for an opportunity—it came to me!

INTERVIEW
with the Stars

Explain!

⋙ Esther

Some of you may be familiar with this story, but there was a Jew-hating official in the king's court called Haman. He hated us so much (my uncle in particular) that he hatched a plan to wipe us out. Haman was able to convince the king that the Jews were different and needed to be destroyed. Whether I liked it or not, I was the one person who could make a difference in this situation.

And what did you do?

⋙ Esther

I have to confess I was reluctant at first until my uncle told me, "Who knows whether you have come to the kingdom for such a time as this?" He reminded me that this was my opportunity to choose to make a difference. And I did. It meant risking my life, but I was able to turn the tables on Haman and give my people a chance to fight for their very lives.

That is some story, Esther. And what an inspiration to anyone who is feeling trapped by decisions others have made. Right now, you may be in a place where you don't want to be. But you still can make a difference. How you respond and the choices you make will determine a lot of the future.

⋙ Esther

That's right. You can choose today to ask God for help. He alone knows what the future will hold. So begin now to make decisions relying on Him. Then you can be sure you'll be heading in the right direction for your future.

REVIEWS

Somebody buy the rights to this book and hire someone to write the screenplay! It's got everything!

You got your drunken parties. You got your major conflicts in the royal family, which result in a year-long beauty pageant to find a replacement queen. You got your little, foreign orphan who sneaks into the contest hiding her true identity. Of course, she wins and becomes queen only to find that the wicked Haman is plotting to kill her one and only relative who raised her. The villain's plan includes an assassination plot for her whole culture (who are exiles in the country). Everything reaches the turning point when this new queen reveals her hidden identity to the king, risking her own life and revealing the villain, at a *dinner party* no less.

Add some jewels, big hair and maybe Salma Hayek, and you've got a show and a half.

You've also got a book of the Bible that doesn't even mention God's name, not even in the credits rolling in the end. And it's in the Bible?

Yep. It is. Because it's a true story about a real life with God's fingerprints all over it. It's a woman making the most of every situation she's in. For Esther, her moment of decision comes when she's asked, "Who knows whether you have come to the kingdom for such a time as this?" (Esther 4:14) At that point Esther is faced with the decision that faces every person. God can help you to do important things, but it'll cost you something—whadda ya' say?

Esther said yes and the ending outmatches every happy-go-lucky Disney flick you've ever seen. The bad guy gets it and the good guys throw a big party.

Maybe in the movie version there's even a sunset at the end...yeah... and a rainbow...

Goldie Ruel

ENCORE

> For insight into what happens to people like Haman, who "make useless plans" against God and his people, read Psalm 2.

> For another story about a strong-minded woman who did the right thing, read the short book of Ruth, another excellent example of the best in Hebrew literature.

Job

Adam	Abraham	Job	Moses	David	Ezra	Jesus Is Born
4000+ B.C.	2100 B.C.	2000 B.C.	1500 B.C.	1000 B.C.	450 B.C.	7/6 B.C.

A rad dude gets jumped

What do you do when life kicks you in the teeth, pulls your hair, sticks its knee in your back and orders you to cry uncle? Simple. You put on a garbage bag, dump ashes on your head and shut your trap. Job is a tale of a guy who isn't suffering quietly. This is all about a guy who's really ticked that he's hurting. He's got a lot of questions. And a few friends who are mildly helpful.

Job has just lost nearly everything he has spent his life working for: his riches, his children, his health. And, he's got just one quick question for God. It's simple. HEY GOD!? WHAT ARE YOU DOING? Yep, Job probably yelled it, just like that. Job was smart, but even his wisdom couldn't get into the head of God. He knew and trusted God, but what he was losing was too much. His questions finally get answered. Well, kind of answered. Job doesn't get his stuff back, but he does get comforted.

Ever been there? Been beat up by life? Your teacher gives you a C when you know you deserved an A. Your parents yell at you when you didn't do anything wrong. Your unsaved friend dies suddenly. We've all been where Job was. We've asked the same questions. We've questioned God's motives. We've not too often felt like we got the answer we needed. In this book, we get to watch Job struggle with the same issues we face.

QUOTABLES

"Naked I came from my mother's womb, and naked I shall return" (1:21, NKJV). Job's reaction after hearing his children have been killed in a windstorm and his vast flocks stolen by raiders.

"I have escaped by the skin of my teeth" (19:20, NRSV). Job's analysis of how close he has come to dying.

SNEAK PREVIEW

> Mark
> Jesus' life was an action verb.

BEHIND the SCENES
of Job

STARRING ROLES

Job, a rich guy who loses his money, children, and health (1:1)
Eliphaz, the first of three of Job's friends who try to convince him that he sinned (2:11)
Bildad, the second of Job's friends to speak (2:11)
Zophar, the third friend to speak (2:11)
Elihu, a bystander who argues with Job and his friends (32:2)
Job's wife, who tells her husband to curse God and die, so the suffering will end (2:9)

PLOT

Job is a rich guy who owns a lot of animals and has a really large family. He's really happy. But then, (get this) a bunch of bad things happen that ruin everything. First, raiders take his herds and kill his servants. Then, a windstorm crushes a house where his children are eating and all of his kids die. Then, Job gets a wicked skin disease and his body breaks out in ulcers (open bleeding sores... Yuck!). His friends come to comfort him, but add to his misery by insisting he must have committed some horrible sin for which God is punishing him. In the end, God sets the record straight and ends Job's torment.

STAGE DIRECTIONS

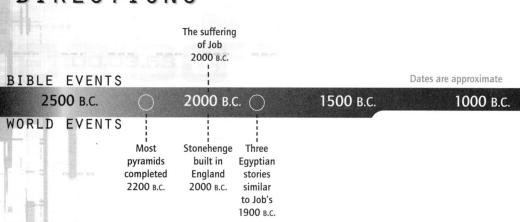

The suffering
of Job
2000 B.C.

BIBLE EVENTS

Dates are approximate

| 2500 B.C. | 2000 B.C. | 1500 B.C. | 1000 B.C. |

WORLD EVENTS

Most
pyramids
completed
2200 B.C.

Stonehenge
built in
England
2000 B.C.

Three
Egyptian
stories
similar
to Job's
1900 B.C.

AUTHOR AND DATE

Scholars suspect that the person who wrote this book was an Israelite, but no one knows for sure. Here's what we *do know* about this book. This story might have been passed down by word of mouth for generations before someone wrote it down in the 900s BC. That makes sense because it was during that time when a lot of these kinds of stories were finally being recorded. And, in the second century BC other Jewish writings were referring to Job. This shows that the book of Job was well known and respected by then.

Here's something else we know. The story is sometime in the era of Israel's founding fathers: Abraham, Isaac, and Jacob. How do we know this? In Abraham's day, his wealth was measured by his herds, (the same way Job's wealth was measured) and he acted as the priest for his family by offering sacrifices to God (just like Job). Job makes one thing very clear: Really rich people, or really "righteous" people will suffer too. They're not exempt from death, poverty, or really stinky boils.

ON LOCATION

This almost invisible, but very real story takes place in the mysterious homeland of Job, "the land of Uz" (1:1). No one knows where that is. Some guess it was in Edom, a region southeast of Canaan, along the border of what is now Israel and Jordan. Two clues suggest this: one of Job's friends comes from Teman, an Edomite city; also, Edomites were famous in ancient times for their wisdom (and, since the book of Job is considered wisdom literature, this makes sense).

WHAT TO LOOK FOR

- **The format.** Check out the debates in this book. Each cycle goes like this: friend #1 talks, Job replies, friend #2, Job, friend #3, Job. (OK, for the most part. There is one exception at the end of the third cycle, when friend #3 doesn't speak. Instead, a bystander adds his thoughts about the matter.) This semi-debate routine takes up most of the book.
- **"I Am Innocent!!"** Like a lot of people in his day, Job believes that you're really blessed by God if you're healthy and wealthy. So, when you have disease and you're poor, you must have sinned. And, since Job knows that he hasn't sinned, he's left wondering why God is putting him through all this. Bitterness begins to invade his heart.... He sarcastically complains, "God destroys the innocent along with the guilty. When a good person dies a sudden death, God sits back and laughs" (9:22–23). Do those sound like the words of an angry, upset, and confused man?

INSIDE SCOOP

Aunt Jemima owes her name to Job's oldest daughter, of his second-chance family (42:14).

"Patience of Job" is a phrase that comes from the story of Job's suffering. Actually, he isn't all that patient. "How I wish that God would answer my prayer," he moans, "Why should I patiently hope when my strength is gone?" (6:8, 11). "Tenacious as Job" is a better match. In spite of the catastrophes that hit him, and his three nagging friends who insist he's to blame, Job won't budge from his plea of innocence or his faith in God.

There aren't a lot of references to life after death in the Old Testament. But Job speaks so clearly of a resurrection that he sounds like a New Testament apostle: "I know that my Savior lives, and at the end he will stand on this earth. My flesh may be destroyed, yet from this body I will see God. Yes, I will see him for myself, and I long for that moment" (19:25–27).

The book of Job contains more rare and archaic words than any other book in the Bible. This suggests it was written a long time ago. It has also made the book hard to translate.

EXTREME SCENES
from Job

⋙ Job's life hits the skids (1:1-2:10)

Job lives with his huge family, livestock, and farm on a large piece of land near the desert (probably what is now Israel). He's not only rich in property, he's got a lot of servants to tend to his possessions. He is also rich in children, with seven sons and three daughters. Satan, however, decides to test Job's loyalty to God. Satan goes to God and asks for permission to test Job. God allows it. And, Job is in for the ride of his life. First, a wandering band of evil do-badders kill the herdsmen tending Job's flocks and then steal Job's livestock. Then, his oldest son and all of his children die when a a windstorm crushes the his oldest son's home. Job gets the news, tears his robe, and shaves his head. Then, in a moment of agony he utters the words "The Lord gave, and the Lord hath taken away; blessed be the name of the LORD" (1:21, KJV).

⋙ The final blow

His children are dead. His herds are gone. You'd think this was it. Enough, right? Nope. Job gets infected with a disgusting skin disease that covers his body with open, festering sores. This is one guy you wouldn't want to sit next to on the bus. What caused the disease? Who knows. Whatever it was, it was totally repulsive and very painful. Job's wife can't stand to see him suffer. "Why do you still trust God?" she asks. "Why don't you curse him and die?" In other words, "Job, you dummy. Death is better than this! One word and you're a dead man, and you're in a much better place then this."

Job's response? "Hush!" (OK, that's not *exactly* what he says. But you get the idea.)

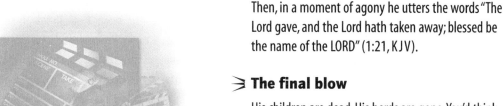

DIRECTOR'S NOTES

If anyone asks you the same pas question that Bildad asked Job, the answer is no. The papyrus plant grows in the water of swamps and marshes. Papyrus stalks are about the thickness of a person's wrist and can reach as high as twelve feet. More than anything else, papyrus resembles an oversize piece of grass. The Egyptians used papyrus to make paper, blankets, sandals, and rafts. Job 8:11

⇥ Three friends come to comfort Job (2:11–37:24)

With everything lost or dead, and with his wife giving him sour advice, you'd think this would be one guy who could count on his friends. Whelp...not exactly. Three of Job's friends DO come and sit silently with him for seven days. When Job finally speaks, he's a broken man. He says, "I wish I had been born dead and then buried." So, what do his friends say? Something encouraging? Nope. They're certain that he's sinned. They tell him he needs to repent. The conversations go back and forth. Job feeling abandoned by everyone including God. His friends feeling like they've got an unrepentant sinner on their hands. In one heated moment, Job strikes at them and says, "Miserable comforters are you all!" (16:2). Ever felt like saying *that* to a friend?

DIRECTOR'S
NOTES

The people of the ancient Middle East were expert miners. Archaeologists have found that the Egyptians dug mining tunnels more than one hundred feet deep. They carried the ore they discovered to the surface in baskets. In addition to precious metals like gold, copper, and silver, the miners brought up valuable resources like gemstones. Job 28:1, 2

⇥ The Lord answers Job (38:1–42:9)

As the friends drone on, a storm begins rolling in. Suddenly, from out of this storm, God speaks to Job, raising questions no human can answer. "How did I lay the foundation for the earth?" (38:4) BOOM! "Where is the home of light, and where does darkness live?" (38:19) BOOM! BOOM! God's been listening. His first few responses rocket through Job and his friends. He's got a lot to say. He's angry at Job. He's angry at his friends, who were no help at all. So, what does God say? Face it. There are some things that human beings can't understand. Suffering is one of those things.

One real happy ending (42:10-17)

⇥ In the end, Job regains all of his wealth. He has ten more kids. He gets back all of his wealth. And, he lives another one hundred and forty years. That's a long time.

REVIEWS

Have you ever had one of those days where you said, "if they made a movie of this, nobody would believe it all really happened"? That's sorta' what the book of Job is like.

If anyone has heard of Job at all they usually know that a lot of stuff went wrong in his life and that he was really patient about it. In reality there was a lot more to it than that. Check it out:

Scene one: A behind the scenes look at the kind of conversations God has with Satan. Here, in this humble little book is an amazing inside scoop on the stuff that goes on outside of earthly dimensions, which affects the lives of people like me and you.

Scene two: Job's life falls apart piece by piece, to prove whether his strength of faith has to do with his prosperity or with a real understanding of God's love and power in the world. It's in this scene that Job's wife (I see someone named Roseanne in this part) advises Job to "curse God and die." Now there's a positive message.

Scenes three through thirty: Hard to believe, but through all these chapters, Job's three friends—Eliphaz, Bildad and Zophar (what were *their* parents thinking?) give him advice, and more advice, and more advice. Really, the fact that Job didn't punch out these three guys is the reason he gets the patience award. What a bunch of goofs. They might as well be named Moe, Larry, and Curly, but that wouldn't be as funny as their *real* names.

Next to last scene: God says, "enough." He also says, "Who do you think you are?" Then he says, "Who do you think I am?"

Closing scene: Job's life is restored: kids, cattle, land, wealth, servants. Oh if life only did work out this way on a regular basis. Maybe if we had as much faith as Job, it would.

There are a lot of lessons that can be learned from Job, like . . . life can be unfair, but God is good, and even if we can't see them, God has reasons for everything that happens. I have something to say to Job about helping God to prove an important point to Satan. Ready? Are you sure? OK, here goes . . . It's tough, Job, but somebody's gotta do it. (Please put the tomato down.)

Aleck Smart

Want more evidence that suffering and sin were closely related in the Bible? Check out the story of Jesus healing a blind beggar. The disciples asked Jesus if the beggar was suffering because of his own sins or the sins of his parents. Take a look at how Jesus responds.

Is Job the only dude in the Bible who got all confrontational on God? Nope. Read Habakkuk. This guy asked God why he was going to punish the unrighteous Jews by sending an invasion of the even more unrighteous Babylonians.

Ever felt like YOU were suffering and God was hiding? Not sure what to say in those moments? Try reading Psalms 10 and 22. These Psalms might say what your mind and mouth can't.

Psalms

SCHEDULE OF SCENES

Adam	Abraham	Moses	David	First Return from Babylon	Ezra	Jesus Is Born
4000+ B.C.	2100 B.C.	1500 B.C.	1000 B.C.	538 B.C.	450 B.C.	7/6 B.C.

Trying to touch God

So, God has blessed you. Groovy. What words will you use to tell him how you feel? Or, you feel attacked...broken...abused or abandoned. What will you say to God to get him to protect you. Better still...you've sinned one huge sin and BLAMO, you saw the wall fall between you and God. What will you shout over the wall to convince him to smash it?

The psalms are a songbook. But, they're not just happy, peppy love songs from us to God. They're songs that reflect the real lives we live. They're written from people who have blown it big time, fallen deeply in love with God, or need rescuing. They're from us, to God using words...the only means we have to express to God how we feel.

QUOTABLES

Make a joyful noise unto the Lord, all ye lands (100:1, KJV).

Thy word is a lamp unto my feet, and a light unto my path (119:105, KJV).

SNEAK PREVIEW

2 Kings
The decay of a nation. A people exiled. A culture almost ground to dust.

BEHIND the SCENES of Psalms

STARRING ROLES

David, the source or inspiration behind nearly half the 150 psalms (18:50)

PLOT

OK, you got us. There's no real plot here. These songs were written over a lllooonnnggg time. How long? Several centuries. Now, within each Psalm there *is* somewhat of a plot. For example, complaint songs carry the theme of complaining all the way through. Love psalms explore the theme of love throughout the psalm. So, there's no plot to the book of Psalms. However, each psalm expresses its own story. Each one contains its own plot. Okay, that's 150 psalms. That's 150 plots and 150 themes. Whew. That's a lot of plots.

STAGE DIRECTIONS

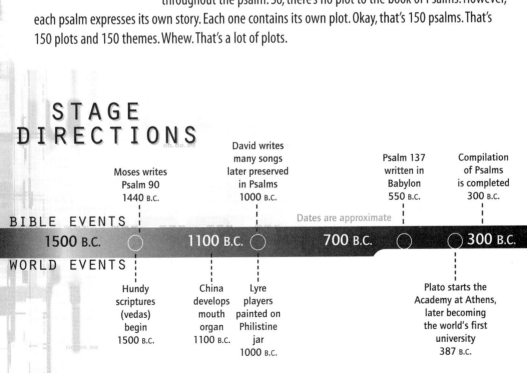

BIBLE EVENTS

Moses writes
Psalm 90
1440 B.C.

David writes
many songs
later preserved
in Psalms
1000 B.C.

Psalm 137
written in
Babylon
550 B.C.

Compilation
of Psalms
is completed
300 B.C.

Dates are approximate

1500 B.C. — 1100 B.C. — 700 B.C. — 300 B.C.

WORLD EVENTS

Hundy
scriptures
(vedas)
begin
1500 B.C.

China
develops
mouth
organ
1100 B.C.

Lyre
players
painted on
Philistine
jar
1000 B.C.

Plato starts the
Academy at Athens,
later becoming
the world's first
university
387 B.C.

AUTHOR AND DATE

The psalms attribute 73 songs to David. But the Hebrew phrase (The psalms were originally written in Hebrew) can mean "by David," "dedicated to David," or "in the style of David." In other words, not all "Of David" psalms are actually "Of David." Other songs are attributed to Solomon, Moses, and Asaph, chief musicians during the reign of David and perhaps Solomon. Some songs remain anonymous.

The psalms were written throughout Israel's history, some from the time of Moses in about 1440 B.C., others from the time of King David in about 1000 B.C., and others after Babylon defeated the Jewish nation and exiled many of the citizens in 586 B.C.

The book exists to give people the words to express their deepest spiritual feelings, privately or in group worship.

ON LOCATION

Not only were these written over a long period of time, they were written throughout a lot of real estate. The songs are set throughout the Middle East, from the Sinai desert where Moses leads the Hebrews, to Israel where David builds a powerful Jewish nation, to Babylon where the defeated Jews spend 50 years in exile. The locations these songs were written from stretch over 1,000 miles (from Egypt to Babylon) and the time they were written in stretches over 1,000 years (from the Exodus to the Exile).

WHAT TO LOOK FOR

- **Repeated thoughts, not sounds.** Ever try listening to someone without the gift of storytelling try to tell a story? Well, that's what Hebrew poetry can sound like. This style of poetry repeats itself a lot. For example, the writer will say something in one line, then, they'll repeat themselves a few lines later. Later in the same psalm, they'll offer a contrasting idea. So, they repeat thoughts a LOT. Once you know this, a lot of psalms make a lot more sense. Try reading Psalm 51:7 as an example.
- **Radically different topics.** Consistency isn't what you'll find here. There aren't collections of love songs, followed by collections of songs crying out to God. They're all mixed up. Just like the CDs you probably buy. Popular musicians mix up their jams to keep us interested, and to reflect their range of emotion. The Psalms do that too. And, what about the topics you'll find? You'll find songs praising God for his gorgeous universe. And you'll find songs for weddings, worship services, pilgrimages to Jerusalem, the crowning of a king, and soldiers on the march. There's a lot of stuff here. Read slow. Read often.

EXTREME SCENES
from Psalms

God's creation is awesome (8:1-9)

God made an unbelievable world. In a song attributed to David (the shepherd boy who spent tons of time outdoors) Psalm 8 praises God for creation and expresses anger that he would entrust such majesty to human beings. Basically, it says, "We've got a great gift here God, why did you leave it to us to mess up?"

God's invisible shield (23:1-6)

When you're hurting, God's got your back. In a song expressing deep trust in God—a song that is perhaps the most loved in all of literature—David compares God to a shepherd who protects His flock. He's watching. He knows when we hurt.

DIRECTOR'S NOTES

The heart's not simply a hollow, muscular organ, as far as Bible writers were concerned. They believed the heart is the center of a person's character. They believed it's the source not only of emotions, but also of thoughts and decision making. They believed that both good and evil actions get their start in the heart. Psalm 4:4

Making powerful music (33:1-3)

Music is a powerful force. It can lift us, it can depress us. When the Jews assemble to worship God, professional musicians add their support by filling the temple courtyard with music. Some psalms are written to be accompanied by certain kinds of instruments. In fact, the word psalm comes from the Hebrew word psalmos, which means "twanging of strings."

Holy hunger (42:1-11)

What's worse than feeling cut off from God? Nothing. In a private, passionate prayer for help, the psalmist expresses deep sorrow because he feels cut off from God. Perhaps he is among the thousands of Jewish exiles forced to live in Babylon, far from home. Or, maybe he's just missing his Creator. Whatever it is, these psalms express for us a longing that we sometimes can't vocalize.

Unashamed actions (63:4; 134:1-2)

Does God really listen to fugitives? Can He hear people who are hiding? Sure. In an uninhibited show of praise to God, or an unrestrained plea for help, the Jews sometimes address Him with arms raised. David, a fugitive in the desert expresses his confidence in God. He raises his hands. He shouts his praise.

Holy shout out (66:1-20)

The psalms prove to us that you don't have to have a really great voice to sing for God. You don't even have to have a recording contract. What does it take? A broken heart. A desire to connect with God. Though sacrifices and prayer are an important part of worshiping God, so is singing. The people sing about God when they're alone, and when they gather at the temple or synagogue. Sometimes, gathered for worship, they take turns singing to each other.

Going home (84:5)

Jerusalem was home for the Jewish nation. Three times a year—spring, summer, and fall—every Jew who is able travels to Jerusalem to celebrate important Jewish holidays: Passover and two harvest festivals. Fifteen songs, Psalm 120-134, are written especially for people going to their Jewish home. The songs are called "songs of ascent," because Jerusalem is on a hill (and it's surrounded by hills). And, no matter how you approach it, you're going to have to climb. Travelers likely sing these songs as they walk to the Holy City.

Unbelievable protection (91:1-16)

The Jews sing of God's ability to protect them, no matter what the odds. This doesn't mean God will always keep them from harm, but it means he has the power to protect. Yet when suffering comes, he is still in control and will help in ways that human beings can't fully understand.

Hiding the word (119:1-8)

Just like sacrifices, prayer, and music, studying the laws of God is an important feature of worship. At home and in groups, the Jews read aloud their scripture and memorized parts of it. Here's a quick stat for you. Psalm 119, the longest chapter in the Bible, has 176 verses. And, every one of these verses speaks about God's law. When you set it to music, it becomes a song urging people to nurture their faith by thinking about God's word.

Unending tears (137:1-9)

The psalms contain songs, praises, tough emotions, fears, etc. But, the largest group of psalms emote about people crying to God out of pain or sorrow. Whatever has happened...they're hurting. They want help. And, when you read these psalms remember this: You're reading someone's tears. You're reading about their deep hurts. You're allowed in to a family moment. In one psalm, an anonymous writer and a Jewish exile in Babylon paint a vivid and heartbreaking scene about the pain of exile, their mocking captors, and their anguish for release.

REVIEWS

The book of Psalms is like a big songbook—like a "Best of Collection" from the ancient church. Some of them even have liner notes attached, who wrote it and what for, that kind of stuff. If anyone could find a B.C. top forty chart, the Psalms would be right there (DJ voice: Allriiight, that was the Amorites with "I Wanna Steal Your Land." Before that, the False Gods with "Where Have All the Followers Gone?" Next up, New Jews on the Block singing their hit single from the album Psalms. It's number five with a spear this week. But first, this message from Saul's gentile-y used camel lot")

There's also an important lesson to learn in Psalms. These days, we think of church music as music that deals only with the spiritual parts of life. Not so, if you look at what David and the other church musicians wrote. Oh sure, there's plenty of worship tunes, but that's not all. Just about every part of life is covered. In fact, if the Psalms prove anything to us it's that we can connect with God at any point in our lives. Some of David's Psalms were written at his most depressed. He poured his heart out to God no matter how bad he felt. He wrote some of the others when he was feeling really good and in a worshiping mood. Still others are pure praise to God. And believe it or not, there are some that really go off on injustices of the world (see Psalm 140 if you don't believe it). The lesson is that God is a part of your *whole life,* not just the parts you spend in active worship. You can go to him at any time, for any reason or for no reason at all.

Don't sweat it that the Psalms don't rhyme in translation. They didn't even rhyme in their original language. Hebrew poetry was a whole different thing than the Western poetry of today. They didn't have any "Roses are red, violets are blue...." It was more like beatnik, free verse stuff.

The first line usually expressed the central thought. Then the second line repeated or built on that thought. Often each line then continued to build, but on that same central thought. It was logical poetry instead of rhyming poetry. No matter which culture or what part of history you jam in, music is a way of expressing all kinds of feelings. ("And that was the Babble-Ons with 'Blah, Blah, Blah', now here's King Solomon's Mimes with 'If Silence is Golden, I Wish You Were Rich'...")

Kay C. Kasum (I wasn't there, but I think Dick Clark was.)

ENCORE

> To see how New Testament writers use Psalms to identify Jesus as the promised messiah, compare Psalm 22:1, 6–8, 12–13, 28 with Matthew 27:36–46, Luke 23:35–36, and 1 Corinthians 15:23–24.

> For another Hebrew song, read Habakkuk 3.

Proverbs

SCHEDULE OF SCENES

Adam	Abraham	Moses	David	Solomon	Hezekiah	Ezra	Jesus Is Born
4000+ B.C.	2100 B.C.	1500 B.C.	1000 B.C.	971 B.C.	700 B.C.	450 B.C.	7/6 B.C.

QUOTABLES

Those who spare the rod hate their children (13:24, NRSV). Source of the old saying, "Spare the rod, spoil the child." This isn't necessarily a command to spank children; it's an encouragement to discipline them in some way. Shepherds carry a long staff, or rod, to reach out and nudge sheep in the right direction—not to club them.

Pride goes before destruction (16:18, NKJV).

Trust in the Lord with all your heart, and lean not on your own understanding (3:5, NKJV).

Train up a child in the way he should go: and when he is old, he will not depart from it (22:6, KJV).

Smart stuff from old people

Imagine this: You're really smart... or, you're really old. And, you've got a lot of stuff you want to advise people about. What do you do? Simple. You write Proverbs.

This book isn't known for its seamless, easy to read writing style. The book reads like a lifetime collection of someone's Chinese fortune-cookie messages, scribbled down in the order they came out of the bag. However disjointed these snappy one-liners and two-liners are, they contain the wisdom of the ages, condensed for the quickly bored.

In the time it takes to read one sentence, we're dished up a life-tested insight on any one of a thick menu of everyday topics: good women, bad women, spoiled kids, lazy slugs, etiquette at dinner meetings, dating, money, controlling our temper, and even avoiding the wrong crowd.

Yeah. Lots of advice from old people. Lots of great topics, too. This advice is sometimes easy, sometimes difficult to swallow. Like any book of wise sayings, who is speaking is really important. (After all, would you really want "wisdom" from a shmo?) The primary source for Proverbs is Solomon—the Israelite king about whom God said, "I'll make you wiser than anyone who has ever lived or ever will live" (1 Kings 3:12).

He's worth a listen.

SNEAK PREVIEW

> Ecclesiastes
> What do you give a man who has everything ... literally?

BEHIND the SCENES
of Proverbs

STARRING ROLES

Solomon, the wisest king of Israel and author of most of the proverbs (1:1)

PLOT

Hey, look, don't blame us, but these proverbs are mostly two-liners. Short, smart sayings. Quick advice. General wise sayings on a variety of topics. They're not arranged according to any noticeable pattern or theme. An example you say? Consider these two that follow one another, but have nothing in common:

All crooks are liars,
but anyone who is innocent will do right.
It's better to stay outside on the roof of your house
than to live inside with a nagging wife (21:8–9).

See? Really great advice. Not much organization. You get the picture.

STAGE DIRECTIONS

Solomon writes
most of Proverbs
950 B.C.

King Hezekiah's
scribes
compile
proverbs
700 B.C.

BIBLE EVENTS

Dates are approximate

1000 B.C.	**900** B.C.	**800** B.C.	**700** B.C.

WORLD EVENTS

Calendar of
farming cycles,
oldest example
of Hebrew writing
1000 B.C.

Homer writes the *Iliad*
and the *Odyssey*
800 B.C.

AUTHOR AND DATE

Proverbs is a collection of pithy sayings from several wise men. Most are attributed to King Solomon, who is reported to have composed 3,000 proverbs (see 1 Kings 4:32).

The book does mention two other guys: Agur (30:1) and a king named Lemuel (31:1), who says he is passing along the advice of his mother. And, there are other proverbs that come from "sages." Sages were an important part of Jewish society. They served as consultants to kings, and as teachers to young men. These sages grappled with practical and philosophical problems, while priests and prophets specialized in religious matters.

Solomon reigned from about 970–930 B.C. And, as time went on, other people added other proverbs. 250 years after Solomon was king, scribes working for King Hezekiah began compiling the proverbs of Solomon (25:1). And, other proverbs were probably added later on. It's uncertain when the book was completed, but Bible experts think the work may have continued until as late as the 300s B.C.

ON LOCATION

Most proverbs were apparently written by Solomon in Israel. But some of the other proverbs could have come from anywhere throughout the Middle East. Similar collections of wise sayings from about Solomon's time have been uncovered in both Egypt and Iraq.

WHAT TO LOOK FOR

- **General truths.** The proverbs state general principles, not promises from God. For example, it's often true that "A soft answer turns away wrath" (15:1). But don't count on it every time.
- **A nine-chapter introduction.** Check out the first nine chapters. They form a poetic essay contrasting wisdom with foolishness. A lot of scholars consider this a *nine chapter introduction*. Yikes! That's a long intro. After this comes a long string of one-line and two-line sayings, each of which sums up a truth gleaned from life. These truths are universal, not just for God's people. Any person who follows the advice will likely live a better, more radical (and happier!) life.
- **Poetry.** The Proverbs don't get in your face with a bunch of cold truths. They follow the characteristics of Hebrew poetry. They don't have rhyme or rhythm, but they have parallel thoughts. The second half of the proverb might repeat the idea in the first, or expand it, or perhaps contrast it. This style of poetry *can* read along with a cool rhythm. It can also drive you nuts if you don't understand it. Read this, it'll give you an idea:
"Better is a dry morsel with quietness
Than a house full of feasting with strife" (17:1).

INSIDE SCOOP

> The 1960 film *Inherit the Wind,* starring Spencer Tracy as a lawyer who argues to let public educators teach the theory of evolution, takes its title from Proverbs. "He who brings trouble on his family will inherit only wind" (11:29, NIV).

> "God helps those who help themselves" is not in Proverbs, or anywhere else in the Bible. Neither is "Cleanliness is next to godliness," or "Early to bed and early to rise make a man healthy, wealthy, and wise." These are proverbs that Benjamin Franklin published in *Poor Richard's Almanack* during the mid-1700s.

EXTREME SCENES
from Proverbs

⮞ Don't sleep around (5:1-23)

Whoever wrote these proverbs knew what they were talking about when it comes to sex. Immorality kills. It hurts the heart. It puts the body in jeopardy. It damages relationships. Here's a proverb that talks straight about adultery.

"For the lips of an immoral woman drip honey. And her mouth is smother than oil.

But in the end she is as bitter as wormwood, sharp as a two-edged sword." (3-4).

Sounds like someone knew what they were talking about, huh?

DIRECTOR'S NOTES

In most ancient Israelite families, meat was served only on special occasions, such as when they were entertaining guests or celebrating a religious festival. Only the wealthiest people in the land could afford to eat meat regularly. The rest ate mostly fruits, vegetables, and grains. Proverbs 15:17

⮞ Be careful with your cash (6:1-5)

Like sex, money is the cause of many troubles in life. So Proverbs is full of advice about money matters. One persistent piece of advice is to avoid debt—especially another person's debt—like a deer avoids the hunter.

"My son, if you become surety for your friend, If you have shaken hands in pledge for a stranger, you are snared by the words of your mouth; you are taken by the words of your mouth. So, do this, my son, and deliver yourself; For you have come into the hand of your friend." (1-3).

⮞ Teach kids the right stuff (22:6)

The proverbs are known for urging people to teach their children the right things. They almost command people who raise or teach children to raise them in the right ways.

For example...

"Train up a child in the way he should go, and when he is old he will not depart from it." (22:6)

Laziness gets you in a heap of trouble (20:30-34)

If you want to get in a heap of trouble, be real lazy. The proverbs have a lot to say to people who lay around, eat candy, and do nothing with their lives. Here's one, just to show ya how they feel. (Hint: If you *are* a lazy person, you might want to skip this section. Otherwise you'll feel real convicted.)

"I went by the field of a lazy man, and by the vineyard of the man devoid of understanding; And there it was, all overgrown with thorns; its surface was covered with nettles; its stone wall was broken down. When I saw it, I considered it well; I looked on it and received instruction: A little sleep, a little slumber, a little folding of the hands to rest; So shall your poverty come like a prowler, and your need like an armed man." (24:30-34)

Wanted: Rad chicks (30:10-31)

The book ends with a poetic tribute to a good wife. These are the words of a queen mother, passed along to her son, King Lemuel, unknown outside of this one reference to him. However, these words are still a great reminder about what makes a powerful wife. If you're looking for the description of your dream girl. Or, if you're interested in being someone's dream girl, read these words.

"Who can find a virtuous wife? For her worth is far above rubies." (10)

"She watches over the ways of her household, and does not eat the bread of idleness. Her children rise up and call her blessed; Many daughters have done well, but you excel them all."(27-29).

Oh yeah! What a woman!

DIRECTOR'S NOTES

The roof was one of the main features of ancient Israelite houses. Some people used their roof as a deck or terrace. Others covered it with a layer of grass to keep rain from soaking through into the house. Still others used it to dry foods s figs and corn in the sun. Usually people reached the roof via an outside staircase. A railing or low wall usually ran around the perimeter of the roof to keep people from falling off. Proverbs 21:9

INTERVIEW
with the Stars

The wisest fool

Back to the Bible's next subject is a man who achieved all kinds of worldly success, but failed in the one area of his life that mattered most—his own personal life. Solomon is a name that is synonymous with wisdom. Yet his biggest downfall was in neglecting his own advice. Let's see what wisdom we can learn from someone who started out so promising, but failed to live up to his potential. Solomon, tell us about becoming king.

⇒ Solomon

When I became king, I had a dream. In my dream, God told me to ask for *anything* I wanted. So I asked for wisdom. It was, truly, the wisest thing I had ever done. And with it, I accomplished a lot for the kingdom of Israel.

What were some of your achievements?

⇒ Solomon

I organized and built a great temple for God in Jerusalem. I enlarged the borders of our nation, and I applied my wisdom to develop a system of public works and foreign diplomacy. My wealth and my wisdom was known throughout the world, and dignitaries from foreign countries would travel thousands of miles to talk with me. No other king or queen came close to what I achieved.

INTERVIEW
with the Stars

So what happened?

≥ Solomon

I guess I forgot to listen to my own advice. I started to live as if the things I was teaching others really didn't apply to me. You know, like marriage. I wrote all sorts of proverbs about marriage, yet I totally ignored them all and ended up having more than 700 wives. A lot of them I married for political reasons. They brought their foreign culture and gods with them into the palace. I guess I got a little sloppy in my attitude toward God and I started to chase after their gods as well.

Your autobiography in the book of Ecclesiastes paints a very disturbing picture of someone who wakes up and realizes what a mess they have made of their life. Is that an accurate description?

≥ Solomon

I guess you could say that. I was in an unique situation—I had all the resources and all the opportunities to try to have anything. And I did. But, truthfully, when it came right down to it, I was like that man chasing the wind. I think Jesus put it better in Matthew 16:26: *"What profit is it to a man if he gains the whole world, and loses his own soul."* I had the whole world, but in the end, I had nothing because I had failed to live for God.

Thank you for your candid answers, Solomon. Your story is a sobering lesson for any young Christian. Many will start out the race well, but finish poorly. Those who will make the biggest difference are the ones who don't give up once they start living for God.

REVIEWS

ENCORE

➤ Jesus used proverbs throughout his ministry. Check 'em out by reading the Sermon on the Mount in Matthew 5–7, especially the Beatitudes in Matthew 5:3-10.

➤ Proverbs includes real life advice you can use. To read advice for pastors, turn over to 1, 2 Timothy and Titus.

If you're looking for a categorized, indexed, alphabetized rule book for life, this ain't it.

The book of Proverbs is like a bunch of different wise statements, all shook up in bag and then dumped out on the table. It's organized the way life is organized—in a jumble. There are no brightly colored tabs or book dividers and no table of contents.

So when you read Proverbs you just take it as it comes. One minute you're reading something about obeying your parents (Man, am I still working on *that* one!) and the next you could be reading something about not eating like a pig in front of a king (or is it not eating like a king in front of the pigs? Guess I'm due to read that one again). Get what I'm saying? It's just all in there together, like a box of chocolates…or a set of legos…or a spiritual piñata.

One thing I love about Proverbs is that it is divided into 31 chapters. If you've looked at a calendar lately, then you know that means you could read a chapter of Proverbs a day and start over each month (and for you who have to have every question answered, just leave off the last chapter in the 30-day months). It's really a good plan because you're taking that wisdom in overtime.

If Proverbs has any kind of theme to it, it's the theme of wisdom—not just being smart, not getting good test scores, not one-upping your great aunt in Trivial Pursuit—but wisdom, the ability to live life well. If that's not important to you, skip it and have fun being miserable. If living well and being wise is something that sounds like fun, you won't find a much better how-to book than Proverbs.

And when you think about it, why should wisdom be categorized and alphabetized anyway? Life isn't and never will be. So dive into Proverbs and just see where it takes you. Open up a page, close your eyes, and see where your finger lands on the page. You might find something there that might help you find your way today, when life gets in its usual jumble.

Oh, and you can just forget about February. That way I don't ever have to come up with an answer for which chapters to read on a leap year. Honestly, some people.

Tribal Chief Moe Burning Bush

Ecclesiastes

SCHEDULE OF SCENES

Life: What's the point?

Turn on some soft music. Dim the lights. Light a candle. Put on your favorite jimmies. Let's get ethereal for a moment. What's the meaning of life? Ever thought about that? Hey, look, it's probably not a question you've asked yourself *unless* you've faced a near-death experience, or faced really hard times.

When you read Ecclesiastes, you're reading someone's quest to find meaning in life. The first words out of the writer's mouth don't leave us with a great sense of his ability to answer the question. He begins by saying something like, "Nothing makes sense! Everything is nonsense." And goes on from there. Gee. That's real uplifting, isn't it?

Well, don't form an opinion too fast. First, this guy seems really upset. But, through the book you read his inner thoughts. His deep emotions. His careful analysis. He lays out what he sees in life. Then, in the end, he answers the question by pointing directly to heaven. Life, he concludes, is a mysterious gift from God. We should learn to enjoy the gift, and to show our gratitude to the Giver.

Amen.

QUOTABLES

Eat, drink, and be merry (8:15, NKJV).

To everything there is a season, a time for every purpose under heaven (3:1, NKJV).

Cast your bread upon the waters (11:1, NKJV). Which means "be generous."

There is nothing new under the sun (1:9, NKJV).

SNEAK PREVIEW

Zephaniah
My name is Israel.
I'm a nation in sin.

BEHIND the SCENES
of Ecclesiastes

STARRING ROLES

Solomon, the wisest king of Israel and possible author of Ecclesiastes (1:1)

PLOT

Solomon seems to be performing an experiment—he's analyzing life. He examines the cycles of life, the reasons we stress ourselves out, the pleasures we pursue. And he reaches the dead-end conclusion that everything is meaningless. Dude! Everything? Yup.

What Solomon ultimately concludes is that everything (get that? EVERYTHING) that's done without God leads to dissatisfaction and meaninglessness. So, want meaning? Want purpose? Need direction. Do this: Include God.

STAGE DIRECTIONS

Solomon
begins his
40-year reign
970 B.C.

BIBLE EVENTS

Dates are approximate

1000 B.C.   **900 B.C.**   **800 B.C.**

WORLD EVENTS

Eastern
North Americans
grow crops
1000 B.C.

Greek city
of Corinth
is founded
800 B.C.

AUTHOR AND DATE

The first verse gives it away. The writer identifies himself as "the son of David," "king in Jerusalem," and "known to be very wise." That's Solomon. Hey, it certainly sounds like Solomon, especially when you add a bunch of other clues from chapter 2—such as foreign rulers bringing him "silver, gold, and precious treasures" (as the queen of Sheba did) and his "many wives" (he had a thousand).

OK, get ready for a debate. Many Bible experts, however, say the style of Hebrew words suggests it was written many centuries later, maybe as late as 300 B.C. (and, so NOT by Solomon). There's some truth to this because some passages don't sound like something Solomon would say. Like when he blames the king for overtaxing the poor (see 5:8-9). That would be Solomon complaining about himself! Fragments of the book found among the Dead Sea Scrolls were copied in about 150 B.C., suggesting Ecclesiastes was accepted at least by then.

If Solomon wrote this book, he may have done so late in his reign, after he had allowed his foreign wives to coax him away from God and into worshiping their gods. Perhaps Solomon got to the point in his life where he realized that even with all his wealth, power, and wisdom, he was empty without God.

ON LOCATION

If Solomon wrote the book, the setting takes place in his capital city of Jerusalem.

WHAT TO LOOK FOR

- **An honest guy's search for real meaning.** If you read this like a story that goes from introduction to neatly wrapped-up ending, you'll be frustrated. One minute Solomon says life is unfair, and is really messed up. The next minute he's saying we should live life to the extreme, work hard, and obey God. What you're reading are the honest confessions of a man struggling with doubt, disillusionment, and despair. Fortunately, he works his way through the struggle and ends with a sense of comfort worth sharing.

The name of the book comes from the word the writer uses to describe himself: Teacher or Assembly Leader. In Greek, this word is ekklesiastes.

The Ernest Hemingway novel *The Sun Also Rises* takes its name from Ecclesiastes 1:5.

EXTREME SCENES
from Ecclesiastes

⟩ Who wants blisters? (1:1-18)

Solomon takes a long, hard look at life. And he doesn't like what he sees. Nothing makes sense. Everything is meaningless. And, in the midst of all this turmoil humans continue to work. Why? Solomon doesn't know. And, sometimes we don't know either.

DIRECTOR'S NOTES

Solomon was something of a celebrity during his lifetime. During his forty-year reign as king, people would come to Jerusalem from faraway countries just to hear Solomon say something wise. Not only did Solomon know a lot about human nature and the scientific world, he is also considered to be the most important and influential philosopher of the ancient Near East. Ecclesiastes 1:16

⟩ The beat goes on (3:1-22)

Hey, God is in control. Deal with it. Whatever is happening now, is happening for some reason. And, whatever isn't happening, isn't happening for a reason too. God is in control of the life cycle. We can't do anything to change that. No hard work will affect what God has in mind.

⟩ Money leaves you wanting (5:10-17)

Getting attached to the green will leave you wanting. You'll never be satisfied. The more you have, the more people want. And, others are more likely to spend your money for you. In the end, Solomon says, wealth is worthless to human beings. Can you take it with you? No. Will it make you happy? No. What good is it? None.

⟩ Go for the gusto! (5:18-20; 9:7-9; 12:13)

Imagine Solomon pushing his body back in his favorite chair. Thinking about his life. After living a long and luxurious life, Solomon concludes that it's the simple things that matter most. When Solomon's analysis of life is complete, the main conclusion he reaches—the core of everything he has ever been taught—is this: Respect God. Obey God. You want to live life to the extreme? Solomon, after years of thinking and reflecting finally figured it out. Honor God. The rest takes care of itself.

REVIEWS

ENCORE

> Want to read more about how you can be fulfilled? Read the parables of Jesus about the kingdom of heaven. You'll find them in Matthew 13. Reading these will give you perspective about your life, and challenge you to give your attention to things of greatest value.

> You want MORE practical advice about living, really? Okay. Read James, often described as the Wisdom book of the New Testament.

Talk about lifestyles of the rich and famous. Here's a story about a guy who had more stuff than the richest guy in the world today. Sure he lived in a time without electricity, so his gadgets weren't as sophisticated. (He didn't have a cell phone, he had a "Saul" phone, a guy named Saul who had a good memory and ran really fast) The Bible says that he made silver as common as stones. He was surrounded by gold. He had hundreds of wives and more wannabe wives. He lived in a huge palace. There was almost nothing that he wanted that he couldn't have.

It's the life we all dream of, right? Solomon's story goes deeper than that, though. Zoom in past the interior decorating, the servants, the bankroll. Zoom past the finery and the palm-leaf-waving handmaidens (zoom just a little slower past the handmaidens, if you don't mind), zoom in on the heart of the man who had it all. What do you find?

Emptiness.

Ecclesiastes is the reality check from a guy who "made it" writing back to the old 'hood, "It's shinier toys, but inside it's all the same. What's life about...really?"

I'm not saying that cool stuff and money and all that isn't fun. It can be, if you've got the important stuff too. Stuff like love and a sense of purpose, a reason to live and something to look forward to, even when you die. Stuff like...God.

So enjoy the tour of the man who had it all: fame, fortune, women and wealth. But look close and you'll see him yawn when no one is looking. Listen close and you'll hear the boredom in his voice. Um...hey, Solomon? Since you're not enjoying all that stuff anyway...ah, never mind. This book always makes me feel lucky to be right where I am, just being me and being happy. Not that I'd turn down a palace and maybe just a few hundred servants and a couple gazillion dollars. I just wouldn't trade any of the good stuff for it.

Without God "everything" really is the same as "nothing." Do that math, would you? I guess the truth is that if you take an empty space and build a house around it and fill it with fancy stuff, it's still an empty space. That's what our hearts are without God's presence—just an empty space.

Berry Richman

Song of Songs

Adam	Abraham	Moses	David	Solomon		Ezra	Jesus Is Born
4000+ B.C.	2100 B.C.	1500 B.C.	1000 B.C.	971 B.C.		450 B.C.	7/6 B.C.

A romantic work of art

Passion! Love! Romance! Need a little? You're in the right place. But, make sure you're old enough first. In ancient times, Jews wouldn't let a man read it until he was 30 years old. Jewish elders didn't worry about the women because, unfortunately, most of them couldn't read.

Ever wonder why your pastor doesn't preach out of this book? Well, it might be a little too steamy for Sunday mornings. This is an erotic poem. The theme is for adults only. The major players are a man and woman in love, and this poem graphically and explicitly praises the physical features of each other and reveals their shared fantasy about making love. Their words are not vulgar or obscene. They *are* sexual, sensual and intimate. Yikes!

No, because this book is in the Bible you don't have God's permission to watch racy movies. Many godly people, in fact, have argued that it never should have been added in the first place. So, why's it even in the Bible? Consider this book God's gift to sexuality. This book gives us a cool reminder that human sexuality is a gift of God. It also paints a wonderful picture of what romance can be. So, read this as God's little romance instruction book.

QUOTABLES

I am the rose of Sharon, and the lily of the valleys (2:1, KJV).

I am my beloved's (7:10, KJV).

SNEAK PREVIEW

Romans
Amazed that faith can move mountains? Wait 'til you see what it does to your heart.

BEHIND the SCENES
of Song of Songs

STARRING ROLES

An unnamed woman, from the countryside of Israel (1:2)
An unnamed man, the woman's true love (1:8)
Solomon, king of Israel (1:1)

PLOT

On the surface, the plot for this book is simple. First, you've got a guy. Then, you've got a girl. Then, you've got love. And, the rest is magic. The tale is of two people, deeply in love, and ready to express how they feel.

However, this is also a poem with a ton of highly symbolic language. So Bible experts don't agree on the story behind the poem. Here's a few ideas.
• Solomon chooses a country girl for his bride, but the young lady refuses the king in favor of her country lover.
• Solomon and the country lover are the same man.
• The unnamed country lover is the only man in the story, and when he comes to the woman, she looks upon him as a glorious king—a kind of knight in shining armor.

In ancient times, many Jewish and Christian scholars didn't take the poem literally. Jews saw the poem symbolizing God's love for the Jewish people. Christians later saw it as Christ's love for the church.

STAGE
DIRECTIONS

Solomon begins his 40-year reign 970 B.C.

Dates are approximate

BIBLE EVENTS

1100 B.C.   1000 B.C.   900 B.C.

WORLD EVENTS

Egyptian love songs written 1100 B.C.

Greeks worship many gods including Aphrodite (goddess of love) 1000 B.C.

AUTHOR AND DATE

Bible scholars aren't certain who wrote the book. The Hebrew phrase in verse one that attributes the poem to Solomon can mean it was written by him, for him, or dedicated to him. It is possible Solomon did write it. And he is said to have written 1,005 songs altogether (1 Kings 4:32). But it's also possible that a professional musician wrote the song for one of Solomon's weddings. Or, it may have been written for weddings in general, and dedicated to the memory of the king with a thousand wives.

It's uncertain when the poem was written. If it was composed by or for Solomon, it was probably written sometime during his reign: 970–940 B.C.

ON LOCATION

The setting is Israel. The young woman addresses the "women of Jerusalem." And the two lovers occasionally compare one another to landmarks in Israel. Can you imagine saying to your girlfriend, "Your head is like Mount Rushmore"? Yeah, kind of unbelievable today. But that's exactly what the man said to his beloved in Song of Songs 7:5. Those ancient people really knew how to compliment each other, huh?!

WHAT TO LOOK FOR

- **Passion**. Lots of passion. This is a passionate, erotic celebration of love between a man and a woman. And, what's really interesting is that the man nor the woman feels the least bit inhibited about expressing their most intimate feelings and desires. So, it's not only passionate (did we mention that?) it's also unrestrained, unashamed passion. The man lovingly, poetically compares the body of his beloved to a garden filled with sweet aroma and brimming with delicious fruit. So, we've got passion. We've got intimacy. And we've got fruit. Interesting.

> Like the book of Esther, the Song of Songs doesn't mention God.

> The title of the book comes from the introduction, "Solomon's most beautiful song" (1:1). So it's called the Song of Songs just as Jesus is called the "King of kings."

EXTREME SCENES
from Song of Songs

⇒ Eye of the beholder (1:1-17)

"Kiss me tenderly!" a young and beautiful peasant woman tells the man of her dreams. "Your love is better than wine, and you smell so sweet." Wow. These are the captivating, opening lines of a passionate song about sexual intimacy. What follows is an exchange of compliments, in which each lover boldly praises the physical attributes of the other.

DIRECTOR'S NOTES

You may be wondering why the author would compare his beloved to a dove, of all things. The ancient Israelites appreciated the faithfulness, the beauty and especially the gentleness of the bird. A dove is one of the few creatures that will not attempt to defend itself when it's attacked. Instead, it will simply call out in distress. Song of Songs 1:15

⇒ The big day (3:6-11)

On the day of the wedding, friends of the bride are the first to notice a dust cloud rolling in from the desert. It is the groom, arriving with his procession. This man may actually be Solomon, coming to marry the young woman. Or the poetic description may be a way of saying the young peasant couple is so deeply in love that their humble wedding feels to them like the majestic ceremony of a king and a queen.

⇒ Mood setting words (4:1-5:16)

After the wedding, the groom praises the beauty of his bride by comparing her to some of the most natural beauty he has ever seen. Her hair flows gracefully upon her shoulders, like a flock of goats moving in rhythmic union down a mountainside. Her teeth shine as white as freshly washed wool. He doesn't get the only say. She has a lot to say about the way he looks.

⇒ The honeymoon (7:1-8:14)

The passionate compliments continue flowing, as husband and wife praise each other and even more boldly describe their physical desires. The intensity of their expression heats up, crossing the border into sensuality that is neither obscene nor ashamed.

REVIEWS

If Song of Songs was expanded for the big screen there would be plenty of kissing scenes. There's just no getting around it. It's downright mushy. It's a love poem about a couple (King Solomon and his bride). They are infatuated. They are in love. They are romantic. They are crazy about each other. This one is way past puppy love.

You might be surprised to know that when this book was written, it wasn't unusual for its day. Similar but even older songs have been recovered from the Middle East. So love songs have been around a long time. Probably as long as love has...but probably not longer.

Does it surprise you to find this kind of stuff in the Bible? Think about it. You can learn something important about God from this. He created us to need each other. He created romance. He created sex. He even told His people to "be fruitful, and multiply." Sex is a very, VERY powerful thing. One of God's greatest powers is the power of creation and one of God's greatest miracles was creating people. With sex, he gave us the power to do the same. Just remember, with all that power comes a LOT of responsibility. Don't believe me? Baby-sit a six-month-old kid for a few days. By the end of the first day, you will be exhausted and covered with baby barf. By the end of the second day, you will be WISHING the worst thing babies did was barf. By the third day, sleep will be a distant memory, and you will be going over pamphlets to decide which monastery to join, if one will take you in your present condition. Jokes aside, you get the picture, right? It's all good...in its place. Sometimes the parent types are trying so hard to keep you out of trouble that they forget to say, "God was the one who made romance up. He was the one who had the big idea for it all."

ENCORE

> To read about the prophet Hosea wooing back his unfaithful wife, as a symbol of God trying to win back the affection of Israel, turn to Hosea 1—3.

> To see how the New Testament writers speak of the church as the bride of Christ, read Matthew 9:15; 25:1-13; Revelation 19.

REVIEWS

Early on, godly Jews and Christians asked what such a book was doing in the Bible. You know, each book included in the Bible went through a major screening as to the power of the book and who wrote it. All kinds of stuff. Each book had to pass the test of time and authenticity before it was included. Somehow this one made it. Some people see it as a symbolic kind of book. For some Jews, the husband in the story symbolizes God and the wife symbolizes Israel. For Christians, the husband could represent Jesus, and the wife could represent the church. There's probably a lot of truth that can be learned by looking at it that way, but there's a lot of truth to be gained from the book just like it is. Sometimes the differences in the language and times make for a good laugh, too. Check out the parts where he says her teeth look like sheep.

It's a story of two people in love with each other and enjoying every minute of it. So look the other way if mushy gushy stuff makes you wanna hurl. This book's full of it. And if you are gonna hurl, do me a favor and do it somewhere else...baby.

Virginia Vestalius

Isaiah

SCHEDULE OF SCENES

Adam	Abraham	Moses	David	Fall of Israel	Fall of Judah	Ezra	Jesus Is Born
4000+ B.C.	2100 B.C.	1500 B.C.	1000 B.C.	722 B.C.	586 B.C.	450 B.C.	7/6 B.C.

A prophet sees Jesus

You want bizarre in God's Word? Okay. You got it. How about a guy who lives 700 years before Jesus walked the earth, and yet he writes like he knows the guy. Scattered throughout Isaiah's oracles are vivid descriptions and graphic scenes that read as if they flowed from the pen of a poet who saw the miraculous birth of Jesus in Bethlehem, his crucifixion, and his resurrection. Isaiah's strangeness doesn't end there. How about walking around naked for three years. That's strange too.

This book has become a classic. Not just because it talks about a naked prophet. But because Isaiah's Jesus connection seemed so real. The first disciples of Jesus didn't miss the connection. The Gospels are full of their comments about Jesus fulfilling one prophecy of Isaiah after another. Jesus didn't miss the connection either. When he stood in his hometown synagogue, in Nazareth, he opened the scroll of Isaiah and read the first two verses of chapter 61. Then he told his listeners, "What you have just heard me read has come true today" (Luke 4:21).

Even though this is really fascinating, the book of Isaiah is far more than a sneak preview into the life of Christ. It's a study of sin—of how it slowly destroyed two Jewish nations and of how God will one day wipe it from the face of creation.

QUOTABLES

Unto us a Child is born, unto us a Son is given; and the government will be upon His shoulder. And His name will be called Wonderful, Counselor, Mighty God, Everlasting Father, Prince of Peace (9:6, NKJV).

They shall beat their swords into plowshares (2:4, NKJV).

"Here am I! Send me" (6:8, NKJV).

Though your sins are like scarlet, they shall be as white as snow (1:18, NKJV).

"Come now, and let us reason together" (1:18, NKJV).

SNEAK PREVIEW

Exodus
To what lengths will God go to set His people free?

BEHIND the SCENES
of Isaiah

STARRING ROLES

Isaiah, prophet whose ministry spans four kings (1:1)
Hezekiah, godly Judean king who usually follows Isaiah's advice (1:1)

PLOT

Ever had a vision? Isaiah had one. In an amazing moment, God calls Isaiah to become a prophet during a tough time in Middle Eastern history. Assyria will destroy the northern Jewish nation of Israel, and the southern nation of Judah (Isaiah's country) will face the same threat. Isaiah's job is to deliver God's messages to his fellow Jews. No small task!

The prophet warns sinners of both Israel and Judah that God will punish them, using the Assyrians, then the Babylonians. But Isaiah also predicts that when the punishment has ended, God will send a Prince of Peace (a.k.a. Jesus) to restore the nation. Woven into the Plot are implications about the end of human history, when God punishes the entire world for sin, then makes a new world for the people who have been faithful.

STAGE DIRECTIONS

	Assyria destroys				
God selects Isaiah to become a prophet 740 B.C.	northern Jewish nation of Israel 722 B.C.	Hezekiah revolts against Assyria 705 B.C.	Assyria seizes Judah but can't capture Jerusalem 701 B.C.	Babylon destroys Jerusalem 586 B.C.	Jewish exiles return to Jerusalem 538 B.C.

BIBLE EVENTS

Dates are approximate

800 B.C.   **700 B.C.**   **600 B.C.**   **500 B.C.**

WORLD EVENTS

First recorded Olympic games 776 B.C.	King Romulus founds Rome 753 B.C.	Assyrians choose Nineveh as capital and start rebuilding it 705 B.C.		Jewish exiles return to Jerusalem 539 B.C.

Chinese history confirms solar eclipse 775 B.C.

AUTHOR AND DATE

Most people believe that Isaiah is the author. You'll find him throughout this book. You'll see him doing strange things. You'll read about him being God's mouthpiece to a sinning nation. This book covers a LOT of time. The first 39 chapters deal with Isaiah's time. Chapters 40–66 tell the story of Judah's exile in Babylon (and the return home) 150 years later. This leads many Bible experts to think that the book was written by two or three authors. Others think Isaiah wrote the later chapters by drawing on what God showed him about the future.

Isaiah's ministry spanned at least the last four decades of the 700s B.C., during the reigns of four kings: Uzziah, Jotham, Ahaz, and Hezekiah. Isaiah apparently lived at least another 20 years because he reports the murder of Assyrian King Sennacherib, who was killed by his own sons in 681 B.C. Now for the gross stuff. Jewish legend says Isaiah was sawn in half at the order of Manasseh, who reigned from 696 to 642 B.C. What a way to go!

ON LOCATION

Isaiah prophesies in the southern Jewish nation of Judah and probably lives in the capital city of Jerusalem. Later in the book the setting changes as Isaiah tells about the coming defeat of Judah, followed by the people's long exile in Babylon.

WHAT TO LOOK FOR

- **Messages from God in the first person.** Isaiah was God's mouthpiece. That means when he spoke for God, he spoke as God would. Isaiah won't say, for example, "God is sick of your offerings." Instead, he speaks the very words of God: "I am sick of your offerings." However, he introduces most prophecies with the phrase, "The Lord has said." Just so people know who's going to tell them off.
- **Promises about a coming messiah.** There are more references about the Messiah in Isaiah than in any other Old Testament book. New Testament writers often quote Isaiah to show that Jesus fulfilled prophecies about the promised Messiah.
- **Poetry and prose.** This is a literary type thing. The prophecies are printed in poetic form and are usually indented. The stories and sermons are printed in paragraph form.
- **Vivid images.** Isaiah is a genius of imagery. He's especially fond of treating inanimate objects as though they live and breathe. In his book, mountains sing and trees clap (55:12). He knows how to evoke emotion in us by painting great pictures. But, remember: These are *images*. Don't take all the images literally.

Isaiah   **195**

EXTREME SCENES
from Isaiah

⇥ The making of a prophet (1:1, 6:1-13)

Sometime during the year that King Uzziah died, in about 740 B.C., a young man described only as "Isaiah," has an incredible, bizarre vision. He sees God seated on a high throne in a temple. Surrounding the throne are glowing, heavenly beings. God asks "Is there anyone I can send? Will someone go for us?" Isaiah quickly replies, "Send me!" (Would you have said this?). God's instructions? Call the people of Judah back to obedience. No small task. God warns that they won't listen. With this promise of failure, Isaiah begins his ministry.

DIRECTOR'S NOTES

A hair weaving business would have been a hit with men in ancient Israel, because they took great pride in their hair. Baldness was considered an embarrassment. For the most part, the only people who shaved were Levites, victims of skin disease, and people in mourning. To be shaved (involuntarily) by someone else was a tremendous insult. Isaiah 7:20

⇥ Northern Israel destroyed (8:1-10)

A few years later, the northern Jewish nation of Israel unites with Syria to fight for freedom from the Assyrian Empire. When Judah refuses to join the coalition, Israel and Syria try to force the issue. Isaiah tells Judean King Ahaz to stand his ground because God says the kings of Israel and Syria are "nothing more than a dying fire" (7:4). Ahaz apparently doesn't trust God alone, so he calls on help from Assyria. The Assyrians come and in 732 B.C. conquer Syria. Ten years later, they return and destroy Israel, burning the capital city and deporting tens of thousands of the leading citizens. Judah pays dearly for trusting an alliance with Assyria instead of trusting God's promise: they lose their freedom and must pay taxes to Assyria each year.

⇥ The Jesus prophecy? (9:2-7)

In a prophecy possibly delivered at the coronation of Hezekiah, one of Israel's most godly kings, the prophet Isaiah reflects back on the birth of the king and portray this birth as a sign of hope. New Testament writers saw this and interpreted it as a signpost, pointing to the promised Messiah, Jesus.

Peace: What you really need (11:1-16)

In another prophecy that may have been delivered at the coronation of one of Judah's kings, Isaiah speaks of the day when a ruler from the family of King David will lead the nation into an era of enduring peace. Jesus? Yup. Early Christians associated this with the coming kingdom of Jesus, in which God will defeat sin and restore the original beauty of creation.

Burning Babylon (13:1-22)

In Isaiah's time, Babylon is a baby powerhouse. Isaiah sees a time in the future when it will become powerful and majestic. And, he also sees that it'll level Jerusalem in 586 B.C. The *cause* of the destruction was the sins of Jerusalem. Even so, the Jews slam God for punishing them with a nation that is even more sinful. The pain is coming for Babylon. Isaiah promises that Babylon will face its own Judgment Day. The devastation will be so thorough that "even nomads won't camp nearby." Did it happen? Sure did. Babylon, 60 miles south of Baghdad, has been completely deserted since A.D. 600s.

The sky is falling (24:1-23)

God promises to get rid of sin. This purging begins with the punishment of a long list of nations. Among the many that will suffer are Judah, Assyria, Babylon, Egypt, and Arabia. Then Isaiah says the entire planet will suffer. Isaiah promises that the destruction will feel like God is dismantling His physical creation. Many experts think Isaiah is speaking about the end of human history. After the end comes a new beginning, a new creation. First the end. Then, a new beginning. But first, the end.

From doom to comfort (40:1-31)

The first 39 chapters are mostly doom and gloom, you're all gonna burn. After this, the threats of doom turn to promises of comfort. The scene moves in fast-forward, 200 years into the future. Jerusalem is destroyed, and the people of Judah are suffering through half a century of exile in Babylon.

The wounded servant (53:1-12)

Someone was coming. Isaiah knew it. Isaiah tells about a servant who would be despised, rejected, full of sorrow and familiar with suffering. Who was this? Jews reading this text in Babylonian exile may have thought Isaiah was talking about them, the outcast Jewish nation. But the New Testament writers also saw this as a portrait of Jesus (Matthew 8:17).

A new crib (54:1-17)

What do you do when your home is destroyed? Simple. You dream about a new home. The Babylonians had reduced Jerusalem to a pile of rocks, burned timber and shattered pottery. God gives Isaiah a picture of the Holy City restored by God. The Jews needed this. Isaiah gets creative with his language for the Holy city (read about it in 54:11-12).

    The first readers of these words may have considered the prophecy fulfilled when the Jews returned from Babylon and rebuilt their nation. But the meaning could reach well beyond this, to a time when God brings salvation to everyone, and once again God can look at his creation and declare, "It is good."

REVIEWS

ENCORE

➤ For another prophet's perspective on what life was like at the time, read the seven-chapter book of Micah.

➤ For a glimpse into how New Testament writers interpreted the words of Isaiah as prophecies about Jesus, read these texts: John 12:37-41; Acts 8:26–39; Romans 15:7-21.

When you think of Isaiah, think of a big ol' Billy Graham crusade...the wisdom, the teaching, the crowds. If most Americans were going to go listen to someone about spiritual stuff, it would be Billy Graham. If any Hebrew was going to listen to someone about spiritual stuff it would have been Isaiah. He was educated. He was wise. He met with kings and preached to his people.

Isaiah could have easily had his own weekly religious talk show. It wouldn't have been cheesy either. He would have talked about real issues that mattered to God and to people. He would have had guests that weren't just the famous people, but were the "together" people, the ones who were making a difference in their world.

Isaiah didn't get his own show though. In fact, tradition says that he was executed during the reign of evil King Manasseh...by being sawn in half (Manasseh would not have been a guest on Isaiah's show, although he might fit better on some of today's talk shows. "Evil Kings who saw people in half, tonight on Springer.") Big price to pay for telling the truth. Brave dude.

The first part of Isaiah's prophecy was pretty harsh. He didn't cut the people any slack (on the other hand, he didn't cut them in half either). The second part was about the coming Messiah, Jesus.

Isaiah was amazingly specific as a prophet. He actually named Cyrus—the Persian king who came along 200 years later—as the leader who would "set my people free" (45:13). This really freaks some people out. They say, "How could this book be written by a man 200 years before Cyrus was even king. It must have been written by someone else." But, given Isaiah's prophetic abilities and God's ability to do whatever He wants to (Oh yeah, there is THAT, isn't there?), Isaiah could have known Cyrus' name. Stranger things have happened and probably will again.

All I know is that if Isaiah led a crusade in my town, I think I'd buy a ticket and go (of course, Isaiah wouldn't have charged money anyway). And I think I'd listen really close and go away a little more intent on obeying the God that Isaiah described.

Graham Williams

Jeremiah

SCHEDULE OF SCENES

Adam	Abraham	Moses	David	Fall of Israel	Josiah	Fall of Judah	Ezra	Jesus Is Born
4000+ B.C.	2100 B.C.	1500 B.C.	1000 B.C.	722 B.C.	640 B.C.	586 B.C.	450 B.C.	7/6 B.C.

The doom predictor

Imagine this: You're a witness to the most tragic event in your nation's history. You watch your friends slaughtered, with survivors herded up and taken away. You watch your city burn. You watch your friends die. Actually, he had seen all this coming for 40 years. And he knew it didn't have to end like this. The people in Jerusalem had a choice. Honor the agreement their ancestors had made with the Lord. Honor their obligations, which are summed up in the Ten Commandments. God would honor His by protecting and blessing the people. But, they chose to dishonor the covenant. God was bound by the agreement to punish them. The rest is history.

No one likes a guy who constantly predicts bad things. That was Jeremiah's role. He reminded people of their commitment to God. Sin had consequences; it was written into the covenant. Jeremiah gives us a chance to learn from the mistakes of his era, for he opens a window that allows us to take a long, hard look at the wages of sin.

QUOTABLES

Can a leopard remove its spots? (13:23).

"I will write my laws on their hearts and minds. I will be their God, and they will be my people" (31:33).

"Like clay in the hand of the potter, so are you in my hand, O house of Israel" (18:6, NIV).

The heart is deceitful above all things, and desperately wicked (17:9, NKJV).

SNEAK PREVIEW

> Daniel
> A glance to the future
> through the eyes of an exile.

BEHIND the SCENES
of Jeremiah

STARRING ROLES

Jeremiah, a prophet who witnesses Jerusalem's fall (1:1)
Baruch, the scribe who writes Jeremiah's dictated prophecies (32:12)
Jehoiakim, king who cuts up Jeremiah's first scroll of prophecies (1:3)
Zedekiah, last king of Judah; he takes his army and abandons Jerusalem (1:3)

PLOT

The prophet Jeremiah, a young guy, begins his job of telling people what God thinks about them during a spiritually upbeat time in Judah's history. King Josiah, a godly ruler, is leading the nation in a revival. That's awesome, but it's a little too late. The effects won't last, and the Jews will go back to worshiping idols and treating each other like crud.

    God is sending a world of hurt on Judah. It'll come from the Babylonian army, but it's from God. In the midst of this spiritually weird time, Jeremiah delivers this heartbreaking message. Unfortunately, his is one of the few hearts broken. Most people ignore him and treat him like crud too.

STAGE DIRECTIONS

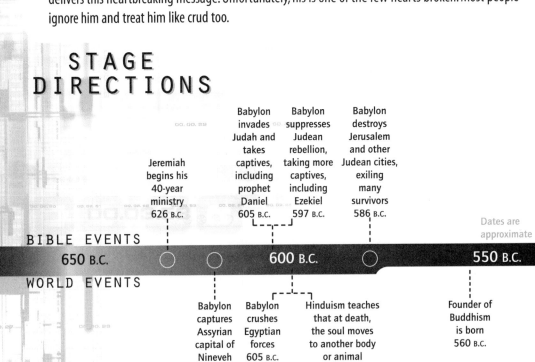

	Jeremiah begins his 40-year ministry 626 B.C.	Babylon invades Judah and takes captives, including prophet Daniel 605 B.C.	Babylon suppresses Judean rebellion, taking more captives, including Ezekiel 597 B.C.	Babylon destroys Jerusalem and other Judean cities, exiling many survivors 586 B.C.	Dates are approximate

BIBLE EVENTS

650 B.C.   **600 B.C.**   **550 B.C.**

WORLD EVENTS

Babylon captures Assyrian capital of Nineveh 612 B.C.	Babylon crushes Egyptian forces 605 B.C.	Hinduism teaches that at death, the soul moves to another body or animal 600 B.C.	Founder of Buddhism is born 560 B.C.

AUTHOR AND DATE

Jeremiah had a secretary. He dictated (which means, he spoke, his secretary wrote down what he said) these prophecies to his assistant named Baruch (36:4). Some people believe that Baruch added some of the poetry later. That would make him a great, but sneaky secretary.

Jeremiah prophesied in Judah for about 40 years, from 626–586 B.C. He dictated his prophecies, the heart of the book, during the reign of King Jehoiakim (609–598 B.C.).

This is a confrontational book. It confronts the Judeans with their sin. It gives them a chance to repent. Then (when they don't repent) it records the horrifying consequences. You'd think a huge "THE END" was written when Jerusalem fell. Well, not exactly. At the end of the book, Jeremiah offers the promise that the nation of Israel will rise again.

ON LOCATION

Jeremiah delivers his prophecies in Jerusalem, capital of Judah. When Babylonian invaders conquer the land, they move much of the population to Babylon, a city near what is now Baghdad. Jeremiah and a group of survivors who remain in Judah later escape to Egypt.

WHAT TO LOOK FOR

- **Poetry, stories, speeches.** The prophecies of Jeremiah are easy to spot. They're indented because they are poems. You'll also find in the book some stories and sermons or speeches, which are written in regular paragraph form.
- **Poetic repetition.** The prophet Jeremiah understands the powerful impact of repeating a striking phrase or idea. This repetition is the most unique characteristic of Hebrew poetry, which does not rhyme or have rhythm.
- **Jeremiah's complaints.** Scattered throughout the book are complaints and questions Jeremiah raises. Once he complains and wishes he had never been born. (15:10). Another time he questions God's justice. (12:1–2). This is one complainy guy.

Jeremiah has more words than any other book in the Bible.

The prophet acts out many of his messages. For example, on one occasion he wears a yoke to symbolize that God expects the nations of the area to serve Babylon (27:2). Another time God tells him not to attend any funerals or show sympathy to the bereaved. This is to illustrate that God will have no pity on the Jews when it comes time to punish them (16:5).

The new covenant, which New Testament writers said replaced the hundreds of laws that God gave Moses, is first mentioned here: "The time is coming," declares the Lord, "when I will make a new covenant with the house of Israel and with the house of Judah" (31:31, NIV). That time arrived with the death and resurrection of Jesus, says the New Testament (Hebrews 8).

EXTREME SCENES
from Jeremiah

⤏ Off the bench...into the game (1:1-18:23)

Jeremiah (the son of a priest) has no desire to become a prophet. When God calls him, Jeremiah resists. His list is long. "I'm too young." "I'm not a good speaker." God's response? Well, basically, God says, "Yeah, right...you're going anyway!" Later, God tells Jeremiah to go to the pottery shop. Jeremiah goes relying on God's promise to tell him what to say. As Jeremiah and others watch the craftsman at work, they see that when the pottery doesn't shape up well, the potter starts over. Jeremiah, acting on God's instruction, tells the spectators that God can do to the Jewish people what the potter has just done to the clay. God promises to strike them with disaster through the Babylonians. The invasions would last over 20 years. Basically, the Babylonians attacked three times. The first two times, they moved Israelites from their country to Babylon. Then, in the third invasion, they leveled all the major Israelite cities. Not cool.

DIRECTOR'S NOTES

Normally, it would have been easy to tell who was an Egyptian and who was an Israelite, based on appearance alone. The Egyptians preferred a clean-cut look, while the Israelites wore their hair and beards long. For the Israelites, shaving one's hair was a sign of deep distress or mourning. Jeremiah 7:29

⤏ Here comes da king (23:1-8)

Jeremiah verbally thrashes the unrighteous rulers of Judah. Speaking on God's behalf, he accuses them for leading people astray and predicts their destruction. Then, Jeremiah reverses his theme. He lays out a poetic prophecy that describes a coming ruler whom the Jews later associated with the promised Messiah. So, you've got a lot of bad kings. The promise of a powerful and righteous king. Jeremiah is obviously right where God wants him.

⤏ The final ruling (25:1-14)

Jeremiah warned and warned and warned...a lot like the way your mom calls you a hundred times to get out of bed when you're *really* comfortable. He warned them for 23 years. Now their time is up. God has made his decision. He's going to destroy and scatter them.

⤏ A symbolic investment (32:1-15)

The Babylonians capture all the major cities of Judah except Jerusalem, which they have now surrounded. Inside is Jeremiah, under arrest in the palace courtyard for speaking out against King Zedekiah. While the siege is underway, Jeremiah buys a field in his boyhood home nearby. The sale is meant to serve as a symbol to Israel. God tells Jeremiah to put the bill of sale in a clay jar (the ancient version of a safety deposit box). Jeremiah reports what God has told him, "Things look bleak now, but one day you will be able to buy land."

Hot prophecy (36:1-32)

This one involves a cool flashback. About 20 years ago, God instructs Jeremiah to write down all the prophecies he has spoken. Jeremiah dictates the prophecies to his scribe, Baruch. Later, Baruch takes the scroll to the temple and reads it to the people. When King Jehoiakim hears the words in a private reading he is not impressed. As the reader finishes a section, the king reaches over with a small knife, cuts it off, and tosses it in the fire. He does this to the entire scroll. Sheesh! All that hard work! When Jeremiah hears about it, he vows that the king will be killed and thrown out. Jeremiah dictates a second scroll, which becomes the core of the book bearing his name.

A stinky mud home (38:1-13)

Jeremiah's prophecies don't just hit the ears and minds of the people. They attack the hearts. People begin to lose hope – even the soldiers. So, they've got to do *something* with him. There's a brief back and forth conversation. Then, they finally decide to lower him into a cistern. They lower him in and leave him to die. Jeremiah sinks deep into the muddy cistern. Before long, an official pleads with the king to let Jeremiah go. So, Jeremiah leaves the cistern and enters "house arrest" in the palace courtyard where the king asks him for advice about the ensuing battle.

Long live Jeremiah! (39:1—40:16; 52:1–34)

A year and a half into the siege, the Jews are starving to death. So the king and his army make a break for it under the cover of darkness. Babylonian soldiers catch the fleeing king and capture the city. In one memorable scene, King Zedekiah watches his sons' execution. Then he's blinded, locked into chains, and taken to Babylon where he dies a prisoner. The temple, the palace, all the important buildings, and the homes are all set on fire. Then the protective walls of the city are broken down. Everything is laid to waste.

Then, the Babylonian commander locates Jeremiah in a string of chained slaves bound for Babylon. He removes Jeremiah's chains and Jeremiah remains in Judea, under the care of the governor. Sometime later, the Jews assassinate this governor. Fearing reprisal, they flee to Egypt and force Jeremiah to go with them. There, the Jews take up the worship of the goddess Astarte. Jeremiah promises that this

DIRECTOR'S NOTES

You may be surprised to learn that Jerusalem has its share of cold spells in the winter—and even receives occasional snow. In ancient Judah, people who lived in two-story homes usually stayed on the first floor in the winter, then moved to the better-ventilated second floor in the summer. Jeremiah 36:20-22

remnant of Judah will die in Egypt. And (you could guess this, couldn't you?) they disappear from the pages of history, as does Jeremiah.

INTERVIEW
with the Stars

Overcoming weaknesses

What do you think it takes to be a prophet of God? An encyclopedic knowledge of the Bible that comes from years and years of study? Great public-speaking skills? Good looks and a winning smile? **Behind the Bible's** next subject was your typical, man-on-the-street Judean, who woke up one day to find himself called to be a prophet of God. Jeremiah, how did you react when God called you to action?

⋗ Jeremiah

Shocked, absolutely blown away. I had no training; I was young; and worse yet, I was a terrible speaker.

So what did you do?

⋗ Jeremiah

I did what anyone would do in my situation. I pointed out all these things to God...and He *still* insisted that I become His newly appointed prophet.

So what did God say to that?

⋗ Jeremiah

He agreed with me! And then he told me to stop thinking about all the reasons why I couldn't be a prophet and focus instead on how God was going to take care of those things. I'll never forget it. As part of the deal of being a prophet, God promised that he would give me three things: his guidance; his words; and his companionship. Then he gave me three orders: don't use my youth as an excuse; go where he sent me; and don't be afraid.

INTERVIEW
with the Stars

With all that God-power behind you, you must have been very successful as a prophet.

⋗ Jeremiah

You would think so, wouldn't you. But to be truthful, I had to be probably the most unpopular person in all of Judah. No one listened to me. I was thrown in jail. My writings were burned to a crisp. And one guy even dropped me into a well! No, when you look up success in the dictionary, you aren't going to find my picture. At least from the world's point of view.

But what about God's promises?

⋗ Jeremiah

Oh, God kept His promises. He was always with me. In fact, when things got really bad and I couldn't take it anymore, I just would spout off to God and tell Him exactly what I thought. And He always listened. He never left me. He was my constant companion when everyone else had deserted me.

Based on your experiences, what advice could you give to young people today?

⋗ Jeremiah

The main thing is not to let your weaknesses—either real or imagined—keep you from following God's direction for your life. God knows you best. He knows you inside out. And the more open you are to God's direction, the more you will find God using both your abilities and your inabilities to get the job done. Just like God told me in Jeremiah 1:8, *"I am with you to deliver you,"* God will make a difference in you as He is making a difference through you.

REVIEWS

Jeremiah … you gotta' love this guy. He was a bit of an Eeyore, a kind of Puddleglum. In fact, he was called the "weeping prophet." If you were documenting Jeremiah's life you'd shoot it in black and white and make it that really grainy texture, not prettied up at all, because that's who Jeremiah was.

Why was he sad? Because he saw what was coming. For him, it was like walking down a train tunnel in the middle of the night, seeing that light, hearing that whistle and knowing you can't outrun it. Jeremiah was watching his people, the Hebrews, fall farther and farther away from God. He knew the consequences for the way they were living would catch up to them. He knew that they were so weak spiritually that they couldn't stand against any attacks. He tried to tell them over and over. . . .

And all he got for it was a wimpy nickname like the "weeping prophet."

There are some dramatic scenes in Jeremiah. He used visuals to communicate. Have you seen those commercials where someone takes an egg and says, "This is your brain." Then they break the egg into a hot frying pan and say something like, "This is your brain on drugs."

Jeremiah actually did an ancient version of that commercial. He got a clay pot and stood in front of his people. He said something like, "This is your life." Then he threw the pot to the ground and it broke, of course, into little pieces. Then he said something like, "This is your life without obeying God's law."

The saddest thing about Jeremiah is that he was right. His story is one that will leave you walking out of the theater with your popcorn half-eaten and a somber look on your face. He wasn't really about entertainment. He was really about a message.

Regis "Wise Guy" Solomon

ENCORE

For more on this era in Judah's history, read 2 Kings and 2 Chronicles 34–36.

For the words of other Judean prophets who lived during Jeremiah's lifetime, read the books of Habakkuk, Zephaniah, and Nahum.

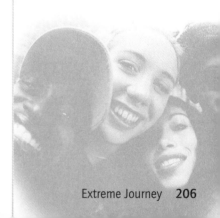

Lamentations

SCHEDULE OF SCENES

Adam	Abraham	Moses	David	Fall of Israel	Fall of Judah	Ezra	Jesus Is Born
4000+ B.C.	2100 B.C.	1500 B.C.	1000 B.C.	722 B.C.	586 B.C.	450 B.C.	7/6 B.C.

It's OK to cry

Caution: If you're depressed, don't read this book.

Agony. Death. Spiritual pain. Lamentations has it all. This book can be depressing. But, if you want a window into the emotions of the ancient mind, reading this book will feel like an education. It's the best place to go in the Bible if you want to understand how people feel when they've suffered an indescribable loss. The writer of this book has lost nearly everything but his life—and he could lose that as quickly as a master could kill a slave. His country is gone, the cities burned, and the leaders dead or arrested. The citizens are gone, slaughtered by Babylonian invaders or deported to faraway lands. Perhaps many of the writer's friends and close family members are among the dead. And perhaps he's all alone now. This book reads like the diary of a P.O.W. Lots of pain. Lots of loss. Little comfort.

Whadya do when you're hurting?" The writer of Lamentations made a tough move. He reached inside himself. He searches for a response to all this tragedy. And, in the process of his search, he turns up a surprising revelation.

"The Lord is all I need" he says. Can you relate? In the midst of despair we're flooded with the divine reminder that God is our everything. He soothes the aching soul.

QUOTABLES

Great is thy faithfulness (3:23, KJV).

SNEAK PREVIEW

> **2 Thessalonians**
> How to keep busy while you're waiting for the big party to begin.

BEHIND the SCENES
of Lamentations

STARRING ROLES

Survivors of Judah, a nation defeated and dispersed (1:3)

PLOT

This book is a "life song". It describes pain, hurt, death, loss, and the results those tragedies have on us. No plot here. Just a sad song about the death of the Jewish nation.

In a collection of five poems, the writer captures the intensity of his feelings about the unspeakable suffering he has witnessed. He knows his nation has sinned, but he can't understand why God has responded so viciously. He yells at God with questioning accusatory statements. He weeps. The plot here is really more like a process. It's the process of finding truth in pain. Reason for suffering.

STAGE DIRECTIONS

BIBLE EVENTS			
Babylon destroys Jerusalem 586 B.C.		Jewish exiles return to Jerusalem 538 B.C.	Temple rebuilt 516 B.C.

Dates are approximate

600 B.C. — — **550 B.C.** — **500 B.C.**

WORLD EVENTS

Babylon crushes Egyptian forces 605 B.C.

Cyris Cylinder confirms return of Jews 539 B.C.

AUTHOR AND DATE

Since ancient times the writer has been identified as Jeremiah. How do we know? The writer would have been a witness to the fall of Jerusalem and the suffering that followed. For example, it seems likely that an eyewitness would report starvation becoming so intense in Jerusalem that mothers would have boiled and eaten their children (4:10).

Lamentations also reads a lot like Jeremiah. Because the pain is so much on the surface of the writing, and without any clue that relief is in sight, most Bible experts say the songs were written shortly after the fall of Jerusalem in 586 B.C., and before the rebuilding of the temple 70 years later.

ON LOCATION

Some songs are set in Israel, as the Jews suffer near-annihilation. Others are set abroad, as survivors are forced to live in exile in Babylon (now Iraq). At least one group of survivors, Jeremiah included, escapes to Egypt.

INSIDE SCOOP

➤ This is the saddest book in the Bible, the only book made up entirely of mournful songs.

➤ This collection of songs, along with some heart-wrenching songs in the book of Jeremiah, has earned Jeremiah the nick-name, "the weeping prophet."

➤ Many Jews today read this book at the Western (Wailing) Wall, where they still lament the destruction of the temple, and pray for the day it will be rebuilt.

WHAT TO LOOK FOR

- **Twenty-two-verse chapters**. There are five chapters in this book, and all but one have 22 verses (the only exception is chapter 3, which has 66 verses—3 times 22). There's a reason for this. In the 22-verse chapters, each verse begins with a letter of the Hebrew alphabet—starting with aleph, followed by beth, and continuing through the 22-letter alphabet. So each chapter forms an acrostic, using the Hebrew alphabet. Chapter three is a bit different; it begins every three verses with a new letter from the alphabet. Chapter five is not an acrostic, but it follows the concept by limiting itself to 22 verses. Imagine the thought it took to create these acrostic songs. Why would he have done this? Possibly to help people remember the songs better.
- **Poetry with a beat.** Lamentations has a rhythm...one thing Hebrew poetry is not known for. There's a beat that you can see not only in the original language, but in many English translations as well. The beat is usually 3–2, with three beats in the first line and two beats in the second line. It's got a beat...but you really can't dance to it.

EXTREME SCENES
from Lamentations

⇒ Jerusalem implodes (1:1-22)

Somewhere in exile a homesick poet writes songs about his Jewish nation lying in ruins. A strong nation has lost its strength. Jerusalem is a city of rubble. The Israelites have gone from city-dwellers to enslaved people suffering in a foreign land. The poet knows that his nation is being punished for its horrible sins, and that if God had not been merciful, the entire nation could have been destroyed. Even so, he longs for an end to the torment.

DIRECTOR'S NOTES

Abandoned city gates in ancient times would have seemed as unusual as empty freeways during rush hour today. Usually the gates of ancient cities were crowded with people and bustling with activity. The city gates were where most business and legal transactions took place. In addition, there was the constant flow of caravan traffic in and out of the city. Lamentations 1:4

⇒ Hey, God...Wassup?

The poet finds it impossible to understand how God can allow such depth of suffering to go on for so long. He wants God to forgive Israel. He pleads, begs and cries to God. The poet doesn't know how God will respond. But somehow, somewhere he finds a calming, healing assurance. God is all he needs. Tough, huh?

REVIEWS

ENCORE

⋙ For more songs of grief about the fall of Jerusalem, read Psalms 74, 79, and 137.

⋙ Jesus' lament over the impending disaster of Jerusalem fits the emotion of Lamentations (Luke 13:34-35).

⋙ For the history behind Lamentations, read Ezekiel and Zephaniah.

Do you know what a funeral dirge is? It's a sad, depressing song. It's the kind of music you listen to after you get dumped by someone you've been dating for a year. Know the kind I mean?

Have you ever heard that song that goes, "Nobody likes me, everybody hates me, guess I'm gonna eat some worms..."? That's pretty close to the feeling of a dirge if you sing it really slow and look at the ground.

Or look at it this way. Lamentations was like the Hebrews' Blues music. They didn't have harmonicas or guitars. But they had some blues to sing about. They were captives in a foreign land, not sure if they would ever get to go home again.

The saddest part was that they had been told from the beginning that this would happen if they didn't live their lives the way God wanted. As long as the Hebrews stayed strong spiritually, they were strong as a nation. But when they let the spiritual stuff go to pot, everything else went with it. (this happens to people too, 'nuff said).

Since Jeremiah was one of the main prophets who warned the people about their coming predicament, he is most often credited with writing Lamentations. Who better than a weeping prophet to write the We-knew-we-were-screwing-up-but-did-it-anyway Blues?

Today it might go something like this. HIT IT BOYS....

(ba DAH duh dum) Shoulda listened to God,
(ba DAH duh dum) And the prophets too,
(ba Dah) Now we got the sad and lonely homeless Jew blues,
Yeah we got the blues,
Jeremiah warned us too,
We used to be such happy Hebrews,
Now we cry and sing these homeless Jew blues.

Jerry "Blind Pomegranate" Myer

Ezekiel

SCHEDULE OF SCENES

Bones that talk

You want strange in God's Word? Sci Fi meets the Divine? Okey Dokey. Try reading Ezekiel.

This is no bedtime story. It's full of strange and unsettling images. In a vision of the throne room of God, Ezekiel reports seeing humanoid creatures, each with four faces, four wings, human hands, and calf-like hooves. Later, he records his most famous vision: His spirit is transported to a valley filled with the scattered bones of human beings. Right before his eyes, these bones begin to rattle, snapping together to form skeletons. Muscles and skin then erupt onto the bones, quickly spreading and covering them to form lifeless corpses. Finally a wind begins to blow, breathing into the bodies the breath of life. This, God promises, is what he will do for Israel, destroyed by Babylon. As a nation, Jews will be resurrected.

OK. That's just weird. Get this. God is an incredible science fiction writer. He uses motivating images to get us to pay attention, and to convey His message. What messages? Well, for starters, God would rather forgive than punish. And, He'll never give up trying to win back the loyalty and love of those who have turned their backs on Him. This is Ezekiel recording God's message of love in strange images. Yeah, it's strange at times. But *so* worth reading.

QUOTABLES

Like mother, like daughter (16:44, NRSV).

Dry bones, hear the word of the Lord! (37:4, NIV).

There shall be showers of blessing (34:26, KJV).

The fathers have eaten sour grapes, and the children's teeth are set on edge (18:2, KJV). Ezekiel refutes this old adage, saying that God does not punish children for the sins of the parents. People are accountable only for their own sins.

SNEAK PREVIEW

1 Samuel
The first king of a baby nation. Royal intrigue, jealous insanity.

BEHIND the SCENES
of Ezekiel

STARRING ROLES

Ezekiel, Jewish prophet, priest, and prisoner in Babylon (1:1)

PLOT

Ezekiel is a 25-year-old priest in Jerusalem. Babylonian soldiers arrive to suppress a rebellion and they take Ezekiel (and 10,000 other upper-class Judeans away) and enslave them. Five years later, in a bizarre vision filled with strange-looking creatures from heaven, God calls Ezekiel to become His prophet and to deliver His messages to the Jews in exile. For the next 20 years, Ezekiel does just that. He does that for eight years. Then, when the end arrives, Ezekiel radically changes his message. He switches from doom to hope. He promises that the exiled people will return to Jerusalem. The city and temple will be rebuilt. And the nations that hurt Israel will suffer big time.

STAGE DIRECTIONS

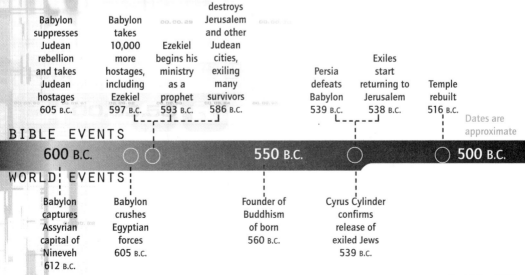

| Babylon suppresses Judean rebellion and takes Judean hostages | Babylon takes 10,000 more hostages, including Ezekiel | Ezekiel begins his ministry as a prophet | Babylon destroys Jerusalem and other Judean cities, exiling many survivors | | Persia defeats Babylon | Exiles start returning to Jerusalem | Temple rebuilt |
| 605 B.C. | 597 B.C. | 593 B.C. | 586 B.C. | | 539 B.C. | 538 B.C. | 516 B.C. |

Dates are approximate

BIBLE EVENTS

600 B.C.   550 B.C.   500 B.C.

WORLD EVENTS

| Babylon captures Assyrian capital of Nineveh 612 B.C. | Babylon crushes Egyptian forces 605 B.C. | Founder of Buddhism of born 560 B.C. | Cyrus Cylinder confirms release of exiled Jews 539 B.C. |

AUTHOR AND DATE

The prophet Ezekiel wrote this book to Jewish exiles living in the Babylonian Empire. Before God called him, Ezekiel was a priest. Ezekiel was 30 years old when God called him, and five years into his exile that probably began in 597 B.C. So the prophecies recorded in this book began in 593 B.C., about eight years before the fall of Jerusalem.

ON LOCATION

Ezekiel lives near the Chebar River, close to the Babylonian Empire's capital city of Babylon—about 50 miles south of the modern Iraqi capital, Baghdad. That's about a thousand miles from his home in Jerusalem by way of the ancient caravan routes. In chapters 47 and 48 he charts the division of the land after the exile.

WHAT TO LOOK FOR

- **Prophecies acted out.** Get this. Ezekiel was an actor. To help people see what he's talking about, Ezekiel sometimes acts out his prophecies. Check out these three examples of his strange way of prophesying.
- Once, when his wife dies, he refuses to follow the Jewish mourning customs. He doesn't cry, put on torn and ragged clothing, or cover himself in dirt. When his neighbors ask why, he says the Jews are about to suffer something so horrible that it will leave them in a state of shock; they won't even be able to cry.
- Another time, he shaves his head and beard. Some of the hair he burns, some he cuts with a sword, and the rest he scatters to the wind. This, he explains, is what will happen to the Jewish people.
- Another time, he sleeps on his right side for 40 days, to symbolize that the Jews have 40 more years to suffer the consequences of their sins.
- **A lot of vivid symbolism.** Don't always take Ezekiel literally. Instead of saying something like, "You're going to die soon!" Ezekiel might say, "Your days will be as a pizza at an all nighter with your church" In other words, you won't be alive too much longer, buster. Sometimes it's easy to see his symbolism. Other times, it's not so easy. Don't let Ezekiel's symbolism confuse the message. It's actually supposed to help you understand his message better.
- **Bad news first, good news last.** The book divides into two parts. Chapters 1–24 contain Ezekiel's prophecies of warning made before the fall of Jerusalem. Using really rough language, he condemns the Jews for rebelling against God, and he warns them that judgment day is coming soon. Then in chapters 25–32, he pronounces doom on the wicked countries that destroy the Jewish nation. After the fall of Jerusalem, Ezekiel's message changes completely. He begins spreading good news for Judah. In the final 16 chapters, 33–48, he promises the exiles that they will one day return to Jerusalem.

INSIDE SCOOP

➤ The song about the "foot bone connected to the leg bone" comes from one of Ezekiel's strange visions (37:1–14).

➤ "Son of man" is how God addresses the prophet—about 90 times in all. This title spotlights Ezekiel's humanity and his dependence on God. The prophet Daniel, however, uses the term to describe the future Messiah (Daniel 7:13). Jesus used this title more than any other to describe himself.

➤ The last word in the book of Ezekiel is the symbolic name of the new Jerusalem: "The-Lord-Is-Here."

EXTREME SCENES
from Ezekiel

⇒ Scroll Eaters Anonymous (2:3-3:3)

Ezekiel's calling to be a prophet is filled with symbolism. While living in Babylon with other upper-class Jewish captives, God selects him to become a prophet. Ezekiel will deliver God's message to the Jews in exile. To symbolize that Ezekiel's words will come from God, he is handed a scroll "filled with words of sadness, mourning, and grief." He's told to eat it. Ezekiel eat is, and says it tastes sweeter than honey.

DIRECTOR'S NOTES

If someone ever tries to sell you a book from Old Testament times, don't buy it—it's a fake. Ancient documents were not written in book form, they were written on long pieces of paper or leather called scrolls. Since most scrolls were usually thirty-five pages or longer, ancient librarians discovered that the best way tot store them was to roll them up on a stick (like toilet paper). A tag with the title written on it was attached to the scroll. Ezekiel 2:9

⇒ God checks out (10:1-22)

In an incredible vision that begins in chapter 8, Ezekiel is transported to the Jerusalem temple. What he witnesses there becomes part of the tragic, unbelievable message he must deliver.

First, a little background. The temple represents the presence of God in Israel. The temple's back room represents the earthly throne of God. It's the holiest site in Judaism. The Jews believe that God's presence has been there ever since King Solomon dedicated the temple. Ezekiel sees the light of God's exit temple and ascend into the heavens. God takes off. And, the Jews are left to be destroyed.

⇒ Jerusalem + temple = large rubble pile (21:1-32)

What could be worse than God leaving the nation? Simple, God comes back with a sword. God tells Ezekiel to tell the Israelites that He's coming back with a sword. Is it *really* God who'll do the slashing? Nope. He's hired the Babylonian soldiers to do it. Ezekiel tells the Jews that Babylon will build dirt ramps to the top of Jerusalem's walls, invade the city, kill the people, and tear down the walls. The city—and the sacred temple—will smolder in ruins. That's a lot of work just to destroy a city. God must have been really ticked!

⇒ Valley o' bones (37:1-14)

Here's where the comfort begins. Imagine standing on the edge of a valley filled with skeletons. Does that sound like comfort? Not really. God transports Ezekiel to a valley filled with dried-out human skeletons, broken and scattered about. The place looks like the site of a massacre long years ago. God tells Ezekiel to speak to the bones. He does. And then (get this...hold on!) he hears a rattling throughout the valley. Bones snap into joints. Muscles spontaneously grow. Skin envelops them. Then a wind sweeps into the valley, blowing across the corpses and bringing them to life. Before long they all stand up. This is dramatic symbolism. It's God saying, "OK. You're destroyed. You deserved it. But I'll bring you back."

DIRECTOR'S
NOTES

There was nothing special about the city of Jerusalem before Solomon chose it as the site of God's temple. The Hittites and Amorites had built the city long before the Israelites arrived in Canaan. When construction of the temple was finished, however, the city became the center of Israel's religious life. Ezekiel 16:3

⇒ A new casa for the peoples (40:1-43:27)

The year is 573 B.C. (40:1). 13 years after the temple was destroyed Ezekiel is standing on a mountain. Ezekiel sees a new and glorious temple. More importantly, he sees the presence of God returning to this holy place. Two very important happenings for the Jews. Ezekiel sees the Lord's glory come through the east gate and into the temple, filling it with brilliance. God has returned to His people, and His people have returned to Him.

The Jews hearing this would have been comforted. New life would have flooded their hearts. This symbolic message would have made them alive again.

REVIEWS

ENCORE

➤ The prophets Jeremiah and Daniel lived at the same time as Ezekiel. Read their books for more insight into the turbulent times.

➤ Some Bible experts believe that the writer of Revelation borrowed the strange and highly symbolic imagery from the books of Ezekiel and Daniel. Revelation also borrows some of the content. For example, both books talk about a new Jerusalem.

Fire up the special effects and get out the 3-D glasses because you're going to need them. Imagine trying to explain something that you have never seen before, that is made out of substances that don't exist and that functions in dimensions that are not a part of this world (Star Trek comes to mind: replicators, wormholes, transporters, but that's nothing compared to what happens here). So if you saw a bunch of stuff like that, and then tried to explain it to other people, it might turn out a bit confusing, don't you think? And don't you think that you would end up making a lot of comparisons? "It was like this, except..." "It was sort of like that, only it didn't..." If you can deal with that kind of explanation then read the book of Ezekiel. Way cool.

Ezekiel opens with a bang. He has a vision of spinning wheels of fire in the sky and creatures made from all different people and animal parts. They shone like bronze. They had four faces and wings. They had hooves like calves. They moved like lightning. Are you getting this image? Break out the computer graphics and have a ball. I bet you thought Steven Spielberg invented these kinds of effects. Spielberg is good, God is GREAT. The stuff he shows Ezekiel blows away anything you've ever seen in your whole life.

One of my favorite parts of Ezekiel is seeing a song coming to life. Remember that old spiritual "Dem bones." You know, "the ankle bone connected to the shin bone, the shin bone connected to the knee bone, now hear the word of the Lord." That song came from Ezekiel. God transported Ezekiel to a valley full of old dry bones. Then God does his thing and the bones start rattling together, growing muscle and skin. God was giving Ezekiel a picture of the hope of Israel. God was saying, it's never too late. You'd think it was too late for these old bones, wouldn't you? But look what I can do with old dead things. "Now hear the word of the Lord."

This is a really good book to read in the daytime, if you get my drift. 'Scuse me a minute, I'm gonna go turn on a few lights. What? Oh, like YOU never get creeped out.

Lucas George "Sky" Walker

Daniel

SCHEDULE OF SCENES

Adam	Abraham	Moses	David	Daniel to Babylon	Cyrus releases Jews	Ezra	Jesus Is Born
4000+ B.C.	2100 B.C.	1500 B.C.	1000 B.C.	605 B.C.	538 B.C.	450 B.C.	7/6 B.C.

A meal the lions skipped

You probably heard these stories when you were young. Remember Daniel in the lion's den? How about Daniel in the fiery furnace? Remember that one? Well, this is the book. You're in the right place.

These stories are classic. And, they're classic tales of God at work in the young prophet – Daniel. It might be easy to think that the lions had just eaten seventeen bean burritos and weren't hungry. It might be just as easy to believe that the furnace was more like a sauna. Well, that's just not true. The lions were hungry, and proved it the next morning by scarfing up Daniel's accusers. The furnace was super hot and instantly torched some soldiers. Daniel's strange happenings are joined with equally strange visions in the second half of the book. The prophet tells some weird visions concerning the future, and of angels explaining what the vision meant.

This is a short book. These twelve chapters were intended to comfort exiled Jews who wondered if God had forsaken them. However, this book *could* comfort you. Through Daniel's stories and visions, God reminds us that He is Lord of creation. He has used His power to invade human history. And He will use that power to direct the future. In the end, God will rule forever. From Lions to the Millennium. . . God is the man!

QUOTABLES

"My God knew that I was innocent, and he sent an angel to keep the lions from eating me" (6:22). Daniel's explanation to the king of how he survived a night in the lion's den.

I saw what looked like a son of man coming with the clouds of heaven. . . . He will rule forever, and his kingdom is eternal (7:13–14). One of Daniel's end-time visions, which New Testament writers say refers to the second coming of Jesus.

SNEAK PREVIEW

1 Peter
Rock solid faith
in a stone cold life.

BEHIND the SCENES
of Daniel

STARRING ROLES

Nebuchadnezzar, Babylonian king who deports Daniel (1:1)
Daniel, Jewish prophet exiled in Babylon (1:6)
Shadrach, Meshach, Abednego, Daniel's friends who survive a fiery furnace (1:7)
Belshazzar, ruler who sees the handwriting on the wall (5:1)

PLOT

As a young nobleman in Jerusalem, Daniel is arrested by Babylonian soldiers. Daniel is taken with many other Jewish leaders to Babylon and forced to live there. The Babylonians quickly realize how intelligent he is, and put him through a three-year training program to become a royal advisor. With his pals, Shadrach, Meshach, and Abednego, he agrees to serve the king. The king demands that they reject God. These four guys refuse. When they're ordered to worship an idol and to stop their daily prayers, they don't give in. They're punished. Tossed in a furnace. They survive. Daniel is thrown in the lion's pit. He survives. Then, for 50 years or more Daniel serves various kings, first Babylonian, then Persian.

STAGE DIRECTIONS

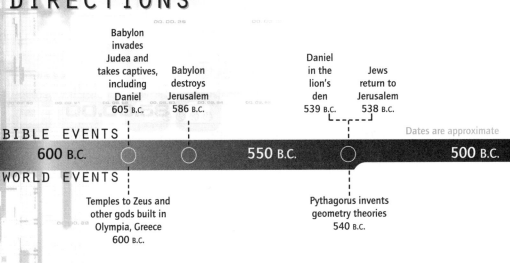

Babylon invades Judea and takes captives, including Daniel
605 B.C.

Babylon destroys Jerusalem
586 B.C.

Daniel in the lion's den
539 B.C.

Jews return to Jerusalem
538 B.C.

Dates are approximate

BIBLE EVENTS

600 B.C.   550 B.C.   500 B.C.

WORLD EVENTS

Temples to Zeus and other gods built in Olympia, Greece
600 B.C.

Pythagorus invents geometry theories
540 B.C.

AUTHOR AND DATE

Many believe Daniel wrote the book sometime after Cyrus defeated Babylon in 539 B.C., because that's one of the last events described in the stories about Daniel. Others say the book was written and compiled centuries later.

ON LOCATION

The stories and visions take place in Babylon, the capital city of the Babylonian Empire. It's the same place where Daniel and his friends are taken after the first Babylonian invasion of Judah in 605 B.C.

> The old saying, "I could see the handwriting on the wall," comes from Daniel's story of a terrified king watching a disembodied hand write a message on the palace wall (5:5).

> Old Testament writers rarely speak about life after death. But Daniel does, offering the Old Testament's clearest insight into the resurrection: "Many of those who lie dead in the ground will rise from death. Some of them will be given eternal life, and others will receive nothing but eternal shame" (12:2).

WHAT TO LOOK FOR

- **God in control.** These stories and visions point out one thing: God has your back. He's in control. He was in control of everything that happened to Israel. And, he's in control of everything that's happening to you too.
- **Easy Parts.** The book is divided into two parts, and they're easy to spot. The first six chapters are stories about Daniel and his friends. The remaining six chapters are about the mysterious visions of Daniel. See? Easy.
- **Apoca-who?** Daniel's visions are written in a writing style called apocalyptic literature. This type of writing is filled with stories about spirit-world creatures delivering messages to human beings concerning future events. It's full of symbolism that needs explaining or interpreting. And, even the interpretations are sometimes hard to understand. The point of the visions is not to provide a coded road map to the future, but to assure us that God's doing the driving.

EXTREME SCENES
from Daniel

⋝ God in the hot house (3:1-30)

When Babylon became a superpower, it stole some really smart people: Shadrach, Meshach, and Abednego. Because they're so smart, they're trained to work in the palace.

Later, at a palace event, they refuse to bow to a new idol built for the king. So, they're thrown into a hot furnace. How hot? It's so hot that it burns people *outside* the furnace. The guys didn't burn. They even got a visit from God. The king sees that these guys have been protected and vows to protect their right to worship God.

DIRECTOR'S NOTES

What's in a name? You decide. *Belteshazzar* means "Bel Will Protect." (Bel, also known as Marduk, was the chief god of Babylon.) *Daniel* means "God Is My Judge." Which name do you supposed Daniel preferred? Daniel 4:8

⋝ The case of the mysterious handwriting (5:1-30)

This one's straight from "Tales from the weird and mysterious". Before long, a new king throws a banquet for a thousand of his top-ranking officials. He parties a little too much and gets drunk. Then, he orders drinks served in the sacred cups stolen from the Jerusalem temple. Suddenly a human hand appears and writes these words on the plastered palace wall: "Numbered. Numbered. Weighed. Divided." The king is terribly frightened. The kings calls on Daniel to interpret the happening. Daniel says that God has measured you, and you're not even close to what it takes to be a king, and he warns that God will divide the kingdom. Does that happen? Yup. That night Babylon gets tackled by the Medes and the Persians.

⋝ Wanted: Lion tamer (6:1-28)

Daniel worked his way up to become one of the top three officials in the Persian palace. He had a lot of power. Jealous officials began a plot to kill him. They shrewdly convince King Darius to order the people to pray only to the king for the next 30 days, or face the lions. When the officials catch Daniel praying openly to God, they turn him in. The king is upset and tries to find a way to save Daniel. Since he can't go back on his law, Daniel is doomed. That night he's tossed in the pit with the lions. He's protected by an angel and survives. After a sleepless night, the king rushes to the den to find Daniel alive. The king orders Daniel removed and his accusers thrown in. The death they wished upon Daniel is the death they receive.

INTERVIEW
with the Stars

Taking the heat

Behind the Bible's next subjects are three young men whose names are never mentioned alone. These three friends are always together, no matter how hot things got serving King Nebuchadnezzar—and in this particular situation, the heat definitely was on. Shadrach, why don't you introduce your two companions and give us the background on your situation.

⋟ Shadrach

Myself, together with Meshach and Abed-Nego, served the king of Babylon, Nebuchadnezzar, as wise men. We had been trained along with Daniel in the king's service, but like Daniel, our highest allegiance was to our God, the Holy One of Israel.

⋟ Meshach

That's right. Usually, our work didn't conflict with our faith. But there were those in the king's palace who hated us. And they tried to create a trap for us by convincing the king to build this humongous statue and then have everyone bow down in worship before it.

⋟ Abed-Nego

We weren't trying to insult the king. But we simply refused to go along with the idea that Nebuchadnezzar was any kind of god. So we refused to bow before the statue.

That probably didn't go over too well with the king, did it?

⋟ Shadrach

You could say that. That's when things got really hot—literally.

INTERVIEW
with the Stars

⇒ Meshach

Yeah, our punishment for refusing to obey the order was to be thrown into a blazing furnace. And the king was so mad at us that he even threw on a couple extra logs to make sure the fire was *really* blazing!

So the heat's on; you're faced with a decision to give in and take a quick bow before this statue or end up as toast. Why not just bow and cross your fingers behind your back? God would know you really didn't intend to worship the king.

⇒ Abed-Nego

Sure that's one way of avoiding the heat. But we knew that our God could deliver us from anything—including a furnace and an angry king. And even if he didn't, we were not going to worship any king or serve any other gods but the one true God. And that's where we took our stand—together in the furnace.

⇒ Meshach

And God stood together with us in the furnace and let that king know without any doubt who was the true king of this universe.

We all face furnaces, whether it's nothing more than the heat of public ridicule or rejection. But when things get hot, remember that God can do amazing things in your lives, too.

⇒ Shadrach

And don't forget this either—you won't always be able to pick your "furnaces," but you sure can pick some good friends who will stand with you and with God.

INTERVIEW
with the Stars

Tough choices; tough stand

Do you think it matters to God if we stuff ourselves with junk food? What about if we're late for class by a few minutes each day? These are the small things that often get overlooked in the big picture, but **Behind the Bible's** next subject knew that even the small stuff mattered to God. Daniel had to make some tough choices in some very difficult situations. Daniel, tell us about your situation.

≽ Daniel

I was part of a group of Hebrew hostages taken to Babylon to work as slaves. Once we were there, my friends and I obviously made a good impression on our captors because we were assigned to training in the palace.

That had to be one of the better assignments to get, wasn't it? It had to be better than being a slave in the stables, for example.

≽ Daniel

Yes and no. Obviously we were well taken care of in the palace. We were given good food to eat and wine to drink, and were trained by the best of the best in Babylon. But being in that kind of environment also meant my friends and I had to make some tough choices.

What do you mean? It sounds like a no-brainer—eat the food, get trained, don't cause any trouble, and you're living like a king.

≽ Daniel

I suppose that's one way of looking at it. And there were plenty of other young men who took that road. But back in Judah, I already had dedicated my life to God. And that meant the choices I was going to make probably were going to look a bit different from the others. For example, my friends and I chose not to eat the rich food the king provided. Why? I felt if we compromised on the small things, like our diet, it would lead to other compromises down the road, and I didn't want to go there.

INTERVIEW
with the Stars

So how did you and your friends handle this? Did you have a protest or go on a fast?

⋙ Daniel

No, not at all. The idea wasn't to bring attention to ourselves and make everyone think we were better than anyone else was. Again, we wanted to find a way to accomplish our goal while honoring the men in charge. I quietly arranged to have our diet restricted to vegetables and water—and told the steward in charge to watch and see for himself if we didn't fare better after ten days. Then he could make the final decision. It was a win-win situation for everyone.

So even the seemingly small decision, like what you were going to eat and how you worked with others, had a big impact.

⋙ Daniel

That's right. You can't spend your life making decisions based on the claim that "everyone is doing it." If you're unwilling to stand alone and be different, then you won't make a difference with your life.

Thanks Daniel for your excellent reminder that God cares deeply about how we live, even down to the tiniest details, and wants us to honor Him in the way we live each day.

REVIEWS

If ever there was a stand-up guy, a real hero, it was Daniel. If he had been a cowboy, he'd be the one with the white hat. If he had been a cable guy, he'd be the one (the ONLY one) who'd be there on time. If he had been a high school football player he would have been one of those that always played fair, gave 110% AND worked hard for his grades too. If he'd been a tax collector…well, you can only take things so far.

But Daniel wasn't any of those things. He was actually a Hebrew teenager who became a prisoner in Babylon and eventually was a government official there. Kind of backwards from the usual, to go from jail into a political office instead of the other way around.

Daniel was a natural born leader. One of the first things he did as a prisoner was to refuse the rich Babylonian food and ask for more healthy kosher cuisine. So in essence he was offered a T-bone and asked for a salad instead. The amazing thing was after negotiating with the guards he got all the prisoners to switch too. He was a force to be reckoned with.

Daniel's leadership abilities didn't go unnoticed either. He became a political figure in Babylon, eventually third in command (pretty good for an ex-con). He interpreted mysterious handwriting on a wall for the king (contrary to what some scholars believe, it did NOT say "Kilroy was here" or "wash me"). He even risked death by lion's teeth because he would only pray to God rather than the king. He hung out with the three guys that got thrown into the fiery furnace for not bowing to an idol. Thanks to God's help, they came out not even smelling like smoke.

Daniel was just one of those people who knew who he was and what was important to him. He didn't get swayed by the opinions of people around him, no matter where he was or who he faced. He was the kind of hero every movie needs and every kid can look up to. He was the clean cut, sports star who really did live a good life (the kind of guy you almost wish you could dislike, but you just can't help liking). Real heroes are hard to find.

We gotta find a script for this. He's just too good to pass up. Look out Stallone and Schwarzenegger, here comes Daniel.

Jose Kanyusee

The stories of heroic Daniel are similar to the stories about earlier Israelite heroes, Joseph (Genesis 39–41) and Mordecai (Esther). Both stories contain dreams and interpretations.

For more of the apocalyptic style of writing, read the visions in Ezekiel and Revelation.

Check out how Jesus interprets Daniel's reference to someone committing sacrilege in the temple in Matthew 24:15–28. (Here's a cool tidbit of history for ya. Jesus tells people to run to the hills when they see this happening. About 40 years later, when Romans planted their idols on the temple mount, many Christians left. They escaped the destruction of Jerusalem in A.D. 70. Neat, huh?!)

Hosea

SCHEDULE OF SCENES

Adam	Abraham	Moses	David	Fall of Israel	Fall of Judah	Ezra	Jesus Is Born
4000+ B.C.	2100 B.C.	1500 B.C.	1000 B.C.	722 B.C.	586 B.C.	450 B.C.	7/6 B.C.

The prophet and the prostitute

Here's one for the record books. Hosea, famed prophet of doom and gloom. A man with a reputation for following God is asked to marry a prostitute. Did he? You bet. But, why in the world would God ask him to marry a prostitute? This is a story that shows God's creativity at getting His message across. It's a story of God's persistent love for the Jewish people. Centuries earlier He had entered into a covenant with them. He would be their God, they would be His people. He would take care of them, they would obey the laws He had given through Moses. That was the agreement anyway.

So, as you might expect, God fulfilled His part of the agreement, but Israel didn't. They totally disobeyed. God appointed prophets to urge people to return to God (again... sensing a theme here with the Israelites?). They listened, right? Nope. They treated the prophets just as poorly as they treated God. So, the story of Hosea is about how God nails the Israelites again. He pounds them into compliance? Demands and gets their obedience?

Not exactly. The story of Hosea is about God's inexplicable, relentless love even for people who treat Him like the enemy. For those who think the Old Testament God is cruel, Hosea reveals a preview of God practicing the compassion that His Son would later preach.

QUOTABLES

They sow the wind, and reap the whirlwind (8:7, NIV). Hosea's way of saying that if Israel doesn't repent, they'll pay for their evil. They'll sow idolatry, and reap annihilation.

You are not my people, and I am not your God (1:9, NIV). God's complaint about Israel stated exactly opposite of the wording in the covenant agreement between Israel and God (Leviticus 26:12).

SNEAK PREVIEW

> Job
> A very good man, in a very bad life.

BEHIND the SCENES
of Hosea

STARRING ROLES

Hosea, prophet to the northern Jewish nation of Israel (1:1)
Gomer, Hosea's prostitute wife (1:3)

PLOT

God tells Hosea to marry a prostitute. Why? To show the Israelites how they've spiritually prostituted themselves by worshiping other gods. When Hosea's wife has three children, only the first of whom is clearly identified as her husband's, God instructs Hosea to give them names that symbolize Israel's potential fate:
- Jezreel, meaning "God Scatters"
- Lo-Ruhamah, meaning "No Mercy"
- Lo-Ammi, meaning "Not My People"

Hosea's wife eventually takes off (maybe because her kids got some super depressing names?) and moves in with another man who treats her as his legal property. Acting on God's order, Hosea buys her back. Again, Hosea prophesies that the people will be punished if they don't quickly change their ways. Even though they refuse to stop sinning, God begs them to come back.

STAGE DIRECTIONS

Jeroboam becomes Israel's king 786 B.C.		Hosea becomes a prophet 750 B.C.	Israel destroyed by Assyria 722 B.C.

BIBLE EVENTS   Dates are approximate

800 B.C.   **750 B.C.**   **700 B.C.**

WORLD EVENTS

	First recorded Olympic games in Greece 776 B.C.		European nomads invent the saddle 700 B.C.

AUTHOR AND DATE

The first verse of the first chapter tells us that Hosea wrote the book. Little is known about Hosea.

Hosea lived and prophesied during the last 20 years or more of Israel's existence, before Assyria conquered the nation in 722 B.C. Hosea said he was called to become God's prophet sometime during the 40-year reign of King Jeroboam II (786–746 B.C.).

ON LOCATION

Hosea's story takes place in the northern Jewish nation of Israel. The Israelites there broke away from the union about 200 years before Hosea's time, during the reign of King Solomon's son.

WHAT TO LOOK FOR

- **Gomer.** The marriage between Hosea and Gomer is totally symbolic. Both Gomer and Israel are unfaithful to their beloved. Both become enslaved, Gomer by an unnamed master (3:2), and Israel by Assyria (10:6). Both are urged back in spite of their unfaithfulness and their abandoning the one who loved them.

EXTREME SCENES
from Hosea

⇒ A sinful marriage? (1:1-11)

God instructs Hosea to marry a prostitute. In that move he places Israel, Hosea, and Gomer smack in the middle of a drama that will be told forever. Why marry a prostitute? Well, the marriage is arranged to serve as a living, breathing symbol that Israel has broken its covenant with God, and has been unfaithful by worshiping idols. Gomer has three kids. Hosea gives them names that will remind Israel of its future: Jezreel, meaning "God Scatters"; Lo-Ruhamah, meaning "No Mercy"; and Lo-Ammi, meaning "Not My People." Even with these names, and, even with God's threat of punishment, God promises that there is coming a day when the people of Israel will be called "Children of the Living God," "My People," and "Shown Mercy." They will return home and enjoy the rich blessings of God.

⇒ Wife for sale (3:1-5)

Gomer leaves her husband and family to return to prostitution. Now, you'd think that would be the end of it. God made His point. Hosea made His prophecies. Everyone's said what they want. Well, not exactly. God has one more creative move. God gives Hosea a second bizarre command. Hosea is to fall in love with Gomer all over again. He's to do this to show that God still loves Israel. By this time, Gomer has shacked up with another man. Hosea needs to buy her back — just like someone would buy a slave. The price is 15 silver coins and about 10 bushels of grain. After this, Hosea warns that if Israel continues on its current course, God will use Assyria to destroy the nation and lead the people into captivity. Forgiveness and their freedom will come at a price. They'll have to give up their idols.

DIRECTOR'S NOTES

Ever had a raisin cake? If so, did you like it? In ancient times, cakes made of dried raisins were very popular. In face, some Israelites used raisin cakes in their pagan rituals as they worshiped a goddess known as the "queen of heaven." Hosea 3:1

REVIEWS

ENCORE

→ For a second opinion into what life was like in Israel during Hosea's day, read the nine-chapter book of Amos. He prophesied just a few years before Hosea.

→ Other prophets who lived and wrote in Hosea's time were Isaiah and Micah, though they ministered in the southern Jewish nation of Judah.

→ To see how other prophets compare Israel to an unfaithful bride, turn to Jeremiah 2—3 and Ezekiel 16, 23.

→ For a New Testament perspective on God's persistent love, read 1 John 4:7-21.

Have you ever been to one of those movies where you watched the story, but you knew that the underlying message was just as important as the story line and the characters? Some stories are not just stories. A story within a story, that's how it worked with Hosea.

If you just watched the movie you'd see a guy who foolishly married a real scuz and lived a life of heartache. Sad enough that he married a woman named Gomer (suddenly I feel like thanking my parents for not naming me Gomer), but she was also a prostitute and probably not a high dollar one. And she wasn't through being a prostitute just because she married a prophet (goh-ol-l-ly). She kept running off. Hosea would bring her home and then she'd run off again (shazam). His life was a plateful just keeping Gomer on the homestead. In the midst of it all they had three children to raise (su-prise, su-prise, su-prise!).

On the surface you say, sad story, horrible name for a wife, silly prophet. But underneath the surface, you'd be missing a big lesson. This lesson was meant for the Hebrew people that Hosea prophesied to.

You see, Hosea's marriage was a picture of the Hebrew's relationship with God. They were unfaithful spiritually just like Gomer was unfaithful physically. The Hebrews kept wandering away from God to the false gods around them. God kept going and bringing them home. But then they wandered off again.

Seems like a big price to pay to preach a sermon, doesn't it? To just what lengths would Hosea go to get his point across? To what lengths would God go to call his children back to a faithful lifestyle?

Some people say, "Hosea didn't really marry a prostitute. It's just a story." Others say, "Why not? As long as it got the point across." Wonder what Gomer and Hosea would have to say about it.

Wonder if she had a sister named Goober?

Anne D. Griffith

Joel

SCHEDULE OF SCENES

Adam	Abraham	Moses	David	Fall of Israel	Ezra	Jesus Is Born
4000+ B.C.	2100 B.C.	1500 B.C.	1000 B.C.	722 B.C.	450 B.C.	7/6 B.C.

Year of the locust

Incredible poetry. Terrifying images. A scary movie? A box office smash horror flick?

Not really. Joel's book is packed with stark images of frightening features. In the opening scene, locusts swarm in from the desert (info tidbit for ya...a single locust swarm can number into the billions...that's a lot-o-bugs!). These bugs are hungry, and begin to eat everything—wheat, barley, figs, grapes, pomegranates—everything an insect can eat. They eat the grass off the pastures. They strip trees bare.

As if this isn't bad enough, Joel warns the people that more trouble's ahead. Israel will be punished for sin. God is allowing an invasion force to assemble somewhere up north. The invasion is on its way, and it'll be a world of hurt on Israel. But there's hope. "It isn't too late," the Lord says, "You can still return to me with all your heart" (2:12). So, we've got a lot of locusts. A sinning nation. And an army gathering to invade the sinful nation. Pretty typical prophet stuff. In Joel, however, comes a somewhat new and different twist. He speaks of a judgment valley. A time when God will try the nations of the world and render His verdict. God promises to punish the guilty and defend the innocent. The Israelites are faced with a choice. It's not an easy one.

QUOTABLES

Beat your plowshares into swords, and your pruninghooks into spears (3:10, KJV). The exact opposite of what happens in the peaceful scene of Isaiah 2:4 and Micah 4:3. Joel warns the enemies of God to get ready for their last battle with Him.

Multitudes, multitudes in the valley of decision (3:14, KJV). A poetic description of the nations assembled for Judgment Day.

The judgment day of the Lord is coming soon (2:1).

Everyone who calls on the name of the Lord will be saved (2:32, NIV).

SNEAK PREVIEW

Judges
The ancient world and the old West. Rugged heroes and raging outlaws.

BEHIND the SCENES
of Joel

STARRING ROLES

Joel, a prophet of God (1:1)

PLOT

Swarms and swarms and swarms of locusts invade Israel, devouring the crops and then laying eggs that will hatch and consume the next generation of plants. OK...that would have just been the grossest thing ever. Can you imagine bugs everywhere? With harvest and pasture gone, people and livestock go hungry. Water holes dry up. Famine scars the land for years to come. Basically, things get pretty ugly very fast.

Joel uses this natural disaster to warn of an even worse catastrophe. Because the people have sinned, a monstrously enormous army will invade the land and strip it bare. Joel may be talking about an ancient invasion, an end-time apocalypse, or both.

It's not too late. And, God makes this really clear. In fact, he even pleads with the Israelites to come back to Him. The math from this point is simple. If they do return to God, they can escape a horrifying judgment that Joel simply calls "the day of the Lord."

AUTHOR AND DATE

The writer is the prophet "Joel, the son of Pethuel" (1:1). He's not mentioned anywhere else in the Old Testament, however, Joel is a really popular name and there are a dozen or so references to Joel throughout Scripture. The only other mention of the prophet Joel comes in a sermon by Peter on the day of Pentecost, when Peter declared that one of Joel's prophecies had just been fulfilled.

We don't have too much solid info about when Joel lived. His book is included among those of the prophets from the 700s B.C., just before Assyria destroyed the northern Jewish nation of Israel. Joel does talk about invaders coming from the north—as Assyria did in the 700s B.C., Babylon in the 500s B.C., and Alexander the Great of Greece in the 300s B.C. But Joel doesn't say who the invaders are, so we're pretty much left guessing the exact date of his lifespan.

ON LOCATION

Joel lived in the southern Jewish nation of Judah, and he mentions it a lot. But he also speaks of Israel. The name "Israel" could refer either to the northern nation of Israel or to the entire Jewish race, in both Israel and Judah (remember folks, they split a long time ago). He may have prophesied in the years before Assyria overran Israel.

WHAT TO LOOK FOR

- **The day of the Lord.** This is an important phrase in Joel, repeated five times in the short, three-chapter book. Many prophets use this phrase to talk about any time God does something to a nation or a generation of people—whether to punish or protect. Joel uses the phrase in both ways. It'll be really nasty when God punishes, and it'll be totally awesome when God saves the faithful.

- **The coming of the Holy Spirit.** A day is coming when God will pour out His spirit. That day arrives about two months after the resurrection of Jesus. Before Jesus ascends to heaven he tells the disciples to wait in Jerusalem until the Holy Spirit comes upon them. On the day of Pentecost the Holy Spirit arrives in an unforgettable scene.

EXTREME SCENES
from Joel

⇒ Land of bugs (1:1-20)

Locusts attack everything. They eat crops. They damage farms. Wheat is gone. Trees are wasted. The food is gone. The rivers are dry. And the livestock wander aimlessly in search of pasture. Would you like to live there? No way! And, even with all of this, Joel warns, the worst is yet to come.

DIRECTOR'S NOTES

At first glance, the locust seems like a pretty unlikely creature of destruction. It looks like a large grasshopper with two sets of wings and a brown-colored body two to three inches long. Nothing to be worried about, right? Did we mention that locusts travel in swarms large enough to blot out the sun in the sky? An average-size swarm of locusts, numbering in the millions, can strip a field completely bare—down to its last leaf—within minutes. Joel 1:4

⇒ Alien troops (2:1-27)

God's judgment is coming soon. Nasty troops are coming that will shake the mountains, the earth and even heaven. Hold up! Says Joel. It's not too late. The people of Judah can escape the disaster if only they will return to God with all their heart.

⇒ Young prophets (2:28-3:21)

Everyone will get God's Spirit. Sons and daughters will prophesy. Old dudes will dream incredible dreams. It is going to happen. But, there's some tough stuff to get though first. The message? Hang on. Return to God. Wait for God's Spirit.

REVIEWS

ENCORE

⇒ To see what Peter said was the fulfillment of Joel's prophecy about the Holy Spirit, read Acts 1—2.

⇒ For what other prophets say about the day of the Lord, read Amos 5:18-27; Zephaniah 1:14—2:3; Isaiah 13:6—14:2. For Jesus' insight, read Matthew 25:31-46.

⇒ Revelation 19:11-21 and 20:11-15 are judgment scenes similar to that in Joel.

Joel's prophecy is a disaster movie big time. You know the kind. There's an earthquake coming and the one lone seismologist tries to warn everyone. Or there's a volcano about to erupt but of course everyone goes to the Luau anyway. Or there's a flood or a fire or a ship turned upside down. Worse yet there's a meteor falling light years away or a tidal wave that is still miles offshore. You know the drill. First the hero has to get everyone to believe that disaster is coming. Then they have to make a plan. Then something has to go wrong with the plan at the last minute after all. Yep, Joel is a disaster waiting to happen. So what's the threat?

Locusts.

Locusts?

You got it. Locusts.

You mean, like grasshoppers? What's the big deal?

The experts disagree on whether Joel was talking about actual locusts or whether he was using the locusts as a symbol for the Assyrian army. Either way Israel would be in a heap of trouble.

Let's think it through. What if Joel did mean actual locusts? This was an farming society. Locusts were known to sweep through a place by the millions, eating the vegetation as they flew leaving it looking like a desert. That wouldn't be good news.

What if Joel meant the Assyrian army? That was even worse. They Assyrians didn't just eat vegetation. They were cruel soldiers who did unspeakable things.

So here's Joel running through town like a madman, "The locusts are coming! The locusts are coming!" while everyone is sitting on their porches sipping their ancient sodas and fanning themselves.

Whether Joel was prophesying insects or militia men, the bottom line for the Hebrews was that God's judgment was on its way. However God chose to judge the people there was no way to get away from it. That should have been an alert, shouldn't it? But you know how it goes. When times are easy, people tend to relax and not get excited.

Eventually the Assyrians did swoop in and disaster struck. I bet being right wasn't much of a consolation for Joel.

R. Miante

Amos

SCHEDULE OF SCENES

Adam	Abraham	Moses	David	Fall of Israel	Ezra	Jesus Is Born
4000+ B.C.	2100 B.C.	1500 B.C.	1000 B.C.	722 B.C.	450 B.C.	7/6 B.C.

God vs rich folk

Wanna know what God thinks about a rich society that exploits the poor and lets money do the talking? You're in the right place. Long before advocacy leaders and civil rights organizers, there was a sheepherder named Amos. With vicious honesty, he condemned rich people who smear poor people and ignore the helpless. Amos even gets into name-calling. He calls women who mistreat poor servants and beggars, "fat cows." (Ouch!) He doesn't stop there. Amos also condemned leaders, nobles, and merchants who cheat honest people, tax them to death, and twist the face of justice until no one can recognize it anymore. *That's* not even all. He strikes at the leaders of Israel. He says, "Guys . . . GET OUT!"

God doesn't stand for this kind of status quo. He stepped into human history and rearranged Israel's system. Suddenly, with the swooping of an Assyrian invasion force, the rich were on the same level as the poor. This book is about God's concern for social issues, his concern for the poor, broken and homeless.

QUOTABLES

Prepare to meet your God (4:12, NKJV).

Let justice roll on like a river (5:24, NIV).

SNEAK PREVIEW

> Philemon
> A runaway slave. A favor owed. A life saved in more ways than one.

BEHIND the SCENES
of Amos

STARRING ROLES

Amos, prophet, shepherd, and fig farmer (1:1)
Amaziah, a priest who chases Amos off (7:10)

PLOT

God calls on Amos, a shepherd and fig grower, to leave his small village at the desert's edge in the southern Jewish nation of Judah. What's the call? Deliver a prophetic message to the northern nation of Israel —a nation packed with cash. Wealthy are getting wealthier at the expense of the poor. In court, the verdict goes to the client with the most money. Father and son sleep with the same prostitute. People go through the motions of worship, thinking rituals are enough to appease God. Things are really, really bad.

Amos' words are simple: "God will crush you." A priest named Amaziah replies, "Amos, take your visions and get out!" (7:12) So, Amos leaves, but not before promising that Amaziah's children will be killed in the war, and the priest will die in a foreign country. As for Israel, Amos leaves the people with a hopeful promise: God will one day restore the nation he has been forced to destroy.

STAGE DIRECTIONS

	Amos begins his ministry 760 B.C.		Israel destroyed by Assyria 722 B.C.

Dates are approximate

BIBLE EVENTS

800 B.C.   750 B.C.   700 B.C.

WORLD EVENTS

Ohio River people build earth burial mounds 800 B.C.	King Romulus founds Rome 753 B.C.	Ethiopia starts 50 year rule of Egypt 716 B.C.

AUTHOR AND DATE

No mistake who wrote this book. The author and his homeland are noted in the first verse of the first chapter. He was both a herder and a farmer, living about 10 miles south of Jerusalem. He was not a prophet, until God gave him this message to deliver to Israel (7:14–15). Apparently, Amos was an educated man. His writing style suggests that he's not just a farmer.

He says he lived when Jeroboam was king of Israel (786–746 B.C.). The national prosperity that Amos talks about fits the conditions during the later part of Jeroboam's reign, beginning about 760 B.C.

ON LOCATION

Amos leaves his hometown and country—Tekoa, 10 miles south of Jerusalem in the southern Jewish nation of Judah—and takes God's message to Bethel, a worship center in the northern nation of Israel.

WHAT TO LOOK FOR

- **Crimes of injustice.** Social injustice is out of control and no one's doing anything about it. The poor are starving. Slavery is growing. Merchants cheat people with rigged scales. Judges are bought and paid for. The poor and powerless don't have a chance.
- **Empty worship.** Many people do nothing more than go through the motions of worship. They think that bringing the appropriate sacrifice is all they need to do to please God.
- **The day of the Lord.** This is a phrase used by many Jews of the time. It refers to a day when God will deliver Israel from harm and punish Israel's enemies. But like other prophets, Amos warns that the day of the Lord is nothing for Israel to look forward to. It'll be a lot worse than they're expecting.

> Civil rights leader Martin Luther King, Jr., drew heavily from the ideas in Amos. In King's famous "I Have a Dream" speech, he said he dreamed that one day "the heat of injustice and oppression" would become "an oasis of freedom and justice."

> Amos was perhaps the first Bible prophet to write down his messages.

EXTREME SCENES
from Amos

On a mission (1:1; 7:12-15)

Remember this: Amos ain't no prophet. He's a farmer. And, he's very quick to remind people of that. He's also quick to tell people that the only reason he's doing the whole prophecy thing is because God told him to do it. His herds are in a different country, the rival Jewish nation of Judah, in the southland. Acting on God's orders, Amos leaves his work. He leaves his village and his country. He travels 200 miles north of his home to Bethel to deliver God's message.

The verdict: You get crushed (2:1-3:15)

The message Amos delivers is blunt. "The Lord said: 'I will punish Israel for countless crimes, and I won't change my mind. They sell honest people for money, and the needy are sold for the price of sandals. They smear the poor in the dirt and push aside those who are helpless'" (2:6–7). The result will be swift. God is going to crush them. You can't outrun it. You can't overpower it. You're in super huge trouble.

Fat cows (4:1-13)

Amos calls the women of Samaria fat cows. This is a man with guts. Actually, he calls them "Cows of Bashan". These were actually famous cows from southern Syria, noted for being pampered, prime stock, well fed and well bred. Amos goes on to accuse these women of mistreating the poor and needy. He reminds them that their time is coming. What's coming? They'll be hooked through the nose and strung together with ropes.

180...Please!! (5:1-27)

The time is late. The judgment is coming. God still gives Israel a chance to mend its ways. He pleads with them to turn back. If they do, they'll live. God won't receive their worship until the Jews stop doing wrong and start doing right. So, what's God after? He wants justice that doesn't end. He wants the scales of justice balanced. No matter how rich you are.

The plumb line (7:1-17)

God gives Amos a vision about how crooked Israel really is. In the vision, God stands next to a wall holding a string with a weight tied to the end of it. The string is used to measure the straightness of the wall. The wall is crooked. God proclaims that the Israelites are crooked too. And, like crooked walls, the Israelites must be taken down.

All isn't lost (9:11-15)

Even if Israel refuses to repent, all is not lost. Even though God's contract with the Jews (remember the Ten Commandments?) gives him the right to annihilate Israel for breach of contract, God refuses to do so. Instead, God gives Israel a hopeful message. He'll rebuild what gets destroyed. Promise.

REVIEWS

Like Joel, Amos saw the coming judgment. Like Joel, he was usually ignored or treated like a freak. Prophets get that a lot. When you start a conversation with "Well, I was talking to God the other day, and He said..." people get a little weird. I mean Moses walking down off the mountain with big stone tablets is ONE thing but, without proof or witnesses, a lot of people would have thought he was SMOKING the burning bush instead of talking to it.

Anyway, Amos saw that the people were screwing up big time. The rich were getting richer, and the poor were getting poorer. It wasn't a new story, but it was an evil one. In fact it was directly against God's law. When God established the Hebrew nation he gave them very specific guidelines for living. Some of those guidelines were directly aimed at making sure everyone got a fair shake. Sure, people could be smart, work hard, and build a business, but not at the cost of letting other people starve or making money off of your neighbor's misfortune. The whole point was that we should love and care for each other like God loves and cares for us. This message is important enough to get repeated a bunch of times throughout the Bible, and from several different angles. If there is a quiz in the afterlife, this WILL be on it. So learn it.

Amos basically confronted the people with their disobedience and hypocrisy. Does it surprise you that the people didn't respond well? Who wants to be reminded of their failures and faults when things seem to be going so well? It was easier for them to call him a nutcase than to look into their own hearts and see the truth.

Amos was in the right, though. The whole identity of the nation was based on a covenant with God. The people were not keeping up their end of the agreement. Amos' prophet radar was on full red alert because he knew that judgment was on the way.

He was right. About 40 years later Assyria made Israel's life miserable. Too bad nobody listened.

Nita A. Lender
Nora B. Borrower

ENCORE

> Besides Amos, two other prophets known for their concern about the poor and other social justice issues are Micah and Isaiah.

> You'll find social justice themes addressed in the New Testament by Jesus (Matthew 5–6; 25:31-46) and throughout the short book of James.

Obadiah

Payback

It's no fun to watch the bad guys win. We seem to have this inner sense of justice that makes us want to go after the evil dude who's winning.

Obadiah had this same feeling. He saw injustice about as bad as it gets. He saw what happened after invaders swarmed on Judah. Jewish refugees ran for their lives to the neighboring country of Edom. Did Edom embrace them? Nope, Edom ambushed them. Then Edom arrested them, turned them over to the invaders, and scavenged Judah for anything left behind. Creeps!

The Jews didn't live to see Edom get what it deserved. All they had was God's promise that they'd pay for what they did. God settles His accounts. And he does it justly. Sooner or later, sometimes later, sin is punished. Always. That's the message of Obadiah. Payback...it just ain't no fun.

QUOTABLES

As you have done, it will be done to you (Verse 15, New International Version). Obadiah's warning to the country of Edom is the flip side of the Golden Rule: "Treat others as you want them to treat you" (Matthew 7:12).

SNEAK PREVIEW

> Acts
> Sometimes a revolution begins in the most unlikely places...like back rooms and broken hearts.

BEHIND the SCENES
of Obadiah

STARRING ROLES

Obadiah, a prophet who warns the people of Edom that they'll get the punishment they deserve (1:1)

PLOT

Invaders attack and destroy the southern Jewish nation of Judah. Edom, Judah's neighbor south of the Dead Sea, decides to get its kicks. Edom even arrests the Jewish refugees and turns them over to the invaders. Then Edom raids Judah to steal anything the attackers may have missed. Obadiah promises that Edom will be wiped out and Judah will be restored.

STAGE DIRECTIONS

BIBLE EVENTS

Babylon invades Judah and takes captives
605 B.C.

Babylon suppresses Judean rebellion, taking more captives
597 B.C.

Babylon destroys Jerusalem
586 B.C.

Jews start returning to Jerusalem
538 B.C.

Dates are approximate

600 B.C.   550 B.C.   500 B.C.

WORLD EVENTS

Temples to Zeus and other gods built on Olympia, Greece
600 B.C.

Chinese philosopher Confucius is born
551 B.C.

AUTHOR AND DATE

Obadiah is the prophet who wrote this book. We know nothing about him except that he had a common name that means "worshiper of the Lord."

Because Obadiah talks about Edom's treachery against Judah, we assume the book was written sometime after 586 B.C. That's when Babylon conquered Judah, with support from Edom.

ON LOCATION

The events unfold in the southern Jewish country of Judah, and in Edom south of the Dead Sea. When Babylon conquered Judah, the Edomites collaborated with the invaders, working against their Hebrew cousins.

WHAT TO LOOK FOR

- **Part 1 is doom, Part 2 is hope.** Verses 1–14 talk about how God will punish the people of Edom for their cruelty. The rest of the short book (verses 15–21) promises that the Jews will one day return to their land, and will even capture the land of their enemies, including Edom.

INSIDE SCOOP

> The Jews and Edomites were related. Jews descended from Jacob. Edomites descended from his twin brother Esau.

> Obadiah is the shortest book in the Old Testament, with only one chapter and 21 verses.

> Edom was famous for its wise men. One of Job's well-educated friends came from there (Job 2:11).

EXTREME SCENE
from Obadiah

Edom: You're goin' down!

The people of Edom lived in secure mountaintop fortresses. That doesn't stop God. He vows to bring them down regardless of their wimpy fortresses. God vows to wipe them out and give away their land. The reason? The Edomites, (descendants of Esau), celebrate and even contribute to the destruction of Judah. And, to be even more cruel, the Edomites go around stealing all their friends' stuff. Then, they turn in the refugees. Here's the interesting thing: Israel is being punished...that's why they were invaded. Now, Edom is being punished for taking advantage of the Israelites on the run. Both are being punished. But, one day, Israel will ultimately conquer and will be restored.

DIRECTOR'S NOTES

There was no love lost between the Edomites, the descendants of Esau, and the Israelites, the descendants of Jacob. Apparently the sibling rivalry that existed between the two brothers was passed on to their descendants. When the Israelites were on their way to the Promised Land for the first time, the king of Edom refused to let them cross through his land. As a result, the Israelites were forced to travel through the desert. The bad feelings between the two countries continued for centuries. Obadiah 1

REVIEWS

ENCORE

→ Read Jeremiah 49:7–22. The message is nearly identical to Obadiah 1-9.

→ For other prophecies against Edom, read Amos 1:11-12; Isaiah 34; and Ezekiel 25:12-14.

Obadiah's prophecy was a little like the game show Family Feud. Ever seen it ? Two families stand on opposite sides of the stage and try to outdo each other. They answer questions. They huddle. They cheer. They hope that the other team will flub a question so *they* can get the points.

Obadiah's prophecy was addressed to the Edomites. Remember who they were? Let's go on a little history expedition. The Hebrews were called Israelites because they all descended from a man named Israel. Before his name was changed to Israel it was Jacob. Jacob had a twin brother named Esau. Jacob was a bit of a swindler back then. One day he tricked Esau out of the family birthright. Jacob got the biggest share of the inheritance and the role as family leader. Esau got left out in the cold. Esau's name was later changed to Edom. Is it becoming clear?

So here you have these two nations, Israel and Edom, living side by side with their own brand of family feud still alive and well even after hundreds of years (some old habits *really* die hard). When something bad happened to the Hebrews, Edom would cheer from their side of the stage. When something good happened to the Hebrews, the Edomites would "boo" and look disappointed. Eventually, this got on God's nerves. (Which is not something you want to do. Remember the big flood? Sodom and Gomorrah? If I was going to tick someone off, I wouldn't pick the guy who invented lightning, tornadoes, and earthquakes. Maybe that's just me.) Obadiah's prophecy was God's way of telling the Edomites, "Enough! Quit picking on my kids or you'll be sorry". He wasn't kidding.

The bottom line of Obadiah's prophecy was that Edom would eventually be completely destroyed, wiped out, left in the dust. About 400 B.C. the Arabs did drive the Edomites out of their land (get this...most of them ran to Judah for asylum). By A.D. 70 Edom disappeared from history.

So all you have to do to know if the Old Testament prophets knew what they were talking about is stop by a map. Look for the land of Edom. You won't find it. The empty space where it used to be is proof that nobody should mess with God's children. God's side ALWAYS wins in the end. Lucky for the Israelites that they were His family in this "Family Feud." I wonder if he'd be my "phone a friend" if I was on "Who Wants to be a Millionaire"? Could there BE a better "lifeline"?

Philemon T. Hall

Jonah

SCHEDULE OF SCENES

Adam	Abraham	Moses	David	Divided Kingdom	Fall of Israel	Ezra	Jesus Is Born
4000+ B.C.	2100 B.C.	1500 B.C.	1000 B.C.	931 B.C.	722 B.C.	450 B.C.	7/6 B.C.

Prophet overboard

It's a fish story gone wild. It's a boat trip gone wrong. It's a prophet on the run. This is not your standard book of prophecy. This is the only book in which a prophet gets swallowed by a fish. And it's the only prophetic book that doesn't have a collection of prophecies. Instead, it serves up a minuscule one-sentence prophecy, which turns out wrong.

God tells the prophet Jonah to go east and deliver a message of doom to Assyria. Instead, Jonah chickens out and runs west. He boards a ship on the Mediterranean. Why the heck does he do this? He might have been afraid of the Assyrians. The Assyrians were ruthless. For entertainment, Assyrian soldiers cut open the stomach of live prisoners, inserted a live cat, and swiftly sewed the stomach back up. Then they watched the cat claw its way out. Pretty gruesome, huh? I'd be running, too. Maybe he was afraid that his prophecy wouldn't come true. Maybe he couldn't get enthusiastic about delivering death threats to an empire that thought fine art was stone carvings showing captured enemies getting impaled on stakes. Maybe he was in search of breath mints. Who knows.

Jonah is the only prophet of God whose ministry was not directed to the Jews. Despite his reservations, Jonah took his ministry to Assyria. This book sends a clear message: God's love is available to everyone.

QUOTABLES

The Lord sent a big fish to swallow Jonah (1:17).

SNEAK PREVIEW

> **Deuteronomy**
> What kind of heart does God want us to have toward him?

BEHIND the SCENES
of Jonah

STARRING ROLES

Jonah, a Jewish prophet who reluctantly takes God's message to an Assyrian city (1:1)

PLOT

God tells Jonah to go to Nineveh, a huge city deep within the feared Assyrian Empire. Jonah's assignment is to warn the citizens that God will trash their city in 40 days.

Jonah, totally afraid, boards a ship, and heads in the opposite direction. A fierce storm erupts. To appease God, the sailors throw Jonah overboard. The prophet is swallowed by a large fish. Three days later the fish pukes Jonah onto a beach. From there, Jonah walks to Nineveh and delivers the message. And, hey. Guess what?! The people repent and God spares them. Jonah gets ticked that the prophecy hasn't come true and goes to the desert for a one-man pity party. The book ends abruptly with God explaining that He has a right to show mercy on the 120,000 citizens of Nineveh.

STAGE DIRECTIONS

Jeroboam begins his 41-year reign
786 B.C.

Jonah goes to Nineveh, perhaps before end of Jeroboam's reign
746 B.C.

Dates are approximate

BIBLE EVENTS

800 B.C.   **750** B.C.   **700** B.C.

WORLD EVENTS

Solar eclipse confirmed in Chinese history
775 B.C.

Assyrians choose Nineveh as capital, and start rebuilding it
705 B.C.

AUTHOR AND DATE

We don't know if Jonah wrote the book. But the story **is about** Jonah, the son of Amittai. His dad was a prophet from a village near Nazareth. Jonah also supported King Jeroboam's successful efforts to expand the borders of Israel in the late 700s B.C. (2 Kings 14:25).

If Jonah wrote the book, he probably did it during the eighth century B.C., maybe during the reign of Jeroboam (786–746 B.C.). It is possible that someone else recorded this short, dramatic story. It could have been passed along by word of mouth for generations.

ON LOCATION

The story begins in Israel, continues somewhere aboard a ship in the Mediterranean Sea, then inside a fish. It ends in Nineveh, an Assyrian city in what is now northern Iraq.

WHAT TO LOOK FOR

- **One Quick Prophecy.** Books by other prophets contain a lot of prophecies. Not Jonah. It has one prophetic sentence: "Forty days from now, Nineveh will be destroyed!" (3:4). The rest of this short book tells the story of what leads up to this prophecy, and what happens afterward.
- **God's Compassion.** Many Jews in Bible times consider themselves to be not just the chosen people of God, but the only people of God. The only ones who can worship Him. The only ones He cares about. Not true! The story of Jonah confirms that God cares deeply about non-Jewish people as well.

EXTREME SCENES
from Jonah

➢ A quick dip (1:1-2:10)

When Jonah runs, he gets creative. He buys a ticket on a boat and heads in the opposite direction. God churns up a storm that nearly sinks the ship. Finally, in desperation, the sailors turn to prayer. Jonah confesses that he is the cause of their trouble, and he advises them to throw him overboard. At first they refuse. Then, to protect themselves, they toss him overboard. The sea calms down. Jonah is swallowed by a huge fish. He remains inside for three days, praying a prayer of thanks to God for rescuing him. Then the fish vomits him up onto a beach. Jonah becomes a partner in the first whale hurl.

➢ Jonah finally obeys (3:1-10)

Finally, Jonah walks to Nineveh and delivers the assigned message: "Forty days from now, Nineveh will be destroyed!" (3:4). For whatever reason (maybe because he was covered with whale puke?) the Assyrians believe him. The Assyrians (even the king) stop eating and drinking, dress in ragged clothes, and sit in the dust. They do this to show their sorrow. They won't even let their animals eat or drink. This is serious repentance! When God sees this, he has pity and does not destroy them as he had planned.

DIRECTOR'S NOTES

Ninevah was the largest city in the ancient world. In fact, the area referred to as Ninevah probably included several other cities. The wall around Ninevah stretched for almost eight miles. Each of its fifteen gates was "guarded" by a statue of a bull. Jonah 3:3

➢ Mad, mad Jonah (4:1-10)

Jonah is super ticked. He complains to God. "You are a kind and merciful God, and you are very patient. You always show love, and you don't like to punish anyone, not even foreigners. Now let me die! I'd be better off dead" (4:2–3). Ironically, Jonah is one of the few prophets in the Bible who is successful. He convinces the people to repent. Yet he thinks he's a failure. God disagrees. The point of the entire story is that God deeply cares about everyone, and He is eager to show mercy to anyone genuinely sorry for the wrongs they have done. Anyone. Even those covered with whale vomit.

REVIEWS

ENCORE

➤ For another story about God showing mercy to a non-Jew, read the short book of Ruth.

➤ For more about God's concern for non-Jews, read Genesis 12:1-3; Isaiah 42:6-7; 49:6; Romans 10—11.

➤ For background on what life was like in Israel during Jonah's day, read the book of Amos. The two prophets ministered about the same time.

The story of Jonah is like the show "Survivor," except that instead of a bunch of people against the elements and each other, it's one guy against God's will (who do you think will win?). On one side, you have a prophet who is so caught up in his own hate and prejudice against Nineveh that he would rather run from God than preach there. On the other side, you have God, who wants Jonah to bring His message to Nineveh as much for Jonah's good as theirs. God was calling Jonah to preach to his enemy. Nineveh was the capital city of Assyria. Assyria was a nation of wicked, mean Nazi types that deserved every bad thing that came their way, and they were *always* picking on the Israelites.

God, who loves everybody (even the ones He has to punish) saw a way to help both the delinquent prophet and the evil empire. Jonah could help the Assyrians change their evil ways and, in doing so, learn to let go of the hatred that was in his heart.

The first round seems to go to the prophet when he hops a ship that's headed the opposite direction from anywhere near Nineveh. Seems to, that is; God just sends a storm to stop the boat and, a REALLY big fish, which swallows Jonah and gives the prophet three days to evaluate his choices. Three days INSIDE the fish, that is. Talk about "time out."

At the end of round one, Jonah does go to Nineveh (big surprise).

That's the most famous part of the story, but in round two is the real test. Once Jonah preaches to Nineveh, much to his surprise, they actually LISTEN AND BELIEVE. They repent of their sin and God puts off their destruction. A happy ending? Not yet. Jonah is still so full of hate for these people that he is disappointed that they repented. Did you get that? The **prophet** is **disappointed** that the people **repented.** Not only is he disappointed, he doesn't even pretend not to be (can't you just **see** him going "Oh, MAN, why do I hafta be so GOOD at what I do"). Maybe a couple more days in the fish would have changed his attitude quicker, but I'm thinking at that point he wouldn't have been able to get close enough to any Assyrians to preach to them.

Jonah's story is important in that it shows God's grace is meant for everybody, the good guys and the bad guys. It can seem like the Old Testament paints a picture of a God that only cares for Israel, but Jonah's story shows that God cares about every nation's obedience. He was on Jonah's side, even when Jonah wasn't. He's on the side of what's good for ALL of us, even when we're not.

In the human race, it's not important **when** you cross the finish line, just that you **do** cross it. And if you can help some others get there too, you'll cross it in style!

Moe B. Richard

Micah

SCHEDULE OF SCENES

Adam	Abraham	Moses	David	Fall of Israel	Fall of Judah	Ezra	Jesus Is Born
4000+ B.C.	2100 B.C.	1500 B.C.	1000 B.C.	722 B.C.	586 B.C.	450 B.C.	7/6 B.C.

Painting a portrait of God

Micah paints two pictures of God. First, he paints God's holiness. He uses broad strokes that portray God's goodness and justice. Second, he paints bigger strokes to show us God's love. He paints in the details of God's love... His compassion. His forgiveness. His unending passion for his creation.

The book of Micah is like a portrait of God with two distinct meanings. The broad picture: You've sinned and God will punish you. The detailed picture: God loves you and He'll forgive you. Like a painting that's constantly being painted, Micah identifies the sins of the Jews and the consequences they'll have to face. Then he consoles them with the promise that, no matter what, God loves them.

Three times Micah warns the Jews that because of their nation's long-standing sinfulness, the nation will die. Then he promises a saving miracle: one day the nation will be restored. Not because the Jews deserve it for good conduct, but because God loves them and forgives them. This isn't just a history lesson. It's a glimpse into the character of God. What he did for the Jews, He continues to do for all people. He stands against people who do evil, but loves them nonetheless.

QUOTABLES

They will beat their swords into plowshares and their spears into pruning hooks. Nation will not take up sword against nation, nor will they train for war anymore (4:3, NIV).

Bethlehem . . . you are one of the smallest towns in the nation of Judah. But the Lord will choose one of your people to rule the nation (5:2). Because of this verse, some Jews in ancient times believed the Messiah would be born in Bethlehem, birthplace of Jesus.

What does the Lord require of you but to do justly, to love mercy, and to walk humbly with your God? (6:8, NKJV).

SNEAK PREVIEW

Haggai
First things first. What's *your* priority in life?

BEHIND the SCENES
of Micah

STARRING ROLES

Micah, a rural Judean prophet who criticizes the leaders of Israel and Judah (1:1)

PLOT

This is a collection of poetry, so you won't find a whole lot of plot here. Within his poetry, Micah denounces corrupt officials in both the northern Jewish nation of Israel and the southern nation of Judah. These judges take bribes, priests teach God's word only for money, and prophets tell fortunes for profit. Rulers mislead the people, nobles take advantage of the poor, and the masses take their pleas to idols.

Micah promises destruction for what's going on. Assyria, in fact, destroys Israel during Micah's lifetime, in 722 B.C. Assyria also stomps Judah about 20 years later, stopping short of destroying it. But another nation, Babylon, wipes out Judah in 586 B.C.

Micah promises that a time will come when the Jewish nation will be restored and worship God.

STAGE DIRECTIONS

	Micah begins several decades of ministry 742 B.C.	Israel is destroyed by Assyria 722 B.C.	
BIBLE EVENTS			Dates are approximate
750 B.C.	○○	**725 B.C.**	**700 B.C.**
WORLD EVENTS			
	Ivory carving popular in Samaria, Phoenicia, Egypt 750 B.C.	Merchants in Greece prosper, farmers starve 725 B.C.	

AUTHOR AND DATE

The prophecies are from Micah, a rural prophet who lived in a small village about 25 miles southwest of Jerusalem.

Verse one says that his ministry took place during the reigns of three Judean kings: Jothan, Ahaz, and Hezekiah. These men reigned between 742 and 687 B.C. Decades later, the prophet Jeremiah quoted Micah, confirming that during the days of Hezekiah, Micah predicted "Jerusalem will be plowed under and left in ruins" (Jeremiah 26:18; compare to Micah 3:12). Micah lived to see the Assyrians destroy Israel.

ON LOCATION

Micah delivers his prophecies in the southern Jewish nation of Judah. But he criticizes both Judah and the northern Jewish nation of Israel, often addressing them by the names of their capital cities: Jerusalem (Judah) and Samaria (Israel).

WHAT TO LOOK FOR

- **A pattern of doom and salvation.** The prophecies are arranged in an obvious pattern: doom (1:1–2:11), salvation (2:12–13), doom (3:1-12), salvation (4:1–5:15), doom (6:1–7:7), salvation (7:8–20). Like the other prophets, Micah warns that sin gets you in a heap of trouble with God. But Micah also assures that punishment is not the last word. God still loves the people, and when the punishment is over he will prove it.

- **Charges of injustice.** Micah criticizes the leaders and nobles for misusing their power. He gets kinda disgusting in 3:1-3 and uses some pretty hairy images to describe how evil the leaders have become. Using this kind of stark, symbolic imagery, Micah attacks the rich and powerful for abusing their wealth. Not only do they leave the helpless to fend for themselves, the leaders make dishonest decisions against the poor. They cheat families out of homes and land. They worship wealth, not God. They revere power, not justice. They admire achievement, not mercy. All in all, they're pretty mean people.

EXTREME SCENES
from Micah

⇒ Truth twisters (1:1-16)

Because they've sinned so much, both Jewish nations will be destroyed. God's gonna trash Samaria. He's going to leave it in ruins. (1:6–7). That's not all. Whatever He does to Samaria, He's going to do to Jerusalem. (1:9). So, what are the charges anyway? The people hate justice. They're cruel. Leaders accept bribes. Priests teach only for money.

These are people who have lost perspective, and are totally clueless about what God can do to set them straight.

DIRECTOR'S NOTES

The Israelites like to wear their hair and beards long. They thought it made them look attractive and manly (or womanly, depending on the sex). To them, a clean-shaven head was something to be ashamed of. Aside from priests and Levites, the only Israelite man who would have considered shaving his head was one who was going through a time of extreme sadness or mourning. Micah 1:16

⇒ S-T-O-P! (5:2-5)

God refuses to abandon the Jewish people because of their sins. They will have to face punishment, but not forever. In the future the Jewish people will repent of their sins, stop doing evil, and return to God. In return, God will bless them by sending a chosen leader, a Messiah, who would lead them into peace. He even mentions Bethlehem as being the birthplace of the person who will eventually rule.

Guess what! Seven hundred years later, wise men from an eastern nation followed a light to Israel. When they arrived in Jerusalem and asked King Herod if they could see the child who had been born king of the Jews, Herod was upset. After all, he was the king of the Jews, and he had no newborn son. He would kill this newborn threat, if he could. Herod turned to the religious leaders and asked them where the Messiah would be born. They turned to the book of Micah and found their answer: Bethlehem. Ooooohh. Spooky!

REVIEWS

ENCORE

⤍ Amos was another prophet concerned about social problems.

⤍ Read Matthew 2:1-16 to see how the Jews of Jesus' day interpreted Micah's prophecy about a Jewish leader coming from Bethlehem (5:2).

⤍ To read more about the two sides of God—judgment and mercy—turn to Nahum.

⤍ For more about the kind of social concern that Micah expressed in 6:8, read Isaiah 1 and the Sermon on the Mount (Matthew 5:1–7:29).

Micah was a cable-access sort of prophet (Cue Music: GOD'S WORLD, GOD'S WORLD, PARTY TIME, EXCELLENT !!!). After the nation of Israel divided into the northern and southern kingdoms most of the prophets spoke only to one kingdom or the other. Sort of like choosing a network to appear on. But not Micah. He preached to anyone who would listen. He had no affiliates, he only had a message.

His message was as wide as his audience. He was one of those guys who could talk hellfire and brimstone but make you feel loved at the same time. His message included *loads* of judgment. God was going to judge the sins of Israel and Judah. There was no getting around it, but there *was* hope of getting through it. Micah never let hope get too far away.

Micah's reputation was as a down-to-earth kind of guy. He didn't preach against sin as a generality. He got down and dirty with it. He spent a lot of time dealing with social sins like fraud, theft, hypocrisy, injustice, extortion and lying. He wanted his people to stop hurting each other and stop breaking God's heart in the process. Peace, love and flowers, man. . .OR ELSE !

I get the impression that Micah was one of those preachers who could explain to me in detail the whys and wherefores of an argument, yet could put the argument aside and have me over for supper. Sort of like he was a leftover from the hippies (did Israel experience the '60s WAY before the rest of us?) who never figured out that the love revolution was over (He was right. It's NEVER over). While most of his contemporaries had learned to put on the suits (and tunics) and play the game, Micah just never did. He kept on believing that God meant what he said (imagine that). He kept on believing that people should obey God. All people. He kept right on preaching to whoever would listen.

I think if Micah were living today he'd be the preacher who would lead the church congregation on Sunday morning, work at the homeless shelter in the afternoon, read goodnight stories at the orphanage and then go to bed wondering if he should have done more.

Harry Proffit

Nahum

SCHEDULE OF SCENES

Adam	Abraham	Moses	David	Fall of Israel	Fall of Ninevah	Fall of Judah	Ezra	Jesus Is Born
4000+ B.C.	2100 B.C.	1500 B.C.	1000 B.C.	722 B.C.	586 B.C.	586 B.C.	450 B.C.	7/6 B.C.

The end of terror

Get this. Nahum's name means comfort. So, you'd expect that his book is filled with messages about pillows, flowers and people resting in God's forgiveness. Right? Not really. Actually, Nahum delivers a message that sounds entirely vindictive. It's cutting against the Israelites. But, Nahum's words are pointed directly at the Assyrians. He wants them to know that their reign of terror over the Israelites is over. The language Nahum uses is like little verbal jabs.

Evil is real. The Jews knew that. God's justice is real. They knew that, too. (After all, they'd had prophets galore yelling that at them for years...how could they miss it!) Eventually, evil is stopped and the guilty are punished. It's in the deliverance from evil—not the punishment of the guilty—that the Jews found comfort.

So, in the meantime, while they wait for God's justice to fall from heaven, the Jews relax, knowing that God is good, and he's a great protector when life gets really tough. And hey, look. We can take comfort in that too! When times are tough...God is there. We might get a little biffed up, but we won't get squashed completely. Here's the truth...We live on, evil doesn't. Congrats! We win!

QUOTABLES

The Lord is slow to anger (1:3, KJV).

Your people are sheep without a shepherd (3:18).
Nahum's description of Assyria, whose leaders have been killed by invaders.

SNEAK PREVIEW

> Colossians
> Faith doesn't come with accessories.

BEHIND the SCENES
of Nahum

STARRING ROLES

Nahum, Judean prophet who vows that God will punish Assyria for its cruelty (1:1)

PLOT

For centuries the Assyrian Empire (located in what is now northern Iraq) has been terrorizing the Middle East. They crush nations. They almost completely crushed the northern Jewish nation of Israel in 722 B.C. Survivors are deported to central Assyria—especially craftsmen, teachers, and other skilled people who can make a valuable contribution to the empire.

Roughly 100 years later, while Assyria is still bullying the Mediterranean world, the Jewish prophet Nahum has a vision about the empire. He sees its savagery and its defiance of God. And he hears God saying that he's going to send the Assyrians to the grave. The Israelites were being forced to pay taxes to this rude and overpowering empire. Nahum delivers this message to his people...offering them hope and comfort.

STAGE DIRECTIONS

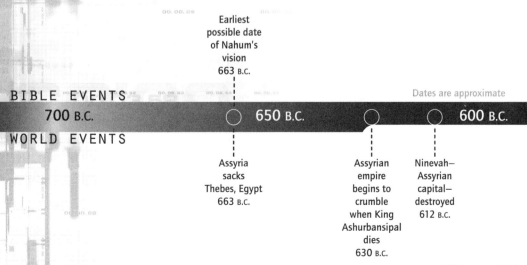

Earliest possible date of Nahum's vision 663 B.C.

BIBLE EVENTS

Dates are approximate

700 B.C.   650 B.C.   600 B.C.

WORLD EVENTS

Assyria sacks Thebes, Egypt 663 B.C.

Assyrian empire begins to crumble when King Ashurbansipal dies 630 B.C.

Ninevah—Assyrian capital—destroyed 612 B.C.

AUTHOR AND DATE

We know nothing about Nahum, except that he wrote this book. He's not mentioned in any other book of the Bible. Even the location of Elkosh remains a mystery.

Nahum probably had the vision described in this book sometime between 663 and 612 B.C. He said Thebes, Egypt had already fallen (3:8-10); it fell to Assyria in 663 B.C. And he predicted the fall of Nineveh, which Babylon and coalition forces captured in 612 B.C. This time frame places Nahum alongside two other prophets: Zephaniah and a young Jeremiah.

ON LOCATION

The Assyrian Empire, centered in what is now Iraq, is the target of Nahum's prophecy. But the message seems intended for the people of Judah, to assure them that God will soon put an end to Assyria's tyranny.

WHAT TO LOOK FOR

- **Assyrian terror.** Nahum describes an empire vicious and brutal....it's as evil as evil can get. When the Assyrians capture a city, they are merciless. They take babies by the ankles and hit them head first like clubs against stone walls. Members of enemy royal families are auctioned off to the highest bidder, or tortured and executed.

- **Poetic justice.** Nahum uses poetry and graphic symbolism to describe the coming destruction of Assyria. Hey, be careful. Don't read these descriptions literally. They are meant to express the seriousness of Assyria's crimes and the satisfaction that the Jews and the rest of the world will get when they find themselves freed from this international bully.

INSIDE SCOOP

English poet Lord Bryon (1788–1824) in his poem The Destruction of Sennacherib portrays the fierceness of the Assyrian army: The Assyrian came down like the wolf on the fold, and his cohorts were gleaming in purple and gold.

About 100 years before Nahum, the prophet Jonah told Nineveh it would be destroyed in 40 days. The people repented and were spared.

EXTREME SCENE
from Nahum

➢ Nineveh hits the skids (2:1-13)

To Assyria's complete surprise the combined forces of Babylonians and Medes strike at the heart of the empire. Nineveh falls. The Israelites are stoked. Why? Because Assyria had been the evil superpower of the Middle East for centuries. It took whatever it wanted, whenever it wanted. It took the northern Jewish nation of Israel in 722 B.C., swallowing it whole and deporting the citizens. Afterward the empire had allowed the southern nation of Judah to survive, but only if Judah joined other countries in annually feeding money into the Assyrian treasury at Nineveh.

DIRECTOR'S NOTES

Chariots were a pretty scary sight to an army heading into battle. These intimidating war machines were powered by two or more horses, and usually held two or three soldiers. One person drove, while the other(s) fired arrows at the enemy. Sometimes one soldier served as a shield bearer. Nahum 2:3, 4

God promised He would send an army to level them. The Babylonians and Medes arrived at Nineveh's doorstep in 612 B.C. Nahum had said that when this happens, "the river gates fly open" (2:6). This might have been a reference to the Khoser River that ran through the city. Ancient writings mention that a flood washed away some of the walls of the city. Perhaps the invaders broke a dam for this very purpose. Nineveh is so utterly destroyed that its massive ruins do not resurface until 1845, when archaeologists finally uncover them.

REVIEWS

ENCORE

To see God showing compassion to Assyria, read Jonah.

To read more about the two sides of God—judgment and mercy—turn to Micah.

Just as Nahum portrays God as a divine warrior who will rescue his people from tyranny (1:2–10), so does the prophet Habakkuk (3:3–15).

Nahum's prophecy is a final showdown. You can see Nahum walking out into the dusty street, six-shooters at his side, hands dangling, squinty-eyed and ready to draw. He heads out by the corral ready to face his enemy . . . Assyria. Um . . . dude? Don't you think you want to back up on this one?

Oh, that's right, GOD is your backup. Never mind, y'all have fun. I'll be over here behind this barrel.

Assyria, and particularly its capital, Nineveh, was like an old western town without a sheriff. The bandits had taken over and there was no justice to be found. The men were mean and the women were meaner. It was not a place you'd want to raise kids or even ride a wagon through. It was a savage place where decency was ridden out of town before sunset a long time ago.

Assyria was cruel and vindictive. The Assyrians tortured people for sport. Their national seals showed their enemies with rings in their noses being pulled around like cattle (so THAT'S what those are for). They were bloodthirsty and heartless. Assyrian soldiers would impale captured enemies on wooden spikes as thick as a fencepost (you KNOW that's gonna leave a mark). Some Assyrian kings ordered the corpses stacked like cord wood beside the city wall. Assyrian king Shalmaneser III (BOO . . . hsss) built a pyramid of decapitated heads in front of a besieged city (ooh, pretty . . . pretty INSANE, that is!). Assyrian kings bragged about their battlefield ferociousness by hiring artists to re-create the grisly scenes in stone carvings mounted on the palace walls. (See, Bob, here's where I cut off his arm and BEAT him with it. He was NOT a happy camper, let me tell YOU . . .)

Through Nahum, God was laying down the law. "There's not room for both of us in this town. You are going down." You'll find some vicious language in Nahum. You almost expect it to be written in blood. God had changed tactics from back in the days when he compassionately sent Jonah to preach to Assyria's capital, Nineveh. That was then. This was now. Enough was enough.

REVIEWS

God promised the Assyrians humiliation. Nahum's words went something like this, "I'm gonna pull up your skirt and make a spectacle of you." As humorous as that might sound, don't you get some satisfaction out of the mean, old, gangsta Assyrians running around with their skirts over their heads trying to find their way home? God said, "I'll make a spectacle of you." International humiliation was on the way. The showdown was at hand. By the way, a LOT of people wore "skirts" in those days. Kinda like Scottish kilts or the long part of a bathrobe. Still sounds kinda funny though, doesn't it? A bunch of tough guys running around in skirts.

As you read Nahum you can see the mother's gathering their children out of the streets. You can hear the jingle of spurs as the prophet turns to face his enemy square in the face.

Did Assyria listen to Nahum? We don't rightly know. But you can imagine how good it felt to the people of Israel to hear Nahum's prophecy. It must have felt like the Sheriff had ridden into town and the posse was gathered. For Israel, Nahum's raging message held a lot of hope.

Dylan Marshall

Habakkuk

SCHEDULE OF SCENES

Adam	Abraham	Moses	David	Fall of Israel	Fall of Ninevah	Fall of Judah	Ezra	Jesus Is Born
4000+ B.C.	2100 B.C.	1500 B.C.	1000 B.C.	722 B.C.	586 B.C.	586 B.C.	450 B.C.	7/6 B.C.

The problem of pain

So, why does God sit by and do nothing when good people suffer at the hands of the wicked? Why does he allow us to experience pain? Why do really evil people seem to win more than really good people? That's Habakkuk's question for God.

Judah had become a moral sewer. Its people were experts at extortion. They were violent. They were a criminal factory. Habakkuk wanted it to stop. So what does God do? He decides that Judah should suffer at the hands of the Babylonians. Here's the problem: Judah was a nation of saints compared to the Babylonians. Sure, the Judeans ignored the laws of God and all . . . but the Babylonians didn't even pretend to worship God. They stole entire countries. They raped women and girls to death.

Habakkuk asks his question. God answers . . . but that's not good enough for Habakkuk. He's got one more question that reads a little something like, "God . . . are you nuts? Why the Babylonians?" God didn't give a direct answer. He did assure Habakkuk that the Babylonians would eventually face their own judgment. Basically, God said, "I'm in charge . . . shut your trap" (2:20).

God is telling Habakkuk this: When you can't understand what's going on, understand this: the Lord is in control. That was all Habakkuk needed to hear. Already—some 2,600 years ago—God had a reputation for knowing what He was doing.

QUOTABLES

The just shall live by his faith (2:4, KJV). God's expressed desire that people learn to trust him. Martin Luther zeroed in on this idea, as paraphrased in Romans 1:17, to launch the Protestant movement. Luther argued that people are saved by faith in God, not by performing church rituals.

Fig trees may no longer bloom, or vineyards produce grapes . . . but I will still celebrate because the Lord God saves me (3:17–18).

SNEAK PREVIEW

Amos
A new way of measuring the good life.

BEHIND the SCENES
of Habakkuk

STARRING ROLE

Habakkuk, a prophet in Judah who asks God why he's not punishing the wicked (1:1)

PLOT

Habakkuk has a vision of talking with God. The prophet begins by asking God why he's allowing Judah to go unpunished for unbelievable sins against him. God says He'll punish them using the Babylonians. Habakkuk tells God He shouldn't use the Babylonians to punish the Jews. God replies that He will punish the Babylonians later. But in the meantime He wants his people to learn to trust Him. Habakkuk responds with a masterful and moving song of confidence in God.

STAGE DIRECTIONS

| Habakkuk predicts the fall of Jerusalem (earliest likely date) 612 B.C. | Babylon invades Judah, takes captives 605 B.C. | Babylon suppresses Judean rebellion, taking more captives 597 B.C. | Babylon destroys Jerusalem and other Judean cities 586 B.C. |

Dates are approximate

BIBLE EVENTS

625 B.C.   600 B.C.   575 B.C.

WORLD EVENTS

| Athens gets a code of laws 621 B.C. | Babylon begins 70-year dominance of Middle East 612 B.C. | Babylon defeats Egypt at battle of Carchemish 605 B.C. |

AUTHOR AND DATE

Habakkuk wrote this book, but he's not mentioned by name outside this book. The New Testament quotes the phrase (which later helps launch the Protestant Reformation) "The just shall live by his faith" (2:4 Compare that with Romans 1:17; Galatians 3:11; and Hebrews 10:38).

Habakkuk likely prophesied in the years just after Assyria had fallen (612 B.C.) but possibly before the Babylonians had defeated Egypt (605 B.C.) to assume the role of top superpower in the Middle East. Babylon defeated Judah three times in the next 20 years, carrying off hostages each time: 605 B.C., 597 B.C., and 586 B.C. when Jerusalem was leveled. Other prophets Habakkuk may have known are Jeremiah, Zephaniah, and Nahum.

ON LOCATION

Habakkuk's conversation with God takes place "on the watchtower," probably somewhere along the walls of Jerusalem (2:1). It is here he gets word that the nation of Judah will fall to Babylonian invaders who "laugh at fortresses" (1:10). Judah becomes absorbed into the Babylonian Empire and many of its citizens are relocated.

INSIDE SCOOP

A legend recorded in Bel and the Dragon, a book of the Apocrypha, reports that Habakkuk took a bowl of stew to Daniel in the lion's den. An angel reportedly transported Habakkuk from Judah to Daniel's location in Babylon, then home again.

Among the ancient library known as the Dead Sea Scrolls is a commentary on Habakkuk. The author, who lived when Rome occupied Israel, said Habakkuk's references to Babylon stood for Rome. In fact, as Babylon destroyed Jerusalem in 586 B.C., so did Rome in A.D. 70.

WHAT TO LOOK FOR

- **A divine discussion.** This is an unusual book of prophecy. Habakkuk questions God. So the book is not so much an oracle from God or a story about the life of a prophet as you'll find in other books of prophecy. It's a record of the dialogue between Habakkuk and God.
- **A song of trust in God.** The third chapter in this book is a song of confidence in God. Though Habakkuk is bummed by the news that Babylon will conquer his homeland and destroy the holy city of Jerusalem, he praises the miracle-working God of creation and pledges unwavering allegiance to him. The song eventually is used in worship.

EXTREME SCENES
from Habakkuk

> ### Waiting and waiting and waiting...(3:1-19)

Habakkuk's country is stuck in sin. He cries out to God. He expects God to send some righteous nation to level the people. Instead, according to Habakkuk, God makes a mistake and decides to send the wrong army. The Babylonians were more disgusting than the people Habakkuk is complaining about. However, God assures Habakkuk that after the Babylonians finish their job of punishing Judah, they will be punished for their own sins. While they wait, the righteous are called to live by faith and trust God. Habakkuk promises that no matter what happens he will trust in God. And if the Babylonians take everything—stripping vineyards, groves, and fields, and stealing all the livestock—Habakkuk will lean on God. This is one dude who knows how to trust God.

DIRECTOR'S NOTES

Let's set the time frame for this conversation between Habakkuk and God. The Babylonians (or Chaldeans, as they were also known) were on a roll, having defeated both Egypt and Assyria in battle. In 612 B.C., they destroyed the city of Nineveh, the capital of Assyria. Less than thirty years later, the Babylonians, led by King Nebuchadnezzar, would conquer the city of Jerusalem and burn down the temple built by Solomon.
Habakkuk 1:6

REVIEWS

The book of Habakkuk is almost like a debate. Almost. Habakkuk was addressing God himself. I don't know that you can call that an official debate. Nevertheless, Habakkuk knew there was only one place to get the answers he needed, so he asked the hard questions to the only One who would know.

Habakkuk wasn't breaking new ground arguing with God. He was joining a town hall meeting filled with inquisitive, respected biblical leaders. Moses had argued with God that he wasn't a good enough speaker to confront Pharaoh (WRONG!). Gideon couldn't believe God was calling him to lead an army, so he asked for — and got — miracles to prove that God would help him (POOF, now do you believe?). Job insisted that he didn't deserve the horrors that had robbed him of his children, flocks, and health (not even what this is about, Job. NEXT!). Jeremiah resisted becoming a prophet, arguing that he was too young (um... listen to God on this one, dude. Prophets don't even HAVE curfews).

It was Habakkuk's turn to lose an argument with God.

Habakkuk, like most prophets of his day, fully expected God to punish Judah for becoming such a sinful country. But he was shocked when God told him that He would use their neighboring nation, Babylon, to do the punishing. Babylon was more godless than Judah, for goodness sake! This was like assigning Hitler to execute a convicted war criminal, or Jeffrey Dahmer to be a judge.

One of the great lessons from Habakkuk is that God can use evil things to do good. It happened in other places in the Bible. After Joseph's brothers sold him to slave traders, Joseph ended up in Egypt, second in power to the king. There, he was responsible for keeping the people from starving during a famine. When his brothers came to Egypt for grain, Joseph told them not to be afraid: "You tried to harm

ENCORE

> Habakkuk's description of God's power (chapter 3) is much like the description in Nahum 1:2–8.

> For insights from other prophets of the day, read the books of Jeremiah, Zephaniah, and Nahum.

> To see how the New Testament interprets Habakkuk's phrase, "The just shall live by his faith" (2:4), read Romans 1:17; Galatians 3:11; Hebrews 10:38.

me, but God made it turn out for the best, so that he could save all these people" (Genesis 50:20). Through Joseph's brothers' cruelty, the whole nation of Israel was saved from starvation. This is one of the coolest things about God. I *love* watching the bad guys get frustrated when God takes their evil deeds and make good things happen with them. It is *too* funny.

One of the interesting things about Habakkuk's prophecy is that he began with hard questions but he ended with worship. That happens a lot if you sit with God long enough to hear his answers and to trust them. After Habakkuk listened to God, he accepted God's control over the situation. Like a good dad, God basically said, "You're going to have to trust Me on this one." Habakkuk did.

Babylon did wreak havoc on Judah. But they didn't get away with it. If you go today to the place where the mighty Babylon was, it's just a mound of dirt.

T. Able Turner

Zephaniah

SCHEDULE OF SCENES

Adam	Abraham	Moses	David	Fall of Israel	Josiah	Fall of Judah	Ezra	Jesus Is Born
4000+ B.C.	2100 B.C.	1500 B.C.	1000 B.C.	722 B.C.	640 B.C.	586 B.C.	450 B.C.	7/6 B.C.

Good-bye, human race

Imagine this: You're sitting in your home, watching the news. And, the announcer has just announced that a humongous meteor is heading for earth. One third of the population will be wiped out. You say to yourself…"Hmm. I might die, or get seriously hurt. I think I'll read Zephaniah." Probably not.

Why? Well, because Zephaniah makes some pretty depressing claims. Things like, "I will utterly consume everything from the face of the land." (1:2). Not real comforting words here. Zephaniah lived in a day when most Jews didn't worship God. However, they worshiped gods of other nations, and even sacrificed their children to appease the idols. They cheated each other to get richer. They hated the people God loved and commanded them to take care of widows and orphans.

See, God gave the Jews centuries to change their ways. He sent prophet after prophet to warn them about the consequences of their sins. Now, God had seen enough. Zephaniah said the Lord would punish the Jewish nation and ultimately bring an end to life on this planet. Even so, the end is not the end. The prophet also said that God will gather up the faithful to live in a mysterious time and place where sorrow is no more. Zephaniah's last words are that those who love the Lord can trust Him, even when they can't trust anyone else.

QUOTABLES

I will wipe out the entire human race (1:3). God's promise of a coming judgment. Some scholars see this as extravagant exaggeration, common in ancient poetry, and say it refers to the imminent decimation of Judah. Others take it more literally, saying it refers to the end of humanity, when the faithful are gathered into heaven.

SNEAK PREVIEW

Leviticus
Ever seen a Hebrew survival and worship guide?

BEHIND the SCENES
of Zephaniah

STARRING ROLE

Zephaniah, a prophet who predicts the destruction of Judah and the surrounding nations (1:1)

PLOT

The three-chapter book of Zephaniah is not a story with a plot, but a prophecy written as a poem. The theme for this poem? Punishment for sin...real uplifting huh?! Judah will be defeated for their sins. But the wrath of God doesn't stop there. Zephaniah names countries to the north, south, east, and west of Judah—perhaps symbolizing the four points of the compass—and declares that the Lord will destroy them all. The graphic descriptions read like those of an end-time apocalypse. Then, Zephaniah speaks of an assembly of righteous survivors hanging out in a restored Jerusalem. This might be their earthly city rebuilt. It might be a heavenly city. Wherever the city is, it's new, fresh, and God is there. Hey, do you think there's an ice cream shop too?

STAGE DIRECTIONS

King Josiah begins 31-year reign
640 B.C.

Zephaniah delivers his prophecy
630 B.C.

Jerusalem destroyed by Babylonions
586 B.C.

BIBLE EVENTS

Dates are approximate

650 B.C.   600 B.C.   550 B.C.

WORLD EVENTS

Japan founded, says a legend
660 B.C.

Assyrian Empire begins to crumble when King Ashurbanipal dies
630 B.C.

Horse racing becomes Olympic event
624 B.C.

AUTHOR AND DATE

Zephaniah is the prophet behind this book. The four-generation genealogy in the first verse adds credibility to the theory that Zephaniah carried the royal blood of King Hezekiah. The prophet says he received his message from God during the reign of King Josiah (640–609 B.C.). Josiah assumed the throne at age eight, and by age 20 began making religious reforms, such as tearing down pagan altars (2 Chronicles 34:3).

Because Zephaniah describes the rampant idolatry in Judah, he probably prophesied before the reforms began, in about 628 B.C. It's quite possible that Zephaniah's warning of a global disaster may have been a catalyst for the spiritual reform. Zephaniah predicted the fall of Nineveh, so he delivered his message before 612 B.C., when this prophecy was fulfilled.

ON LOCATION

Zephaniah delivers his prophecy in the southern Jewish nation of Judah, perhaps in the capital city of Jerusalem.

WHAT TO LOOK FOR

- **Doom, doom, and more doom.** A big fat fire was coming. It would consume Judah, Philistia, Moab and Ammon, Ethiopia, and Assyria. The day of the Lord will engulf the entire planet. This whole Day of the Lord theme is like a reverse of the creation. Everything God created he was planning on destroying.
- **Joyful survivors.** Like all other prophets in the Bible, Zephaniah adds a message of hope. After the punishing destruction, God promises to gather up the scattered survivors, who are his true worshipers. These people of God will celebrate the end of sorrow, violence, and injustice.
- **Poetic symbolism.** Zephaniah's style is captivating. His poetic style uses vivid and exaggerated images. He can be difficult to interpret sometimes. For example, It's clear that he's talking about God punishing the southern Jewish nation of Judah for worshiping idols. It's also clear that Zephaniah foresees God punishing the surrounding nations. But, is he also predicting the end of human history and the beginning of a new age in a celestial "Jerusalem"? Who knows?

INSIDE SCOOP

God sings. Zephaniah says God "celebrates and sings because of you" (3:17). This may be only a poet's way of describing God's joy. On the other hand, it doesn't seem too far-fetched to believe that the One who inspires so many songs could also sing them.

Zephaniah was probably a prince. He's identified as the great-great-grandson of Hezekiah—likely the Hezekiah who was the former king of Judah (1:1).

EXTREME SCENE
from Zephaniah

Total global destruction...Have a nice day! (1:2-3)

Want a jaw dropper? How 'bout this. Listen to these snippets from Zephaniah's first chapter...

"I will consume everything"

"I will consume man and beast."

"I will cut off man from the face of the land."

Now...that's encouraging! Zephaniah goes on to describe the doomed fate of his own country of Judah, along with the surrounding nations. All are destined for destruction. Judah will be demolished and plundered for abandoning God and worshiping the stars and idols. The other nations will be wiped out for worshiping their own pride, threatening the Jews, and mocking God. Yet somehow, after God has destroyed the earth He brings together His true worshippers. And with this, a new age dawns. People will live right. They'll never fear again.

DIRECTOR'S NOTES

When it came to pagan gods, the Israelites weren't choosy. They worshiped just about anything. Baal was the chief god of the Canaanites, but the Israelites adopted him as their own. The followers of Milcom (or Molech, as he was also known) sacrificed children as part of their worship rituals. That didn't bother the Israelites, who were eager to join in the disgusting proceedings, despite the fact that God had specifically forbidden human sacrifice. Not satisfied with merely worshiping idols, the Israelites also got involved in astrology and started worshiping the sun, the moon, and the stars. As part of their worship, they poured out drink offerings and burn incense on their rooftops. Zephaniah 1:4, 5

REVIEWS

ENCORE

⇒ To learn about what Judah was like during Zephaniah's day, read 2 Kings 21—23 and 2 Chronicles 33—35.

⇒ For more about the "the day of the Lord," a Judgment Day theme central to Zephaniah, read the book of Joel, which also emphasizes this idea.

⇒ For more prophecies about what appears to be the end of human history, read Isaiah 24—27, a passage known by Bible experts as the Apocalypse of Isaiah.

Zephaniah's style wouldn't have been a feature length film or even a movie of the week. It wouldn't have been a weekly series or even an instructional video. It would have probably been more like a sandwich sign. Ever seen one of those?

It's two big signs with two straps across the top. You let the straps hang on your shoulders so that one signs hangs down in front of you and one in back. Then you can walk around downtown or wherever and draw attention to your message.

On the front of Zephaniah's sign it would have said, "Judgment is coming!" On the back it would have said, "Deliverance is on its way, eat at Joe's!"

Like most of the Old Testament prophets Zephaniah gave his message on two levels. The first was the immediate. Judah had disregarded God and there were consequences on the way. Zephaniah was one of the last prophets to warn Judah before judgment fell in the form of exile into Babylon about 40 years later.

But Zephaniah also had a long-term message of hope. The Messiah was coming. This was the hope that the Jews had held on to since their beginning. It was actually a hope that God had given us as early as Adam and Eve's screwup in the garden.

When Judah's judgment came, it was bad. King Zedekiah was forced to watch his sons executed, then his eyes were gouged out. Babylon torched the cities of Judah after looting them. The Babylonians knocked over the buildings and walls, then deported the surviving citizens. Within a few decades, Judah was overrun and burned to the ground.

Some of Zephaniah's prophecies won't be fulfilled until the end of the world as we know it. Until then, the sandwich sign will have to do.

Joseph Dinar (Sponsored by Joe's Diner)

Haggai

Get back to work!

It's easy to put important things on hold, isn't it? Life gets busy, the pursuit of happiness weighs in better than the pursuit of spirituality. Hey, if religion has taken a backseat to other things in your life, like making a living, the prophet Haggai has a word from the Lord for you.

Haggai lived about 2,500 years ago at a time when worship was the key element in the life of a Jew. Every day they'd head to the temple and express their faith. There they'd sing praises, listen to the instruction of the priests, and offer sacrifices in thanks for God's goodness, or in sorrow for their sins. But there was no temple anymore. The Babylonians had destroyed it before deporting the Jewish citizens. When they finally returned to Jerusalem, their first task was to lay the foundation for a new temple. But opposition from outsiders forced them to stop. For the next 18 years the Jews went about their private business, abandoning the temple.

So, here comes Haggai with a message from God for the Jews, and for us. Don't neglect the Lord. Don't exclude Him from your life. Talk to Him. Sing to Him. Offer Him expressions of your gratefulness and your sorrow. Worship Him with an assembled community of believers. In other words...people! Rebuild the temple...fast!

QUOTABLES

"Is it right for you to live in expensive houses, while my temple is a pile of ruins?" (1:4) God's complaint to the Jews returned from exile.

"I am with you, says the Lord" (1:13, NKJV).

SNEAK PREVIEW

> 2 Peter
> It's easy to turn on each other when your back is against the wall.

BEHIND the SCENES of Haggai

STARRING ROLES

Haggai, prophet who urges Jews returned from exile to rebuild the temple (1:1)
Zerubbabel, Persian-appointed governor of Judah and descendant of King David (1:1)
Joshua, high priest, not the Joshua who led the Israelites into the Promised Land (1:1)

PLOT

After the Jews return from exile, they lay the foundation for a new temple. But neighboring communities convince Persian leaders to order the work stopped. Almost 20 years pass, and nothing more has been done to rebuild the temple, even though a new Persian king supportive of religion is on the throne. Times get tough, and Haggai tells the high priest and the governor of Judah that the reason the people have been suffering from crop shortages is because the temple has not been rebuilt. God will bless the people once they resume work on the temple.

About three weeks later, the rebuilding begins.

Though Haggai does not report the completion of the project, perhaps because he does not live to see it finished, Ezra says it takes about three and a half years (Ezra 6:15). The new temple is dedicated in the spring of 516 B.C., 70 years after Solomon's temple was destroyed.

STAGE DIRECTIONS

BIBLE EVENTS			
King of Persia decrees the exiled Jews can return home 538 B.C.	Jews complete the foundation of the temple 536 B.C.	Haggai urges the Jews to complete the temple 520 B.C.	The temple is completed 516 B.C.

Dates are approximate

550 B.C.   **525 B.C.**   **500 B.C.**

WORLD EVENTS			
Cyrus of Persia conquers Babylon 539 B.C.	Actor Thespis wins first prize in a tragedy competition in Athens 534 B.C.	Darius succeeds Cyrus as king 522 B.C.	Buddha, in India, preaches his first sermon 521 B.C.

AUTHOR AND DATE

The prophecies are from Haggai, a Jewish prophet whose name means "festival" (which means he might have been born on a Jewish holiday). Another prophet, Ezra, said that Haggai and Zechariah both urged the Jews to rebuild the temple (Ezra 5:1; 6:14).

Haggai may have been over 70 years old when he delivered this message.

Haggai delivered several prophecies from August through December in 520 B.C., "the second year that Darius was king of Persia" (1:1). Darius reigned from 522 to 486 B.C. The dating is unusu-

ally precise because Haggai reported the month and day of each prophecy, as well as the date that the Jews resumed work on the temple.

ON LOCATION

The story takes place in Jerusalem.

INSIDE SCOOP

> Haggai is the second shortest book in the Old Testament, after Obadiah.

> If this book reports all the prophecies of Haggai, his ministry covered less than four months.

WHAT TO LOOK FOR

- **Obedience and prosperity.** Haggai bluntly tells the religious and civic leaders of Judah that the people are suffering from a bad harvest and a sour economy because the temple hasn't been rebuilt. If they'll obey, God will bless them. This isn't a theme you'll find all over the Bible. But there are times when God makes it clear that financial hardship is the result of disobedience.
- **Making a point.** Haggai emphasizes key points by raising questions and by repeating important phrases. For examples of this, see 1:5, 1:13; 2:4, 7; 2:15, 18, 2:6, 21.

EXTREME SCENE
from Haggai

⤳ Laying the foundation (1:1-15; 2:18)

When the Jews finally return from the exile, many of them move into really expensive homes. However, they've not taken the time to rebuild the temple. Because of this, the people have been suffering from mildew, mold, and hail that have devastated the crops.

   The announcement to rebuild the temple comes in late August, near the end of a pitiful harvest. Within about three weeks the Jews have organized a workforce and began laying a new foundation. They finish the foundation before winter. Pleased with their progress, Haggai assures the people that in the seasons ahead God will bless them with abundant harvests. And, he reassures them that there is a day coming when nations will bring their treasures to Israel, the new temple will be more glorious than Solomon's, and peace will reign in Jerusalem.

DIRECTOR'S NOTES

If you had to be held prisoner by a foreign king, Darius was the kind of king you'd want on the throne. Like Cyrus before him, Darius allowed his captives to practice their own religion. Not only did he let the Jews who had returned to Jerusalem continue rebuilding the temple, he also sent money to help with the construction, and livestock to be used as sacrifices. Haggai 1:1

REVIEWS

ENCORE

For more about the rebuilding of the temple, read the books of Ezra and Zechariah.

The prophecy of Haggai is kinda like one of those infomercials. You know, the people buy time on TV and make it look like a program, but it's really an ad? They aren't really trying to entertain. They are trying to tell you something they think is important. The difference is, Haggai *did* have something important to tell us and he was *giving* it away. Free information—straight from God. Sure beats $4.99 a minute to talk to a "psychic," huh?

Haggai's prophecy came after the Jews had been carried off to Babylon and spent 50-70 years there. That was long enough for a whole new generation or two to come into its own. Then a new king took over and said, "OK, you Jews can go home now." Home? Wasn't Babylon home by that point?

So Haggai's people (some of them at least) headed back to Jerusalem to find their city in ruins. They had been back in Judah ten years when Haggai appeared on the scene.

Haggai's message was really about priorities. The people had rebuilt their homes and businesses but had only started on the temple. Only started? It had been ten years! Aren't you guys EVER going to learn? God is important. With Him, you've got it all. Without Him, bad times are comin' and I don't mean maybe.

It wasn't that a church building was soooo important. But then again it was. This was a time before Jesus came and loosed God's presence in a new way. For the Jews, God's presence was at the temple. It had been that way since they left Egypt to start an earlier trip back home. They built a portable temple called a tabernacle. For them, that was how they knew God was with them.

In light of all that, for the people to have left the temple in ruins was a major goof. It meant that even after their exile they were still just doing the minimum to get by. Hello? Is anybody out there listening?

D. Anwar Wikke

Zechariah

SCHEDULE OF SCENES

Adam	Abraham	Moses	David	Fall of Judah	Decree of Cyrus	Ezra	Jesus Is Born
4000+ B.C.	2100 B.C.	1500 B.C.	1000 B.C.	586 B.C.	538 B.C.	450 B.C.	7/6 B.C.

Jews rebuild their temple

Back at home from a long exile, the Jews began to stretch their legs. But, after 20 years they were still spiritually bankrupt, financially selfish and politically corrupt. Their temple lay in ruins. So did their harvests. Even their independence was gone again: Persia swallowed them up. So, what could the Jews possibly do to turn all this around?

QUOTABLES

Strike the shepherd, and the sheep will be scattered (13:7, NIV). Jesus quoted this to describe what would happen to Him and his disciples (Mark 14:27).

Everyone in Jerusalem, celebrate and shout! Your king . . . is coming to you. He is humble and rides on a donkey (9:9). A verse the New Testament says was fulfilled on Palm Sunday, when the crowds cheered as Jesus rode into Jerusalem (Matthew 21:2-9; John 12:14-15).

Nothing. That's the bad news.

The good news is that God is in control. That's the inspiring, motivating message of Zechariah, expressed in visions and prophecies. Zechariah promises that God is going to see to it that the temple is rebuilt, prosperity returns to the land, and Israel is ruled by the king of peace.

Strangely enough, when the people start to believe this, they suddenly find themselves with strength and determination to finish the temple. That's what happened in Jerusalem. It's still happening among those who believe that God is the sovereign Lord over all creation.

SNEAK PREVIEW

John
God in the flesh.
Love in a Hebrew tunic.

BEHIND the SCENES
of Zechariah

STARRING ROLE

Zechariah, a Jewish prophet and priest born in exile, in Babylon, but among the first Jews freed to return to Israel (1:1)

PLOT

It's hard to get a plot out of Zechariah's eight visions and prophecies for the Jews who have returned to Israel, after enduring several decades of exile in Babylon. Basically, though, the theme goes something like this. The Jews still haven't rebuilt the temple. They had started the project right away, with the Persian king's blessing. But they abandoned it when local opposition convinced a new king that if the Jews rebuilt the city, they would rebel. Now with another king on the throne Zechariah urges the people to finish what they started.

Zechariah's visions encourage the people to trust that God will help them rebuild not only the temple but the nation. The prophecies in the second half of the book are messages of punishment for the ungodly and salvation for the faithful. The closing prophecy looks forward to an end-time age when God defeats evil and reigns unopposed as the king of creation.

STAGE DIRECTIONS

Zechariah and other Jewish exiles return to Jerusalem
538 B.C.

Zechariah's first reported message from God
520 B.C.

Jerusalem temple rebuilt
516 B.C.

BIBLE EVENTS   Dates are approximate

550 B.C.   **525 B.C.**   **500 B.C.**

WORLD EVENTS

Temple of Artemis built in Ephesus
550 B.C.

Darius succeeds Cyrus as king of Persia
522 B.C.

AUTHOR AND DATE

The book was written by the prophet Zechariah, beginning in October or November of 520 B.C. We know that's when he wrote this book because Zechariah said the word of God came to him in the second year and eighth month of Persian King Darius' reign. The eighth month on the Jewish calendar covers the end of October and the beginning of November. Zechariah's ministry spans at least two years, because his prophecy beginning in chapter 7 is from the fourth year of Darius' reign (518 B.C.).

ON LOCATION

Zechariah ministers at Jerusalem in Judah. Though Judah was once a nation, now it's just a small province in the growing empire of Persia.

WHAT TO LOOK FOR

- **The Messiah.** This book talks about the Messiah more than any other Old Testament book (with the exception of Isaiah). New Testament writers, and Jesus Himself, often quote Zechariah to show that Jesus fulfilled what was predicted. Here's a partial list of the prophecies, and the New Testament fulfillment:
  - Ruler on the throne (2:10–13)—Revelation 22:1–5.
  - Holy priesthood (3:8)—1 Peter 2:5.
  - Heavenly high priest (6:12–13)—Hebrews 8:1–2
  - Riding a donkey (9:9–10)—Matthew 21:4–5
  - Betrayal price: 30 pieces of silver (11:12–13)—Matthew 26:14–15
  - The money is used to buy a potter's field (11:13)—Matthew 27:9
  - Body is pierced by spear (12:10)—John 19:34, 37
  - Good shepherd killed, sheep scattered (13:6–7)—Matthew 26:31
- **Angels.** Angels appear to Zechariah in all eight of his visions. These angels serve as God's messengers, who help the prophet understand what each vision means.
- **Part 1, Part 2.** The book divides into two sections that are so different from each other that some say they are the work of two writers. Part 1 (chapters 1–8) deals with the visions of Zechariah concerning the rebuilding of the temple. Part 2 (chapters 9–14) contains prophecies about God punishing Israel's enemies and rescuing Israel.

INSIDE SCOOP

> "Never again" is a phrase that many say in response to the Holocaust. God uses this phrase to describe a future age, perhaps after His people are assembled in heaven: "Never again will an oppressor overrun my people" (9:8, NIV).

> Though Zechariah has only 14 chapters, it's the longest of the 12 minor prophets.

EXTREME SCENES
from Zechariah

Holy motivation (1:1-17)

In a series of visions given to the prophet Zechariah, God motivates the Jews who have returned from exile in Babylon to finish rebuilding the temple. This is a job the Jews had started 18 years earlier, but one they halted because of local opposition. The Jews need to get off their hineys and get to work..

DIRECTOR'S NOTES

Ancient documents were not written in book form; they were written on long pieces of paper or leather called scrolls. Since most scrolls were usually thirty-five pages or longer, ancient librarians discovered that the best way to store them was to roll them up on a stick (like toilet paper). You may not be familiar with ancient measuring units such as cubits, so we'll do the calculations for you. A scroll twenty cubits by ten cubits would have been about the size of a billboard. Zechariah 5:1, 2

Jerusalem...where the party is (1:17–2:5)

There's a lot going on here. Not only is God promising that the temple *will* be rebuilt. He promises that the cities of Judah will prosper again—especially the city of Jerusalem, his "chosen city." Eventually the population will expand beyond the walls. The Lord has promised to be a protective wall of fire surrounding Jerusalem. Zechariah's message must have struck a nerve. The people began rebuilding the temple, and saw it through to completion four years later.

The King of peace (9:9-10)

Zechariah looks deep into the future (more than 500 years) to the time of Jesus. The Messiah will come in riding a donkey. Peace will rule. People in Jerusalem will celebrate.

Matthew and John both say this prophecy is at least partly fulfilled on the Palm Sunday when Jesus rides a donkey into Jerusalem, while crowds cheer his arrival as the promised Messiah (see Matthew 21:9; John 12:13-15). Though God's kingdom of peace was not fully established then, it has started. And Zechariah promises that what God has started, He will finish.

REVIEWS

The first part of the Zechariah's message was like a pep rally:

Gimme an

S-P (S-P)

I-R (I-R)

I-T (I-T)

GOT SPIRIT? (GOT SPIRIT!)

HOLY SPIRIT? (HOLY SPIRIT!)

THEN LET'S HEAR IT! (OK!)

The people that Zechariah was preaching to had returned home after an exile in Babylon. They felt overwhelmed with the work that had to be done. Their town was in ruins. The temple was destroyed.

Zechariah stepped in to say, "It'll be worth it! Let's get to work."

"TWO BITS, FOUR BITS, SIX BITS A DOLLAR

BUILD THAT TEMPLE OR I'LL STAND UP AND HOLLER!"

(and holler... and holler... and...)

The second part of Zechariah's message contained more prophecies about the Messiah than any other Old Testament prophet. If prophecy was baseball, Zechariah would have beat Sammy Sosa.

Let's check out his stats:

He prophesied that Jesus would ride into Jerusalem on a donkey (9:9), which he did.

He prophesied that Judas would betray Jesus for thirty pieces of silver (11:12), which he did.

He prophesied that Jesus would have scars in His hands and side (13:6) and that he would be arrested and deserted by His disciples (13:7), which He did and he was and they did.

He prophesied that Jesus' side would be pierced (12:10) and that His blood would cleanse our sin (13:1) which it was and it does.

Zechariah also prophesied that Jesus would return a second time to reign on earth, (14:4), which He will.

Now that's a lot of balls to hit out of the park. You go, Zechariah.

GIVE ME A Z. . . .

Bob Eucharist

> For another perspective on what was happening in Jerusalem during Zechariah's day, read Haggai, a prophet who lived and ministered alongside Zechariah. The 10-chapter book of Ezra also reviews the history, though Ezra lived a generation or so later.

> Zechariah's sixth vision speaks about an evil woman. This concept is expanded in Revelation 17:1–19:4.

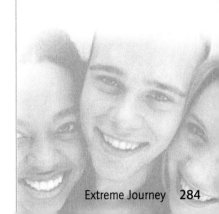

Malachi

SCHEDULE OF SCENES

Adam	Abraham	Moses	David	Ezra	Jesus Is Born
4000+ B.C.	2100 B.C.	1500 B.C.	1000 B.C.	450 B.C.	7/6 B.C.

Frauds and freeloaders in God's house

Malachi gets what everyone wants...the last word. Malachi is the final word in the Old Testament—the last message left stirring in the minds of people through the 400 years until Jesus was born. So, you'd think Malachi would have something important to say. He does, but it doesn't look like that at first.

His message is simple. He tells the people to stop sacrificing sick, crippled animals. Worshipers who offer these cheap-o types of sacrifices weren't giving their best to God. They were merely going through the motions of worship. He also reminds the people to bring 10 percent of their harvest and herds to the temple. Why? Because God's laws required it, and they weren't doing it. See? They had really let things fall apart. They didn't seem to care about obeying God's sacrificial laws. They certainly didn't care about giving God what He deserved.

OK. So we don't sacrifice animals anymore. Most of us aren't farmers, and we can't lead Bessie, our prizewinning sow into the temple and give it to God. That's true. Malachi still pushes us toward true worship, just like it did for its original audience. God doesn't want us to simply go through the motions of worship. He doesn't want us to take our time with Him lightly. He wants all of us. He wants the best of us. This verbal bookend to the Old Testament challenges our hearts and actions to be as sincere as possible. And, it encourages us to help our eyes on the horizon...the Messiah is coming!

QUOTABLES

The sun of righteousness will rise with healing in its wings (4:2, NIV). Malachi implies that in a future age, God will heal the sin-damaged creation by defeating evil and restoring justice.

SNEAK PREVIEW

Revelation
Wanna' see who wins in the end?

BEHIND the SCENES
of Malachi

STARRING ROLE

Malachi, a prophet who condemns insincere worship (1:1)

PLOT

A century after the Jews have returned from exile in Babylon, they are again losing respect for God. They still go through the mechanics of offering sacrifices. But these sacrifices come from the bottom of the barrel and are really no good. Even the priests give these raunchy sacrifices their stamp of approval. Through Malachi, God asks the people to stop wasting their time. God isn't impressed with their pitiful attempts. Malachi urges the people to treat God with the respect due Him. They're to treat each other with respect, too: not cheating in marriage, or lying in court, or taking advantage of employees, or ignoring the poor, or swindling foreigners. In the end, Malachi says, God will settle all scores.

STAGE DIRECTIONS

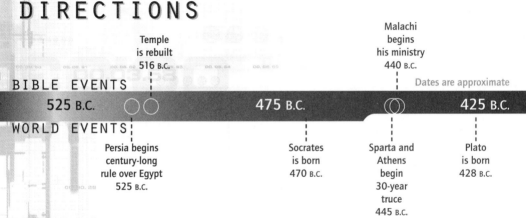

Temple
is rebuilt
516 B.C.

Malachi
begins
his ministry
440 B.C.

BIBLE EVENTS
Dates are approximate

525 B.C.   475 B.C.   425 B.C.

WORLD EVENTS

Persia begins
century-long
rule over Egypt
525 B.C.

Socrates
is born
470 B.C.

Sparta and
Athens
begin
30-year
truce
445 B.C.

Plato
is born
428 B.C.

INSIDE SCOOP

AUTHOR AND DATE

We know for sure that Malachi wrote this book, but we don't know anything more about him than that. Some Bible experts think "Malachi" is a title, not a name. The word means "my messenger."

The book was written sometime after the temple was rebuilt (516 B.C.). Malachi's description of a decaying sacrificial system and his concern about Jews marrying non-Jews seems to fit the conditions around the time of Ezra and Nehemiah, roughly 450 B.C.

ON LOCATION

The prophet is one of several who addressed Jews in Jerusalem.

WHAT TO LOOK FOR

- **Insincere worship.** Throughout this short book, Malachi complains that the people go through the motions of worship as though it's the motion that God wants. They miss the point. God wants the motions to flow out of an inner sense of devotion and love. These people don't feel devoted. They feel obligated.
- **Elijah.** Malachi is the only prophet to announce that God will send the prophet Elijah as a messenger to prepare the way for the Lord's arrival, and the salvation to follow (3:1; 4:5). Jesus later explains that John the Baptist fills that role (Matthew 11:7-14).
- **Judgment day.** Malachi vows "the day of judgment is certain to come" (4:1). When it does, justice comes with it. Evil is trampled and the righteous will be likes kids on a playground.

EXTREME SCENES
from Malachi

⇾ Go ahead...insult God! (1:6-2:3)

God is insulted. He has allowed the Jewish people to return home from exile and to rebuild their temple and capital city. After some 100 years they've become lazy in their worship. God wants sacrifices that are without defect (Leviticus 22:18-23), but their sacrifices are blind, crippled, and sick. The priests are guilty too because they let all of this stuff go on. God warns them...take Me seriously. He probably waves His finger at them too.

D I R E C T O R ' S
N O T E S

Here's how tithing worked in ancient times: The Israelites were commanded to give 10 percent of everything they had—including crops, livestock, and money—to God. The Israelites gave their tithes to the Levites, the people who worked in the temple. The Levites, in turn, gave 10 percent of everything they received to the priests. The priests offered a sacrifice to the Lord for their tithe. The third-year tithe was given to help support the poor and needy. Malachi 3:10

God robbers (3:8-12)

Wimpy sacrifices aren't their only problem. The Israelites stopped giving their tithes. Basically, the tithe (10 percent from the best of their crops) belonged to God. You didn't mess with the tithe. If you didn't give it, you were in a world of hurt. God equals the withholding of their tithe to robbing Him. And, robbing God really isn't a good idea.

After this, Malachi (and the Old Testament) concludes with the promise that the Lord is coming, on the heels of a messenger who will prepare the way for Him. Then the New Testament picks up the story of God's work among the human race. Jesus is born. And when He grows up, His ministry follows that of John the Baptist. Malachi says, "Get ready!" Then, John the Baptist says, "Get ready!" Then, Jesus begins His ministry. Gee, maybe God *DOES* have a plan after all!

REVIEWS

The book of Malachi is the Old Testament prophets' season finale, the big cliff-hanger. It's the connection between the Old Testament (The Messiah is coming!) and the New Testament (aaaand heeeeeerrre's Jesus).

Malachi prophesied after the people of Judah had returned home from exile in Babylon. They were in the process of rebuilding their life and reconnecting to their roots. Malachi was the voice reminding them to connect with their *spiritual* roots. When you think about the Jews you realize that almost all of their roots are spiritual. After all, their whole existence came from a promise kept between God and Abraham.

It was ironic then that Malachi found his people in the sorry shape they were in. Religion had become a vitamin to them, a minimum daily requirement: "Here, take this much so you won't go to hell or get carried away to Babylon." God seemed so distant from them that they were promising Him their best cattle as offerings and then bringing their damaged or crippled animals to give. What were they thinking? Did they think God was fooled? Did they think He wasn't watching or had they given up on their faith completely?

I guess that's really what Malachi was asking. "What are you thinking?"

It's easy to look down our noses at the Jews in this scenario. Pretty dense for them to think that they could pull one over on God. But it's really not quite so hard to believe. All of us do it. We do the right thing so that the wrong people are impressed. As long as those people think we're doing OK, we feel pretty good about things. We so easily forget that God can see right into us and *that's* the relationship we should be worried about. Lucky for us, God knows how *stupid* people can be and sent us Jesus so that even idiots and bookworms can live good lives and go to heaven (math teachers too, if you can believe *that*).

Micah reminded his people over and over again to live their faith with sincerity. His prophecy is still a good reminder. When the next season opens (Matthew kicks it off with a biography of the life of Jesus), you can see how the Jews fared in their journey. The nice thing here is you can go right to Matthew without waiting through the summer reruns. Two thumbs up for the Old Testament.

Shekel and Hebrew

⮞ Malachi quotes God as saying "I hate divorce" (2:16). For more on God's feeling about divorce, read the words of Jesus in Matthew 19:3–9.

⮞ To see how the New Testament portrays John the Baptist as the promised Elijah, turn to Matthew 17:1–13.

⮞ For more about the Jewish law of tithing, read Leviticus 27:30–32 and Numbers 18:21–24.

Matthew

SCHEDULE OF SCENES

Jesus Is Born	Jesus crucified / Pentecost	Temple Destroyed	Matthew Written	Death of John
7/6 B.C.	A.D. 30	A.D. 70	c. 75	A.D. 100

Jesus and His teachings

Imagine this. You've just reclined on a soft clump of grass on a Galilean hillside. The air is crisp and warm. Your schedule is clear... nothing to do but listen. You're there with thousands of others who have arrived to hear Jesus teach. Your mind is ready to drink in all that Jesus has to say. Your heart is eager for a divine touch. As Jesus begins to teach, suddenly it's just you and He. No more thousands of people. Just you.

That's the spirit of Matthew. The book was intended for hundreds of thousands of millions of people. But it reads like it's for one person. You.

Matthew is the first of four New Testament books about Jesus. Like any collection of stories about one person, each version is different. And there's something unique enough about Matthew's story to inspire Christian leaders long ago to put this ahead of all others in the New Testament. So, what's so unique?

In Matthew, you won't find as much dramatic action as you'll discover in Mark, or as many spotlights on compassion like in Luke, or even as much proof of the deity of Jesus as you'll uncover in John. But in Matthew, you'll find the most complete record of what Jesus taught. And you'll learn how His teachings grow out of Old Testament scriptures. Matthew's book is like an encyclopedia of Jesus. This is the total good news. Totally complete. Totally true.

SNEAK PREVIEW

Numbers
A forty-year long very bad day in the life of God's people.

BEHIND the SCENES
of Matthew

STARRING ROLES

Jesus, God's son in a human body, and the Messiah that prophets said God would send to Israel (1:1)

12 apostles, working-class men whom Jesus recruits to become His disciples (4:18; 10:1–4)

PLOT

The amazing life of Jesus begins with His birth. Astrologers arrive, saying they have followed a star they believe is a sign that the future king of the Jews has just been born. Herod is going nuts, and fears that the Messiah could overthrow his rule as king. So, Herod kills all the male children two years old and younger. Jesus' family moves him to Egypt and they live there until Herod dies.

STAGE DIRECTIONS

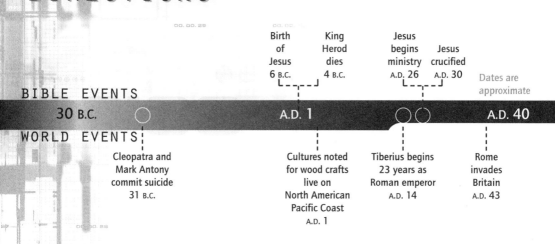

| | Birth of Jesus 6 B.C. | King Herod dies 4 B.C. | Jesus begins ministry A.D. 26 | Jesus crucified A.D. 30 | Dates are approximate |

BIBLE EVENTS

30 B.C.   A.D. 1   A.D. 40

WORLD EVENTS

| Cleopatra and Mark Antony commit suicide 31 B.C. | Cultures noted for wood crafts live on North American Pacific Coast A.D. 1 | Tiberius begins 23 years as Roman emperor A.D. 14 | Rome invades Britain A.D. 43 |

BEHIND the SCENES
of Matthew

At about age 30, Jesus' ministry begins. It's a busy schedule for the next few years. His ministry begins with His baptism. Then, He begins preaching and calls 12 men to join Him as disciples. From that point, He begins preaching, teaching, and healing for the next three or four years. His most famous sermon, recorded only in Matthew, is called the Sermon on the Mount, a masterful summary on how to live for God on the earth.

That's the good stuff. Here's the tough part. Jesus predicts His death and begins to head towards Jerusalem...healing and preaching the whole way. In Jerusalem He faces a bunch of grouchy combative Jewish scholars who love their religious traditions more than they love God. When Jesus reveals that some of these traditions have no basis in Scripture, and (even worse!) that the leaders are hypocrites misleading the people, they get majorly ticked off. They plot to kill Him, but realize they have to do it secretly because He is really popular.

During His prayer time one Thursday evening, Jesus is arrested, interrogated throughout the night, and tried as a criminal the next morning by Pilate, the Roman governor. Even though He doesn't buy it, Pilate gives in to the wishes of the assembled Jews and sentences Jesus to death. The execution is carried out immediately, and Jesus is dead before sundown. On the following Sunday morning, he rises from the dead and appears to women who have come to His tomb. Later He meets with His remaining disciples and gives them what is now called the Great Commission: "Go to the people of all nations and make them my disciples" (28:19).

AUTHOR AND DATE

This book is named Matthew, but no one's really sure who wrote it. Both the author and date it was written are uncertain. Christians writing in the second century said the book was written by Matthew, a tax collector who became one of the 12 original disciples of Jesus.

There's a bunch of clues within the book that make scholars think it was written near the end of the first century, sometime after the Romans destroyed the Jerusalem temple in A.D. 70. Without the temple, there was no need for priests because there was no place to offer sacrifices. So the Jewish scholars, called Pharisees, rose to prominence. The book seems written especially to a Christian Jewish community trying to define and defend itself against traditional Judaism that— before the century was over—excommunicated Christian Jews from all synagogues. One clue that the Christian Jews faced such persecution appears in Matthew 23:34, which says the Jews "kill them or nail them to a cross or beat them in your meeting places or chase them from town to town."

ON LOCATION

The story of Jesus unfolds in what is now Israel, beginning in His hometown region of Galilee, and continuing southward through Samaria and into Judea, where he dies and is resurrected in the city of Jerusalem.

WHAT TO LOOK FOR

• **The Jewish angle.** This Gospel was written to convince Jews that Jesus is the Messiah that the prophets said was coming. That's one reason it comes first in the New Testament, right after Malachi, which ends with the promise of the Lord's coming. Matthew quotes Old Testament prophecies about the Messiah, to show that Jesus fulfilled them. In fact, he quotes the Old Testament more than 57 times (Mark's the runner up quoter...he refers to the Old Testament 30 times).

INSIDE SCOOP

In the family tree of Jesus are three women with tarnished backgrounds—not the kind of people Jews expect in the family tree of the great Messiah. There's Rahab, a pagan prostitute; Bathsheba, an adulteress; and Tamar, who becomes pregnant by her father-in-law. These memories of scandal would challenge the too-rosy memory of Jews conceited about their pedigree. And they would also counter attacks on the virgin Mary by reminding Jews that women with bad reputations are in the family tree of the great King David, forebear of the Messiah.

- **Lots on the death of Jesus.** There's a ton of stuff here on the suffering and death of Jesus. How come? Well, Matthew has His work cut out for Him. People weren't expecting the Messiah to be crucified like a common criminal. The Messiah was supposed to restore the glory of Israel, not be killed by it. Matthew takes the Jews back to the prophets, who portrayed a humble Messiah, rejected by leaders, and sacrificed for the sins of others.
- **Five teachings of Jesus.** The book is woven around five sets of teachings by Jesus. Some scholars believe these teachings were the original core of the book, provided by Matthew, and that the story line was added later.

  The teachings are broken into these five sections:
  - The Sermon on the Mount (chapters 5–7)
  - Commissioning the 12 disciples as ministers (10)
  - Parables revealing what the kingdom of heaven is like (13)
  - Guidelines on how to live as citizens in God's kingdom (18)
  - Warnings about the end of the age and judgment day (24–25).
- **The kingdom of heaven.** God's revolution and change is coming. Matthew, and other Gospel writers call this "the kingdom." Both the miracles and the teachings of Jesus show that God's reign applies not only to heaven and the future, but also to earth right now. Imagine this: When Jesus gets up to deliver the Sermon on the Mount, it's a lot like a president getting up to give an inaugural address. Because, in that sermon, Jesus outlines the policies of God's administration, showing people how to live as citizens of this kingdom.
- **Different responses to Jesus.** Despite his life-changing miracles, compassion and revolutionary teachings, not everyone likes Jesus. His unique interpretation of Old Testament Jewish laws make Him seem like a threat to Jewish traditionalists who grip their false understanding of tradition too hard.

EXTREME SCENES
from Matthew

⇥ Smart guys with candy (2:1-12)

Jesus is born. Within about two years, wise men from the east arrive in Jerusalem. Through their actions and their questions they recognize that this baby is no ordinary child. They search throughout Jerusalem...looking for baby Jesus. (Here's what's weird...the non-Jews recognize Jesus before the Jews do. Cool!) King Herod (who killed his own brother to protect the throne) is instantly worried. Herod learns that the Messiah will be born in Bethlehem. He tells the wise men if they find the kid to tell him so he can worship the baby too. The wise men find Jesus, but in a dream are warned not to return to Herod. When Herod realizes the men aren't coming back, he orders all the boys who are two years old and under, living in the Bethlehem area executed. Jesus and his family escape to Egypt.

DIRECTOR'S NOTES

At the time of Jesus' birth, the Roman Empire included pretty much the entire known world. Obviously, that's a lot of area to rule. To maintain control, the Roman senate selected governors to rule over various regions in the empire. Herod was selected to rule Judea in 37 B.C. Look up the word *paranoid* in the dictionary and you may find a picture of Herod next to it. This guy was so desperate to hang on to the throne that he killed anyone he suspected of even wanting to become king. That included three of his own sons. Matthew 2:1

⇥ Jesus gets dunked (3:13-17)

John the Baptist (the guy who's job it was to tell everyone that the Messiah was coming) halfheartedly baptizes Jesus. He doesn't feel worthy. John's baptism was unique. It was intended to be a symbol of their spiritual cleansing after repentance. Jesus is baptized to endorse John's ministry and, as a representative of all humanity, to be an example of humble obedience to God. God's opinion of Jesus' baptism? He's stoked. He sends a dove (a symbol of His spirit) to rest on Jesus. And says, "This is my own dear Son, and I am pleased with him." After His baptism, Jesus goes into the desert where He is tested by Satan. After He passes the test His ministry begins.

⇉ Jesus' first sermon…It goes well! (5:1-7:29)

Matthew spends a lot of time telling us what Jesus taught. The most famous sermon of Jesus is called the Sermon on the Mount, delivered somewhere on
a hillside possibly near the Sea of Galilee, where many of his disciples had worked as fishermen. This sermon is well known for the world famous beatitudes, which show that God's kingdom is not full of the high and mighty, but of people who are poor in spirit, humble, pure in heart, and sometimes persecuted. There's also stuff here about adultery, divorce, revenge, loving your enemies, helping the needy, prayer, worry and judging others. Instead of laying out a list of rules for people to follow, Jesus gives broad principles that define the life of the believer. Not sure how to act? Do what Jesus says…Act like God would act.

DIRECTOR'S NOTES

Think of the Pharisees and Sadducees as rival gangs. Instead of fighting with guns and knives, though, these rivals fought with words and ideas. The Pharisees were ordinary, middle-class people who emphasized the importance of obeying the Law God had given Moses. The Sadducees were wealthy and powerful individuals, many of whom served as priests. These two groups of Jewish scholars interpreted Scripture differently and argued over issues, such as the resurrection of the dead and the existence of angels. Because they knew so much about Scripture, members of both groups tended to take pride in themselves and to criticize others. Matthew 3:7

⇉ Dead as a doornail? (9:18-26)

As he's teaching, a government official rushes to Jesus. His daughter is dead. He needs a miracle. When Jesus arrives at the man's house, a crowd of mourners has already gathered. Jewish custom requires speedy burial, usually the same day. Jesus tells the people to leave. "The little girl isn't dead," He says. "She is just asleep." Suddenly, cries of sorrow erupt into heckling laughter. The people eventually leave the house. Jesus takes the girl by the hand and helps her up. News of the miracle spread. Many people are drawn to His message. These supporters praise God for the miracles of healing they see Jesus perform. But others believe that He's the leader of the demons. (9:34).

⇉ Twelve gutsy dudes (10:1-42)

Jesus gathers the 12 disciples together to give them instructions for a mission they are about to undertake. They've been following Jesus around. Listening to Him teach, watching His actions and following His instructions. And, planning on continuing His work when He is gone. These are 12 fishermen. Working class dudes. Matthew is a tax collector (a profession hated among the Jews). The mission Jesus wants them to go on is short term. Maybe even a trial-run for the ministry they will perform when Jesus is gone.

He sends them out to teach about the kingdom of heaven, heal the sick, exorcise demons, and even raise the dead. They are to take no pay. And, they can leave when they're not welcomed. Jesus encourages the disciples not to be afraid at what they're about to do.

The story of the weeds (13:24-30, 36-43)

Jesus used stories (called parables) to communicate a spiritual meaning. The parables in chapter 13 reveal mysteries about God's kingdom. The parable of the tall-growing mustard seed and of the yeast show that the kingdom will emerge suddenly in the world. The parables about the hidden treasure and the pearl show that people have to decide whether or not to become citizens of the kingdom. And the parable of the weeds in the wheat field reveal that people will be rewarded for choosing the kingdom and punished for rejecting it. In this parable, Jesus compares Himself to a farmer sowing good seeds that produce "people who belong to the kingdom." The weed seeds are those who belong to the evil one." At harvesttime (an expression of end-time judgment) the wheat is gathered in. But the weeds are separated and burned.

5000 hungry students (14:13-21)

In a memorable scene told in all four Gospels, Jesus and His ministry-weary disciples sail away from the crowds for a rest. But the people on shore keep the boat in sight and follow it. When Jesus and His men arrive at a remote site, they are met by 5,000 men, not counting the women and children. Even though He's wiped out, Jesus is moved with compassion and heals everyone who is sick. The disciples suggest asking the crowds to go home and eat. Jesus looks at the disciples and says, "You feed them." All that the disciples manage to round up is one boy's lunch: five pieces of barley bread and two small fish. Jesus takes it, looks to heaven and gives thanks for it, then hands it to the disciples to distribute. The people eat their fill, and the disciples collect 12 large baskets of leftovers.

So THAT'S who You are! (16:13-20)

While in Caesarea Philippi, north of the Sea of Galilee, Jesus asks the disciples who people say He is. They reply that some think He's the spirit of John the Baptist, who was recently beheaded. Others say He is the spirit of Elijah, Jeremiah, or some other Old Testament prophet. When Jesus asks who the disciples think He is, one disciple boldly replies, "You are the Messiah, the Son of the living God." Jesus gives this disciple, Simon, the new name of Peter, which means "rock." Then Jesus says, "On this rock I will build my church" (16:18). Later, on the day of Pentecost, when God sends the Holy Spirit to empower the disciples, guess who preaches the sermon at the event? It's Peter. The rock! (Acts 2).

Jesus changes in public (17:1-13)

Jesus begins preparing His disciples for His death. He takes His three closest disciples—Peter, James, and John—to a hilltop. There they see Jesus changed into His glorified, heavenly form: "His face shone like the sun, and his clothes became as white as the light" (17:2). Suddenly, the prophets Moses and Elijah appear, also as beings of light, talking with Jesus. A glowing cloud rolls overhead, and from it a voice says, "This is my beloved son, in whom I am well pleased. Hear him!" (17:5). The disciples hear and drop to the ground terrified. But Jesus tells them not to be afraid. When the men look up, Jesus is alone. He tells them to say nothing about this until after His resurrection.

Homecoming (21:1-11)

Jesus arrives in Jerusalem just before His Friday crucifixion. Crowds who had heard of Him cheer, welcoming him as the long-awaited Messiah who would save them from their enemies and restore righteousness to Israel. He enters riding a donkey, just as the prophet Zechariah said the Messiah would arrive in Jerusalem (Zechariah 9:9). The people respond by laying down a carpet of palm branches and cloaks. The kind of entry fit for a king. Many believe they are witnessing the arrival of the Messiah.

Housecleaning (21:12-17)

Jesus heads for the temple. When He enters the courtyard of the temple, He sees the place filled with merchants selling sacrificial animals and exchanging foreign currencies for the Hebrew coins required in temple offerings. Jesus gets really angry. The Jewish officials have set up a sacrificing scheme, and a skewed money-changing operation designed to cheat people. Jesus turns over the tables in the courtyard. Later, Jesus prophesies that the temple will be destroyed. It was (by the Romans, in 70 A.D.) and they haven't had a temple since.

You a sheep? (25:31-46)

Jesus and his disciples leave Jerusalem and head towards Bethany. They stop and rest on the Mount of Olives. There Jesus warns them about the coming fall of Jerusalem and the later end of the human age, saying He will return to take the citizens of God's kingdom to their eternal home. He goes on to say that everyone needs to live in a state of readiness, since no one knows when this will happen. To illustrate this, Jesus tells a story about sheep and goats. The sheep, symbolizing godly and compassionate people who help the needy, are rewarded with "eternal life." The goats, representing the godless and selfish, "will be punished forever."

The Last Supper (26:17-30)

Officials in the Jewish government begin to plot strategies for arresting and executing Jesus. The high priest and other members of the Sanhedrin all get involved. They're upset at Jesus' unorthodox interpretation of Scripture. The night of the arrest, Jesus arranges to eat a final meal with his disciples. There's total symbolism throughout this meal. Jesus introduces the idea of communion. He breaks bread and tells the men that it represents His body, which will soon be broken. Then He gives them wine and says it represents His blood, "poured out, so that many people will have their sins forgiven." After singing a hymn, the group goes to a garden on the Mount of Olives to pray. There Jesus betrayed by Judas and arrested. The disciples scatter. Peter waits outside the home of the high priest, but repeatedly denies knowing Jesus. Judas hangs himself.

Clean hands...but no backbone (27:11-26)

The Sanhedrin holds an emergency session and spends the night interrogating Jesus. They bring lying witnesses, but their testimony isn't enough to warrant execution. Frustrated, the high priest asks Jesus, "Are you the Messiah, the Son of God?" (26:63). Jesus confirms He is. The court charges Him with blasphemy and takes Him to the Pilate. Pilate is the only person who can order an execution. Pilate doesn't understand why Jesus needs to be executed, but he eventually gives in to the early-morning crowd of Jesus' opponents. The opposing crowd is screaming, "Nail him to a cross!" Pilate publicly washes his hands, saying he is innocent of this man's blood. Then he orders Jesus to be killed.

The execution of Jesus (27:33-66)

Jesus is transferred to soldiers who now have custody of Him. They know all about Jesus' claims to be the Messiah. So, they dress Him in a robe of scarlet, the color of royalty, then make Him a crown from branches of a thornbush. They beat Him. They force Him to make a humiliating march through the city. They tie the cross-beam of the cross to Him and force Him to carry it as He marches through the city. The vertical beam is fixed at the execution site outside the city walls. They nail His hands and feet to the cross. Once crucified, Jesus hangs between two criminals. Above His head is a sign that reads, "This is Jesus, the King of the Jews."

When Jesus dies, His last words quote the beginning of a song about a servant of God who suffers and is later proven righteous. Instantly, the earth shakes so violently that a soldier exclaims, "This man really was God's Son!" Because Jesus had claimed He would rise on the third day, the Jewish leaders convince Pilate to seal the tomb and post a guard. This way Jesus' disciples can't steal the body and claim He rose from the dead.

DIRECTOR'S NOTES

What's a wineskin? Good question. A wineskin was a bag used for storing liquids. Did we mention that the bag was made of the hide (or skin) of a goat or another animal? When grape juice was stored in a new wineskin, the fermentation process (the chemical changes that cause grape juice to become wine) made the wineskin stretch and swell. The older a wineskin got, the more stiff and brittle it became. When grape juice was poured into an old wineskin, often the container would break. Matthew 9:17

Alive! (28:1-20)

Jesus' mom wasn't allowed to prepare His body for burial. It was sundown on the Sabbath, and the work had to wait until Sunday morning. So, early Sunday morning, when Sabbath is over, several women followers of Jesus go to the tomb to finish preparing his body for burial. But by this time, an angel appeared and rolled back the stone, then sat on it. The guards were so terrified they passed out. When they woke up, they reported to the Jewish priests, who bribed them to keep quiet.

When Mary Magdalene and at least two other women arrive, the angel is still there. "Don't be afraid!" the angel says, "For I know that you seek Jesus who was crucified. He is not here for He is risen." (28:5–6). As the women turn to leave, Jesus greets them. "Tell my followers to go to Galilee," He says. "They will see me there." Jesus meets His disciples in Galilee. There, He gives them what has become known as the Great Commission. "Go to the people of all nations and make them My disciples," He says, "I will be with you always, even until the end of the world."

INTERVIEW
with the Stars

The Extreme Teen

What *does* it take to be an extreme teen? *Behind the Bible* goes straight to the source for the answer to this key question and welcomes Jesus, the true extreme teen, as our next subject. Jesus, there's a lot in the Bible about Your birth, Your ministry years as an adult, and certainly Your death and resurrection. But what about Your teen years? Can You tell us about them?

⋙ Jesus

Definitely. To find out anything about me as a youth in the Bible, you'll have to read between the lines. By age 12, I was considered a whiz kid when it came to Bible knowledge. I talked about it; I read it; I lived it. I understood early on that obeying God's Word was the key to life.

How were you able to do that at a time when most young boys were either learning their father's trade or working out in the fields?

⋙ Jesus

I spent as much time as possible with the religious leaders. When my family went to Jerusalem for the festivals, like Passover, I went straight over to the temple. I listened to the adults talking about God's Word and I asked questions. I think at first they tended to not take Me too seriously because of My age, but my questions and comments amazed even them!

INTERVIEW
with the Stars

What about at home? How did knowing God's word impact your relationships there?

⇒ Jesus

That was difficult at times. I knew that I had come to earth for a purpose. Sometimes I was in a hurry to get on to the bigger things, like when I stayed on at the temple in Jerusalem and forgot all about My mom and dad. But I practiced obeying God by obeying My parents. I learned just like most kids have to at that age, that life isn't just about what I wanted to do. I had to cooperate with My folks, and I did spend time learning My dad's trade.

Did you ever feel like your youth was just marking time until you began fulfilling your real purpose in coming to earth?

⇒ Jesus

Not at all. The time spent learning God's Word, living out my faith in my daily relationships, all helped Me grow and mature. Listen to what Dr. Luke had to write about My teen years, "*Jesus increased in wisdom and stature, and in favor with God and men*" (Luke 2:52).

Based on Your own experiences then, what advice would You give to 21st century teens on how to be extreme?

⇒ Jesus

You really want to be extreme? You want to shock people and make them sit up and notice you? Try being interested! Ask questions! Dig for the truth! Anyone can be bored and disruptive. It takes work to learn. But if you do, you'll find you'll make a huge difference in at least one life—your own!

INTERVIEW
with the Stars

Daring to be different

Are there people you know who try really hard to be different by looking different and acting different? Typically, they hang out with others who are "different," just like them. Sound familiar? *Behind the Bible's* next subject is different. He looked different. He acted different. But he chose to be different because *God* called him to be different. John the Baptist, tell us about your call.

⮞ John the Baptist

I'm sure you know the story. But God's purpose for my life was laid out even while I was still in my mother's womb. I was called to be a messenger. To tell others that the Messiah was coming and to get ready by turning from sin. That's it. My entire purpose in life and nothing was going to distract me from accomplishing it.

Is that why you chose to wear camel skins and live in the wilderness?

⮞ John the Baptist

Exactly. I wasn't out to start any trend or call attention to myself because of what I wore, or where I lived, or how I acted. The only trend I wanted to start was a trend of people getting ready for the coming of Jesus by cleaning up their act. It didn't matter who they were—rich, poor, soldiers, the king—they all needed to turn from their sin.

INTERVIEW
with the Stars

And were you successful?

⋟ John the Baptist

I suppose not by the world's standards. Only a handful of people really listened to what I had to say and made an effort to prepare their hearts. But it was enough in God's eyes.

Apparently, because Jesus Himself said about you, *Assuredly, I say to you, among those born of women there has not risen one greater than John the Baptist; but he who is least in the kingdom of heaven is greater than he* (Matthew 11:11).

⋟ John the Baptist

True. What's important in God's eyes is not how you look or how you act. What's important is how you respond to His calling for *you*. That's what will ultimately make a different—and make you different. Being different for God as *He* instructs and leads will take courage. It will take even more determination. Have you set out to be all that God has called you to be?

REVIEWS

ENCORE

➤ The Gospels of Mark and Luke are similar to Matthew's. John's Gospel is more theological, emphasizing the divinity of Jesus more than retelling the highlights of His life's story. But all three add depth to Matthew's portrait.

➤ Read some of the Old Testament prophecies that Matthew says Jesus fulfilled. For example: Jesus is Immanuel, God with us (1:23; Isaiah 7:14); born in Bethlehem (2:6; Micah 5:2); a healer of diseases (8:17; Isaiah 53:4).

➤ Read Acts to find out what happens after Jesus ascends into heaven.

The first rule of selling anything in *any* kind of media presentation is that you gotta' believe in the product. The second rule is you've gotta' know the product inside and out. Matthew does a bang-up job on both counts. He's pitching Jesus Christ as the promised Messiah, the One that the whole Old Testament pointed to, and you can tell by reading what he wrote that he believed 110 percent AND he did his research too.

Selling rule #3, you have to know your market. Matthew does. He was writing to the Jews of his day and most of the information he used is from Old Testament prophecies in the Jewish Holy books. I can just see him doing a slide show on his laptop with charts and tables and facts and figures to back up everything he said. Here's a few highlights from his presentation.

"Micah 5:2," he would have said. "The Messiah would be born in Bethlehem." (click the remote to change frames)

"Matthew 2:1," he would have continued, "Jesus was born in Bethlehem."

And so he would have continued walking everyone through prophecy after prophecy.

He would have walked them through Isaiah 53, practically an eyewitness kind of account of the suffering and death of Jesus: "He suffered and endured great pain for us.... He was wounded and crushed because of our sins.... He was condemned to death without a fair trial.... The Lord decided his servant would suffer as a sacrifice to take away the sin and guilt of others" (4, 5, 8, 10).

REVIEWS

He would have quoted Zechariah:"Everyone in Jerusalem, celebrate and shout! Your king has won a victory, and he is coming to you. He is humble and rides on a donkey" (9:9). Then he would tell the story of the first Palm Sunday (21:1-9) in which Jesus rode into Jerusalem on a donkey with the people cheering.

Convincing the Jews was definitely the plan when Matthew wrote his Gospel. Rule # 4, some people just aren't buying no matter what. Some of his potential "customers" pointed out a few prophesies that, at least as far as they could tell, hadn't happened yet. So even though Matthew made a lot of converts, some of the old school Jews just weren't ready to believe. The big shame here is that believing was the only "cost" for what Matthew was selling. Sounds like a bargain at twice the price, especially when you count in that, as part of the deal, Jesus will pay off all your sins. Personally, I couldn't pass this deal up. Best thing ever purchased for me. (And true faith doesn't scratch or dent.) Lifetime guarantee? How 'bout FOREVER? Is THAT long enough? BUT THAT'S NOT ALL, when you buy now, he'll throw in peace, joy, and abundant life at absolutely no extra cost.

God is standing by to take your call.

Will "Pearly" Gates

Mark

SCHEDULE OF SCENES

Jesus Is Born	Jesus Crucified Pentecost	Mark Written	Temple Destroyed	Death of John
7/6 B.C.	A.D. 30	A.D. 62/63	A.D. 70	A.D. 100

Non-Stop Jesus

If you're looking for a great action-packed story about Jesus, you've come to the right place. Here you'll find Jesus moving from place to place...healing to healing...miracle to miracle. Mark follows along, and doesn't miss a beat.

Mark's Gospel is the shortest in the New Testament, but it includes so much information in such a short amount of chapters, it feels a lot bigger than it is. And, guess what. Mark's Gospel was highly influential in the development of Matthew and Luke. When Matthew and Luke sat down to write their Gospels, they had probably already read Mark. Their books show signs of borrowing from the book.

This story makes one thing crystal clear—Jesus suffered on our behalf. Almost 40 percent of this short book lays out details of the final, traumatic week of Jesus' life. And the earlier part of the book throws the spotlight on the pain Jesus endured from the very beginning of his ministry: confrontation with hostile spiritual forces and with human beings intent on humiliating and then killing him. It even describes the suffering and rejection he endured from his family and lifelong friends. Words alone can't accurately convey all that Jesus went through to help us understand how much God loves us. But, this action story about his life is an excellent place to begin.

QUOTABLES

Many who are now first will be last, and many who are now last will be first (10:31). Jesus tells his disciples that in the afterlife, some of this world's most respected people will be humbled, and the least respected will finally receive the honor due them.

I will make you fishers of men (1:17, NIV). What Jesus says to Peter and Andrew, the fishermen He is inviting to become His disciples.

Give to Caesar what is Caesar's and to God what is God's (12:17, NIV). The answer Jesus gives to Jewish leaders trying to trick Him into a traitorous quote by asking if Jews should pay taxes imposed by the Romans.

SNEAK PREVIEW

1 Timothy
Like an ancient E-mail from the person you respect the most...

BEHIND the SCENES
of Mark

STARRING ROLES

Jesus, God's son, who has come to earth in human form (1:1)
12 apostles, men Jesus invites to join His ministry as disciples (1:16; 3:14–19)

PLOT

Mark skips the childhood of Jesus altogether and begins with John the Baptist preaching in the desert. This makes total sense since John fulfills the Old Testament prophecy of the messenger who is to prepare people for the Lord's arrival. Get it? From Old Testament promise to New Testament fulfillment.

Jesus arrives, is baptized by John, then retreats into the desert, where He overcomes several temptations by Satan. Immediately afterward, Jesus begins His ministry in Galilee (northern Israel) by choosing four fishermen as the first of 12 disciples. Then He amazes people with miracles like casting out demons and healing the sick. After a few of these, He calls the rest of the disciples. Jesus' ministry

STAGE DIRECTIONS

Birth of Jesus
6 B.C.

Jesus begins ministry
A.D. 26

Jesus crucified
A.D. 30

Dates are approximate

BIBLE EVENTS

10 B.C.   A.D. 1   A.D. 40

WORLD EVENTS

Trial by combat used among German tribes
A.D. 1

Cremation preferred burial method by wealthy Romans
A.D. 30

Nero is born
A.D. 37

BEHIND the SCENES
of Mark

of teaching and healing continues with amazing results. Jesus draws a crowd wherever He goes. His teachings draw them in. His miracles astonish them. But, within these astonished people mingle skeptics, scholars, and religious leaders. They don't agree with Jesus' teachings. They make a lot of attempts to humiliate Jesus.

When Jesus heads to Jerusalem, these skeptics begin to make their move. It all happens fast.

Jesus enters Jerusalem on a Sunday, amid cheering crowds who give Him a royal welcome. Five days later, by 9 A.M., He is nailed to a cross. By about 3 P.M., he is dead. But come Sunday morning, His tomb is empty, and an angel dressed in white is declaring that Jesus is alive and preparing to visit His devastated disciples. And His skeptics, well, they're just a bit confused.

AUTHOR AND DATE

The writer never says, "Hi, I'm Mark, and I'll be writing this book." However, Christian leaders in the early second century said it was written in Italy by John Mark, and was based on the memories of Peter. John (his Hebrew name) was also called Mark (his Latin name). We don't know if he ever met Jesus (see 14:51–52), but he did know the apostles. Peter went to John Mark's mom's house after an angel released him from prison one night (Acts 12:12). Her home was a meeting place for Christians, and a group was praying there when Peter arrived.

Most Bible experts say Mark was the first Gospel written, and that the writers of Matthew and Luke had access to Mark's manuscript, and borrowed from it. Matthew, for example, repeats 601 of the 678 verses in Mark. Most believe Mark was written in Rome by the early 60s. The story does contain Latin terms, and it explains Israel's geography and some Aramaic words, both of which would have been familiar to people living in Israel. The biblical evidence and early Christian writers indicate that both Peter and John Mark were in Rome during the Christian persecution of the 60s.

More than 1,000 years after Jesus, knights of the Crusades searched Israel for the Holy Grail—the cup of wine over which Jesus spoke the words, "This is my blood, which is poured out for many" (14:24). People in the Middle Ages collected sacred relics, which they believed had mystical power. Any trace of the blood of Jesus, they thought, would be the most powerful relic of all.

ON LOCATION

The story takes place primarily in what is now Israel, though some of the scenes show Jesus ministering east of the Jordan River, in what is now northern Jordan. The early part of Jesus' ministry takes place in his hometown region of Galilee, in northern Israel. His last week takes place in the Jerusalem area, in the region of Judea.

WHAT TO LOOK FOR

- **Tons of action.** Mark focuses more on what Jesus did than what he taught. In fact, this Gospel contains fewer teachings of Jesus than any of the four Gospels. Like any action-packed stories, this is fast paced. Mark jumps from one scene to the next, saying something like, "Immediately after that…" This conveys the image of a super busy Jesus, and it leaves the rest of us with the weariness that he and his disciples must have experienced.

- **A suffering Jesus.** There are only 16 chapters in this short book, and the last 6 are devoted to the final week of Jesus' life: his suffering and crucifixion.

  So, why does Mark devote so much of the book to the last days of Jesus' life?
  - **First,** the Jews of Jesus' day can't conceive of a suffering Messiah. They expect a king. The Old Testament prophets have spoken of a suffering servant sent from God, but the Jews apparently don't associate these passages with the Messiah. Instead, they latch onto prophecies about the Messiah's glory days, which are yet to come.
  - **Second,** this book might have been designed to help early believers. The was written about A.D. 60. In A.D. 64, Rome catches fire and Emperor Nero blames the Christians. This begins an empire-wide persecution of Christians. Many believers are martyred or executed in really gross ways. The followers of Jesus would have benefited from reading about a suffering Messiah.
- **What's the big secret?** Throughout this book, Jesus constantly tells people not to say anything about who He is. When demons begins to say who He is, He orders them to be quiet. When He heals a man of leprosy, He asks the man not to tell anyone. He probably does this to keep opposition to a minimum. Not everyone liked what Jesus was doing. Jesus also uses parables as coded messages to followers. The messages within the parables wouldn't have made any sense to the people opposing Jesus.
- **Son of Man.** This is Jesus' favorite way of describing Himself. He uses it 14 times in Mark. By calling Himself this, Jesus is fulfilling the prophecy in Daniel 7:13–14. The image in Daniel is that of a royal, victorious Messiah. Many believe that this image will fully unfold at the Second Coming, when Jesus returns to earth (Matthew 24:30).

EXTREME SCENES
from Mark

⟩ Jesus goes fishing (1:14-20)

Before Jesus begins His ministry, he's baptized, then heads into the desert to pray. He knows what's coming. Satan tempts Him, trying to get Him to abandon His mission. Jesus proves Himself stronger than Satan. He eventually leaves the desert to begin His work. He begins His work by calling a group of 12 men to be disciples. He finds the first four men working as fishermen on the Sea of Galilee. As Jesus is walking along the shore, he sees the brothers Andrew and Simon casting a net.

Jesus says something like, "You wanna catch fish? Great! Let Me teach you how to be fishers of men." Both men join Him immediately. Probably because they've already heard His preaching and witnessed His power. Farther down the shore Jesus invites another team of brothers, James and John (later nicknamed "Thunderbolts"). Just like Andrew and Simon, they leave their nets and follow Jesus. (Later, Jesus selects His remaining disciples: Philip, Bartholomew, Matthew, Thomas, James son of Alphaeus, Thaddaeus, Simon, known as the Eager One, and Judas Iscariot, who would later betray Him.)

DIRECTOR'S NOTES

The mustard seed is proof of the old saying, "Big things come in small packages." One tiny mustard seed—a seed much smaller than a kernel of corn—is capable of producing a plant up to fifteen feet high. Mark 4:31

⟩ Evicted demons (1:21-28)

Jesus had unbelievable fortitude. Before he faces humans that are really nasty, he faces unseen, spiritual forces. These demonic beings aren't necessarily after Jesus. But, they're not happy when He sets out against them. While Jesus is teaching in a synagogue at Capernaum a demon-possessed man storms into the service and interrupts...yelling and screaming. The conversation goes a little something like this:

"Jesus from Nazareth," the demon yells, "what do you want with us? Have you come to destroy us? I know who You are! You are God's Holy One."

"Be quiet," Jesus replies, "and come out of the man!"

Jesus takes control. The evil spirit shakes the man, screams, and takes off. All the people who witness this otherworldly encounter are confused and wonder where Jesus gets His power. News of Jesus spreads quickly through the town and beyond, and people begin coming to Him for healing. Lepers, lame, blind, demon-possessed—Jesus heals them all.

Jesus breaks the rules (2:23-3:6)

Jesus does something that makes the Pharisees really mad. One Sabbath, the disciples pick some heads of grain as they follow Him through a field. A group of Pharisees sees this and confronts Jesus. The Pharisees believe that plucking even a few heads of grain is harvesting, which is work (and . . . working on the Sabbath is a big no no). Jesus disagrees and tells them the Sabbath was made to benefit people, not deprive them. Later, Jesus does more "work" on the Sabbath by healing a man with a crippled hand. Rather than marveling at Jesus' obvious power, the Pharisees go nuts with anger and start making plans to kill Jesus.

Gardening 101 (4:1-20)

Jesus isn't just a clever teacher, He's a strategist. He knows that not everyone will accept His teachings. He tries to convey what He knows in a story about a farmer sowing seeds.

Basically, the story (with a quick explanation) goes like this: Some seeds fall on the road and are taken by birds. These seeds symbolize people who hear Jesus' message but are snatched away by Satan. Some seeds land in shallow dirt resting on stones; the seeds spring up quickly but die. These are people who accept the message but don't develop spiritual roots. Some seeds land among thorns and get choked. These are people who accept the message but let it get squeezed out by preoccupation with other things, such as making money. Finally, some seeds land in good soil and produce a great harvest. These are people who accept Jesus' message and pass it on.

Through parables like this, Jesus is able to reveal mysteries about the kingdom of God to His followers. His followers understand because they have faith in Christ. However, Jesus' opponents are often mystified by these seemingly simple tales.

DIRECTOR'S NOTES

Salt wasn't just used for flavoring in Jesus' day. It was also used in sacrifices and as a preservative. Most salt in Galilee came from the Dead Sea, which is nine times saltier than ocean water. It wasn't like the salt we use today, though. Because it contained many impurities, salt in New Testament times became stale pretty quickly. Mark 9:49-50

An eager woman (5:21-34)

While Jesus is walking in a crowd, a woman who has been suffering from bleeding for 12 years decides that even touching the robe of Jesus will bring her healing. When she touches Him, Jesus feels a release of power. Jesus knows what happened. He questions the disciples, who think that He's crazy . . . they're in a mob and a lot of people are touching Him. Jesus turns to the woman and says, "You are well now because of your faith." Throughout His ministry, faith is the response Jesus looks for. Through faith, strangers and non-Jews are healed. But without faith, even Jesus' family and the Jewish leaders experience nothing.

Leftovers (8:1-10)

Earlier, Jesus fed 5,000 people with five loaves of bread and two small fish. This time, he feeds a crowd of 4,000 with seven patties of bread and a few fish. But the result is the same: the people eat their fill, and the disciples collect many basketfuls of leftovers.

Later on, the disciples show their ignorance by apologetically only bringing one loaf of bread with them on a trip. Check out Jesus' response in 8:17-19.

Telling Peter off (8:27-33)

Jesus and Peter have a little disciple-Messiah confrontation. It's not much, but it's enough for Jesus to tell Peter off. Jesus was telling the disciples that the Messiah (He) would suffer a lot (he was predicting His rejection and murder) but would rise from the dead three days later. The disciples can't conceive of a suffering Messiah—only a victorious one. When Peter advises Jesus to stop talking like this, Jesus responds, "Satan, get away from me! You are thinking like everyone else and not like God." Then Jesus tells them that if they are to be his followers, they have to be willing to give up their lives. If they do this, Jesus assures them, they will preserve their souls. Six days later, Jesus gives Peter, James, and John a glimpse into the afterlife by allowing them to see Him in His glowing, heavenly body as He talks with Moses and Elijah (9:2–8).

Jesus likes kids (10:13-16)

In Bible times, people believed that a blessing can unleash an unbelievable power in someone's life. One day, while Jesus is teaching, some parents come forward, hoping to have Jesus bless their children. The disciples can't believe it. They're amazed that these parents would have the guts to bother Jesus. Jesus ignores the disciples and blesses the children. By doing this, Jesus shows the kind of compassion he wants them to imitate. Then he reveals how to become a citizen of God's kingdom. The disciples (true to form) just don't get the fact that the Kingdom of God is spiritual…not physical.

Jesus goes home (11:1-11)

Up to this point, Jesus has told the disciples that he's going to die. And still they haven't gotten the hint. So, when Jesus enters Jerusalem and the people are really happy, the disciples have even more reason to anticipate a happy ending. Jesus even rides in on a donkey, just like Zechariah 9:9 says the Messiah will arrive. The crowd goes nuts when Jesus enters Jerusalem. They lay palm branches on the ground and cheer. Unfortunately, this is the last happy moment Mark records. The trial and death of Jesus are just days away. Following this scene, Mark sets the stage for the final battle between Jesus and the Jewish leaders.

Aftershave for the feet (14:1-11)

The day before Jesus is arrested, he goes to some friends' house in Bethany for a meal.

While he's there, a woman opens a sealed, stone flask full of expensive perfume—worth a year's salary. This kind of perfume is used on special occasions, like to prepare the body of someone you love for burial. The woman pours this on the head of Jesus, and the other guests go a little crazy. They wonder why a woman would waste such expensive stuff on Jesus. Jesus tells them to be quiet. Afterward, Judas goes to the Jewish priests and offers to help them arrest Jesus. The following night, while Jesus is praying in a secluded place on the Mount of Olives, Judas leads temple officers to arrest him.

Jesus is executed (15:1-47)

When the high priest learns that Jesus is in custody, he calls an emergency session of the Sanhedrin, a 70-member legislative court of priests, scholars, and respected elders. They find Jesus guilty of blasphemy (a capital offense). Jesus is ordered to appear before Pilate, who's the only one who can order an execution. Even though he sees no reason to kill Jesus, he orders Jesus crucified. At about 9 A.M., Roman soldiers nail Jesus to a cross. Jewish leaders mock Jesus. At noon the sky turns black and stays that way until three o'clock. About this time, Jesus dies. At that moment, an earthquake rips through the land, strong enough to tear the sacred curtain inside the temple. As Jesus hangs on the cross, a soldier finally recognizes who Jesus is and comments "This man really was the Son of God!"

DIRECTOR'S NOTES

The secret to Rome's success was slave labor. It's been estimated that one out of every five people in the Roman Empire was a slave. Slaves in New Testament times had very few rights. Some were treated worse than animals. The only way a slave could become a free person was to pay a certain amount of money—usually thirty pieces of silver, or about a month's earnings. Mark 10:45

The case of the missing Messiah (16:1-8)

The body of Jesus is taken down before dusk. It's the Sabbath now, and there's no time to carefully prepare the body by anointing it with oil. So, they wrap the corpse in linen and place it in a tomb cut from solid rock. The entrance is sealed with a huge, disk-shaped stone that rolls along a stone-chiseled groove on the ground. Sunday morning, three women walk to the tomb to properly prepare His body for burial. They're worried how they're going to move the heavy stone by themselves. But guess what! The stone is rolled away! Inside the tomb is a white-robed young man (alive...by the way).

"Don't be alarmed," the man says, and He tells them that Jesus is alive.

INTERVIEW
with the Stars

A woman's liberation

Behind the Bible's next subject, Mary Magdalene, is one of six different Marys found in the Bible. Like many other men and women mentioned in the Bible, we don't know much about her. But we do know that she mattered to Jesus and that her life made a difference because of her overarching desire to serve and honor her master, teacher, and friend. Mary, what was behind your devotion to Jesus?

⇒ Mary Magdalene

It's very simple. For years, I had been tormented by not one, but seven demons. My life was literally a living hell. I was untouchable, unlovely, and unreachable—beyond help. Yet, Jesus touched me. He loved me and reached beyond the cultural barriers to help me. How else could I have responded but in total gratitude to the One who liberated me from my prison?

So what did you do?

⇒ Mary Magdalene

I joined a small group of women who traveled with Jesus and the disciples. We took care of their needs—prepared and provided meals, did the laundry, mended their robes, did whatever it took to meet their needs so they could go about the business of Jesus' ministry here on earth. Some of the women were wealthy enough to support Jesus' ministry financially; I had to show my gratitude in other ways.

How did you do that?

⇒ Mary Magdalene

Basically I did whatever I could to show Jesus my love for Him. For example, after that awful, awful day, when they crucified my Lord on the cross, I wanted to properly anoint Jesus' body. There wasn't time to do it right after Jesus had died because of the Sabbath. So first thing in the morning, I went along with several others to His tomb. It seemed like such a small thing at the time, but it led to such a wonderful, miraculous, world-changing event, that even as I recall that moment, I shake like a leaf.

INTERVIEW
with the Stars

Explain to us what happened.

⇾ Mary Magdalene

When I got to the tomb, the stone had been rolled away and the tomb was empty! I thought some of Jesus' enemies had taken His body away and I was so upset. I totally broke down, weeping. I went looking for someone to help me. Nothing could have prepared me for the truth when moments later I was looking into the face of my Lord! He was alive! And is alive! He told me to go and tell the others.

So, you were the first eyewitness to Jesus' resurrection. And your testimony that Jesus is alive sparked that movement of people who came to be known as Christians! Talk about a life that made a difference!

⇾ Mary Magdalene

It's hard to believe that it is all true. Certainly, it is quite an honor to have been the first one that Jesus appeared to, but all that was on my mind that morning was to be obedient and do the right thing. I wanted to honor Jesus' buried body; God had something far greater in mind. The most important thing you can do with your life is put yourself in God's plan and pathway by doing what is right. Honor and fame don't always follow obedience, but obedience has to be there first. Make sure you are where God is at work—and leave the rest up to Him!

INTERVIEW
with the Stars

A simple gift/the gift that kept giving

Behind the Bible's next subject is one of those people in the Bible who we know little about. We don't know his name. We don't know where he lived or what became of him after this event that is mentioned in all four Gospels. All we know for sure about this young boy is what he had for lunch and what he was willing to give to Jesus—and the totally jaw-dropping event that occurred because of this boy's simple gift. Young man, can you fill us in on a few of the details?

⇒ Boy with lunch

I'm originally from the Galilee area, and we had heard about this Jesus. News had even reached our tiny village about miraculous healings and this man's powerful teaching. I convinced my mom to let me go and join some of the other men from the village who were going to hear Him teach. I didn't know how long we were going to be gone, so my mom packed me a lunch, not much, two fish and five loaves of bread. It was enough to keep me going for a few days.

What happened when you finally reached the place where Jesus was teaching?

⇒ Boy with lunch

I couldn't believe it! The crowd was huge! I had never seen so many people in one place at one time before. My village is only a couple hundred people. There had to be thousands of people there listening to Jesus. There were people everywhere.

How were you able to get close to Jesus and His disciples with so many people there?

⇒ Boy with lunch

Being so short, I couldn't see or hear anything from the edge of the crowd, so I snaked my way through the crowd until I got a great seat front and center. I was so close, in fact, that I could even hear Jesus' disciples arguing with Him.

INTERVIEW
with the Stars

What was the argument about?

⋗ Boy with lunch

Well, it appears that Jesus told His disciples to feed the crowd and they basically were telling Him to get real—there was no way they could possibly pay for enough food to feed all these people. They wanted Jesus to send everyone home. I had forgotten all about my little lunch until then, but I thought if it could help feed a few people, that was better than nothing. So I went up and offered Jesus and the disciples my lunch.

Most of us are probably familiar with what happened next, but why don't you describe the scene in your own words.

⋗ Boy with lunch

I remember a few of the disciples snickering when I came up with my lunch, like, who is he kidding? Two fish and five loaves of bread? But I will never forget Jesus' face. He turned to me with such a look of love and kindness. He took my fish and bread and He blessed them. The next thing I knew the disciples were handing out basketfuls of fish and bread! All from my lunch! It was totally an amazing thing to see.

The lesson we can learn from your story is so obvious, but it bears repeating. Why don't you give us your take on what you learned from this occasion?

⋗ Boy with lunch

Well you can view yourself like how the disciples viewed my lunch—not worth bothering about. Or you can view yourself how Jesus did my lunch—in His hands, *anything* can happen. The choice is yours!

REVIEWS

You better buy your popcorn early and hit the restroom before you go in because once this show begins there's not even time to breathe until it's over. Talk about action adventure. The camera work is amazing. No panning, just straight shots between scenes. No scenic landscape moments. Each angle just zooms to the next. Mark tells the story of Jesus much like the disciples must have told it right after the Resurrection.

Imagine it. You witness the execution of the most influential person you've ever known. You are powerless to help. You bury Him and mourn His death. You wonder how life will ever be the same. Then someone comes running up, breathless, and tells you that He's alive again. How would *you* tell it? I can almost imagine ol' doubting Thomas holding the camera on himself, hands shaking, saying " I am SOOO sorry."

As Mark told the story of Jesus' life he concentrated on what Jesus did rather than what he said or thought or felt. Mark had the opportunity to watch a lot of it from behind the scenes. He wasn't a disciple but the disciples met at his mom's house. Mark got to be close friends with the disciple named Peter. Mark's cousin was Barnabas, who later worked and traveled with Paul. Mark even traveled with Paul and Barnabas once on one of their missionary journeys. Mark really had access to the real scoop in ways that other researchers of the time didn't. Why did he focus so much on the "hard" facts and action/adventure parts of the story?

Mark's target audience was the Romans. The Romans? Many were soldiers, conquerors. They would be interested in

ENCORE

> For more insights about Jesus, read the other three Gospels: Matthew, Luke, and John. For the Gospel least like Mark, read John.

> Read Acts to see how the disciples respond to their newfound faith that Jesus is the Son of God.

REVIEWS

the intrigue of Jesus' life, not so much the lessons. They were "show-me" kinds of guys. It says a lot about Mark that he even wanted to write a gospel for them.

Get this, though. Even though Mark was writing for a tough audience, he presented Jesus as a servant leader. So he showed both sides. He showed the power of Jesus' miracles, but also the humble guy He was. Some Roman soldiers probably *were* impressed with the story of this tough, scrappy guy fighting for what He believed and giving up everything—power, friends, his *life* to defend those beliefs. The highest purpose and the greatest honor a soldier can achieve is to sacrifice his life defending others. Jesus sacrificed His life so that we can all live FOREVER. Soldiers were bound to be interested in a story like this. I know I'm impressed, how 'bout you?

Capt. O. Mysol

Luke

SCHEDULE OF SCENES

Jesus Is Born	Jesus Crucified Pentecost	Temple Destroyed	Luke Written	Death of John
7/6 B.C.	A.D. 30	A.D. 70	c. 75	A.D. 100

The tale of two physicians

Everyone likes a baby. Especially if the baby has superpowers. Like, if the baby could be the fulfillment of a prophecy...that would be cool. And, if the baby had the power to make blind men see, and lame people walk...that would be even cooler. Yeah, everyone likes a powerful baby.

Luke's Gospel might feel like the same old story repeated again. Actually, the elements are the same. But, Luke's account is absolutely essential. It recorded the birth of the world's most powerful baby —Jesus. Luke, a physician, is the only one who reports the birth of Jesus in such moving detail.

There are great stories here. There's the story of the loving shepherd, leaving his 99 safe sheep to look for the lost one. And the story of the prodigal son, squandering his share of the family wealth, then returning home to the open arms of a loving father. And the story of the good Samaritan, a half-breed who shows compassion to an injured man after blue-blood Jews, supposed men of God, walk on by. In fact, there are fourteen of these stories that are only found in Luke. Oh yeah...there are also six miracles and ten leper healings too. Yep...lots of stories here. And, all of them point us to Jesus...the most powerful baby ever.

QUOTABLES

Our Father which art in heaven, hallowed be thy name (Luke 11:2, KJV). The first sentence of the Lord's Prayer.

Glory to God in the highest, and on earth peace, good will toward men (2:14, KJV). The praise of angels in a shepherd's pasture on the night of Jesus' birth.

Physician, heal thyself (4:23, KJV). The words of Jesus, anticipating the command of his hometown critics, wanting to see him perform in Nazareth the miracles they hear he has done elsewhere.

I am sending you out like lambs among wolves (10:3, NIV). The warning of Jesus to 72 followers he is sending on a mission of preaching and healing.

SNEAK PREVIEW

Nehemiah
A brave band of underdogs reclaim their city.

BEHIND the SCENES of Luke

STARRING ROLES

Jesus, God's son, who has come to earth in human form to offer salvation from sin, and eternal life to everyone who has faith in Him (1:31)
12 apostles, men Jesus invites to join his ministry as disciples (5:10; 6:13–16)

PLOT

The angel Gabriel makes dramatic appearances to announce the coming birth of two men who will change history: John the Baptist and Jesus. A month later, Gabriel tells Mary, a teenage virgin from a low-income family, that she will miraculously give birth to Jesus. Both children are born. John begins his ministry, urging people to repent of their sins and then be baptized to show their devotion to God. Jesus is baptized and begins His ministry. A short time later, John's ministry ends when He is arrested and beheaded for criticizing Herod's marriage to his brother's wife.

STAGE DIRECTIONS

BIBLE EVENTS

Birth
of Jesus
6 B.C.

Jesus
begins   Jesus
ministry crucified
A.D. 26   A.D. 30

Dates are
approximate

40 B.C.   A.D. 1   A.D. 40

WORLD EVENTS

Rome names
Herod the Great
king of Jews
40 B.C.

Druids in Britain
believe they
descended from
a supreme being
A.D. 1

Romans make
first known
reference
to diamonds
A.D. 16

BEHIND the SCENES
of Luke

Jesus teaches and heals throughout His home region of Galilee for several years, establishing a following of people who believe He is the Messiah. He makes the Jewish leaders mad because He doesn't share their interpretation of Scripture on many key points. They keep close tabs on Him, follow Him everywhere and constantly bug Him. As Jesus heads toward Jerusalem, His ministry is drawing to a close. But He continues preaching and healing, even among non-Jewish groups such as the Samaritans. When he finally arrives in Jerusalem, crowds welcome Him as the promised Messiah-king. Thursday evening, while praying, He is arrested and rushed to the Jewish leaders who try Him all night, condemn Him to death, then at daybreak on Friday they insist that the Roman governor issue the death sentence.

That same morning, Jesus is nailed to a cross. By early afternoon, He is dead. On Sunday, however, He is raised to life and later appears several times to the disciples. Some time afterward, on the Mount of Olives, the disciples watch Him ascend into the sky.

AUTHOR AND DATE

Luke wrote this book. He's a physician and a friend of the apostle Paul. Even though the book never says it's written by Luke, Christian leaders in the second century said he wrote it. Both the Gospel and its sequel are addressed to "Honorable Theophilus," probably a Roman official who asked for information about Christianity. In response, Luke produces a really great account, drawing from material gathered from a variety of sources, including eyewitnesses.

The book may have been written as early as the late 50s, before the execution of Luke's friend, Paul. But the book's emphasis on the fall of Jerusalem (which happened in A.D. 70) hints that the book was written a lot later.

ON LOCATION

The story takes place primarily in what is now Israel, with some scenes east of the Jordan River, in what is now northern Jordan. Much of Jesus' ministry takes place in His hometown region of Galilee, in northern Israel. His last week takes place in the Jerusalem area, in the region of Judea.

INSIDE SCOOP

> Luke is believed to be the only non-Jewish writer of Scripture. His literary contribution of the Gospel of Luke and its sequel, Acts, amounts to nearly one-fourth of the New Testament.

> Legend says Luke was an artist, and that in A.D. 590 Pope Gregory the Great used one of Luke's paintings to lead a procession that stopped a plague. An angel is said to have appeared, sheathing its bloody sword, ending the plague. Luke, at least, was a painter of vivid word pictures that inspired many artists.

> John the Baptist and Jesus were related, though the Bible doesn't say how (1:36).

WHAT TO LOOK FOR

- **The way of salvation.** So, what really drives this Gospel? One thing — Jesus is the savior of the human race. What Luke chooses to report about Jesus—events, miracles, and teachings—all point to this single truth.
- **The most comprehensive story of Jesus.** This Gospel is 100 percent Jesus. It covers more detail about Jesus than any other Gospel. In fact, there's so much info about Jesus that a lot of scholars call Luke the first Christian historian
- **Good news for everyone.** Luke uses many techniques to show that salvation through Jesus is available to everyone. Check out some of his moves:
  - Luke reveals that Jesus came not just for the Jews but also as "a light for revelation to the Gentiles." Get it? Everyone has the chance to be saved.
  - Unlike Matthew, Luke traces Jesus' genealogy back to Adam. He doesn't stop with Abraham, like a lot of others do.
  - Luke reports Jesus' parable of the good Samaritan, which commends a race that many Jews hate.
  - Luke identifies a bunch of women. This is really cool because in ancient times women were barely regarded at all.
- **A non-Jewish audience.** Luke's not a Jew. And, he aims this book for non Jews. He barely makes any references to the Old Testament (The Gentiles wouldn't have known it) and he doesn't use the word Rabbi (Gentiles wouldn't have necessarily understood that word).
- **Jesus' compassion for the needy.** Luke's Gospel is full of stories showing how much Jesus cares about the poor and the social outcasts. Jesus is drawn to sinners, and even eats with tax collectors. Luke writes down His encounters with these people.
- **The prayer life of Jesus.** Prayer is important to Jesus. He prays throughout this Gospel, including after His baptism, before selecting disciples, and before dying. He also teaches the disciples how to pray and tells the crowds several stories about the importance of taking requests to God.

EXTREME SCENES
from Luke

A magnetic baby (2:1-20)

The miraculous story of Jesus' birth reveals that the first to visit the Savior were not wealthy rulers or prestigious Jewish leaders, but humble shepherds guarding their sheep near Bethlehem. They got an invitation they couldn't refuse: angels filled the night sky with the brightness of God's glory. The shepherds rush to the place and tell Mary and Joseph what the angel said.

Lost at the party (2:41-52)

Each spring, Mary and Joseph take Jesus and their other children to Jerusalem, to celebrate the Passover festival that commemorates Israel's freedom from slavery in Egypt. One year, when Jesus is 12, He accidentally gets left in Jerusalem after the festival. Mary and Joseph think He's with them and their family. But He's not. When they realize that Jesus is back in the city, they get frantic and head back to Jerusalem and search for three days. They finally find Him sitting in the temple courtyard, talking with teachers who are astonished at the lad's insight. When Mary asks her son why He stayed behind and caused her such terrifying worry, Jesus replies something like, "Mom! Didn't you know that I would be in my Father's house?"

Jesus is dissed (4:14-30)

One day, as Jesus is beginning His ministry, Jesus is sitting in a synagogue in His hometown. His friends and family are there to hear Him. He begins reading from a scroll from Isaiah where it says, "The Spirit of the Lord is upon me, Because he has appointed me to preach the gospel to the poor; He has sent me to heal the brokenhearted, to proclaim liberty to the captives and recovery of sight to the blind to set at liberty those who are oppressed." (4:18). People are happy, right? Nope. They're actually very upset at what He says. He closes the scroll and says, "What you have just heard me read has come true today." The people can't believe their ears. As far as they are concerned, Jesus is Joseph's son—not the Messiah. Furious at His blatant blasphemy, they try to throw Him from a cliff, but He slips through the crowd and leaves town.

Lowering for a miracle (5:17-26)

One day as Jesus is teaching in a house, some men can't get their paralyzed friend in . . . the house is packed! So they remove the roofing tile and lower their friend through the ceiling. Jesus is so impressed by this show of faith that he says, "My friend, your sins are forgiven" (5:20). And, as you might expect, Jewish scholars instantly object. Only God can forgive sins. And, they're convinced that Jesus isn't God. Jesus asks which is easier—to heal the man or forgive his sins. Jesus says he has the power to do both.

"Pick up your mat and walk home," Jesus tells the man. The man does, and everyone is amazed.

Long distance healing (7:1-10)

A Roman soldier who is not a Jew convinces some Jewish friends to do him a favor. They ask Jesus to heal a servant of his who is deathly sick. Jesus agrees and begins walking to the soldier's home, but he is intercepted by others bearing a second message from the officer. The message is that Jesus doesn't *really* need to come over. He can heal the girl from a distance if he wants. The guy's faith impresses him and heals the servant.

Groggy, but still in charge (8:22-25)

One evening Jesus decides to leave Galilee and sail across the lake, called the Sea of Galilee, to an area where mostly non-Jews live. Jesus has become so weary that he falls into a deep sleep. He doesn't even wake up when a storm tosses the boat around. Even though they're skilled fishermen, the disciples start to freak out. They're convinced they're going to drown. They wake Jesus up. He tells the storm to be quiet and everything calms down.

A daring Samaritan (10:30-37)

Jesus is questioned Jewish scholar who wants to know what the two most important laws are. Jesus replies with this now very famous story of the Good Samaritan.

A man walking the deserted, 15-mile path from Jerusalem to Jericho is attacked by robbers, stripped, beaten, and left for dead. Later in the day a priest approaches, but walks right on by. Then comes another temple worker, but he walks by also. Finally a Samaritan arrives, helps the man, takes him to an inn, and pays the innkeeper to take care of the victim until he recovers. (By the way, Samaritans are considered half-breeds by the Jews, and they don't like them very much.) "So," Jesus asks, "Which one of these three people was a real neighbor?" The scholar replies, "The one who showed pity." "Go and do the same," Jesus says.

Addressing God (11:1-4)

Jesus prays a lot. After one time of prayer, one of His disciples asks that He teach them all how to pray. Jesus responds with an example that has become known as the Lord's Prayer.

Welcome home! (15:11-32)

People kept questioning Jesus about His mission on earth. Either they didn't get it, or they were trying to trick Him. In response to them bugging Him nonstop, He tells this story about the Prodigal Son. The idea is to give them an accurate picture of what He's here to do. In this story, a son asks for and is given his share of the family property. He leaves home and spends all the money in wild living. He spends himself broke and lowers himself to eating pig food to survive. He decides to go home and ask his father for a job, since even the servants are better off than he. On the son's last stretch home, his father spots him a long way off and takes off running, arms wide open. You want a great description of what Jesus is here to do? Read this story.

A hated little man

Tax collectors routinely overtax and keep the extra money. No one likes them. As Jesus is passing through Jericho on His way to Jerusalem a crowd meets Him and begins walking with Him. Like others, Zacchaeus has heard of Jesus and wants to get a look at Him. But Zacchaeus is too short. So he runs ahead and climbs a tree. When the crowd approaches the tree, Jesus stops, looks up, and says He'd like to stay the night at Zacchaeus' home. By the time Jesus leaves Jericho, Zacchaeus is a changed man. He offers to give half his money to the poor and to repay everyone he has cheated. Pretty cool change, huh?!

A willing widow (21:1-4)

Jesus arrives in Jerusalem and he's greeted by a huge crowd laying down palm branches (you guessed it, Palm Sunday!). While in Jerusalem, Jesus stands with the disciples in one of the temple courtyards. There, they watch people dropping their offerings into temple collection boxes. Some donors are rich, and make the size of their gift as conspicuous as possible. When Jesus sees a poor widow give what He knows is all she has, he turns to the disciples and says, "This poor woman has put in more than all the others."

Private prayers of a dying man (22:39-46)

On Thursday evening, Jesus eats a final meal with his disciples. Then He leads them to the Mount of Olives, where He prays passionately for God to spare Him from the crucifixion. Judas arrives and the scene turns sour real quick. A bunch of temple guards arrive and arrest Jesus. They take Him to the home of Caiaphas, the high priest, who convenes an emergency session of the Sanhedrin. After an all-night trial, they convict Jesus of blasphemy for claiming to be the Son of God. At daybreak, the assembly leads Jesus to Pilate, the Roman governor, who alone has the authority to condemn a local prisoner to death. When Pilate refuses, not agreeing that blasphemy is a capital offense, the Jews charge that Jesus is an insurrectionist, stirring up the crowds for a possible revolt. Pilate remains unconvinced, as does Herod, who is also in town. But Pilate eventually gives in to the persistent assembly and orders Jesus executed immediately.

Final moments (23:26-56)

As Jesus is nailed to a cross He prays, "Father, forgive these people! They don't know what they're doing." People in the crowd hurl insults at Him. One of the two criminals hanging beside makes fun of Jesus. Jesus dies about 3 P.M. and His body is given to a Sanhedrin member who had objected to the council's sentence. Jesus is buried in this man's newly cut tomb, but by Sunday morning He is raised from the dead.

Walking a long road (24:13-35)

On the day of His resurrection, Jesus joins two dejected travelers on their way to Emmaus, a village seven miles from Jerusalem. The two men don't recognize the Lord. They tell Him about how the Crucifixion has dashed their hopes in Jesus, whom they had thought was the Messiah. But Jesus, without revealing His identity, replies, "Didn't you know that the Messiah would have to suffer before He was given His glory?" Then He teaches them a Bible lesson, proving His point by quoting the books of Moses and the words of the prophets. Only later, as He breaks bread for them during a meal, do they recognize who He is. Then He disappears. Cool!

INTERVIEW
with the Stars

The right response

Behind the Bible's next subject is yet another Bible character who needs no introduction. Mention the name Mary and instantly a picture of a young woman cradling a tiny baby in a rude stable comes to mind. But think about it. What do you *really* know about Mary as a person? What were her dreams? What did she like to do when the house was quiet and the chores done? What *did* she think about her firstborn? Most of what we know about Mary comes from her *responses* to the surprises in her life. And she had quite a few of those! Mary, can you tell us about that day when you had probably the biggest surprise of your life.

⇒ Mary, mom of Jesus

I guess getting a visit from an angel ranks pretty high on the scale of the unexpected. I certainly wasn't expecting anything unusual that day. It started out like any other day. But when Gabriel appeared before me, I can tell you, it certainly got my attention! And if having a conversation with an angel isn't amazing enough, what he had to say to me was even more unbelievable.

Tell us about that. What did you think?

⇒ Mary, mom of Jesus

The only thing I could think of was how? How was this going to happen? How could this be possible? The idea of having a child with God's help certainly wasn't a new concept to me. Our history is filled with women who gave birth because God had promised them a child—Sarah, Hannah, and the Shunmanite woman, to mention a few. But at least those women had husbands! I didn't have a husband yet. How was this going to happen?

INTERVIEW
with the Stars

So what did Gabriel tell you?

⋙ Mary, mom of Jesus

His instructions were specific, but simple. Do nothing. Nothing. God's spirit was going to do it all. That was good enough for me. Gabriel made it clear that I didn't need to worry about the details, the hows, the whens, even the whys. All I needed to know was that God was in control. He would take care of everything. All I had to do was cooperate and participate in God's wonderful plan. What could be simpler? My response was the only one that made any sense: *Let it be to me according to your word* (Luke 1:38).

Mary, I think the majority of our readers will agree that your response to this remarkable news is nothing short of amazing, too. There would be many others who would react with doubt, confusion, possibly anger that God would mess their lives up in this way. In fact, I think we can learn a lot about ourselves by the way we react to the unexpected.

⋙ Mary, mom of Jesus

Certainly God wants to make a difference in and through each one's life. The key is to *expect* God to guide. And be prepared—God's guidance may come in surprising or unexpected ways. I know. It did for me!

INTERVIEW
with the Stars

Sister act

Some people like to do solo acts; they do their best work alone. But **Behind the Bible's** next two subjects discovered early on that they worked well as a team. Mary and Martha were a sister act—together they formed an outstanding hospitality team, whose frequent guest was none other than their good friend Jesus. Each brought different skills to the table that worked well together—most of the time. Tell us a little bit about yourselves. Martha, why don't you begin?

≥ Martha

Thank you. It probably would be more appropriate for Mary to begin because she's the conversationalist. She's the one who would make sure our guests felt comfortable by talking with them or listening. Right, Mary?

≥ Mary

Yes, but you are the original Martha. You were the genius behind getting the food prepared, making sure our guests' needs were met. You took care of all those little details.

It sounds like you two had all the bases covered. So where did the problems come in?

≥ Mary

As you know, Jesus was a frequent guest. He was a good friend of our brother Lazarus, and often when he was coming through Bethany, he would stop in with his disciples. It was one of those evenings when Jesus was there with His 12 disciples. Martha was frantic, trying to get things ready, and . . .

INTERVIEW
with the Stars

⋙ Martha

And there was Mary, sitting at Jesus' feet, hanging on His every word. I mean there's nothing wrong with that, but there were things to get done. The table wasn't set; there was food to get ready. I couldn't do it all by myself! And I was getting downright frustrated! So finally, I got in Jesus' face and told Him to make Mary help me!

And what did Jesus do?

⋙ Mary

That's the wonderful part of this story. And he had such a beautiful way of dealing with it, didn't he, Martha?

⋙ Martha

He sure did. Made me stop in my tracks. All He said was, "Martha, you are worried about so many things. But look at Mary. She's chosen what is best—the only thing that really is important, and it won't be taken away from her." He reminded me oh so gently, yet firmly, that I had forgotten the reason behind why I was so busy.

⋙ Mary

You see, Jesus wasn't telling Martha that she shouldn't have been busy. But he was reminding her that she had shifted her attention from her guest, Jesus, to herself. That's why she resented me so much.

INTERVIEW
with the Stars

So Jesus helped you with a little attitude adjustment.

≥ Martha

You could say that. He helped us be a team again, that's for sure. Later on, we're with Jesus again. I'm still serving, but hey, that's what I do best.

≥ Mary

And I'm still sitting at Jesus' feet, focused on him, but serving him by washing his feet with my perfume. Together, we made a difference for our guest.

So the point is that each one of us, you, Martha, me, and our readers, bring something very special to offer God—ourselves. And we don't have to worry about meeting the expectations of anyone else other than our God. Is that right?

≥ Mary

You got it. The only way to accomplish the purpose God has set out for you most effectively is to keep your attention focused where it needs to be—on God, and not on yourself.

REVIEWS

Of the four Gospels, Luke is the most like a documentary. Luke was a doctor: very detailed and organized. He wrote his Gospel that way. It was important to him to get the facts straight and to let you know exactly how things happened. He set out to document the facts of Jesus' life in order to make the point that Jesus was fully God, but also fully human.

Luke wanted his readers to know that Jesus was born a baby like we all were (Well *most* of us. I think my little brother was *hatched)*. He grew up as a child like we all do (except my brother, who may *never* grow up). He was a teenager before He was an adult (DUH!). He had a human body. He had human emotions. If He cut himself it hurt physically. If His friends let him down, it hurt emotionally.

Because Luke was writing from the perspective of the wonder of Jesus' humanity, he included some human interest stories and interesting facts that the other Gospel writers didn't include. He gave insights into Christ's childhood. He documented Christ's compassion in dealing with the people around Him. Luke made the point that Jesus wasn't too high and mighty to get down and dirty when ministry demanded it. Luke painted the picture of a Jesus whose priority was to become a part of our journey and teach us a better way.

Luke revealed Jesus' friendships. He mentioned more women than any other Gospel. He told the story about Martha (the organizer) and Mary (the people person). They practically fought over time with Jesus at a dinner party in Bethany.

It was Luke that revealed to us that Jesus was accused of being a party-er. What?!? That's right. Jesus complained to the Pharisees saying, "John the Baptist came neither eating bread nor drinking wine, and you say, 'He has a demon.' The Son of Man has come eating and drinking, and you say,

> Acts shows how the disciples boldly continued the work Jesus began, starting the Christian church.

> Matthew and Mark are two similar accounts of the life of Jesus. John also focuses on Jesus, but emphasizes primarily the teachings and miracles that show he is the Son of God.

'Look, a glutton and a winebibber, a friend of tax collectors and sinners!'" (Luke 7:33-34) Do you get what that means? It means that Jesus wasn't this spaced-out, wild-eyed, on the fringe, holy guru type who kept Himself away from fun of any kind. Jesus was the kind of guy you'd invite to a party. He could sit down with anyone and just hang out and talk. The Pharisees, on the other hand, would probably be the guys to call the cops right after they left and make up stuff to get everybody in trouble. One of the most impressive things about Jesus is that He did most of His miracles and great works *and* sacrificed Himself for us while he was a person like you or me. You expect God to be able to do the impossible, but Jesus was a man, with friends and feelings and everything else, who did the impossible anyway. If you get that, then Luke would be happy. It's what he really wanted you to know about Jesus, the Messiah. So if He can do all that, maybe I can be just a *little* nicer to my little brother. He might turn out to be human yet.

Joe A. Verage

John

SCHEDULE OF SCENES

Jesus Is Born	Jesus Crucified Pentecost	Temple Destroyed	John Written	Death of John
7/6 B.C.	A.D. 30	A.D. 70	A.D. 85	A.D. 100

Extreme faith for the thinker

This is the gospel for smarty-pants. It's written for people who are thinkers. If the action-packed Gospel of Mark was written for shorter attention spans, John has a different kind of person in mind. This book is for people who enjoy peeling off layer upon layer of dramatic, insightful symbolism, and people who want extensive, detailed teaching sessions led by the Master Teacher.

John wrote this with one reason in mind: to convince us to have faith in what he cannot possibly explain. The unexplainable is that Jesus and God are one, and that when Jesus lived on earth, He was both truly God and truly human. You know, that thought almost doesn't even fit inside your head. John doesn't even try to explain how this could be. He simply reports that it is. He provides testimony from a ton of witnesses, including Jesus Himself. And he leaves us with a convincing series of miracles that prove who Jesus is.

QUOTABLES

"I was blind but now I see" (9:25, NIV). A man's response to Jewish leaders who hope to prove that Jesus hasn't cured any blindness.

"For God so loved the world, that he gave his only begotten Son, that whosoever believeth in him should not perish, but have everlasting life" (John 3:16, KJV). Jesus' explanation of why he has come to earth.

"I am the bread of life" (6:35, NIV). Jesus' claim to be the source of spiritual nourishment that produces eternal life.

SNEAK PREVIEW

2 Corinthians
Sometimes straight talk is the only kind of love.

BEHIND the SCENES
of John

STARRING ROLES

Jesus, God's son, who was present at the Creation of the world and who has come to earth in human form to offer eternal life to everyone who has faith in Him (1:17)

12 apostles, men Jesus invites to join his ministry as disciples (1:40–45)

PLOT

John gets serious with this story. He doesn't begin with the birth of Jesus — he takes us all the way back to Creation. John says Jesus was there. He was with God. He is God. This leads John to this message: Jesus is no ordinary prophet, and, He's not *just* the Messiah. He's part of the Trinity. He's the Son of God. No Joke!

From the Creation, John introduces John the Baptist who calls Jesus the Lamb of God.

Jesus selects 12 disciples and begins His work. Even though Jesus challenges and wins deep discussions about God with Jewish scholars, most Jewish leaders remain unconvinced that He is anything but a fraud. The second half of the book tells about the final week in the life of Jesus. The book concludes by expressing the hope that readers will believe Jesus is the Son of God, and that through faith they will enter into the kingdom of God and live forever.

STAGE DIRECTIONS

	Birth of Jesus 6 B.C.			Jesus begins ministry A.D. 26	Jesus crucified A.D. 30
BIBLE EVENTS			Dates are approximate		
10 B.C.	○	A.D. 1		○	A.D. 30
WORLD EVENTS					
		Druids in Britain believe they descended from a supreme being A.D. 1		Pilate begins 10-year rule as governor A.D. 26	Tiberius' 16th year as Caesar A.D. 30

AUTHOR AND DATE

Most scholars believe that John is the writer of this Gospel, even though the book doesn't bear his name. When the book was published, probably near the end of the first century, the church accepted it as the authentic testimony of the apostle John.

No one knows for sure when the Gospel was written. Some believe John wrote it around the middle of the century, perhaps the same time some of the other Gospels were written. Others suggest John wrote it late in the century, A.D. 85 or later, to supplement the other Gospels. Some Christian writers in the second century say this is exactly what happened, that an elderly John wrote it in Ephesus, a coastal city in western Turkey.

ON LOCATION

The story takes place primarily in what is now Israel, with some scenes east of the Jordan River, in what is now northern Jordan. Much of Jesus' ministry takes place in His hometown region of Galilee, in northern Israel. His last week takes place in the Jerusalem area, in the region of Judea.

WHAT TO LOOK FOR

- **Jesus portrayed as God.** John describes Jesus as the "Word" from the Greek term "logos," which can mean a lot of different things. The Jews think of it as the power of God. The Greeks think of it as cosmic reason, the well-designed frame on which the universe is built. Guess what…Jesus is both of these—the power of God, and the One whose signature is stamped on the universe. But John takes the term still further. Just as a word reveals a thought, Jesus is the expression of God, physically revealing the invisible, spiritual presence of God.
- **What's missing?** Notice what John leaves out. You won't find a single parable. You won't find anything about the birth of Jesus, His baptism, temptation, the Last Supper, His agonizing prayer on the night of His arrest, or His ascension into the sky. Why? John probably doesn't want to repeat most of the stories that have been circulating for decades. Instead, he focuses on Jesus' deity, using carefully selected miracles and teachings that propel this theme.

- **Seven miracles.** John reports seven miracles of Jesus, which he calls "signs" that prove Jesus is God.
  - Jesus turns water into wine (2:1-12). This shows he is the source of physical life who can take one substance and make it into a new creation.
  - He heals a soldier's son by long-distance (4:46–54), showing He is not limited by geography.
  - He heals a lame man on the Sabbath (5:1-17), revealing He is not limited by time.
  - He feeds 5,000 people (6:1-14), then declares He is the bread of life—the source of both physical and spiritual nourishment.
  - He walks on water (6:16-21), as Lord of nature.
  - He heals a blind man (9:1-41), proclaiming Himself the light of the world that can overpower any form of darkness.
  - He raises Lazarus from the dead (11:17-45), revealing His power over death.
- **Seven "I am" descriptions of Jesus.** Jesus describes Himself with seven revealing statements. All begin with "I am."
  - "I am the bread that gives life!" (6:35). Jesus says He is the source of spiritual nourishment: "No one who comes to me will ever be hungry."
  - "I am the light for the world! Follow me, and you won't be walking in the dark" (8:12).
  - "I am the gate for the sheep" (10:7), the only entrance into God's eternal kingdom.
  - "I am the good shepherd. . . . I give up my life for my sheep" (10:14–15).
  - "I am the one who raises the dead to life! Everyone who has faith in me will live, even if they die" (11:25). The body will die, but the soul that trusts in Jesus will live forever.
  - "I am the way, the truth, and the life! . . . Without me, no one can go to the Father" (14:6).
  - "I am the true vine" (15:1). Anyone cut off from Him will wither and die, like pruned branches.
- **Several layers of meaning.** John's language is packed with symbolism. One truth can often mean several different things.

  For example, when Jesus calls himself "the bread that gives life," people would have had different thoughts about that. Here are some of the ways they'd interpret that statement.
  - They might think wheat or barley bread, one of their staple foods.
  - They might think of the manna that God sent the Israelites in the desert.
  - They might think of the bread they eat each Passover to commemorate how God saved them from slavery.
  - They certainly think of the Last Supper, when Jesus breaks a loaf of bread and tells His disciples that this represents His body, which will be offered as a sacrifice for the sins of humanity.

EXTREME SCENES
from John

Jesus is really really old (1:1-18)

John begins his Gospel by saying that Jesus was present at the Creation. Since humanity first sinned God has been working His plan to purge this contamination—to remove sin and its destructive effects. By associating Jesus with the first Creation, John also portrays Jesus as the one who will establish the New Creation, the kingdom of God.

Living water makes wine (2:1-11)

Jesus attends a wedding at the small village of Cana. When guests drink the last of the wine, Jesus' takes the opportunity to help out a little. He instructs the servants to fill six stone jars with water. Then He tells them to dip some out and take it to the reception coordinator. The coordinator says this new wine is the best wine of the feast. Wine? Huh? Yep . . . Jesus changed the water into wine. Imagine the amazement of the people at the wedding! This miracle is the first of seven "signs" or proofs that John reports. These signs are intended to convince people that Jesus is God in the flesh. By turning the water into wine, Jesus shows he is the source of creation and the sustainer of life. And that He likes a party.

DIRECTOR'S NOTES

In New Testament Israel, you could work eleven hours and still not qualify for overtime. The Jewish work day lasted twelve hours, from sunrise to sunset. John 11:9

Open air evangelism (4:1-42)

Jesus has been traveling for a long time. He's tired. So, He decides to sit by a well in a small town in Samaria. He waits for someone with a bucket. When a woman arrives, Jesus asks for a drink of water. But she says she can't understand why He's talking to her, since Jews and Samaritans don't get along. "You don't know who is asking you for a drink," Jesus replies. "If you did, you would ask me for the water that gives life" (10).

Before the visit is over, this woman has brought the entire village to Jesus, and the people have declared, "We are certain that He is the Savior of the world!" (42). One simple conversation and everyone heads for the well to meet the Living Water.

What everyone craves (6:1-59)

Because Jesus is doing so many amazing things, huge crowds are drawn to Him. One day, 5,000 people approach Him in an isolated field along the shores of the Sea of Galilee. When they grow hungry, Jesus miraculously feeds them, using only five small loaves of barley and two fish. Everyone has plenty to eat, and the disciples gather up 12 large baskets of leftovers.

Lazarus ain't dead...really! (Luke 10:1-44)

John 11:

As Lazarus lies dying, his sisters send word to their friend Jesus, expecting him to come quickly. But Jesus delays, telling his disciples that Lazarus' illness "will bring glory to God and his Son" (11:4). By the time Jesus arrives, Lazarus has been dead four days. Jesus orders the tomb opened. As the group of mourners watch, Jesus shouts, "Lazarus, come out!" Lazarus emerges. Guess what... Jesus has the power over death!

God gets humble (13:1-17)

Before eating the Last Supper, Jesus performs the humble chore of washing the feet of His disciples. It is something servants do for guests, or disciples for their rabbi. And, look, this was one really tough job. Everyone wore sandals in this day... and everyone walked everywhere. Can you imagine how smelly and dirty their feet were? This is not just an object lesson in humility. It's also a symbol of the spiritual cleaning that Jesus makes available to everyone. When Peter objects to the washing, Jesus gives a stern reply. "If I don't wash you," he says, "you don't really belong to me" (8).

Peter makes a huge mistake (18:15-27)

At the Last Supper Jesus predicts that Peter will three times deny knowing Him. He'll do it that night before the rooster crows. Later, when the officers arrest Jesus and take him to the high priest, Peter stands outside the priest's home with soldiers and servants, warming himself by a fire. One by one, throughout the night, people ask Peter if he is a disciple of the man inside. And one by one, Peter denies it. At the moment of the third denial, a rooster begins to crow. Peter is majorly upset at what he's done.

The rejected King (19:28-42)

It seems like everyone wants Jesus dead. Pilate tries to talk the Jews out of the execution. A mob forms and Pilate feels a little threatened. So, he hands Jesus over to be killed.

Thomas is wrong! (20:24-31)

On Sunday morning, a resurrected Jesus appears to His disciples who are hiding behind locked doors. Thomas is not there. Later, when the disciples tell him they've seen Jesus, Thomas says he'll believe it when he can touch the spear wound in Jesus' side and the nail scars on His hands. A week later, Jesus returns. This time, Thomas is there. Thomas gets his chance. He touches Jesus' wounds. He believes. Jesus gently rebukes Thomas for needing proof—after all he has seen. And He commends those in years to come "who have faith in me without seeing me."

REVIEWS

John's Gospel focuses a little less on the story of Jesus' life and a little more on why we should believe Jesus was the Son of God.

John wasn't as concerned that we know about what Jesus did (and in what order) as much as he wanted us to know Jesus, Himself, and to love Him as John did. John wanted us to believe the mystery of Jesus' deity, that even though He was a person, He was really and truly God, too. Because of that John wrote in this style that was part philosopher, part poet and part guy-next-door.

The other Gospels were already written by the time John sat down to have his say. John didn't need to rewrite the same things. So instead of starting with Jesus' birth or even God's promise to Abraham, John started with the Creation of the world. Since Jesus was God, Jesus was there when the world was created.

John is the only Gospel that recorded Jesus' first miracle at a wedding in Cana. They ran out of wine. At the request of His mother, and with a little negotiation between them, Jesus changed some plain old well water into wine so the host wouldn't be embarrassed (John 2:1-11). It's sort of a twist that the God of all creation would incarnate into a human and the first miracle was to keep the party going and save a dad from embarrassment. And you know, Jesus was a little reluctant to even do the miracle, but his mom put the pressure on.... ("But, MOM, everybody's gonna look at me funny if I do a miracle." "No they won't. Now do what mama says. Go on.")

I bet EVERYONE invited Him to their parties after THAT little miracle.

John shows us Jesus' anger about the temple. From the beginning of His ministry, Jesus ferociously confronted the men who made the temple into a marketplace. He defended the temple as His own turf (John 2:12-25). That should have told them something, don't ya' think?

ENCORE

➢ Other New Testament books traditionally attributed to John are the short letters of 1, 2, 3 John and the mysterious end-time prophecy of Revelation.

➢ Read Matthew, Mark, and Luke for additional details about the life and ministry of Jesus.

➢ Acts begins where the ascension of Jesus ends, with the disciples boldly reporting what Jesus taught them.

REVIEWS

It was John who told us about Nicodemus, a Pharisee himself, sneaking around at night to learn from Jesus. It was during this conversation that Jesus firmly established the concept of being "born again." It's also where Jesus spoke the famous words we now know as John 3:16—God so loved the world, that he gave his only son... (John 3:1-21)

John was also the only writer to tell the story about the Samaritan woman at the well. It was so politically incorrect for Jesus to even talk to her. He not only talked to her but met all her friends. (John 4:1-42)

John gave us a lot of insight into what Jesus did with His power as God in human form. He did his best to lay out a mystery so that we could accept by faith. That's a pretty tall order, but John does a really good job at it.

Bart Elson James

Acts

SCHEDULE OF SCENES

Jesus Is Born	Jesus Crucified Pentecost	Temple Destroyed	Acts Written	Death of John
7/6 B.C.	A.D. 30	A.D. 70	c. 80	A.D. 100

A baby church

Everyone likes a baby. Its skin is so soft. Its legs and hands are so small. It's curious and tentative at the same time. Acts is a book about a baby church. It's a curious church. Even though it's hands are still small, it's willing to serve.

Acts is the well-known sequel to the Gospel of Luke. It tells of Jesus' ascension into heaven, then gives us some really cool snapshots of what happens next. There's the first sermon by a disciple. Then, the first miracle by a disciple. All of this is followed by the first major steps toward organizing a Christian movement. Acts also reports on the persecution of the Christians, the first Christian martyr, the first non-Jewish convert, and the first missionary trip. You could call it an important book of firsts.

And, there's really cool stuff here, too. Remember the disciples? In the Gospels they were really important figures. Well, in Acts, they're almost invisible. The disciples are still respected, but other leaders become well known and begin leading the church. Acts introduces these leaders, like Paul. It also introduces us to the miracles believers can do through the Holy Spirit. God's Spirit making bold witnesses out of ordinary people is the reason behind the phenomenal success of the first-generation church. And, hey. Don't forget that this same God who did all of this in Acts does it for us today. He's behind our success. He's with us, just like He was with the baby church.

QUOTABLES

It is more blessed to give than to receive (20:35, KJV). Paul quoting a proverb of Jesus that does not appear in any of the Gospels.

Everyone who calls on the name of the Lord will be saved (2:21, NIV). Peter announcing that this prophecy of Joel's is now fulfilled.

"You will receive power when the Holy Spirit comes on you; and you will be my witnesses in Jerusalem, and in all Judea and Samaria, and to the ends of the earth" (1:8, NIV). The last words of Jesus to his disciples, spoken as He ascends to heaven.

SNEAK PREVIEW

Lamentations
Sad songs say so much.

BEHIND the SCENES
of Acts

STARRING ROLES

Paul, one-time Jewish persecutor of Christians, who converts to become missionary and advocate for non-Jewish Christians (13:9; in 7:58 by his Hebrew name, Saul)

Peter, leader of the 12 original disciples, who preaches the first sermon after Jesus' resurrection (1:13)

Stephen, the church's first martyr, killed by a Jewish mob (6:5)

Barnabas, Paul's missionary colleague (4:36)

PLOT

The Gospel of Luke leaves us at the ascension of Jesus. Jesus gives His final instructions to the disciples. Then He disappears. So, the disciples do what Jesus says. They wait in Jerusalem for the Holy Spirit. When He finally descends on them the coolest stuff happens. They speak in different languages. Peter preaches, and 3,000 people become followers of Jesus. There

STAGE DIRECTIONS

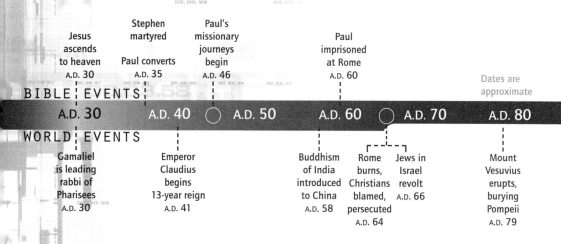

Dates are approximate

BIBLE EVENTS

Jesus ascends to heaven A.D. 30	Stephen martyred A.D. 35 / Paul converts	Paul's missionary journeys begin A.D. 46	Paul imprisoned at Rome A.D. 60	

A.D. 30   A.D. 40   A.D. 50   A.D. 60   A.D. 70   A.D. 80

WORLD EVENTS

Gamaliel is leading rabbi of Pharisees A.D. 30

Emperor Claudius begins 13-year reign A.D. 41

Buddhism of India introduced to China A.D. 58

Rome burns, Christians blamed, persecuted A.D. 64

Jews in Israel revolt A.D. 66

Mount Vesuvius erupts, burying Pompeii A.D. 79

BEHIND the SCENES
of Acts

are tons of new believers running around now…and things *could* get a little confusing. But, they don't. The believers begin to organize, selecting leaders to help the apostles. When the Jewish council hears about this (the same icky group that arranged for Jesus to be executed) they get upset and scared…mostly because the movement is growing. So, they begin persecuting the believers and try to toss them in prison. The persecution gets bad, and believers begin leaving Jerusalem.

A Jew named Saul tries to hunt them down. On his way to find more hiding believers, Saul meets Jesus and converts to Christianity. His name is changed to Paul and after a while he becomes a leader of a church in Syria. Paul joins with other missionaries and begins spreading the gospel throughout Cyprus and Turkey. He has amazing results. He also faces really tough persecution. He's eventually captured in Jerusalem and sent to Rome for trial.

AUTHOR AND DATE

Most people believe that Luke wrote this book. Yup...the same guy who wrote the Gospel of Luke. Even though the book never really says, "Hi, I'm Luke, and I'm going to write this book for you", Christian leaders in the second century attributed this book to Luke. The book is addressed to "Theophilus,"...no one knows exactly who this dude was. Maybe he was a Roman official who asked for information about Christianity.

Like most New Testament books, this one's difficult to tag a date on. The book may have been written in the early 60s, before the execution of Paul, during Nero's persecution of Christians beginning in A.D. 64. But emphasis in the Gospel of Luke on Jesus' prophecy about the fall of Jerusalem, fulfilled in A.D. 70, suggests to many experts that both books were written later.

ON LOCATION

There's a lot of history in the making here. Acts covers the first 30 years of Christian history, beginning in Jerusalem. The apostles witness the ascension of Jesus and experience the Holy Spirit radically changing their lives and doing amazing things through them. They begin to preach. Thousands convert. The church quickly expands beyond Jerusalem into most of the Roman Empire. Within three decades Christians are worshiping in house churches throughout the land. The church even spreads 2000 miles away. Unbelievable!

WHAT TO LOOK FOR

- **Paul Gets Bold.** Okay, in the first six chapters you get the disciples you had in the Gospels. Same old dudes. But, by the sixth chapter new leaders begin to creep onto the scene. Them, in chapter 13, Paul emerges and the head honcho missionary example that either sets the example for living right in Christ, or evangelizing others. Paul's the man, and most of Acts tells why he's such a success.

- **God – The Promise Keeper.** Luke stresses this fact very heavily. Luke points out how the apostles are fulfilling Jesus' commission of Jesus. He makes sure that we know all of the facts of how the church is spreading. He does all of this to show that God is fulfilling his mission for believers, and is redeeming lost sinners.

- **Look out…it's the Holy Spirit!** Just as the Holy Spirit fills Jesus at the beginning of his ministry (Luke 4:1), the Spirit also fills the apostles and other followers of Jesus. This filling gives the apostles supernatural powers that help convince many about the truth of their message (see 2:4, 43, 47). And, the Holy Spirit doesn't stop there. He continues filling believers from all walks of life, not only performing wonders through them but also helping them make important decisions (see 15:28; 16:6–7).

- **God's attacks.** One thing's for sure: God goes around knocking down barriers in the early church. And Luke makes sure he records God's work. Want some examples? Here's three:

- **Customs fall.** Jewish Christians argue that all Christians need to observe Jewish dietary laws restricting what people eat. God shows Peter a vision that repeats what Jesus had taught earlier: under God's new covenant with humanity, all food is kosher (see Mark 7:19; Acts 10).

- **Racism falls.** The Gospel is extended to the Samaritans, a race of Jewish half-breeds that pure-blooded Jews hate (see 8:4–17).

- **Vengeance falls.** Even enemies of God can be citizens of heaven. There's no such thing as vengeance…even from God (see chapter 10).

EXTREME SCENES
from Acts

There goes Jesus (1:1-11)

Forty days after the resurrection, Jesus is still with the disciples. He leads them to the Mount of Olives and says, "Wait here". Then, he rises into the clouds and disappears. The disciples stare into the clouds. Two angels suddenly appear with this comforting message: "Jesus has been taken to heaven. But He will come back in the same way that you have seen him go." Wouldn't you have been a little confused? Maybe even felt a little abandoned? The disciples wait. They're a little unsure about what to do next.

A strange filling (2:1-13)

The disciples finally give up staring at the sky, return to Jerusalem. They've got to find a replacement for Judas, so they pick Matthias. Ten days later, the Holy Spirit drops in on them and changes their lives. He floods the room. He hovers above each person's head like a flame. You'd think these dudes would run and hide. They don't. It's like they're expecting this to happen. The Spirit's arrival marks a turning point in the way God communicates with human beings. Now, everyone (yeah...even you!) who calls on God will receive His presence. What a promise!

DIRECTOR'S NOTES

Why were young men in such a hurry to bury Ananias? Actually, quick burials were a necessity in the ancient Middle East. The hot climate caused the corpses to decay (and stink) pretty quickly. The bodies of wealthy and powerful people were placed in tombs cut out of rocky hillsides. A stone was then placed in front of the tomb to protect the body from scavenging animals. Acts 5:6

One huge revival (2:14-47)

So, you've got the Holy Spirit falling on twelve frightened men in a room. Does it end there? Nope. Not on your life. These twelve dudes go out and change the world. The twelve guys now speak all kinds of languages. What a coincidence! Foreign-speaking Jews from all over the world are in town to celebrate the harvest festival of Pentecost.

At 9 A.M. Peter boldly addresses the crowd, which includes Jewish leaders (these are the same dudes that killed Jesus 50 days earlier). Remember how Peter denied Jesus before? Welp, not this time. Peter gets up and proclaims that Jesus is Messiah and Lord, and that "God has raised Jesus to life!" He just goes to town...totally unloads his gospel barrel on them. Guess what?! 3,000 of the people believe what they hear. The converts repent of their sin, are baptized, then spend time with the apostles learning more about Jesus.

The church is born.

Holding back is a real bad idea (5:1-10)

The baby church takes on a mission: compassion. When someone has a need, others sell property and possessions and bring the money to the apostles, who oversee the compassionate ministries. That means...if you lived back then and someone had a need, you'd sell your skateboard and give them the money. Yowza! Well, two people get this whole idea totally wrong. Ananias and his wife Sapphira decide to sell some property, give part of the money to the apostles, and keep the rest. They talk with Peter. They lie and say they have donated all the money from the sale. When Peter replies that they have lied to God, the accusation catches them totally off guard. They drop dead. What's the message? Dude...don't mess with the Holy Spirit. And, whatever you do...DON'T LIE!

A bad rock concert (7:1-60)

Stephen is one amazing man. He's a gifted communicator. And, he's about to be the church's first martyr. Some Jews have him brought up on charges of saying bad things about the temple and the law of Moses. So...can you guess what happens? Standing before the same Jewish council that tried Jesus, Stephen doesn't defend himself. He gives a heart piercing speech. He reminds the tradition-minded Jews that God is not confined to any temple built by humans. He reminds them that they killed Jesus. As he's speaking, he sees a vision of heaven open and Jesus standing beside God. Then, things get bloody. The angry mob drags Stephen from the courtroom and stones him to death.

Philip's trip (8:4-8)

Just after they kill Stephen, Jews begin looking for other Christians to persecute, toss in prison, or kill. Many believers leave town, taking their teachings about Jesus with them throughout the territories of Judea and Samaria. Philip (one of seven chosen to help the apostles) travels north to Samaria, a region Jews tend to avoid. Philip invites them to become citizens in the kingdom of God. Many accept. God's kingdom grows more and more.

A murderer becomes a target (9:1-19)

Saul is a devoted Christian killer. His job is to find believers hiding from persecution and make their lives really terrible. On one of his trips to find believers to mess with, a brilliant light from the sky knocks him off his horse. Jesus confronts Saul. Saul's life is changed. Jesus orders Saul to go to Damascus and wait for instructions. When the light disappears, Saul is blind. His buds traveling with him take him to the city. God does another amazing thing and calls a believer to go and visit Saul (who was well known for his Christian – killing escapades). As these two men are praying, Saul receives his sight. He goes all over the city and tells people what Jesus has done in his life.

Wacky dreams (10:9-23)

In these times, people often went to their roofs to pray. Peter does that one day at around noon. While he's praying, He a vision. He sees himself running along a sunset lit beach with a daisy in his hair. He's doing one of those slow motion type of runs too. There's even a little classical music playing in the background. As Peter sleeps, he wears a smile. Okay, all that's not true. But, what if it really happened? That'd be cool!

What Peter really saw was a bunch of animals lowered from heaven on a sheet. These are animals prohibited from the Jewish diet since the days of Moses. A voice says, "Get Up! Kill these and eat them!" Peter refuses to break Moses' law. The voice says "When God says you should eat this, don't say it's not good to eat!" Peter's totally confused. While he's sitting there, still totally confused, messengers from a Roman soldier arrive and ask him to come with them. Peter goes, and the soldier's entire household is converted. When these non-Jews receive the Holy Spirit and praise God in other languages, Peter realizes what the vision means: God's new covenant with Jesus' followers now embraces the entire world.

Saul...missionary to the world (13:1-3)

Saul is invited to help lead a growing congregation in Antioch about 100 miles from his hometown of Tarsus. Most of the believers are non-Jews. While Paul is there, the congregation and leaders feel impressed by the Holy Spirit to send him and Barnabas on a mission trip to other places. So, Paul and Barnabas get on a ship and sail for the island of Cyprus, where Barnabas was raised. There, Saul converts a high Roman official. The journey continues into western Turkey, where the men start tiny congregations in one city after another.

Paul gets into it (15:1-21)

Should non-Jews obey the laws of Moses? Should they be circumcised? What are the "right" things to observe? That's what the argument is all about. There are two sides arguing...both have really good points. First, Peter stands and tells the group about his earlier vision with the animals. He argues that this shows God has invited non-Jews to join his people. Paul and Barnabas reinforce this argument by reporting miracles they saw among non-Jews during their recent missionary trip. What happens? It's a split decision.

The council decides against ordering non-Jews to obey Jewish laws. This ruling confirms what many Jewish Christians like Paul have long been teaching: you don't have to be a Jew to be a Christian.

Hey...Who likes prison? (16:16-40)

Paul and Silas are on their second mission trip. They're in Philippi and Paul exorcises a demon-possessed slave girl. This makes her owners really mad (seems they've been making some extra cash off her demonic ability to tell the future. The owners convince city leaders to beat and imprison Paul and Silas for disturbing the peace. Here's where things go from seemingly desperate to way cool. About midnight, as Paul and Silas are singing and praying, a powerful earthquake breaks open the prison doors. The jailer prepares to kill himself (because Paul and Silas are his responsibility). Paul stops him, the jailer recognizes their faith and takes the two men home. That night, the jailer is baptized as a new believer. The next morning, Paul and Silas are released and escorted out of town.

Paul...in the way again! (19:23-41)

During his third and final missionary trip, Paul arrives in Ephesus, famous as the worship headquarters for Artemis (A.K.A Diana), goddess of the hunt, harvest, and childbirth. Her huge temple here is one of the seven wonders of the ancient world. No joke! Paul preaches and, his preaching winds up cramping the business of craftsmen who make silver statues of Artemis. The craftsmen call a town meeting in the theater, then work the city into a riot by claiming that Paul's preaching is not only hurting the economy, but also undermining the worship of Artemis. When Paul hears about this, he wants to defend. He doesn't (which is smart, he'd have been hurt pretty bad if he had tried). When the uproar is over, he slips out of town, leaving behind a committed core of Christians.

Paul: Convict number 5093294 (24:1-27)

Paul heads for Jerusalem, where he's expecting to be arrested. He's carrying an offering for Jewish Christians. The offering is to help ease the tensions between Jewish and non-Jewish Christians. Well, it doesn't. A riot breaks out (starting to get the theme of Paul's life here?) Roman soldiers take Paul into protective custody and take him to Caesarea (about 50 miles away). Paul goes on trial. He's charged with instigating riots and desecrating the temple. Unconvinced that Paul has done anything wrong, Felix placates the Jews by holding Paul in prison for two years, until Festus is appointed governor. After two more indecisive trials, Paul appeals his case to the emperor's court in Rome.

Shipwreck! (27:1-44)

Paul climbs aboard a ship with other prisoners heading for Rome. It's late in the year and sailing can be treacherous. After approaching the island of Crete in the hopes of finding a safe winter harbor, they get caught in a two-week storm that blows them 600 miles west. The ship eventually breaks apart in shallow water near Malta, an island south of Italy and Sicily. Miraculously, everyone survives. Three months later they set sail on a ship that winters in Malta. By spring, Paul arrives in Rome.

In prison...still preaching (28:16-31)

Paul waits for two years for his case to come to trial. Even though he's under arrest and constantly accompanied by a guard, he is free to teach any who come to him. Paul also writes letters to encourage congregations he helped start, such as those in Ephesus and Colossae.

Acts ends without telling us what happened at the trial. That might be because the case hadn't been decided when the book was completed. Or, it might be because everyone knew what happened to Paul. Early Christian writers say Paul was beheaded in Rome. The execution may have taken place after this trial. But Clement of Rome, a Christian leader writing in the late A.D. 90s, says Paul was martyred on his second trip to Rome.

INTERVIEW
with the Stars

The fall guy

How would you like to be remembered forever as the guy who fell out of a third-story window and lived to tell about it? Not much of a distinction. Even less when you find out the guy is young. (Now all the adults reading this are nodding their heads and saying, "Yeah, yeah. That's your typical teen. Goes to a church meeting and falls asleep.") **Behind the Bible** takes a new look at this centuries-old tale and lets Eutychus tell his own story and how it can make a difference in your life! Welcome, Eutychus.

⋙ Eutychus

Thanks. My story is not so much what I did, but more what happened to me. I had gone with a bunch of men from Troas to hear Paul speak. We had gathered to celebrate the Lord's Supper, and then afterwards, Paul began to preach. Since he was leaving the next day, he wanted to make the most of the time he had with us, so he talked until about midnight.

And then what happened?

⋙ Eutychus

I was probably about 14 at the time, so I didn't typically stay up that late. There were a lot of people in the room and a lot of candles lit, so the room was really warm. Even though I was sitting on the windowsill, I was getting really sleepy. Next thing I knew I thought I was having one of those "falling" dreams. But this one was for real!

INTERVIEW
with the Stars

From what I understand, you fell three stories to your death. Is that right?

⋙ Eutychus

I know it's hard to believe, but the story is true. I died instantly, which was immediately confirmed by Dr. Luke (he was traveling with Paul). But fortunately for me, that was not the final outcome. (This probably is a good time to mention that my name means "Lucky.") Paul came running downstairs with the others, but instead of standing around, shaking his head in despair, he held me and prayed. The next thing I knew I was staring into the faces of all those men! It was an incredible moment for everyone.

That is a wonderful miraculous ending, but what does that have to do with life today? I mean teens still fall asleep in church, but you rarely hear of any falling out windows to their death, let alone being brought back to life.

⋙ Eutychus

But that's just the point. Teens do *still* fall asleep in church and that just reinforces the negative impression that some adults have about us young people. But the truth is that after my falling incident, I had a wonderful life-changing story to tell others about what God did in my life. And teens today have similar stories to tell others. Maybe their stories are not as dramatic as being brought back to life. But if God has gotten hold of you, that is no less a miracle as my being revived on the lawn.

So your advice to teens today?

⋙ Eutychus

Wake up a few of those adults in your church by speaking up and telling them what God is doing in your life. You'll be amazed at what a difference it will make to others when they find out how God is making a difference in your life.

INTERVIEW
with the Stars

Answered prayer

Your best bud recently moved away. You've been really down about it and have been praying to God that you will be able to see your best friend soon. The doorbell rings. You answer the door, and it's your best friend standing there. What do you do? Do you... A.) Shut the door and run inside to tell someone; B.) Start screaming and jumping up and down; or C.) Thank God for answering your prayer. **Behind the Bible** is going to take a look at a young girl's response to answered prayer. Sometimes we don't even recognize answered prayer when it comes knocking at our door! Rhoda, tell us what was going on that evening.

⋗ Rhoda

I was only a servant girl at the time, but I was part of those early believers who followed the risen Christ. At first, it seemed that everyone would turn to Christ and follow Him. But then it got ugly, real ugly. Our opponents used confrontations, imprisonment and even death to try to stop the spread of the gospel. No one was safe. In fact, Peter had just been put in jail by King Herod. Herod was going to put him on trial following the Passover.

So what were you doing about it?

⋗ Rhoda

Ever since Peter was thrown in jail, we—that is, the church—had been praying non-stop for Peter's safe release. I was at the house of Mary, John Mark's mother, where we were continuing to pray for Peter's release. While everyone was praying, I heard a knock on the front door. I ran to get it and there standing in front of me was Peter! I couldn't believe my eyes!

INTERVIEW
with the Stars

Your friends must have been ecstatic when you brought Peter into the room with you.

≥ Rhoda

Not exactly.

Why not?

≥ Rhoda

Well, I didn't exactly bring Peter back with me. In all my excitement, I shut the door and ran inside to tell the others that Peter was here.

Hold on, let's get this straight. You opened the door, Peter was standing there, the very man you had been praying for, and you left him standing outside the door? Why?

≥ Rhoda

I guess I fell into that trap of praying for something and not really expecting God to provide it. But I wasn't the only one. When I went back into the room and told the others Peter was outside, they didn't believe me until they went out and opened the door to see for themselves.

That's quite a story and it just goes to show that if you pray for rain, you ought to carry your umbrella. If we were honest, though, there's probably more than a little bit of Rhoda in all of us. God is not bound by our prayers, but He often will answer them with a precision that is easy to miss if we aren't paying close attention.

REVIEWS

ENCORE

➤ Check out the Gospel of Luke. This is Part One in the two-part work of the writer, and the volume referred to in Acts 1:1

➤ The 21 New Testament letters that follow, especially letters by Paul, fill in details about events described in the last half of Acts.

OK, so you finally found the remote down behind the sofa cushions, and you're flipping through the TV channels, and you land on one of those real surgery-in-process shows. You know the kind—facelifts, hernias...but tonight, there's a baby on the way. Oh man, how do people DO this? The pain, the yelling and the not-pushing and then the pushing. Before you realize it, you're breathing with the woman and then...the baby comes. Time stops for a moment in the presence of the miracle and then starts again with the baby's first cry. You let out your breath and realize you were holding it. You reach for the Kleenex with one hand and the cheezy poofs with the other. On screen everybody in the room is all smiles—including the woman who just defied every law of physics, gravity, and modesty. Its a lot of work on everyone involved (or even just watching).

Believe it or not, reading the book of Acts is an awful lot like watching a baby being born. The baby, though, is the church. Before Jesus came, people went to churches called temples. There they learned, worshiped, gave offerings and offered sacrifices. With Christ's death and resurrection, though, church meant something different. Church was no longer a place to go to meet with God. Instead, it was the group of people who made up the family of God and the body of Christ. God was not in a place anymore, he was in people.

When Christ was here on earth he was God in a human body. Since he left, we, the church, have God's representatives in human bodies. Making that transition was and is a lot of work for everyone involved: apostles, disciples, church members, missionaries, pastors, janitors, choir workers, the old lady who gives out the bulletins, etc.

Once you've read the early parts of Acts, and compared them to the closing chapters of any of the Gospels, you can't

help but notice the radical change in the disciples. On Passover weekend, in early spring, they ran for their lives when Jesus was arrested. They were afraid to stand with Him when he faced death. Peter, the lead disciple, wouldn't even admit that he was a disciple.

Fifty days later, each disciple is willing to face death alone on behalf of Jesus. In the temple courtyard, in plain sight of Jewish leaders who plotted Jesus' execution, they speak the same words that got Jesus killed: they proclaim Him Messiah and Son of God. Something happened during those 50 days to change the disciples—something that wiped away their fear of death.

They had seen new life. They had talked with the resurrected Jesus and even eaten with him. Months before, they'd heard His words, "Do not be afraid of those who kill the body but cannot kill the soul" (Matthew 10:28, NIV). But now they *believed* him. And then the Holy Spirit stepped into the picture, changing EVERYTHING, making them even bolder. It's all history to us now, but when it was happening Jerusalem was a delivery room, and a new life was screaming its way into existence. WHEW! Pass the Kleenex please... and the cheezy poofs if, you don't mind.

Dr. Juan Kenobi, Obstetrician

Romans

SCHEDULE OF SCENES

Jesus Is Born	Jesus Crucified Pentecost	Paul's Missionary Journeys Begin	Romans Written	Temple Destroyed	Death of John
7/6 B.C.	A.D. 30	A.D. 46	A.D. 57	A.D. 70	A.D. 100

Paul's masterpiece

If you're looking for an easy read, the book of Romans might not fit the bill. But if you really want to get into the meat of what it means to be a Christian, well, you won't find a better place to look than this letter Paul wrote to believers living in Rome. This letter is Paul's masterpiece, a well-crafted primer on the basics of the Christian faith. It's written after a lifetime of ministry and devotion to being a *real* Christian. Paul didn't just talk the talk; he walked the walk. Here are some of the key lessons he learned along the way:

- Everyone has sinned and needs God's forgiveness (3:23).
- God makes forgiveness available to *everyone* through His son, Jesus Christ. If we simply have faith in Jesus, Paul explains, God "sets us free from our sins" (3:24).
- We should live like we're taking our cues from God, not from the devil. "Dear friends, God is good," Paul says. "Do everything that is good and pleasing to him" (12:1-2).

Romans ends with a few chapters of easy-reading, practical advice about daily living. But the earlier chapters are filled with lots of Godspeak, or theology. Paul throws out a lot of words and concepts like justification and sanctification, but these chapters are critical in explaining why Christians believe and behave the way they do. Believers who understand the reasons behind their faith are better-motivated and more effective servants of God. Romans is a must-read for anyone who takes his or her faith seriously.

QUOTABLES

The wages of sin is death; but the gift of God is eternal life (6:23, KJV).

All have sinned, and come short of the glory of God (3:23, KJV).

All things work together for good to them that love God (8:28, KJV).

SNEAK PREVIEW

Nahum
The final showdown of good vs. evil. Winner takes all.

BEHIND the SCENES
of Romans

STARRING ROLE

Paul, a formerly ultraconservative Jew who becomes the early church's leading minister to non-Jewish Christians (1:1)

PLOT

This is a letter with a theme—salvation—not a story with a plot. But the letter has a background that helps us understand what's on Paul's mind as he writes. Two decades into his ministry, Paul is near the end of his third and final missionary trip. He feels like he has done about all he can do in the eastern Mediterranean. His plans are to deliver an offering he has collected for the poverty-stricken Jewish Christians in Jerusalem, then take the Gospel to Spain. On his way, he'll stop in Rome to meet believers there.

STAGE DIRECTIONS

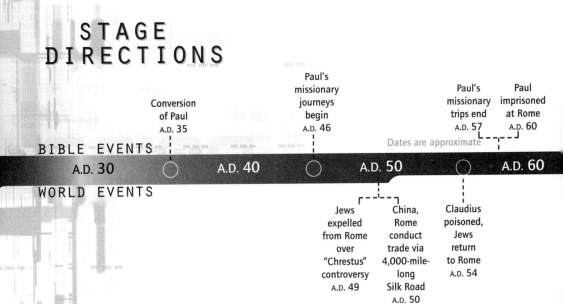

BIBLE EVENTS

Conversion of Paul
A.D. 35

Paul's missionary journeys begin
A.D. 46

Paul's missionary trips end
A.D. 57

Paul imprisoned at Rome
A.D. 60

Dates are approximate

A.D. 30   A.D. 40   A.D. 50   A.D. 60

WORLD EVENTS

Jews expelled from Rome over "Chrestus" controversy
A.D. 49

China, Rome conduct trade via 4,000-mile-long Silk Road
A.D. 50

Claudius poisoned, Jews return to Rome
A.D. 54

BEHIND the SCENES
of Romans

So before returning to Jerusalem—where he eventually will be arrested—Paul writes the Romans to tell them of his plans and to ask for their help. Because Paul wants them to know something about the people they will be helping, he tells them about his beliefs. Paul says that everyone—Jew and non-Jew alike—has sinned and needs the forgiveness and salvation of God. Without these, people are guilty, unable to stand before a holy God. So God is forced to condemn them to an eternity of separation from Him. But Paul says it doesn't have to be this way. God *has* provided forgiveness and salvation through the sacrificial death of Jesus. These gifts are available to anyone who has faith—a characteristic long rooted in Jewish tradition that goes back to Abraham, father of the Jews, who trusted that God would give him a son and make their descendants into a great nation.

When people are saved, Paul says, the Holy Spirit makes Himself at home inside them. The Spirit empowers people to live a godly life—to say no to evil desires that once controlled them like domineering bosses, and to pursue sacred opportunities they would not otherwise have seen.

AUTHOR AND DATE

Paul wrote the letter in about AD 57, possibly in Corinth, Greece, near the end of his third and final missionary journey. "I am now on my way to Jerusalem," he writes, "to deliver the money that the Lord's followers in Macedonia and Achaia collected for God's needy people.... After I have safely delivered this money, I will visit you and then go on to Spain" (15:25–28). Unfortunately, Paul was arrested when he got to Jerusalem and imprisoned for two years. When he finally does arrive in Rome, in about AD 60, he is a prisoner waiting for trial in the emperor's court. It's unclear if Paul is executed after this trial, or if he is released, only to be executed following a later trial in the city after returning from Spain.

ON LOCATION

Paul addresses a Christian congregation in Rome, capital of the Roman Empire. Paul has ministered throughout the eastern Mediterranean, in what is now Israel, Syria, Turkey, and Greece. Now he hopes to visit Rome on his way to taking the gospel to Spain, at the western edge of the empire.

WHAT TO LOOK FOR

- **The reason Paul writes the letter.** Paul has never been to Rome and was apparently not involved in starting the congregation there. But he writes "there is nothing left for me to do in this part of the world, and for years I have wanted to visit you. So I plan to stop off on my way to Spain. Then ... I hope you will quickly send me on" (15:23–24). In this last sentence Paul appears to hint that he would appreciate it if believers in Rome would help back his trip, with prayer and funds. Romans is like an ambassador's letter of introduction, identifying who Paul is ("a servant of Jesus Christ," 1:1) and what message he intends to preach in Spain, in order to prepare the way for a good reception when he arrives.

- **An introduction to basic Christian beliefs.** In short order, Paul's letter starts sounding like a textbook for Christianity 101. Paul's thesis is this: "I am proud of the good news! It is God's powerful way of saving all people who have faith, whether they are Jews or Gentiles" (1:16). Paul then explains what this good news is: "You will be saved, if you honestly say, 'Jesus is Lord,' and if you believe with all your heart that God raised him from death" (10:9). Paul goes on to talk about the radically new life of a Christ-follower, carefully explaining tough religious concepts such as sin, grace, faith, justification, redemption, salvation, sanctification, death, and resurrection.

  On sanctification, for example, a word that means holiness, Paul says that the Holy Spirit makes "Gentiles into a holy offering" (15:16). This doesn't mean they become morally perfect. It means that God has seen their faith and he has separated them from the faithless. "Holy" means reserved for God's purpose. And it's God who makes the reservation, not on the basis of our behavior but on the basis of our faith, which inevitably changes our behavior.

- **Four big ideas.** Paul has created in Romans a study filled with deep theological insight. So Bible experts have broken the work down into many possible outlines—the raw frame on which they believe Paul built the letter. Here's one of many outlines.

  After introducing himself, Paul shows that everyone has sinned and needs salvation (1:18—3:20). He explains how God has made salvation available through Jesus (3:21—8:39). Next Paul assures everyone that there's ample room in the kingdom of God for Jews (9—11). Paul closes with lessons about how to behave (12—15), followed by a chapter of personal notes concerning many individuals.

EXTREME SCENES
from Romans

Time to move on (1:1–17)

After 20 years of ministry in the eastern Mediterranean, Paul feels he has done all he can there and that it's time to move on. Paul writes to the congregation in Rome and tells them he plans to visit them—something he has wanted to do for a long time—and help win other followers to Christ while there. After spending time in Rome, Paul hopes the church there will help send him on to Spain. But because most people in the congregation know Paul only by reputation, he writes a letter introducing himself and his beliefs. Most likely, the letter is read aloud during one of the meetings, which are often held in the larger homes of the more wealthy church members. Because Paul's letter is such a masterfully crafted summary of important Christian beliefs, it is probably copied and circulated among churches throughout the empire.

DIRECTOR'S NOTES

The comparison between sin and slavery probably hit home to many of the people who read Paul's letter. In New Testament times, one out of every four people in the Roman Empire was a slave. People who were captured in battle, whether they were soldiers or civilians, usually became slaves. People who could not afford to pay their debts also became slaves to work off what they owed. Romans 6:19

Jesus is for everyone (4:1–25)

A hallmark of Paul's beliefs is that people become acceptable to God through faith—not through making sacrifices or observing Jewish customs, such as circumcision, dietary restrictions, and annual religious holidays. This is great news to people from non-Jewish backgrounds. Many of them have worshiped God, but have stopped short of converting to Judaism because of the seemingly harsh requirements. On the other hand, most Jews—even Jewish Christians—believe that their traditions come from God and are sacred. They don't believe that mere faith can save anyone.

To prove that faith is enough, Paul reminds his readers that God singled out Abraham to become father of the Jews because of Abraham's faith—not because he followed the rules. Most of the rules, in fact, didn't arrive until several centuries later, during Moses' time. "You cannot make God accept you because of something you do," Paul writes. "God accepts sinners only because they have faith in him" (4:5). As convincing as Paul could be, traditions die hard. And throughout Paul's lifetime and beyond, this remained a touchy topic for Jewish and non-Jewish Christians worshiping together, as they likely did in Rome.

God's plan for sinners (5:12–6:14)

Earlier in the letter, Paul boldly states: "All of us have sinned and fallen short of God's glory. But God treats us much better than we deserve, and because of Christ Jesus, He freely accepts us and sets us free from our sins" (3:23–24). To prove his point, Paul goes all the way back to Genesis. Sin and death entered the world when Adam and Eve disobeyed God and ate the forbidden fruit. God's good creation became contaminated. Because Adam sinned, death entered the world. "Now everyone has sinned, and so everyone must die," Paul explains.

The problem is that a holy God cannot coexist with sin. The sin must be cleansed, or the sinner removed from the presence of God. In Old Testament times, God set up the sacrificial system as a way to allow people to find cleansing and forgiveness. The death of the animal graphically reminded everyone of the deadly seriousness of sin. Later, God sent Jesus as the ultimate and final sacrifice, launching a new means of spiritual cleansing. In a way that we can't fully understand, Christ's sacrifice and resurrection provides a way for us to correct the damage done by Adam. We do that when we have faith that Jesus is the remedy for sin and death. Paul wraps it up like this: "Adam disobeyed God and caused many others to be sinners. But because of the good thing that Christ has done, God accepts us and gives us the gift of life" (5:19, 18).

All God's children (9–10)

Initially, the church gets its start among Jews who believe Jesus came to earth as the Messiah and Son of God. But as time passes and the church realizes that this means the prophesied age of the new covenant has arrived and the age of the old covenant had ended—with all of its laws about circumcision, diet, and rituals—Jews become increasingly hostile toward Christianity. By the end of the century Jews will prohibit Jewish Christians from worshiping in synagogues.

Paul realizes that non-Jewish believers might begin looking down on Jews, including Jewish Christians. But Paul reminds his mostly non-Jewish readers that God has carefully cultivated the Jewish people, just as a farmer cultivates and purposefully prunes an olive tree. "You Gentiles are like branches of a wild olive tree," Paul says, which has been grafted to the "cultivated olive tree" (11:17).

Paul's point is clear. The roots of Christian faith are Jewish. For it is the Jews who have long been drawing spiritual nourishment from God. And it is through Jews—such as Jesus, the disciples, and Paul—that God extends salvation to the rest of the world. Even though most Jews reject God, Paul says, "they are still the chosen ones, and God loves them" (11:28). In the end, Paul adds, Israel will return to God and be saved.

Life as God's children (12:1–21)

Paul explains that when Jesus offered Himself as the sacrifice for our sins, the Jewish sacrificial system became no longer necessary. For all intents and purposes, the Jewish sacrificial system had ended about 40 years earlier when the Romans had destroyed the temple. Since AD 70 the Jews have not had a temple for making sacrifices. (A 1,300-year-old mosque now sits on the temple hilltop.)

Instead of offering animal sacrifices, Paul urges the people to offer their bodies "as a living sacrifice, pure and pleasing. That's the most sensible way to serve God. Don't be like the people of this world, but let God change the way you think. Then you will know how to do everything that is good and pleasing to him" (12:1-2). This letter makes such an impression on the Romans that when Paul finally arrives in Italy, as a prisoner on his way to court, many of the congregation travel 40 miles to meet and accompany him on the last leg of his journey (Acts 28:15).

REVIEWS

ENCORE

➤ Read Galatians for another in-depth, but more freewheeling, emotion-packed glimpse into Paul's beliefs.

➤ For more about how Christianity grows out of the Jewish faith, and fulfills it, read Hebrews.

Romans is like one of those shows where they teach you how to do something like oil painting (with *happy* little clouds and *happy* little trees) or playing guitar or maybe some little artsy-craftsy thing. Whatever it is, they take you step-by-step through something that seems impossible, and they make it easy for you.

With the book of Romans, Paul is explaining to a very non-Jewish community what this Messiah thing is all about. He has to put all the Hebrew prophesies aside and give it to 'em as straight as he can, just the facts. Because of that, this is one powerful how-to faith manual.

First-century Roman historian, Suetonius, (I didn't make up that name but if I had it would be the name of that guy who always dresses up too much for school) says that in A.D. 49 there was such an uproar among Jews over "Chrestus" (probably Christ), that Emperor Claudius expelled the Jews from Rome. The Jews weren't allowed to return until Claudius died in A.D. 54. That was just a few years before Paul reminded the mostly non-Jewish church of Rome that in God's eyes there's no difference between Jew and non-Jew: "No one who has faith will be disappointed, no matter if that person is a Jew or a Gentile," Paul writes. "There is only one Lord, and he is generous to everyone who asks for his help. All who call out to the Lord will be saved" (10:11-13).

This was a HUGE change. The Messiah had always been promised to the Jews. It was their battle cry, their hope for ages. God meant to share salvation with the WHOLE WORLD? Whether they obeyed the Jewish law or not? Yep. God put it on the line—He loved everyone. Faith for eternal life (OK, let's put a little faith on our brush... go like this... and *see*, a *happy* little soul). Salvation may seem like a complicated thing. Just take it step-by-step and you'll find out that anyone who "tunes in" can learn how. Coming up next, tune in and tune up as "the cheerful twanger" teaches you how to play "A Boy Named Suetonius" on guitar.

Hap E. Painter

1 Corinthians

SCHEDULE OF SCENES

Jesus Is Born	Jesus Crucified Pentecost	Paul's Missionary Journeys Begin	1 Corinthians Written	Temple Destroyed	Death of John
7/6 B.C.	A.D. 30	A.D. 46	A.D. 55	A.D. 70	A.D. 100

The un-perfect church

There is no such thing as the perfect church. Period. End of story. As long as human beings are involved in running the show, there will never ever be a perfect church. Consider the church founded by the most notable, influential, successful Christian minister of first-generation believers. Paul didn't just stay in Corinth a few days or weeks like most cities he visited. He stayed there for two years, training and nurturing these spiritual infants. Yet, it took only a couple of years before these Corinthians were behaving like disobedient, rebellious kids who didn't know any better.

Take a look at what was going on: They were arguing over who in the church was most important; suing each other in court; turning a blind eye to incest among the congregation; and showing that they were thoroughly confused about key Christian beliefs, such as the Resurrection. In a blunt, though loving letter, Paul replies to an array of practical questions the Corinthians raised in a letter to him. But he also confronts issues they were apparently too embarrassed to mention.

This is not a boring letter. First Corinthians cuts to the heart of these issues. And it's timely because, unfortunately, there's a little bit of Corinth in every church—and a lot of Corinth in some.

QUOTABLES

Let's eat and drink. Tomorrow we die (15:32). Paul quotes a Greek proverb to suggest what our attitude should be if Christ was not raised from the dead.

O death, where is thy sting? O grave, where is thy victory? (15:55, KJV). A praise of believers who realize that, like Jesus, they too will be resurrected.

God is faithful; he will not let you be tempted beyond what you can bear (10:13, NIV).

Your body is a temple where the Holy Spirit lives (6:19). Paul's reminder to the Corinthians to take good care of their bodies.

SNEAK PREVIEW

Hebrews
Don't miss the gift of God just because it's wrapped in different colored paper.

BEHIND the SCENES
of 1 Corinthians

STARRING ROLE

Paul, leading minister to the non-Jewish world, and founder of the church at Corinth, Greece (1:1)

PLOT

A couple of years after leaving the church he started in Corinth, Paul gets some bad news. Messengers arrive with a letter from the congregation asking for his help in solving a number of divisive problems. Not all the bad news is in the letter. The messengers and other sources report additional problems: power struggles among the leadership, cliques in the congregation, an I-don't-want-to-get-involved attitude about church members engaged in illicit sex, Christians suing Christians.

Paul tackles the tough issues first, since they reflect a deeper misunderstanding about what it means to be a Christian. Then, beginning with chapter 7, Paul addresses the more practical questions that the Corinthians asked—questions about everyday living and worship services, such as "Is it better for people not to marry?" (7:1). And, is it OK to eat "food offered to idols" (8:1), which priests sell wholesale to meat vendors who resell it at a profit in the meat markets?

In all of Paul's advice, he urges the believers to act in unity and love. If they can do this, he teaches, their other problems will disappear.

STAGE DIRECTIONS

	Paul starts church in Corinth A.D. 50		Paul writes 1 Corinthians A.D. 55	Paul's missionary trips end A.D. 57
			Dates are approximate	

BIBLE EVENTS

A.D. 40	A.D. 45	A.D. 50	A.D. 55

WORLD EVENTS

| | London founded A.D. 43 | Some Jews expelled from Rome move to Corinth (Acts 18:2) A.D. 49 | Romans learn about soap from Gauls (France) A.D. 50 | Isthmian Games held at Corinth A.D. 51 | Claudius poisoned, Jews return to Rome A.D. 54 |

AUTHOR AND DATE

"I am signing this letter myself: PAUL" (16:21). This conclusion, along with the introduction, "From Paul," (1:1), clearly identifies who the writer is. Early church leaders included this letter in the New Testament because they believed it came from the pen of Paul, the most influential minister among first-generation Christians.

Paul wrote the letter from Ephesus in about AD 55, two or three years after leaving Corinth. Paul had arrived in the city about five years earlier and started the church during the second of his three missionary trips throughout the eastern Mediterranean. Paul didn't usually stay in a town longer than a few weeks, but he made an exception for Corinth, a busy port city full of international travelers who might hear his message and take it home with them. Paul stayed in Corinth for two years, then returned after writing 1 Corinthians, during his third missionary trip.

> 1 Corinthians is not Paul's first letter to the church at Corinth. It's just the first one that survived. In 1 Corinthians Paul refers to "my other letter" (5:9).

ON LOCATION

Paul's letter is addressed to Christians in a young church he started a few years earlier, during his second missionary journey, in Corinth. Perhaps the busiest city in ancient Greece, located south of Athens, Corinth is near a four-mile-wide land bridge separating the Aegean Sea in the East and the Adriatic Sea in the West.

Eastern trade ships carrying products destined for Rome and other Western cities would often stop in Corinth. If the ship was small enough, it could be hauled up onto a huge wagon, wheeled across the isthmus, then launched into the Adriatic. This saved merchants a 200-mile trip around the tip of Greece, sparing them from storms and pirates. Larger ships unloaded their cargo and had it hauled to other ships waiting at the Adriatic port. Nero started a canal in AD 66, but the project was stopped after engineers doubted it could be done and Corinthians complained that a canal would keep travelers from stopping in the city. The project was completed in 1893 and is still used.

WHAT TO LOOK FOR

- **A power struggle in the church.** The congregation is breaking into factions that prefer one of at least three leaders: Paul, Peter, or Apollos (1:12). Apollos, mentioned in Acts 18:24–28, is an Old Testament scholar and a charismatic speaker. Peter, one of the original disciples of Jesus, may have appealed to Jewish Christians at Corinth. Paul, founder of the church and advocate for non-Jewish believers, maintained a loyal core of supporters. "Don't take sides," Paul advises. "Has Christ been divided up? Was I nailed to a cross for you?" (1:10, 13)

- **Christians behaving badly.** Besides the power struggle, there are other problems in the church—many stemming from Christians behaving as if they had a license to sin. There is a man who has married his stepmother, in defiance of both Roman and Jewish law that considers this incest (Deuteronomy 27:20). Paul is shocked that the congregation lets this man remain in the church, as though he is doing nothing wrong. Though God judges people outside the church, Paul says, Christians have an obligation to judge and discipline their members. Paul advises the Corinthians to stay away from professing believers who are blatantly "immoral or greedy or worship idols or curse others or get drunk or cheat" (5:11). In even sterner advice Paul adds, "Chase away any of your own people who are evil" (5:13).

    Another example of bad behavior is Christians suing each other in "a court of sinners" (6:1). "Can't you settle small problems?" Paul asks. "Why do you take everyday complaints to judges who are not respected by the church?" (6:2, 4)

- **Practical advice about life and worship.** In chapter 7 Paul starts answering a variety of questions the church has asked him. Here's a sampling of the topics:

    Marriage. Paul apparently expects Jesus to return soon, so he advises people not to get married, but he concedes "it is better to marry than to burn with desire" (7:9).

    Eating food offered to idols. Paul says this issue is not particularly important, since all food comes from God. Paul does say, however, that Christians should be sensitive to other believers who have scruples against eating such food (8:1–13).

    Dressing for worship services. People should dress appropriately, Paul says, not as trendsetters, calling attention to themselves, or as lures for the opposite sex (11:1–16).

    The Lord's Supper. This is a shared celebration of the death and resurrection of Jesus, Paul explains. But Corinth has turned it into a segregated potluck, where rich members cluster in cliques to eat rich folks' food, while the poor eat comparative crumbs (11:20–33).

    Spiritual gifts. God gives different abilities to different people, Paul says. Each gift is important and useful in God's work (12:1–31).

- **A beautiful hymn about love.** One of the most famous chapters in the Bible is Paul's lyrical message about love. The poem comes immediately after Paul has talked about other gifts from God, to emphasize that all talent is useless if it doesn't flow from a heart of love. The ability to love others, Paul argues, is the greatest gift of all—greater than hope and even greater than faith (13:13). This is a powerful message especially in Corinth, a city famed for its great temple of Aphrodite, goddess of love.

EXTREME SCENES
from 1 Corinthians

Who's in charge, anyway? (1:10-31)

A few years after Paul leaves the church he founded in Corinth, continuing his preaching trips throughout the eastern Mediterranean, the congregation splits into squabbling factions. Some prefer the guidance of their founding minister. Others prefer the interpretations of Peter, who still observes many Jewish customs and probably lives in Jerusalem. Still others gravitate to Apollos, a brilliant scholar and dynamic speaker living in Corinth. Paul begs the Corinthians to stop arguing, since only Christ is the leader of the church. "Was I nailed to a cross for you?" Paul asks. "Were you baptized in my name?" (1:13). Paul argues that all three leaders are merely servants of God: "Paul and Apollos and Peter all belong to you" (3:22). Comparing God's spiritual kingdom to a garden, Paul says "I planted the seeds, Apollos watered them, but God made them sprout and grow" (3:6).

Tackling the tough issues (5:1-13)

Paul is shocked to find out that a member of the church has married his stepmother and that the church has taken no action to discipline him. By both Roman and Jewish standards, the man has committed incest. "In my other letter [before 1 Corinthians] I told you not to have anything to do with immoral people," Paul says. "But I wasn't talking about people of this world. You would have to leave this world to get away from everyone who is immoral or greedy or who cheats or worships idols. I was talking about your own people" (5:9–11). Paul explains that God judges those outside the church, but believers have a responsibility to protect the name of Jesus by disciplining those who call themselves Christians. Paul's advice: "Expel the wicked man from among you" (5:13, NIV). This harsh judgment is not to banish the man completely, but to bring him to his senses so he will repent and return to Christ and the church.

Taking it to the courts (6:1-11)

Bickering among the church gets so bad that Christians start taking each other to court. Paul reprimands the congregation: "Why should one of you take another to be tried by unbelievers? Aren't any of you wise enough to act as a judge between one follower and another?" Roman courts operated without the ideas that we cherish today, primarily that fairness and justice were blind. In the Roman judicial system, money talked. Roman judges were expected to decide in favor of the wealthier, more influential party. The poor and other persons of low social standing feared being hauled into court, because—guilty or innocent—their misery would surely be multiplied if their accuser was higher-class or wealthier. In banning lawsuits between believers, Paul protects the socially weaker members and calls the whole church to its responsibility to apply God's wisdom to disagreements among themselves.

The love supper or the Lord's Supper? (11:17-34)

In many churches, Corinth included, when believers observe the ritual of the Lord's Supper by eating bread and drinking wine that represents the body and blood of the crucified Jesus, they also eat a full meal called a "love feast." But a problem develops. Instead of having a time that focuses on the reason for the celebrating—the Lord's Supper and bringing the church together—the love feast becomes an exclusive potluck dinner party. The upper crust feast together, while the poor folks dine on just that—crust.

Not only does this dishonor Christ, Paul says, but it also divides the people who should be united in gratitude for what Jesus did for them on the cross. Paul advises the people who are hungry to eat before they come to worship, so they concentrate on the real reason for the meal and thank Jesus for the gift of salvation and the promise of a resurrection.

The greatest gift: love (13:1-13)

Paul writes that God has given the people at Corinth a wide variety of talents, or gifts, such as prophecy, healing, teaching, and speaking in other languages. All of these are important because they allow Christians to help others. But Paul says there is one gift that surpasses all the rest—a gift that channels all our talents in the right direction—the gift of love. Paul writes in the now famous "love chapter": "What if I could prophesy and understand all secrets and all knowledge? I would gain nothing, unless I loved others."

Compassionate love—inspired by Christ's death for humanity—produces a selfless people who are kind and patient, not boastful or easily angered, always supportive and hopeful, never keeping a record of the wrongs that others do. We don't start out this way, though, Paul says. "When we were children, we thought and reasoned as children do. But when we grew up, we quit our childish ways" (13:11). Growing, mature Christians cultivate an attitude of love above all others. Among the three noblest traits—faith, hope, and love—Paul says "the greatest is love."

The final chapter (15:1–58)

Some Corinthians are confused about the resurrection of Jesus and what it has to do with them. Some apparently don't believe that bodies will be resurrected. Instead, these people have adopted the Greek understanding that only the soul is immortal. Paul teaches that Jesus—soul and glorified body—were both resurrected and witnessed by hundreds.

"Unless Christ was raised to life, your faith is useless," Paul explains. "But Christ has been raised to life! And He makes us certain that others will also be raised to life. Just as we will die because of Adam, we will be raised to life because of Christ" (15:20–21).

Paul reveals that some day, in an instant, "our dead and decaying bodies will be changed into bodies that won't die." Our former bodies made from dust will become like that of "the one who came from heaven." When this happens, Paul says, the prophecies of Isaiah and Hosea will be fulfilled, and people will praise God saying, "Death has lost the battle! Where is its victory? Where is its sting?" (Isaiah 25:8; Hosea 13:14).

REVIEWS

ENCORE

➤ Read Paul's follow-up letter:
2 Corinthians.

Corinth was one evil place. Imagine one of those dark movies where smoke comes up out of the sewers and the whole town is full of alleys with all kind of nasty critters hiding there, human and otherwise. Morally, that was Corinth. As a matter of fact, in Paul's day the phrase, "Live like a Corinthian," meant to be immoral.

Corinth was also a trade center. If you wanted to get some information out to the world, Corinth was the place, because people from all over the world came through there. It was a great place to start a church, just a hard place to keep one going.

A cool fact to know about Corinth is that there was something like the Olympics held there, called the Isthmian Games. They were held every four years—including A.D. 51, when Paul was in town. The Isthmian Games featured a wide variety of races by runners, horsemen, and charioteers. It's probably not coincidence then, that Paul used sports images in his letter to the Corinthians. Comparing Christians to runners in a race, Paul says, "You know that many runners enter a race, and only one of them wins the prize. So run to win!" (9:24). "Athletes work hard to win a crown that cannot last," Paul adds, "but we do it for a crown that will last forever" (9:25). The Corinthians could relate to that. (By the way, the winners' crowns at the Isthmian Games were woven from withered stalks of celery. We've come a long way, baby.)

So here's this church in sleazy ol' Corinth trying to be a light in a very dark place. No big surprise that things weren't going too good at first. Christians there were trying to live righteous lives and not get sucked into the evil around them. From what Paul wrote in this letter, they were having a rough time with the not-getting-sucked-back-in thing. Husbands and wives weren't being faithful. People in the church weren't getting along. Things were getting pretty messy. 1 Corinthians was Paul's attempt to get them back on track. From the sounds of 2 Corinthians, it worked.

Benjamin ben John

2 Corinthians

SCHEDULE OF SCENES

Jesus Is Born	Jesus Crucified Pentecost	Paul's Missionary Journeys Begin	2 Corinthians Written	Temple Destroyed	Death of John
7/6 B.C.	A.D. 30	A.D. 46	A.D. 55	A.D. 70	A.D. 100

The Corinth crisis: Part two

When we first meet the church at Corinth, it is in crisis mode. Paul, who has started and trained the church, has been gone for several years and the church is in chaos. Arguments have broken out about who was in church, how Christians should behave, and how they should worship. Paul does some emergency church triage by sending a letter and making a personal visit to address the problems.

It's a year later, and the church at Corinth is facing yet another crisis. Some men who claim to be apostles arrive in Corinth and begin enticing the church leaders away from Paul's leadership. The letter never mentions the specifics of what these false apostles are teaching, but Paul accuses the imposters of repackaging the gospel with "another Jesus," "another spirit," and a "different message" (11:4).

When Paul catches wind of what's going on in Corinth, he goes on the attack. He battles for the hearts and minds of the Corinthians, knowing full well that it's a fight he might lose. Someone concerned about his or her reputation or personal pride, might walk away from this one. But not Paul. He refuses to back off. He genuinely cares about the Corinthian people. And he'll do whatever it takes—regardless of the heartache or humiliation— to win them back to the true Jesus, the true spirit, and the genuine message.

QUOTABLES

God loves a cheerful giver (9:7).

A thorn in the flesh (12:7). Paul's mystifying description of an unnamed problem that tormented him.

SNEAK PREVIEW

Ezra

A little battered and beaten, the people of God dust themselves off and start all over again.

BEHIND the SCENES
of 2 Corinthians

STARRING ROLES

Paul, leading minister to the non-Jewish world, and founder of the church at Corinth, Greece (1:1)

Titus, Paul's associate who carries a letter to Corinth that tries repairing the damaged relationship between Paul and the congregation (2:13)

PLOT

Shortly after the Corinthian Christians receive Paul's letter known to us as 1 Corinthians, some outsiders arrive. Paul doesn't say who these people are, but clearly their take on Christianity differs from his. Paul calls the intruders "false apostles" who "only pretend to be apostles of Christ" (11:13). They apparently represent Jewish Christianity, yet 2 Corinthians says nothing about observing such Jewish matters as circumcision, food restrictions, and religious holidays.

STAGE DIRECTIONS

	Paul begins missionary trips	Paul starts church in Corinth		Paul writes 1,2 Corinthians	Paul's missionary trips end
	A.D. 46	A.D. 50	Dates are approximate	A.D. 55	A.D. 57

BIBLE EVENTS

A.D. 45 — A.D. 50 — A.D. 55 — A.D. 60

WORLD EVENTS

	Famine strikes Jerusalem sometime within next 7 years	Some Jews expelled from Rome move to Corinth (Acts 18:2)	Claudius poisoned by wife, Jews return to Rome
	A.D. 45	A.D. 49	A.D. 54

BEHIND the SCENES
of 2 Corinthians

The relationship between Paul and the Corinthians already was badly strained. The church itself had started fracturing into cliques and arguing over lifestyles and worship practices. After writing 1 Corinthians, Paul makes a visit to the church. But this only aggravates the tension. The situation is ripe for a hostile takeover. Enter the intruders.

Gifted in the art of persuasion, the newly-arrived intruders lob charge upon charge at Paul. All we know of the charges is what we can infer from Paul's defense, preserved in 2 Corinthians. But the outsiders seem to attack his authority and motives. In response, Paul presents himself as an honest and sincere minister of Christ who cares deeply about the Corinthians.

AUTHOR AND DATE

The letter is "from Paul, chosen by God to be an apostle of Jesus Christ" (1:1), along with his associate, Timothy. Paul wrote the letter a few months after writing 1 Corinthians, during his third and final missionary trip. Drawing on clues from the text, some Bible experts speculate that he wrote 1 Corinthians in the spring while staying at Ephesus, then 2 Corinthians in the winter while in Macedonia.

ON LOCATION

Like 1 Corinthians, Paul's letter is addressed to Christians in a young church he started a few years earlier at Corinth, Greece. Located south of Athens, Corinth is near a four-mile-wide land bridge separating the Aegean Sea in the east and the Adriatic Sea in the west. Paul apparently assumes that other churches in the region will read circulated copies of the letter, since he also addresses "all of God's people in Achaia," the Roman province that is now Greece.

WHAT TO LOOK FOR

- **Verbal attacks against Paul.** Religious teachers arrive in town, saying they are Christians. They quickly show they are opponents of Paul, because they begin turning the church against their founding minister. Here are what seem to be several main points of attack, along with excerpts of Paul's defense:

  1. Paul is a self-appointed apostle, not one personally commissioned by Jesus, as were the original disciples. "When I was with you, I was patient and worked all the powerful miracles and signs and wonders of a true apostle" (12:12).

  2. Paul is self-promoting. "We are not preaching about ourselves. Our message is that Jesus Christ is Lord" (4:5).

  3. Paul can't be trusted, since he didn't come to Corinth when he said he would. Paul replies by saying that his last visit was so painful that he decided a cooling off period was in order. "I have decided not to make my next visit with you so painful.... I didn't want to make you feel bad. I only wanted to let you know how much I cared for you" (2:1, 4).

  4. Paul is pocketing money collected for the poverty-stricken believers in Jerusalem. "Unlike so many, we do not peddle the word of God for profit" (2:17, NIV). Paul implies that the intruders are seeking donations for themselves from the Corinthians. Paul had refused to do this (12:13). Instead, he earned his keep by working as a tentmaker (Acts 18:3).

  5. Paul barks boldly in his letters, but in person he's a coward who has nothing worth saying (10:10). "When I am with you, I will do exactly what I say in my letters" (10:11).

- **Paul's reluctant bragging about his sufferings.** Bible experts call 11:16—12:13 the "Fool's Speech" because Paul says "let me be a fool and brag a little" (11:16). Paul feels uncomfortable bragging about anything except the Lord. But he feels that his back is to the wall and his ministry in Corinth will be over if he doesn't speak up. The Fool's Speech might look like self-defensive bragging, but it's not. It's a parody on ancient speeches and letters that commend a person. This is an appropriate defensive technique because the intruder-critics in Corinth have come with letters of recommendation. In a sarcastic reversal of typical commendations, Paul begins bragging about experiences that show him as a victim—a loser by the world's standards. Paul reports suffering one tragedy after another—all because he is doing God's will—and on behalf of the Corinthians. The readers can't help but be reminded of how Jesus suffered for the same reason. For many Corinthians, this speech likely generates a renewed sense of gratitude for what Paul and Jesus have endured on their behalf.

- **Paul's "thorn in the flesh."** In describing what he has suffered throughout his ministry, Paul speaks of a "thorn in the flesh" that torments him and keeps him from getting conceited (12:7, NIV). Paul shows himself to be weak in that, though he asks God three times to remove the "thorn," God refuses. Jesus, too, asked to be spared the suffering of the cross. Because Jesus suffered, Paul is willing to do the same—even if it makes him look weak in the eyes of the world. Paul never says what the "thorn" is. Bible experts have many theories, including some kind of physical problem such as malaria or poor eyesight (he wrote in big letters, Galatians 6:11), or his never-ending persecutions, or his rejection by the Corinthians.
- **Personal information about Paul.** This letter reveals more autobiographical information about Paul than any of his other letters. Much of this comes in chapters 11–12, where he talks about how he suffered as a minister: beatings, jailings, shipwrecks, stonings, public humiliation. The list goes on. He also describes what sounds like a vision or an out-of-body experience in which he caught a glimpse of the afterlife (12:1–6).
- **A passionate fund-raising letter.** Surprisingly, in this letter that includes a defense against charges that he's preaching for profit, Paul asks for money. But the money is not for him. In fact he makes it a point to remind the Corinthians that during the two years he lived among them he did not accept their money. The donation he is now requesting is for poverty-stricken Christians in Jerusalem. This is a special offering Paul has been collecting from churches throughout the eastern Mediterranean. Paul applies some gentle pressure by telling the Corinthians that he has bragged about their generosity.

EXTREME SCENES
from 2 Corinthians

> ## The sweet smell of victory (2:14–17)

Paul begins his emotional letter by saying how glad he is that God always comforts us when we suffer. This is an apt introduction since Paul is going to spend much of the rest of his letter talking about the torment he has endured from the Corinthian church and from others.

DIRECTOR'S NOTES

How much do you know about ancient pottery? Maybe it's time you learned a thing or two. "Earthen vessels" is another name for clay jars that were used to hold oil and grain. Before the clay could be shaped by a potter, stones and other large objects had to be removed from it. After the clay was shaped, the potter had two options for drying it: let the sun do it or stick it in a kiln. A sun-dried jar could hold grain, but it would collapse if it were filled with liquid. A jar heated in a kiln—at temperatures above 900 degrees Fahrenheit—became hard and strong and could be used to store oil and other liquids. 2 Corinthians 4:7

Paul says that followers of Christ in this generation—and especially ministers—should expect hardship, opposition, and rejection because these are what Christ got. To illustrate two extremes in the way people react to the gospel, Paul uses a familiar image to citizens of the Roman Empire. It's the scene of a Roman procession: soldiers marching in a victory parade after a battle. On display are the prisoners of war who will be executed for the emperor's pleasure or sold as slaves. Along the roadway, citizens cheer and fill the air with the sweet smell of burning incense. To the conquerors, this perfumed scent is fragrant and welcome. To the captives, the smell means death.

Paul then paints a picture of himself and other Christian ministers marching in a victory parade led by Jesus. "For people who are being saved," he says, "this perfume has a sweet smell and leads them to a better life. But for people who are lost, it has a bad smell and leads them to a horrible death." Some people welcome the gospel and its messengers. But many reject both and resist them with a vengeance.

> ## Jars of clay (5:1–10)

Paul is amazed that God would entrust a message as important as the gospel to frail human beings. He writes, "We are like clay jars in which this treasure is stored. We often suffer, but we are never crushed. Even when we don't know what to do, we never give up. In times of trouble, God is with us, and when we are knocked down, we get up again. We face death every day because of Jesus" (4:7–11). Paul doesn't have an inordinate fear of death because he believes the only thing to die will be the body, which God will replace with an eternal body. "Our bodies are like tents that we live in here on earth," Paul writes. "But when these tents are destroyed, we know that God will give each of us a place to live. These homes will not be buildings that someone has made, but they are in heaven and will last forever."

⇒ Helping the poor (8:1–9:15)

Since almost the beginning of the early church, disagreements have split the church between Jewish Christians and non-Jewish believers. The Jewish Christians believe that non-Jewish believers should follow the rules regarding circumcision, diet and other traditional practices (Acts 15). Despite a ruling from the Jerusalem Council that says non-Jewish believers don't have to follow these laws, this group dogs Paul's every move and attempts to undo the damage they believe his preaching has done.

To promote unity between the two factions, Paul begins a collection among the predominantly non-Jewish churches to help the poor Jewish Christians in Jerusalem. The Bible doesn't say how the Jerusalem believers got poor. One theory is that the spirit of generosity that started at Pentecost spurred many believers to give away nearly everything they owned (Acts 4:32-37). Another suggestion growing out of Scripture is that a famine hit the region sometime after Paul began his first missionary trip in about AD 46 and before Emperor Claudius died in AD 54 (Acts 12:27–30). Yet another reason may be because older Jews often moved to Jerusalem to spend their final days in the Holy City to be buried there. The church may have had to bear the brunt of caring for women whose husbands preceded them in death.

Whatever the reason for the poverty, the offering for Jerusalem is important to Paul. He pleads with the Corinthians to be generous. "But don't feel sorry that you must give and don't feel that you are forced to give," he adds. "God loves people who love to give" (9:7). Paul later delivers the offering in person, fully aware that he may be arrested and tried for heresy by the same Jewish legislative body that tried Jesus. In fact, Paul is arrested and eventually transported to Rome for trial in the emperor's court. That's the last the Bible says of Paul. Christian writers at the end of the century report that Paul was executed.

⇒ The real thing (11:16–33)

In the closing chapters of his letter, Paul grapples with the biggest problem now threatening the Corinthian church: "false apostles" who have arrived with letters of recommendation and who are winning control of the church (11:13). Paul takes an incredibly creative approach to winning back his congregation. Instead of bragging about his spiritual power and influence—as the intruders have done about themselves—Paul writes a sarcastic parody on self-promotion; he brags about his weaknesses and the humiliations he has suffered.

Once, he admits, he had to sneak out of Damascus like a criminal, lowered over the city wall in a basket to escape Jews who wanted to kill him as a religious traitor (Acts 9:20-25). Paul gives a humiliating litany to show how much he has endured out of love for God—and the Corinthians: "Five times my own people gave me thirty-nine lashes with a whip. Three times the Romans beat me with a big stick, and once my enemies stoned me. I have been shipwrecked three times, and I even had to spend a night and a day in the sea.... My life has been in danger in cities, in deserts, at sea, and with people who only pretended to be the Lord's followers" (11:24–26).

The climax of this parody comes when Paul reveals that Jesus, too, suffered terribly because of the gospel message. "He was weak when he was nailed to the cross," Paul says, but now Jesus "lives by the power of God." The Corinthians should see how only Paul—not the crowd-pleasing latecomers—fits the pattern established by Jesus. Therefore he is their genuine apostle.

REVIEWS

Have you seen those shows where people who are mad at each other face off? They can choose to forgive each other or not. There's usually a lot of crying and hugging. Paul's second letter to the Corinthians is a little like that. Without all the cursing and bouncers.

He had written his first letter to the Corinthians to set them straight on a few issues. They had a choice: They could resent him for it, or they could respond to it. What did they do? They responded to Paul's encouragement and cleaned up their act. So in this second letter Paul gives them the credit they deserve.

Speaking of Paul...have you ever thought of what he looked like? We know from Acts that before he believed in Christ he was an antagonist against Christianity. He seemed to have wielded great power. It might surprise you to know that the impression Scripture gives is that Paul wasn't much to look at. The Bible gives only hints of what Paul looked like, but those hints match up with the earliest surviving description of him in a second-century book.

Writing in the Acts of Paul, a Christian author describes Paul as "a man of middling size, and his hair was scanty, and his legs were a little crooked, and his knees were far apart; he had large eyes, and his eyebrows met, and his nose was somewhat long." Sounds a little like a balding owl.

Paul himself quoted his critics as saying, "Paul's letters are harsh and powerful. But in person, he is a weakling" (10:10). The New International Version translates "weakling" as "unimpressive," while the New Revised Standard Version puts it this way: "his bodily presence is weak." Whatever the description meant, it was no compliment.

ENCORE

> Read Paul's earlier letter to the church: 1 Corinthians.

> For another emotional defense of Paul's ministry, read his letter to the church in Galatia.

> Philippians is another letter in which Paul's gentle tone changes abruptly. In strong language he condemns people who argue that non-Jews must observe the rite of circumcision.

REVIEWS

Paul probably knew what it was to be the weakling, the egghead, the underdog, even if he learned to cover it well. Maybe that was why he spent so much time comparing our weakness with Christ's power. "Although he [Jesus] was weak when he was nailed to the cross, he now lives by the power of God. We are weak, just as Christ was. But you will see that we will live by the power of God, just as Christ does" (13:4).

In other words, the Lord has a remarkable capacity for turning weakness into power. "If Christ keeps giving me his power," Paul adds, "I will gladly brag about how weak I am" (12:9). THAT is one of the best comeback lines I've ever heard. Paul was used to being picked on, even arrested, for believing in Christ but, even though he wasn't very big or strong, he was strong in his faith and stood up to anybody who got in his way. Two thousand years later he's still an important guy, but his critics (excuse me, what were their names again?) are mostly just remembered as *Paul's* critics.

author unknown (ex-Paul critic)

Galatians

SCHEDULE OF SCENES

Jesus Is Born	Jesus Crucified Pentecost	Paul's Missionary Journeys Begin	Galatians Written	Temple Destroyed	Death of John
7/6 B.C.	A.D. 30	A.D. 46	A.D. 54	A.D. 70	A.D. 100

Paul gets angry

Sometimes it might feel that the Bible is devoid of emotion. The cold hard facts of history barely leap off the page. There's little to move your emotion. Well, if you've ever felt that way . . . try this book. It's the most emotionally charged book of the Bible. You can almost see the thick purple veins popping out on Paul's neck as he unloads on the misguided Christians of Galatia.

What's the bid deal? Well, for starters, Paul has taught them God saves them by trusting in Christ alone, not in doing religious things. The people obviously don't buy it. Instead, they've bought into the message of some missionaries who are teaching that Christians have to obey the Jewish laws. Paul is adamant that the Law has nothing to do with salvation now that Jesus has come. So, with an emotionally charged response, Paul reminds the Galatians of the miracles and the gift of the Holy Spirit they experienced when Paul was still in the area. He fires away . . . asking them how they actually received God's spirit. Did they have to work to get it? Nope. How in the world can they be so stupid (hey . . . those are Paul's words!)

It's hard to understand the rage and intensity that drives Paul to say what he does. Paul uses some of the most harsh language in Scripture. Yet in an oddly familiar way, when he detonates his anger all over the Galatians and the people leading them in the wrong direction, he sounds like a furious but loving parent reading the riot act to a child who just did something incredibly stupid and nearly got killed. Sometimes love is silent. But sometimes love is a vein-popping scream, calling one back from the brink of disaster.

QUOTABLES

A man reaps what he sows (6:7, NIV).

"I have been crucified with Christ; it is no longer I who live, but Christ lives in me" (2:20, NKJV). *Paul's declaration that Jesus is in charge of every aspect of his life.*

SNEAK PREVIEW

Habakkuk
What does God's face look like when bad things happen?

BEHIND the SCENES
of Galatians

STARRING ROLES

Paul, an apostle famous for his ministry among non-Jews; founding minister of churches throughout Galatia (1:1)

Peter, leader of the 12 original disciples, who draws a sharp rebuke from Paul for avoiding non-Jewish Christians (1:18)

PLOT

While traveling throughout Galatia, in western Turkey, Paul had told the Jews and non-Jews living there that they needed only faith in Jesus to become Christians. Many had accepted his teachings, which were backed up by miracles. Now, several years later, Paul gets word that other Christian teachers have arrived in the area and are contradicting him. This is a controversial issue previously argued and supposedly settled in Paul's favor at a Jerusalem summit meeting of Christian leaders in about A.D. 49 (Acts 15).

Paul writes in a skilled way, but he's really harsh. Paul argues that the Jewish law was intended to serve only until the Messiah arrived (3:19). With the sacrificial death of Jesus, God established a new covenant that liberated humanity from the law. Instead of needing to follow rules, we're to be guided by God's spirit.

STAGE DIRECTIONS

| Paul starts churches in Galatia on first missionary trip A.D. 46 | Jerusalem council grants Gentiles waiver from Jewish laws A.D. 49 | Paul visits northern Galatia during second missionary trip A.D. 50 | | Paul's third missionary trip ends A.D. 57 | Paul imprisoned at Rome A.D. 60 |

BIBLE EVENTS

| A.D. 45 | A.D. 50 | A.D. 55 | A.D. 60 |

WORLD EVENTS

Dates are approximate

| | Jews expelled from Rome over controversy about "Chrestus" (probably "Christ") A.D. 49 | Romans learn about soap, from Gauls (France) A.D. 50 | | Buddhism of India introduced to China A.D. 58 | |

AUTHOR AND DATE

The letter is "from the apostle Paul" (1:1) to all the churches in Galatia, a Roman province in western Turkey.

No one's sure exactly when Paul wrote this book. The letter doesn't give any clues about the date, where Paul was when he wrote it, or which churches in Galatia he had in mind. Because the theology in the letter resembles Paul's early letter of 1 Thessalonians more closely than his later letter of Romans, Bible scholars speculate that Paul wrote Galatians sometime around A.D. 55 or a few years earlier.

> Whirling dervishes, Muslim monks who dance into a spinning trance while trying to seek God, got their start in the 1200s in a 4,000-year-old city near Lystra, Galatia, where Paul started a church.

> The Roman province of Galatia got its name from the Gauls of western Europe who began settling there about 200 years before Christ.

ON LOCATION

Paul writes to unnamed churches he started in Galatia, a strip of territory roughly 300 miles long and 100 miles wide, located in western Turkey. It's unknown if Paul intended the letter to be for churches he founded in southern Galatia on his first missionary trip (churches named in Scripture), or for churches he started in northern Galatia on his second trip (churches not named in Scripture). Perhaps he had both in mind.

WHAT TO LOOK FOR

- **Anger.** "You stupid Galatians!" (3:1) That's Paul talking. He's more upset in this letter than in any other letter he writes. He's so angry that he skips the note of appreciation and praise that usually begins each letter. Paul jumps on the Galatians' case. He's really really ticked. It's not that Paul had a frail type of ego and was upset that people didn't believe that God followed what he believed. See, if the Galatians believe this new fangled (and *VERY* wrong) message, Jesus would have died for nothing.
- **Makings of the first major split in the church.** The first split in the Christian church came over the very issue that erupted in Galatia. The question was this: Do people have to become Jews before they can become Christians? Paul said no. Many other Jewish Christians said yes, everyone must obey the laws of Moses. If the Jewish Christians had won the debate, Christianity might not have become a major world religion. It could have become just another branch or denomination in Judaism.
- **Paul defending his apostle status.** Paul reminds the Galatians of how God chose him to preach especially to the Gentiles, and of how the original disciples of Jesus accepted him as a minister of equal authority.
- **Paul arguing with Peter.** Paul feels free to argue with Peter when he makes a big mistake. This happens when Peter visits the church that Paul and Barnabas are pastoring in Antioch. Peter, feeling pressured by Jewish Christians who still observe the laws of Moses, stops eating and socializing with Gentile members of the church. According to Jewish law, Gentiles are considered ritually unclean. Jews who come into contact with them have to perform cleansing rituals before they can worship God at the temple. Peter's behavior amounts to religious segregation within the church. Other Jews follow Peter's lead, so Paul confronts Peter.
- **Principles of living, instead of rigid laws.** Although Christians are free of Old Testament rules, Paul says believers must live godly lives nonetheless.

EXTREME SCENES
from Galatians

The throw down (2:11-21)

Jewish-Christian missionaries arrive in Galatia and contradict Paul's teaching that people are saved only by faith in Jesus. Faith in Christ is not enough, they argue. Anyone who wants to be a Christian must also obey the laws of Moses. Paul explains that years ago he had to publicly correct Peter for this same mistaken belief. At first Peter ate with the non-Jewish members and treated them as spiritual brothers and sisters. But later, when other church leaders from Jerusalem arrived, Peter suddenly became afraid of associating with non-Jewish Christians. Apparently these visiting dignitaries believed like other Jews that Gentiles were ritually unclean. Peter would later side with Paul on this matter in a Jerusalem summit meeting of Christian leaders (Acts 15). Even though the summit agrees with Peter and Paul, many Jewish-Christians travel throughout the land and teach this heresy.

DIRECTOR'S NOTES

Many people in New Testament times used secretaries to write letters for them. Some Bible experts believe that Paul needed a secretary because he had very poor eyesight. Apparently, Paul had dictated his letter to a secretary, but then wrote the last paragraph in his own handwriting, so that the churches in Galatia would know it really came from him. Galatians 6:11

Dude, We're all equals (3:26-4:7)

Christians started feeling better than each other. Some believed one way, and felt their beliefs made them superior. Others believed another way and were convinced that they were smarter...even more spiritual. Paul wants nothing to do with a status-conscious Christianity that puts some people ahead of others. Paul's message? We're all equal because of our faith in Christ. Paul also warns that we're all accountable to God. Even though we're free, we're not free to sin. Paul warns that they'll harvest what they plant. If they plant selfishness, they'll harvest destruction. But, if you follow God, you'll have eternal life.

REVIEWS

Have you ever seen one of those paid announcements that end with a deep voice saying, "Paid for by the supporters of Fred Dingleberry"? They usually happen a lot around elections. Basically, they happen because almost anybody can pay for some airtime and speak their mind.

Galatians isn't a paid announcement. Paul wrote it for free. But it sure is his opportunity to have his say.

What did Paul have to rant and rave about? It went like this...

After Jesus' death and resurrection there was a whole new understanding about faith. Instead of righteousness coming through obeying a set of laws and sacrifice, righteousness came through faith in Jesus' sacrifice. Paul spent a lot of his energy communicating that concept. It was a big huge change to the Jewish mindset.

The reason Paul wrote Galatians is because they had accepted this new mindset, but then slipped backwards. Some heretics called Judaizers had stepped in and said, "If you want to be a Christian you have to live by all the Jewish customs and laws."

Paul was totally offended. Only that would cause him to ask a question like, "How could you be so stupid?" (3:3). (Sounds like my dad after I tried to cook eggs, still in the shell, in the microwave.)

He let them have it. He told them not to get sucked into the heresy that anything but faith in Christ could produce righteousness.

Whether Paul let his human emotion get the better of him, only Jesus (who flipped tables of businessmen at the temple and ran them off with a *whip*) can judge (Matthew 21:12). But perhaps, like Jesus, Paul knew when something was a big enough deal to get fired up over.

If only Fred Dingleberry had such passion, huh?

Lisa N. Upp

> For a report of the Jerusalem summit meeting that debated the same issue the Galatians confronted, read Acts 15.

> To better understand Paul's teaching about salvation through faith, read Romans 3:21–4:25.

Ephesians

SCHEDULE OF SCENES

Jesus Is Born	Jesus Crucified Pentecost	Paul's Missionary Journeys Begin	Ephesians Written	Temple Destroyed	Death of John
7/6 B.C.	A.D. 30	A.D. 46	A.D. 60	A.D. 70	A.D. 100

QUOTABLES

Don't go to bed angry (4:26).

Husbands, love your wives (5:25, KJV).

Our struggle is not against flesh and blood, but against the rulers, against the authorities, against the powers of this dark world and against the spiritual forces of evil in the heavenly realms (6:12, NIV). Paul explains there are evil spiritual forces that are every bit as real as the physical world. These forces oppose both God and God's people.

Put on the whole armor of God, that you may be able to stand against the wiles of the devil (6:11, NKJV). To defend against evil spiritual forces, Paul urges Christians to protect themselves with godly attributes such as truth, justice, and faith.

Faith people

Paul had a vision for the church. He intended for it to have a lot of meetings. His hopes were that our churches would be bogged down with heavy agendas. He homed that someday we'd give 100 percent of our time to counting the number of warm bodies in the church.

Not really. Actually, Paul DOES lay out the job of the church in this book, and it has nothing to do with agendas or number crunching. The church's job is to be the people of faith—God's people. So, how do we measure our success? The measuring is God's job. But the goals before us, Paul says, are unity among believers, following the Spirit within us, maturing in our faith, defeating spiritual forces allied against us, and (maybe the hardest job of all) getting along with the people we live with every day. Can the church ever hope to accomplish all of this? Oh yes! But only with God's help.

SNEAK PREVIEW

Joshua
Holy wars. Miracle battles. Extreme risks.

BEHIND the SCENES
of Ephesians

STARRING ROLE

Paul, a traveling minister who starts churches throughout the Roman Empire, and who is most successful in non-Jewish cultures (1:1)

PLOT

Ephesians reads like a beautiful, poetic sermon written for just about any congregation. It's not a story with a plot, or a letter with a problem-solving agenda. It's a compelling meditation with a deep and lasting message: God has a plan to return unity and peace to his creation, and the church will play a leading role in that plan.

STAGE DIRECTIONS

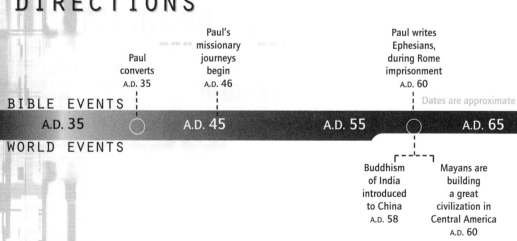

Paul converts
A.D. 35

Paul's missionary journeys begin
A.D. 46

Paul writes Ephesians, during Rome imprisonment
A.D. 60

BIBLE EVENTS

Dates are approximate

A.D. 35   A.D. 45   A.D. 55   A.D. 65

WORLD EVENTS

Buddhism of India introduced to China
A.D. 58

Mayans are building a great civilization in Central America
A.D. 60

AUTHOR AND DATE

The letter claims Paul as its writer (1:1), and speaks in the voice of a prisoner "in jail" (6:20). For about 1,700 years, no one questioned that Paul wrote Ephesians. But in recent centuries, scholars, comparing this letter to others that Paul wrote, have noticed some substantial differences.

Paul may have written this letter during his two-year imprisonment at Rome, which began about A.D. 60. If someone else wrote it in Paul's name, applying his theology to later circumstances in the church, the writing may have occurred in the closing decades of the first century.

INSIDE SCOOP

Unlike the Old Testament, the New Testament has no books that are entire poems. Coming closest is Ephesians, which seems to draw heavily from early church hymns and prayers.

ON LOCATION

Paul may have intended Ephesians as a general letter, for circulation among as many churches as possible. Even though the letter claims to be written "to God's people who live in Ephesus" (1:1), it could have been intended for other churches surrounding Ephesus. The letter doesn't contain any of Paul's characteristic personal greetings to individuals, or references to circumstances in this major port city in western Turkey.

WHAT TO LOOK FOR

- **No problems.** Other letters by Paul contain little scoldings to believers. This one doesn't. Instead, Paul stretches the minds of his readers, helping Christians improve their understanding of what God is doing in the world and how he is doing it.
- **The flow of the letter.** Paul begins by painting a picture of God's plan for all of creation. Next, Paul explains how Christ has made all believers key players in this plan. Then, Paul explains the role that believers play in the church. Finally, Paul tells Christians how to tap into God's unlimited power to defeat evil spiritual forces.
- **Practical advice for everyday living.** The last half of the book lists practical ways for the church to fulfill its role in God's plan. Here are the highlights:
    - Live in unity (4:2-3).
    - Grow spiritually mature and serve others through the church (4:11-13).
    - Seek spiritual renewal (4:23-24).
    - Put others first (5:21).
    - Resist evil spiritual forces (6:12-13).

EXTREME SCENES
from Galatians

⇒ Hey…Get along! (2:11-3:13)

God's intention for us humans is that we live in peace and harmony with Him, and with each other. However, Adam's sin ruined all of that. So, we need God's mercy and forgiveness to get along. By the time Paul writes this letter, Jews are seriously rejecting the Christian gospel, and the church is becoming more and more Gentile. Many non-Jews are developing an us-them attitude, with "them" being the Jews. They begin to seriously dislike the Jews. Paul reminds them that the church is made up of forgiven people…not "Jew"…Not "Gentile". Paul urges them to be unified. It's what God wants. It's the best thing for the church.

⇒ Bag the nasties! (4:17-5:20)

Ephesus believers begin to get nasty with each other. Love for each other goes away. Bitterness rules their hearts. Paul's sick of it. In order for them to be like God, they've got to please him. Their hearts must resemble his. Their actions must mirror his. This doesn't mean Christians never make mistakes and always do the right thing. But it does mean they have accepted their role as human beings devoted to God, their holy father. And it means they live in such a way that others can see the resemblance. No matter what…even though we're sinful. We've got to live like Christ. That means the bitterness and hatred that easily seeps into our hearts has got to go!

⇒ Get comfortable being last (5:21-6:9)

Put others first. Paul's adamant about this. Christians who listen to the Spirit of God will learn to do this in all their relationships. That means, you've gotta put the annoying kid in science class ahead of you. So, does it sound like Paul's got his eye on creating a "perfect society"? Maybe. Paul is clear: This is God working His plan through the church. It may sound unrealistic, but Paul assures his readers that God will make all of this happen.

⇒ Fighting shadows (6:10-18)

We live in a physical world made up of elements we can see and touch and smell and taste. But Paul says there's an overlapping spiritual world that we can't see. And, it's very, very real. In this spiritual world there are two forces at work. There are the forces of God and the forces of Satan. Both can influence us. Paul says the biggest battles we face in this life are not confrontations with other human beings. The biggest battles are those fought in the spiritual world. What do we need to fight these battles? We need spiritual armor — the kind only God can give.

REVIEWS

Have you heard of "Change Your Life" TV? It's part of the current trend to make shows that helps us be better people. If Ephesians had been a TV show, it would have been "Change Your Life" TV.

The expert teaching would have been done by Paul the apostle. I can see the close-up of Paul's face as he smiles at the audience...through prison bars.

That's right. Paul wrote Ephesians, a book of encouragement for the church in Ephesus, while he was sitting in prison. He had been brought up on the charge of "preaching the gospel." That's like being charged for the "crime" of making the world a better place. Sounds like there was no chance of "time off for good behavior." So (here's the cool part) they put him in jail so that he couldn't preach, but gave him parchment and ink to write a few letters home and what did he do? He wrote several books of the Bible. This guy was just *unstoppable*. I've heard about a lot of people finding God while they were in jail, but Paul found a way to free others from their spiritual prisons while *he* was the one in jail.

So what *does* someone write about from prison? Paul wrote about God's unending love. Almost half of his letter to the Ephesians is about how much God loves them. The last half of the letter is about people loving each other: family members or church members or work associates. In the middle of all those chains and bars Paul makes the connection between God's love in us pouring out to the world around. God's love was the part of Paul that was free to go outside the prison walls into the world. God's love *is* freedom, freedom that *no one* can take away from you.

There's a lot of good advice in Paul's letter to the Ephesians. Advice about being patient and loving and forgiving and honest. It's amazing that a prisoner could write a letter to a church in the first century that still changes lives today.

J.L. Houserock

> Colossians, in both writing style and teachings, is strikingly similar to Ephesians.

Philippians

SCHEDULE OF SCENES

Jesus Is Born	Jesus Crucified Pentecost	Paul's Missionary Journeys Begin	Philippians Written	Temple Destroyed	Death of John
7/6 B.C.	A.D. 30	A.D. 46	A.D. 60	A.D. 70	A.D. 100

A letter from lock up

Imagine this. You're locked up in prison. The conditions are rotten. The food stinks. It's dark. Rats crawl over you at night, keeping you awake. You get a chance to write your friends a letter. What might you say? Guess what Paul writes about. He writes about how happy he is.

Nope. Paul isn't nuts. He says he's happy that he has such caring friends. He's even happy that he's suffering for Christ because his suffering is inspiring other Christians to preach more boldly. And he says if need be, he will be happy to die because he will go to be with Christ, which is a much better place than where he is now.

Paul wants the Philippians to experience this same peaceful joy when they reflect on their lives. So, he advises them to discover what it means to be saved. So, what does it mean...according to Paul? It means...be happy. No matter what. No matter where you are. Locked up in prison? Living a terrible life? On the brink of death? Be happy. Shine as a light in a darkened world. Never mind the rats. Smile.

QUOTABLES

At the name of Jesus everyone will bow (2:10).

My God shall supply all your needs according to His riches in glory by Christ Jesus (4:19, NKJV).

For to me to live is Christ, and to die is gain (1:21, KJV). Paul plans to live for Jesus, then enjoy an afterlife of eternity in heaven.

SNEAK PREVIEW

> **2 Timothy**
> How do you say a last good-bye to the person you'll miss the most?

BEHIND the SCENES
of Philippians

STARRING ROLES

Paul, apostle, traveling preacher, frequent prisoner, and founder of the church at Philippi (1:1)

Epaphroditus, a member of the Philippian church who brings gifts from the congregation to jailed Paul (2:25)

PLOT

While Paul is in jail, probably during the early A.D. 60s, a messenger arrives from the church at Philippi, in northern Greece. The messenger carries gifts from a church he helped plant in Philippi almost ten years earlier. The messenger (whose name is Epaphroditus) becomes deathly ill, but manages to recover. Paul sends him home, with a joyful letter of thanks, which we now know as Philippians. In this letter, the apostle expresses joy for the support that the Philippians have given him, and for the recent gifts, as well as for the recovery of Epaphroditus. But Paul also warns the believers that one day they may have to suffer as he is suffering now.

STAGE DIRECTIONS

Paul starts church in Philippi, during second missionary trip
A.D. 50

Paul writes Philippians, during Rome imprisonment
A.D. 60

BIBLE EVENTS

Dates are approximate

A.D. 50   A.D. 55   A.D. 60   A.D. 65

WORLD EVENTS

China, Rome conduct trade via 4,000-mile-long Silk Road
A.D. 50

Rome burns; Christians blamed, persecuted
A.D. 64

AUTHOR AND DATE

Paul, writing from jail in an unnamed city, writes this letter to the Philippians to express thanks for gifts they sent him.

If Paul wrote from Rome, as many scholars believe, then Philippians is a product of his two years of house arrest, beginning about A.D. 60. This would have been during the final years of his ministry, which began with his conversion about 25 years earlier.

ON LOCATION

INSIDE SCOOP

➤ Philippi was named after the father of Alexander the Great, King Philip.

➤ Paul went to Philippi and the surrounding province of Macedonia only after seeing a vision of a man begging him, "Come over to Macedonia and help us!" (Acts 16:9).

Paul writes from prison to a church in Philippi, a large city on one of the main roads connecting Rome with territories to the east. He visited it twice on his third missionary journey. Where Paul is during the writing remains a mystery. He speaks of "Roman guards" (1:13) and employees "in the service of the Emperor" (4:22). So, he could be writing from Rome. But Roman guards and imperial employees are scattered throughout the Roman world. So Paul could be writing from one of many other jails in which he spent time.

WHAT TO LOOK FOR

- **No quotes from the Old Testament.** Paul is a converted Pharisee, a scholar in the Jewish scripture. He would have known the Old Testament very well. It's unusual for him to write about religious matters without quoting the Old Testament. This may be because nearly all the believers in Philippi are non-Jews, unfamiliar with sacred Jewish Scripture.
- **Why Paul writes the letter.** Paul makes several key points in Philippians. Here are a few:
  - Paul thanks the Philippians for their ongoing support, and for their recent gifts (1:3-11; 4:10-20).
  - He warns them that they may have to suffer, as Christ did and as Paul is doing now. But he urges them to stand firm in their faith (1:12-29).
  - He urges them to remain united, and to imitate the humility of Jesus, who "gave up everything and became a slave" (2:7, 9).
  - Paul also warns the Philippians to watch out for Jews who profess Jesus as Lord, but who insist that all Christians must observe the Jewish laws recorded in the Old Testament (3:2).
- **Joy.** For someone writing from prison and facing the threat of death, Paul speaks a lot about happiness. He uses the word "joy" in some form or another sixteen times in this short letter.
- **A moving song about Jesus.** Paul quotes part of what many Bible experts believe is an early song about Jesus (2:6-11). Paul uses the song as an illustration, to urge the Philippians to imitate Christ's humility and his willingness to suffer for others.

EXTREME SCENES
from Philippians

DIRECTOR'S NOTES

Talk about a slow judicial system! Paul lived under house arrest in Rome for two years while he waited for Caesar to hear his case. Since electronic monitoring devices weren't available in Paul's day, he had soldiers guarding him day and night. The guards worked four-hour shifts, with at least one person handcuffed to Paul at all times. Even though he was officially a prisoner, Paul was allowed to receive visitors. That gave him an opportunity to share the message of Christ not only with the people who came to see him, but with the soldiers as well. Philippians 1:7

⋟ Paul shares the love (1:1-29)

The church at Philippi hears that Paul is in prison. They send a courier with gifts. In response, Paul writes a joyous letter of appreciation. Paul spends a lot of time in this letter telling the church how much he loves them. But, after all the lovey dovey stuff, he encourages them. Paul encourages the people not to feel bad about his imprisonment. He writes that his time in prison will spread the gospel even more. And, Paul warns that one day the Philippians may also have to suffer for Christ. If they do, he says, they should be brave and remember that the love of Christ will comfort them.

⋟ You've got it coming to you (2:1-18)

Paul promises a fat reward. Not a huge mound of cash or anything. To illustrate exactly what Paul is trying to say, he quotes a poem about Jesus. He asks them to continue being his pride and joy by getting along with each other and by following his example as he suffers.

REVIEWS

ENCORE

⟩ To read about how Paul started the church of Philippi, turn to Acts 16:11-40.

⟩ Second Timothy is one of Paul's final letters. It includes a moving passage about his approaching death (4:6-8).

If ever there was a book of the Bible that belonged on the Inspirational network it would have been Philippians.

In one sense Philippians was really a thank-you note. Have you had to write any of those yet? Wait until graduation. Here's a little example to give you the idea.

> Dear Aunt Rudilinda,
> Thanks for the lovely book bag. The pink pigs will match the lunch box you sent for Christmas. Now I don't have to worry about being stylish at college next year.
> Yours truly,

Paul was thanking the Philippians for something way cooler than a pink pig book bag, though. They had supported his ministry and offered him a great deal of love and friendship.

So what's inspiring about a thank-you note? Well, first of all, it was written from jail. Now, while you surely would be thankful for a book bag if you were free to use it to embarrass yourself at community college, do you think you'd be as thankful if it might never see the free light of day? Paul was thankful . . . no matter what.

In fact, even though Paul was in prison, what his letter to the Philippians is really about is joy. The art of living above your circumstances. The art of being content no matter what comes. Paul should have been an expert at that. He got plenty of practice at dealing with bad situations.

Inspiration is what the whole Bible is about, but Philippians is bulging with it. You come away from it unsure of what it was you were complaining about anyway. It certainly wasn't the book bag. Now go call your aunt and tell her you love her.

Trudy Light

Colossians

SCHEDULE OF SCENES

Jesus Is Born	Jesus Crucified Pentecost	Paul's Missionary Journeys Begin	Colossians Written	Temple Destroyed	Death of John
7/6 B.C.	A.D. 30	A.D. 46	A.D. 60	A.D. 70	A.D. 100

Fake religions aren't cool

Paul's facing a real challenge. He's discovering a new religion popping up that approaches truth like many of us hit the buffet. It takes a little truth from Christianity, and from other religions too. This religion looks kind of familiar to the people in the area. It teaches that angels exist, it honors religious holidays, and, it urges people to seek God. All this looks so familiar, in fact, that it makes the Christians of Colossae begin to wonder if this new teaching is simply a more insightful way of interpreting old truths.

Paul insists that this isn't a good religion. It's actually just another set of human teachings. For the people who are getting confused about this new religion, Paul has this advice: "Follow Jesus". Simple . . . but often so very difficult to do. This letter was written to warn followers of Christ to stay clear of this deceptive religion.

QUOTABLES

Whatsoever ye do in word or deed, do all in the name of the Lord Jesus (3:17, KJV).

Christ is all, and in all (3:11, KJV). Paul's declaration that Jesus is what matters most in life, and that his Spirit lives in everyone who invites him in.

SNEAK PREVIEW

Isaiah
Sure judgment. One solitary hope for deliverance.

BEHIND the SCENES
of Colossians

STARRING ROLES

Paul, traveling minister who starts churches throughout the Roman Empire (1:1)

Epaphras, founding minister of the church in Colossae, and an associate of Paul (1:7)

PLOT

Paul's sitting in prison, waiting for his trial, when he gets word that Christians in Colossae are confronting a new teaching that could destroy the church. The threatening movement seems to blend elements of many religions into a convincing belief system.

"Don't let anyone fool you," Paul warns. And, he encourages them to stay away from these humanly created religions. Paul reminds the Colossians that they accepted Jesus Christ, and they should now follow him.

STAGE DIRECTIONS

	Paul converts A.D. 35	Paul's missionary journeys begin A.D. 46	Paul writes Colossians, during Rome imprisonment A.D. 60	

BIBLE EVENTS

Dates are approximate

A.D. 35	A.D. 45	A.D. 55	A.D. 65

WORLD EVENTS

Buddhism of India introduced to China A.D. 58

Mayans build a great civilization in Central America A.D. 60

AUTHOR AND DATE

It's very clear who wrote this letter...Paul!
Because of similarities between this
letter and the letter written to the Ephesians, both were probably
written about the same time. Paul probably wrote the letter during
his two-year imprisonment at Rome, beginning about A.D. 60.

ON LOCATION

Paul writes from jail (4:3), perhaps in Rome, to a church he has never visited. Colossae is 100 miles west of Ephesus, where Paul once lived for two
years. The church was apparently started by a student minister Paul sent:
Epaphras (1:7).

WHAT TO LOOK FOR

- **The problem.** Paul hears that a religious teaching that combines Jewish
  beliefs and other religions is making inroads into the church at Colossae.
  It's unclear what the heresy is. Here's what we DO know about it based on
  what Paul writes to the church:
  - Follow rules about food, religious holidays (2:16–17), and circumcision (3:11). These teachings
    may have come from Judaism.
  - Deprive your body, to show you have control over it (2:21–23). This resembles the ascetic prac-
    tices of isolationist religious groups such as the Jewish Essenes, who produced the Dead Sea
    Scrolls, and of Christian monks in later centuries.
  - Worship angels (2:18). This emphasis on having secret knowledge about God and salvation may
    represent the seed of a heresy that develops into a major movement in the second century:
    Gnosticism.
- **The supreme power of Jesus.** Paul attacks this false religion by reminding the Colossians that they
  don't need these lies. Christ is the supreme power on which they can depend.
- **A song about Jesus.** To solidify his statements, Paul quotes a well-known song about Jesus. These
  lyrics, with Paul's additional comments, produce the New Testament's strongest statement about the
  authority of Jesus.
- **Instructions for daily living.** How should we live? Simple. Paul says we should adopt attitudes and a
  lifestyle that reflects a close relationship with Jesus.

EXTREME SCENES
from Colossians

DIRECTOR'S NOTES

In the days of the Roman Empire, any time a Roman guard returned home after a successful military campaign, he was honored with a special ceremony called a triumph. A parade was thrown in his honor, with the general leading the way in his chariot and prisoners of war following along behind it. Those prisoners were then divided into two groups: those who would be executed and those who would become slaves of the Roman Empire. Colossians 2:15

A large segment of the Roman population—anywhere from one-fourth to one-half—was made up of slaves. Slaves in New Testament times had very few rights. Some were treated worse than animals. The only way a slave could become a free person was to buy his freedom. Colossians 3:22

⇒ Jesus is better (1:15-20)

Paul writes the believers in Colossae to refute a nasty false new teaching that's crept into the church. He's concerned that this new teaching will cause believers to stray from the truth. They don't need to pray to angels… they need to pray to God. Paul's on the war path to convince them about this. So long as you have God's free gift of salvation, it's all good.

⇒ Our sins got nailed. Period. (2:6-23)

This senseless new teaching gives people a long to-do list in order to please God. Basically, God's forgiveness comes when they've fulfilled all of their requirements. How wrong is this? It's very wrong. God took away our sins when he "nailed them to the cross" (2:14). We become God's people not by obeying rules, praying to angels, or discovering spiritual secrets in visions. We become His people by trusting Him.

Other than trusting Christ, Christians have no required to-do list for salvation.

⇒ Live it! (3:1-25)

Paul makes his argument short and clear. Then, he tightens the screws a bit. He pushes the Colossians a littler further. It's not enough for them to not have a to-do list. They've got to reflect Christ. And we need to be more kind, patient, and forgiving, all of which are motivated by love. When we're in doubt about what to say or do, Paul offers this suggestion: Do what Jesus would do.

REVIEWS

Colossians is a back-to-the-basics kind of book. It's like those marriage enrichment shows on TV where a guru talks about the foundational thing to make a marriage work—except the writer was talking about faith.

So did Paul write Colossians or not? Some say yes and some say no.

Well, it sure says a lot of the same kinds of stuff that Paul usually taught. Like all believers are equal: "It doesn't matter if you are a Greek or a Jew, or if you are circumcised or not. You may even be a barbarian or a Scythian [people from southern Russia, known for their backwards ways], and you may be a slave or a free person" (3:11). So why is anybody even questioning it? Basically because the wording and the style and some of the other ideas in Colossians don't seem like some of Paul's other work. It's like if your grandma usually writes and says, "Dearest Robert, I hope you are faring well." Then one day she writes, "Yo Bobby, what's the 411, dog?" You might wonder if Grandma really wrote it. Paul usually did things a certain way, like writing a really well thought out argument when he disagreed with someone. Colossians though, is more like poetry than philosophy. It's like a party on paper.

Another thing is some of the things mentioned in Colossians seem like they happened after Paul died. Colossians addresses a heresy (a way of believing that seemed true on the surface, but underneath was just a lie) that sounds a lot like a well-known heresy called Gnosticism. Problem is that Gnosticism doesn't show up on paper until the 2nd century and Paul died during the *first* century. Colossians also talks about Christ being there during Creation (1:16) which was something very few people even *got,* much less wrote about, until years after Paul's death.

You can find Bible experts on both sides of the argument. Some of them say, Paul couldn't have written it, but it's still important truth. Others are like, Hey! Who says Paul couldn't have changed and grown with the times? People start using new words all the time. As for the Gnosticism thing, if it was named in the second century, it probably started in the first one, right? Think about this — maybe the heresy Paul described in Colossians was where Gnosticism came from.

That's what the experts have to say. Read it for yourself.

"Both Sides" Josephus

ENCORE

The letter of Colossians resembles Ephesians in both tone and teachings. Both, for example, have advice for everyday living, and both emphasize the church, which the writer symbolically calls the body of Christ.

1 Thessalonians

SCHEDULE OF SCENES

Jesus Is Born	Jesus Crucified Pentecost	Paul's Missionary Journeys Begin	1 Thessalonians Written	Temple Destroyed	Death of John
7/6 B.C.	A.D. 30	A.D. 46	A.D. 51	A.D. 70	A.D. 100

So...where's Jesus?

Everyone was stoked when Jesus walked the earth. His miracles, His teachings and His service floored them. It wasn't what they were expecting. Now that He's gone, they can't wait to experience all of that again. They want Him to return so they can have a king to look up to. They really can't wait. It's all they think about.

Can you blame them? Without their Messiah they feel left alone on the earth to suffer. They feel like outcasts...like religious criminals. Left alone, this unorganized core of converts united only by their experience of salvation, feeling like kids lost at the county fair. And, even though they are united in their faith, they feel totally alone. They had begun cultivating a lifestyle of holiness while living in a sprawling port city that teems with immorality, greed, and deception. And, their worship of Jesus as God's Son and as ruler of the heavenly kingdom pits them against the Jews who insist that God has no son, and the Romans in the city who worship the emperor.

For Thessalonians, and all Christians who feel out of sync in their world, Paul encourages them not to focus their energy on the return of Jesus. Instead, we are to work hard, live honorable lives, and earn the respect of others. It's OK to be concerned about Jesus' return. It's understandable that they're concerned about persecution. But, Paul's message causes them to refocus their energy away from that and towards a more hopeful message.

QUOTABLES

The Lord will come like a thief in the night (5:2, NIV). When asked about the timing of Christ's return, Paul replies with this phrase, meaning that no one can predict the Second Coming.

SNEAK PREVIEW

> **2 Samuel**
> A man after God's own heart ... his glories and his failures.

BEHIND the SCENES
of 1 Thessalonians

STARRING ROLES

Paul, leading minister to the Gentile world, and founder of the congregation at Thessalonica and other major cities throughout the Roman Empire (1:1)

Timothy, Paul's associate who visits Thessalonica then reports back to Paul about the progress of the new converts and the questions they have (1:1)

PLOT

Paul has an amazing vision. About 1,000 miles into his second missionary trip, he sees a man pleading with him to leave Turkey and come to Macedonia. Paul goes and takes the gospel to Europe. He arrives in Philippi, but stays only a short time before he is charged with disturbing the peace and chased out of town. He proceeds on to Thessalonica, capital and largest city of Macedonia. 200,000 people live in this busy port town on the main east-west trade route to Asia.

Paul preaches in the synagogue for about three weeks before the Jews realize that what he's teaching means the end of traditional Judaism. They riot, forcing Paul to escape to Athens, 200 miles south. But not before some Jews and many non-Jews convert to Christianity.

Within a month or two, while Paul is staying in Corinth, he sends Timothy, to check on the Thessalonian believers. Timothy returns with some good news, but also says that the people in the church are facing persecution, and that they have questions about the Second Coming. By this time Paul is deeply involved in starting the Corinthian ministry; he can't leave. So, he comes up with a great idea. He decides to encourage and teach the believers of Thessalonica by letter.

STAGE
DIRECTIONS

Paul's missionary journeys begin
A.D. 46

Paul starts second missionary trip
A.D. 50

Paul writes Thessalonians while in Corinth
A.D. 51

Dates are approximate

BIBLE EVENTS

A.D. 40 · A.D. 45 · A.D. 50

WORLD EVENTS

Jews expelled from Rome over controversy about "Chrestus" (probably Christ)
A.D. 49

China, Rome conduct trade via 4,000-mile-long Silk Road
A.D. 50

Isthmian Games held at Corinth
A.D. 51

AUTHOR AND DATE

The letter is written by Paul, who is accompanied by his traveling associates Timothy and Silas (1:1). Bible experts agree that this letter reads like other authenticated letters of Paul. Early Christian writers confirm that Paul was the author.

Paul wrote this letter in about A.D. 51, during his second missionary trip, while he was starting a church in Corinth.

ON LOCATION

Thessalonica is a busy trade town in northern Greece. The city profits from a port in the Thermatic Gulf of the Aegean Sea, and from its location on the Via Egnatia, an east-west Roman road that stretches across northern Greece and into Turkey. Paul writes the letter from Corinth, some 250 miles south.

WHAT TO LOOK FOR

- **The Second Coming.** The minds of the Thessalonians are filled with questions about the second coming of Christ. They want to know when He'll return. They want to know if He'll accept them. They are concerned about believers who die before Jesus returns. Paul tells them that no one knows when Jesus will return, but encourages them to trust God while they wait. Paul covers several topics in this short letter, but the Second Coming is the main idea. Every chapter ends with a reference to it.
- **Guidelines for holy living.** Thessalonica is full of really cruddy people. It's a thriving port town on a major trade route. So it has all the sinfulness of any large city, along with a huge emphasis on sex brought with the traveling sailors.

  Paul knows that it's hard to live in a town like this without getting swept into the current of passion and greed. He gently warns the new believers to stand firm in their faith.
- **No quotes from the Old Testament.** Paul was raised a Pharisee, a Jewish scholar. When he talks about religious matters, it's common for him to draw from his expertise and quote the Jewish Scriptures. The fact that he doesn't do this in his letter to the Thessalonians suggests that most of the believers there are non-Jews, unfamiliar with Scripture.

EXTREME SCENE
from 1 Thessalonians

⇒ C'mon...Hurry up! (4:13-5:11)

During Paul's second missionary journey, which takes him into what is now Greece, the apostle spends only a few weeks in Thessalonica. But this is long enough to convince many people that the Messiah has come, been executed, and raised from the dead. It's also long enough to instill in the new converts an urgent sense of expectation; they believe Jesus will return at any moment. So, what do they do? They quit their jobs and wait. Why work if Jesus is on His way back?! When Jesus doesn't come back immediately, they have a bunch of questions.

DIRECTOR'S NOTES

The protective gear that Roman soldiers wore wasn't like the suits of armor you see in medieval castles. Roman armor did not cover the soldier's entire body. Instead, the soldier wore pieces of metal or thick leather to protect his most vital organs. Roman helmets came in all shapes. Some covered the entire head, with a screen covering the face that allowed the warrior to breathe and see clearly. 1 Thessalonians 5:8

Paul assures them that no one knows when Jesus will return. Jesus' return will be like a thief coming in the middle of the night. Then, Paul outlines the events surrounding Jesus' return. There'll be a loud shout. An angel will blast its trumpet. Jesus will descend. Then, those who had faith before they died will rise first. Then every faithful person will go next to meet Jesus in the sky. After that, we'll live forever with God. After reading all that...wouldn't you be ready for Jesus?!

In the meantime, Paul says, believers should not be idle, but should work hard, live godly lives, and patiently endure the religious persecution they'll encounter.

REVIEWS

ENCORE

To learn how the church at Thessalonica began, read Acts 17:1-10.

For Paul's follow-up letter, read 2 Thessalonians.

For Paul's most extensive statement about the return of Jesus, read 1 Corinthians 15.

Sometimes to really get how a book in the Bible goes with history you've got to work it like a jigsaw puzzle. Sometimes you have to put together world history (arghhh!) with Bible history and see what fits where. Every book of the Bible has been through more testing than a senior during finals week. For centuries, experts and bookworms from around the world have gone over every little detail to make sure all the pieces are there without any extras. They even compare who wrote what parts and when with well-known facts about the authors and the times. That way it's nothing but 100 percent pure Bible with no additives or preservatives.

Take 1st Thessalonians for example. Paul was supposed to have written both his letters to the Thessalonians from Corinth around A.D. 51—from jail (The apostles were the rebels of their times. I always picture them wearing leather jackets and riding with another gang called "Heavens Angels.") So, the Bible says he was busted and went to court in Achaia (a state in Greece) where the governor, a guy named Gallio (Acts 18), tried his case. Supposedly, Gallio threw the case out of court (YEA!).

So the first question a scholar (a combination of expert and bookworm) would ask is "Was there a real Gallio? Was he in Corinth at that time?" That's just what scholars do— ask picky questions (Hmmm...I wonder if my mom is a scholar?). Also, scholars *always* (and I do mean *ALWAYS*) want two sources for every fact. So, they read something in the Bible and then they look for something else to back it up (They probably even want footnotes.).

With Gallio, the scholars hit pay dirt. An inscription found at Delphi, near where the action went down, says Gallio was governor of Achaia from about A.D. 51-53. Gallio was also the brother of Seneca, a famous philosopher who gave lessons to Nero (a crazy guy who became emperor of the

REVIEWS

Romans). This is what Seneca had to say about his bro, the Gov: "No other human being is so charming to just one person as he is to all people." Sounds like it all fits. Gallio was so cool he even got along with his own brother. Between that and setting Paul free, he'd have gotten my vote for reelection.

Once you know who a letter was written by you gotta' know why it was written and what it says. Paul wrote to the Thessalonians about Jesus coming back. The Thessalonians was so fired up about it that some quit their jobs just so they'd be ready (4:11-12; 2 Thessalonians 3:6-15).

Know what? Jesus still hasn't returned. Paul finally told the Thessalonians to get back to work because *no one* could really know when Jesus would come back.

Paul's letters to the Thessalonians give us a lot of good information about Jesus' return, just not when. So don't go quitting your day job!

Theophilus

2 Thessalonians

SCHEDULE OF SCENES

Jesus Is Born	Jesus Crucified Pentecost	Paul's Missionary Journeys Begin	2 Thessalonians Written	Temple Destroyed	Death of John
7/6 B.C.	A.D. 30	A.D. 46	A.D. 51	A.D. 70	A.D. 100

Job-quitting waiters

Okay, at this point the believers in Thessalonica have gone way overboard. All they think about is Jesus' return. Instead of telling others about Christ, they hang out and wait for Jesus to come back. They don't just get a little sidetracked, they live a sidetracked life. They quit their jobs. They spend time staring at the sky looking for Jesus. And, in their preoccupation with Jesus' coming back, the mission of the church is sabotaged.

Paul's a little torqued with them. His first letter was nice and encouraging. This letter is a little more blunt. His message is a little something like, "People! You've totally missed the boat on this one. Stop waiting and start working!" And, to help them understand how silly they are, Paul reminds them about everything that has to happen before Jesus returns. This helps them understand that there are things they'll notice *before* Jesus comes back, and they don't have to lie around and wait.

QUOTABLES

If you don't work, you don't eat (3:10). Paul's attitude toward people who quit work so they can wait for the Second Coming of Jesus.

Do not grow weary in doing good (3:13, NKJV).

SNEAK PREVIEW

Obadiah
Final warning: mess with God's people, you mess with God.

BEHIND the SCENES
of 1 Thessalonians

STARRING ROLE

Paul, leading minister to the Gentile world, and founder of the congregation at Thessalonica and other major cities throughout the Roman Empire (1:1)

PLOT

Sometime after Paul writes 1 Thessalonians, Paul writes this letter that arrives perhaps a few months later. The Thessalonians are unbelievably concerned with Jesus' second coming. Partly because Paul taught about it while he was in town. And, believers are facing very violent persecution. So, these people are looking for anything that will give them a quick escape from all of this waiting and persecution.

STAGE DIRECTIONS

	Paul's missionary journeys begin A.D. 46	Paul starts second missionary trip A.D. 50	Paul writes Thessalonians while in Corinth A.D. 51

Dates are approximate

BIBLE EVENTS

A.D. 40	A.D. 45	A.D. 50

WORLD EVENTS

	Jews expelled from Rome over controversy about "Chrestus" (probably "Christ") A.D. 49	China, Rome conduct trade via 4,000-mile-long Silk Road A.D. 50	Isthmian Games held at Corinth A.D. 51

AUTHOR AND DATE

The letter begins by announcing that it comes from Paul and his associates, Timothy and Silas. It ends with Paul's signature statement (3:17). Some scholars believe that one of Paul's helpers might have written this *after* Paul's death. How do they know? Well, because some of the teachings on the second coming differ from the ones in the first letter. And, the writing style of this letter is a little different than the style of the first one.

Because the two letters address the same topics, they were probably written about the same time, perhaps a few months apart. Paul likely wrote them during his two-year stay in Corinth, which began in about A.D. 50.

ON LOCATION

Thessalonica is a bustling trade town in northern Greece. The city profits from a port in the Thermatic Gulf of the Aegean Sea, and from its location on the Via Egnatia, an east-west Roman road that stretches across northern Greece and into Turkey. Paul writes the letter from Corinth, about 250 miles south.

WHAT TO LOOK FOR

- **Second Coming.** Like 1 Thessalonians, the main reason Paul writes this letter is to clear up confusion about the Second Coming.
- **"The wicked one."** Paul aims to calm believers down and get their minds focused on working in this world instead of anticipating the next. Paul reminds them of his earlier teaching about events that will precede the Lord's coming.

Paul mentions that a wicked person will come first, causing a lot of really terrible things to happen (Read 2:3–4, 9–10 for a description of this wicked person). Who is this wicked person anyway? Here are some ideas:

- He may have been an evil religious leader who is an antichrist, opposed to everything Jesus stands for.
- He could be a wicked spiritual entity.
- It could be the Roman Empire, or an emperor. If that's true, Paul would have been smart to not be so specific in this public letter.
- **Persecution.** The Christians of Thessalonica are suffering because they are Christians. It's probably the same kind of violence mixed with legal wrangling that had earlier forced Paul out of town. These harsh conditions would have made the Thessalonians beg Jesus to return quickly.
- **Christians not working.** Since Christians were sure that Jesus was coming right away, some saw no reason to plant crops, work in their shops, or repair their houses. In time, these people began to live off the generosity of others. Paul's not happy about this. And he's very clear about what they should do.

Some of the best-selling Christian books in the past century speculate on when Jesus will return, and under what conditions. Perhaps most famous is the 1976 book, *The Late Great Planet Earth*, which has sold over 11 million copies.

REVIEWS

You've probably seen movies about the anti-Christ. You've watched special effects try to show a big nasty enemy of God making life hell (literally) for everyone around him. This is definitely a case of the book being better than the movie. The monster Paul talks about in 2 Thessalonians is an evil leader who insults God (bad move!) and who shows up before Jesus comes back. This fits in with a lot of stuff in the Old Testament, where the prophet Daniel speaks of an evil leader who will "insult the only true God" (11:36) and of a "Horrible Thing" (9:27) that will desecrate God's holy temple (bad move number two).

Jesus also spoke of this "Horrible Thing" (Matthew 24:15). John, in his Revelation, talked about a coming "beast" (13:5-8) who will claim to be God and who will rule the earth for a while. In the end, John says, the beast will be destroyed. Paul describes the fight like this:"Jesus will kill him simply by breathing on him" (2:8).

By breathing on him? Remember the story of creation? God "breathed life into the man" (Genesis 2:7). Jesus will simply do the same thing in reverse. He'll breathe the life right out of "the wicked one." Pretty cool super powers, huh? It should be a pretty awesome smackdown. How mad would *you* be if someone insulted your dad, trashed your house and tried to make slaves out of most of your family? The anti-Christ hasn't got a prayer.

Paul seems to have figured out the timing better in 2 Thessalonians. He writes about the Second Coming a lot differently than in 1 Thessalonians. In fact, it's so different that some of the experts wonder if a different person wrote the second letter. In 1 Thessalonians, Paul was *urgent*. He believed Christ would come back almost any day. He reminded the church to stay alert and be ready when Jesus comes (1 Thessalonians 5:4-8). In 2 Thessalonians, Paul throws cold water on a bunch of people who quit their jobs and were just hanging out at church waiting around for Jesus. Once Paul had their attention (cold water does that) he basically told them that, while it's a good thing to look forward to Christ's return, they all needed to get a life, quit waiting around and get on with living and serving God. Good call, Paul.

Luke Sky Watcher

ENCORE

Read 1 Thessalonians, the letter Paul wrote the congregation first.

To learn how the church at Thessalonica began, read Acts 17:1–10.

For Paul's most extensive statement about the return of Jesus, read 1 Corinthians 15.

1 Timothy

SCHEDULE OF SCENES

Jesus Is Born	Jesus Crucified Pentecost	Paul's Missionary Journeys Begin	1 Timothy Written	Temple Destroyed	Death of John
7/6 B.C.	A.D. 30	A.D. 46	A.D. 63	A.D. 70	A.D. 100

Pastoring 101

You want to be a pastor? Cool! Well, what should you do? Hmm. Let's see. For starters, you'll need a four-year Bible degree. Then, you'll need at least three years in seminary. Go ahead and pack your bags. Make sure you have your laundry money...and your favorite Bible!

Actually, that's our modern way of preparing people for the ministry. Paul had other ideas. He describes his desires and training for pastors in his two letters to Timothy, and his letter to Titus. Timothy and Titus had each served several years with Paul...following him around and learning from watching him. They went with him on missionary journeys. They delivered his letters. They even served as "answer people" when churches had conflicts or questions. Even after years of experience, both men received continuing education on the basics of ministry, courtesy of Paul.

Timothy and Titus had one incredible teacher. And, hey, so do we! It's through these letters that we discover Paul's ministry fundamentals. We can take these principles and apply them to our lives, or use them to support our pastors. So, you want to be a pastor? Great! Happy reading!

QUOTABLES

The love of money is the root of all evil (6:10, KJV).

SNEAK PREVIEW

1 Corinthians
How to be a stand up person in a sit down world.

BEHIND the SCENES
of 1 Timothy

STARRING ROLES

Paul, traveling minister who covers some 10,000 miles and starts churches throughout the Roman Empire (1:1)

Timothy, one of Paul's most devoted traveling companions, whom Paul appoints to lead the church in Ephesus (1:2)

PLOT

When Paul leaves Ephesus to travel on to Macedonia in northern Greece, he assigns his associate, Timothy, to stay behind and lead the congregation. The Christians there are being confronted and confused by several religious teachings. Paul gives Timothy the job of helping these people sort out the truth and the lies. Sometime later, Paul writes Timothy this letter giving guidance on a lot of issues that surface in local congregations. These topics include conducting worship services, choosing church leaders, ministering to the poor, and even ministering to the rich.

STAGE DIRECTIONS

Paul arrives at Ephesus, staying more than 2 years
A.D. 53

Paul imprisoned at Rome
A.D. 60

Paul writes 1 Timothy, possibly after release from Rome
A.D. 63

Paul executed, possibly after second imprisonment in Rome
A.D. 67

Dates are approximate

BIBLE EVENTS

A.D. 50 ———————— A.D. 60 ———————— A.D. 70

WORLD EVENTS

Rome burns; Nero blames Christians, launches persecution
A.D. 64

Nero commits suicide
A.D. 68

AUTHOR AND DATE

The letter states that it's from Paul. When Christian leaders in the early centuries referred to 1 Timothy, they identified it as the work of Paul. In fact the reason the letter is in the New Testament is because early Christians accepted it as Paul's.

Scholars aren't sure when Paul wrote the letter. Paul might have written it after he visited Ephesus with Timothy. He also might have written it after being released from prison in A.D. 62.

ON LOCATION

Paul addresses his letter to Timothy in Ephesus, apparently writing from the northern Greece province of Macedonia. Ephesus is one of the largest cities in the Roman Empire. The town has a population of somewhere between 200,000 and 500,000. Ephesus is also a Roman seat of government, home to Rome's governor of Asia. In addition, the city is a famous center of worship to Artemis, a fertility goddess whose temple there is four times larger than the Parthenon in Athens.

WHAT TO LOOK FOR

- **Lots of advice for ministers.** The three letters of 1 and 2 Timothy along with Titus are known as the Pastoral Letters because they contain Paul's advice to these two men who are pastoring churches.
- **False teachings.** The Ephesians are dealing with at least three kinds of religious teaching, and all of them are not even close to Christianity's teachings. Here's a breakdown of the teaching they were dealing with.
  - **Senseless stories and lists of ancestors.** This might have come from the Jews, who love to talk about their family trees. They might have also been Jewish legends which were popular in that day.
  - **Forbidden marriage and food.** This points to monk-like people who felt they could be holy by controlling their bodies. But in the process, they treat important elements of God's good creation (like sex and food) like they're sinful.
  - **Stupid Talk.** Many feel that Paul is referring to Gnosticism. Gnostics believe they have received unique knowledge about their true nature, and that this knowledge guarantees them eternal life.
- **How to be a Leader.** Ministers must have a solid reputation, strong social skills, and be able to teach. Paul has harsh words for profiteering preachers who love money and think religion is supposed to make you rich. Church officers who help the minister should be honest, generous, and firm believers in the teachings about Jesus.

EXTREME SCENES
from 1 Timothy

⇟ Paul writes his bud (1:1-20)

Timothy was Paul's friend. And he's learned a lot from Paul during the many years they traveled together. But now Timothy is on his own, pastoring the church in Ephesus. Paul loves this young man like a son; he continues to train and encourage him by offering advice about how to run the church.

D I R E C T O R ' S
N O T E S

It would probably be safe to describe the women of ancient pagan cultures as "high-mainte-nance." They often spent hours creating elaborate hair arrange-ments for themselves. They wore fancy clothing and expensive jewelry to attract attention. We should point out, though, that most of the women who fit these descriptions were prostitutes. In Ephesus, the place where Timothy was working, these women could be found at the pagan temple of Diana. 1 Timothy 2:9

⇟ Leading church ain't so easy! (2:1-3:16)

Paul gives his pal lots of advice. How to cope with false teachings. How to conduct worship services. How to choose church leaders. How to minister to the different kinds of people in the church. He loads Timothy's plate. He doesn't even stop there. He goes on to recommend how people should dress in church.

Then, he makes sure Timothy is clear in his direc-tions for church leaders. They've got to have a good reputation. They need to have a strong marriage. They need self-control, good behavior, friendliness, and an ability to teach. Then, after packing all of this into this short letter, Paul encourages Timothy to be careful with what God has placed in his care.

INTERVIEW
with the Stars

The right role model

Behind the Bible's next subject is a young man who learned early on the importance of picking the right role model. A few twists and turns, and Timothy's life could have turned out completely different. Imagine, for example, if Paul had never traveled through Timothy's hometown, Lystra? What would have happened to him? Even if he had become a Christian, would he have been as effective for the gospel without Paul's mentoring? Timothy, tell us about your childhood background.

⇒ Timothy

I grew up in a racially mixed home. My mother was Jewish, and as a young boy, she taught me all the Old Testament scripture. My dad was Greek, so that gave me a social position that allowed me to move freely in the Roman world. With that kind of background, I could have done practically anything I wanted with my life.

What happened to change your direction?

⇒ Timothy

In a word, Paul. Paul came through Lystra. And as a knowledge-seeking Greek, I was intrigued by the talk about this newfound religion and how it was upsetting Jews everyone in the Empire. So I went to hear him speak. Paul not only talked about the gospel of Jesus Christ, but he also challenged us who knew God's Word to check out the claims of Jesus against the promises and prophecies of the Old Testament. And so I did.

And what did you discover?

⇒ Timothy

The evidence was overwhelming. I was convinced beyond a doubt that Jesus was, in fact, Lord and Savior.

INTERVIEW
with the Stars

What happened then?

⋟ Timothy

I spent so much time hanging around Paul and his entourage that he couldn't help but notice. He recruited me as part of his traveling gospel team, and I served in a number of capacities: messenger, companion, scribe, whatever he needed.

That must have been totally awesome working with Paul. You must have learned a lot.

⋟ Timothy

I did, but it wasn't always easy for me. You have to remember that I was very young at that time, and at times I struggled with the same kinds of temptations that face young people today. I never was totally comfortable being in the limelight, either, like Paul was. He constantly was encouraging me to be bolder in my faith. And that was hard for me at times.

Based on your experiences with Paul, what advice would you give to young believers today?

⋟ Timothy

I think often the younger generation tends to dismiss older believers as not being hip or relevant to their lives. Or they go the other way and are intimidated by older Christians. Yet, the one thing that made the most difference to me was having a mentor like Paul in my life. Without him, I don't think I would have had the same impact for Christ as I was able to have under Paul's guidance. Ask God to give you someone who can guide and encourage you. It'll make all the difference!

REVIEWS

ENCORE

⟩ To read about the founding of the church in Ephesus, turn to Acts 18:18—19:41.

⟩ For insights into the Ephesus congregation by the turn of the first century, read Revelation 2:1—7.

⟩ Paul gives further ministerial advice in the letters of 2 Timothy and Titus.

Timothy was Paul's best buddy and preaching partner. Together, they hit the road and spread the Word in Turkey, Greece, and Italy (sounds like a band on tour). When believers in Thessalonica had questions about the second coming of Jesus, Timothy was the guy Paul trusted to deliver his two letters and help clear things up. While Paul spent two years getting the church going in Corinth, Timothy was right there as his assistant pastor. It was a dangerous time to be a Christian, so having a friend he could trust was a big help to Paul. Sure makes things easier knowing someone's got your back.

Timothy was also the perfect choice for preaching to the Ephesians. His dad was Greek, like they were, and Timothy grew up in Lystra, just 300 miles from Ephesus. His mom and grandma were Jewish (Acts 16:1; 2 Timothy 1:5), so he also knew where he was coming from with the Old Testament stuff and the Jewish community. He was the right man for the job!

Some scholars aren't sure if Paul wrote the two letters to Timothy and the one to Titus. A few of them think that someone else wrote the words after Paul died, maybe using his letters and sermons for the info (ghostwriters in the sky). This happened a lot back then and wasn't any big deal to most people (times sure have changed, haven't they? It'd sure be hard to explain to an English teacher why someone else was writing *YOUR* papers).

One reason some Bible experts think it may have been more than one person writing is the way Paul put different meanings with certain words in different letters. Faith, for instance. In 1 Timothy "faith" is used to mean Christianity in general, but in Paul's other letters it describes a person's trusting relationship with Jesus, a personal faith. I warned you these 'expert' types were picky.

Oh well, you know how it is with people and opinions. Other scholars feel sure that Paul wrote these letters. They say that the differences are just because Paul wrote these letters 10-15 years later than the others and might have learned a thing or two in that time. Maybe the message is what's important. What do *you* think?

Pontiac Pilot

2 Timothy

SCHEDULE OF SCENES

Paul's last words

If you knew you were about to die, what would you say? Would you be a little sappy? Maybe contemplate your mistakes and successes? Check out this letter...it's Paul's last words, just before he dies.

Paul's chained inside a Roman dungeon, awaiting execution. The imperial trial may still be under way, and if so, it's not going well. Paul unrolls a strip of parchment (maybe given to him by Luke, the only person in the area who hasn't abandoned him). Then Paul writes a letter to the man who is his best friend on earth, Timothy.

Paul's strong to the end. He repeats some of what he has said before: Don't be ashamed of the gospel. Don't be fooled by false teachings. Live like children of a holy and loving God. His letter reads like a man heading to his death. He's getting a few final words in before the inevitable happens. Paul's ready to meet Jesus. But, before he goes, he wants to make sure everyone else is, too.

QUOTABLES

I have fought the good fight, I have finished the race, I have kept the faith (4:7, NKJV). Paul's reflection on his life as he sits in prison, expecting to be executed soon.

SNEAK PREVIEW

Ezekiel
Spectacular visuals, riveting commentary on both heaven and earth.

BEHIND the SCENES
of 2 Timothy

STARRING ROLES

Paul, traveling minister who starts churches throughout the Roman Empire, but who is now in jail awaiting execution (1:1)

Timothy, one of Paul's most devoted traveling companions, whom Paul appoints to lead the church in Ephesus (1:2)

PLOT

The end is near for Paul, and he knows it. So he writes this, his last and most moving letter. He addresses it to Timothy, a young friend he thinks of as a son. He's not writing from a comfortable bed in house arrest. He's lying in a cold dungeon. Paul is lonely. He's been abandoned by everyone. He asks Timothy to come see him before he dies. He also warns Timothy that sufferings are bound to come his way, too.

STAGE DIRECTIONS

	Paul imprisoned at Rome A.D. 60	Paul writes 1 Timothy, possibly after release from Rome A.D. 63	Paul writes 2 Timothy, possibly after another imprisonment in Rome A.D. 67	
				Dates are approximate

BIBLE EVENTS

A.D. 50 — A.D. 60 ◯ — ◯ A.D. 70

WORLD EVENTS

	Rome burns; Nero blames Christians, launches persecution A.D. 64	Nero commits suicide A.D. 68

AUTHOR AND DATE

The letter is from Paul, in a jail at Rome (1:1, 16–17). He is writing to his young friend, Timothy, whom he appointed to lead the church in Ephesus. Some scholars say that this letter was written a generation after Paul, perhaps to address Christian persecution going on at that time. Others argue that the deeply personal nature of this letter confirms what early church leaders believed—that Paul wrote it.

It's unclear exactly when Paul wrote the letter. One popular theory is that Paul was released from the Roman imprisonment described at the end of Acts. But after continuing his missionary work he was again arrested, taken to Rome, tried during Nero's crackdown on Christians, and executed in about A.D. 67.

ON LOCATION

Paul writes from a jail in Rome. He addresses the letter to Timothy, pastor of the church in Ephesus, a major Roman city about 1,000 miles east, along the Mediterranean coast of Turkey.

WHAT TO LOOK FOR

- **Intimacy.** Notice how personal the letter is . . . it almost feels a little private. Though Paul intends for the entire church of Ephesus to read it, and he refers briefly to false teachings, end times, and the traits of godly people. The aging apostle is talking especially to Timothy.
- **The approaching death of Paul.** This letter may be the last surviving words of Paul, for he is convinced he is about to die. But in a poignant and inspired moment, Paul expresses his incredible faith (Read 4:6–8 for more info on this).
- **Paul's request for Timothy to come.** Paul's about to die . . . he wants to see his friend.
- **A call to courage.** Timothy is going to face persecution; Paul says he is certain of that. And, Paul gives Timothy instruction for *how* he should act when he's being persecuted. He's to stay calm. That's weird advice, isn't it? Try to be calm even though you're being hurt. Not easy!

EXTREME SCENE
from 2 Timothy

Paul gets serious (3:10–4:18)

As death approaches, the elderly and imprisoned Paul sits alone with his memories. Paul writes his friend. He says he remembers a time when Timothy cried. He remembers laying hands on this young friend, blessing him for ministry. The rancid anti-Christian movement sweeping across the empire, forcing the more timid believers to keep their faith a secret. But Paul pushes Timothy toward courage and boldness: "Don't be ashamed," he says. Not an easy promise to keep. Paul expresses confidence in the Lord even in the face of death. Paul's courage shouts from the prison...and from history. His confidence in the face of death gives us hope that ordinary sinners can stand strong for Christ. Even when they're chained to the wall of a cold, dark cell.

DIRECTOR'S NOTES

Many people in Paul's day were sports fans. They would have appreciated and understood his references to athletics. The Isthmian Games, a forerunner to our modern Olympics, were held every two years in the Greek city of Corinth. People came from all around to see these athletic contests. 2 Timothy 2:5

REVIEWS

Paul gives more advice to ministers in the letters of 1 Timothy and Titus.

This letter tells about some of the awful stuff Christians had to go through in the early days.

The experts and bookworms didn't have to look far to prove that this stuff really happened, because even Roman history books of the time don't try to hide all the mean things they did to people. One of the guys in charge of writing it all down was Tacitus. He didn't like Christians very much. He talked about Christ's followers as having "detestable superstitions" (excuse me, Mr. Tacitus, aren't Romans the ones who thought the sun was pulled by a chariot and the "gods" all lived on a mountain? Talk about superstition!). Tacitus writes about a big fire that burned about two thirds of the city of Rome in A.D. 64 Nero, the Roman emperor, blamed the Christians for the fire and set out to make their lives miserable. Just being a Christian was enough to get somebody arrested, tortured, or even killed. Even ol' Tacitus (who didn't like Christians in the first place) thought Nero was going too far. According to Tacitus, Christians were nailed to crosses, burned alive, and even covered with bloody animal skins and torn apart by starving dogs. Other accounts (including Paul's in 1 Corinthians 15:32) describe Christians being fed to lions and forced to fight wild animals for the entertainment of the Romans (these people needed cable in a bad way). Nero sounds like a real psycho. No big surprise that he committed suicide in A.D. 68.

Unfortunately, the death of the madman didn't stop the madness. For years and years after Nero croaked, the Romans declared "open season" on Christians on a regular basis. One of the worst of the whackos to follow Nero was a dude named Pliny the Younger (he probably hated anybody with a cooler name than his, which was, like, everybody).

REVIEWS

Pliny was the governor of a Roman territory near Timothy's church in Ephesus. In A.D. 112, Pliny (y'know, I think I'd rather have a name like "Wormhead" or "Dogslobber" than Pliny) wrote a report to his boss, the Roman emperor Trajan, that he was accusing people of being Christians and executing them if they said yes.

What a jerk! Pliny was lucky that nobody was executing idiotic Roman governors with silly names anywhere near Ephesus in those days.

Paul wrote about "the last days" like they were just around the corner. He said that in the last days, before Jesus comes back, people will love only themselves and money. They will be proud, stuck-up, rude, and disobedient to their parents. They will also be ungrateful, godless, heartless, and hateful.

Makes you wonder if, in the last days, everyone will be named "Pliny."

Whiny (Pliny's little brother)

Titus

SCHEDULE OF SCENES

Mean, lazy, and downright RUDE!

You've heard the expression, "You're a lousy Cretan," right? Well, if you have (and, hey...even if you haven't!), you're about to learn the history behind this pointed phrase. First, here's a little background.

Paul gave Titus the job of appointing church leaders for the church in Crete who had a good reputation. That was almost like asking Titus to find a supernice person at an angry man convention...it was almost impossible. Cretans were liars, thieves, and all-around bad people. Paul knew this, but, hey, every church has to have a leader.

Paul and Titus knew the reputation of the Cretans and that they deserved it. Paul reminds Titus that Jesus can make a difference for people everywhere, even on Crete, because Jesus made a difference in them. This letter encourages Titus to seek out strong, kindhearted leaders who have had a legitimate change through Jesus. Paul does that, and reminds Titus of how rotten *they* used to be without Christ.

QUOTABLES

"Cretans are always liars, evil beasts, lazy gluttons" (1:12, NKJV). The words of a Cretan writer and prophet, whom Paul quotes apparently to warn Titus that ministry in Crete will be a challenge.

SNEAK PREVIEW

1 Kings
A rich, wild, and glorious kingdom, just before the darkness falls.

BEHIND the SCENES
of Titus

STARRING ROLES

Paul, traveling minister who covers some 10,000 miles and starts churches throughout the Roman Empire (1:1)

Titus, one of Paul's non-Jewish traveling companions, whom Paul appoints to organize the churches on the island of Crete (1:4)

PLOT

During one of his missionary trips, Paul visits the island of Crete, south of Greece. Paul feels the need to continue his journey, but he leaves behind one of his traveling associates, Titus, to appoint leaders. Sometime later, Paul writes this short letter to Titus. Paul may have written it about the same time he wrote 1 Timothy, after assigning Timothy to the church in Ephesus. Both letters cover much the same material.

STAGE DIRECTIONS

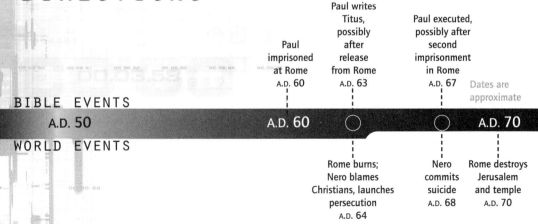

Paul writes Titus, possibly after release from Rome A.D. 63

Paul imprisoned at Rome A.D. 60

Paul executed, possibly after second imprisonment in Rome A.D. 67

Dates are approximate

BIBLE EVENTS

A.D. 50 — A.D. 60 — A.D. 70

WORLD EVENTS

Rome burns; Nero blames Christians, launches persecution A.D. 64

Nero commits suicide A.D. 68

Rome destroys Jerusalem and temple A.D. 70

AUTHOR AND DATE

The letter is written from Paul (1:1) to Titus, who is directing the work of several churches in Crete. Some scholars, however, suggest that one of Paul's associates wrote the letter after Paul died, drawing from the apostle's letters and sermons, then applying the messages to problems that developed later in Crete.

Bible scholars aren't entirely sure when the letter was written. There's no mention of Paul visiting Crete, either in the stories of Acts or in any of his letters outside this one. Some believe that Paul wrote the letter after the events described in Acts.

Half a million people live in Crete today, and most consider themselves members of the Orthodox Church of Crete, a branch of the Greek Orthodox Church. There are more than 3,000 Orthodox churches on the island.

ON LOCATION

Paul addresses his letter to Titus, who is organizing churches on the island of Crete, about 100 miles south of Greece. The island is about 150 miles wide.

WHAT TO LOOK FOR

- **Advice for a minister.** This letter is a seasoned minister's advice to a younger minister. It falls under the group of letters from Paul called "Pastoral Letters." Paul used these letters to counsel men who were once his traveling associates but who are now pastoring churches.
- **Qualifications for church leaders.** Part of Titus's assignment in Crete is to choose leaders for each church on the island. Because Paul knows that a bad leader could ruin a congregation, he gives Titus a list of qualifications. You can read these qualifications in 1:6–9.
- **False teachings.** Titus faced a lot of silly religious arguments…teaching from Jewish Christians that went against what Jesus taught. Paul gives Titus a lot of solid advice he can use to combat these teachings.

EXTREME SCENE
from Titus

Mean dudes in God's house

After Paul arrives on the island of Crete and starts churches in several cities, he decides to move on. So, he assigns Titus to stay behind long enough to appoint church leaders and to clear up confusion about some false teachings that quickly begin to threaten the churches. Paul keeps in contact with Titus by letter, advising him how to choose good leaders and how to fight teachings that undermine Christianity. He urges Titus to teach only what is correct. Then, he tells Titus to stay away from false teachers. In this letter, Paul gives Titus everything he needs to appoint church leaders when everyone seems really mean, and how to wade through teachings filled with misinformed teachers.

DIRECTOR'S NOTES

Paul's reference to genealogies has to do with the obsession of certain Jewish leaders with being able to trace their family tree all the way back to Abraham. Apparently, knowing the name of one's great-great-great grandfather was a big deal to some people in the New Testament times. Titus 3:9

INTERVIEW
with the Stars

Passing the torch

Do you have any heirlooms in your family, treasures that have been passed down from generation to generation? *Behind the Bible's* next subject, Titus, is a man who helped pass along one of life's greatest treasures—the message of the gospel. Although much of Titus's background remains a mystery, he played a unique role as one of Paul's messengers in the development of the early church. Titus, why don't you tell us about your job responsibilities with Paul?

⋙ Titus

Certainly. I was part of Paul's traveling gospel band. Like my colleague Timothy, I served Paul in an official capacity. Often I was given the tougher assignments. For example, when Timothy was having trouble getting the Corinthian church to accept Paul, Paul sent me in to finish the job. My toughest assignment, though, was working with the immature Christians at Crete.

Would you say that was your unique role, being a top troubleshooter for Paul?

⋙ Titus

Actually, no, although that was a role I stepped into many times. I think what made me unique is that I was a Greek believer. I had no Jewish upbringing like Timothy. I guess you could say that I was a living example of what God could do in the life of a non-Jewish person.

INTERVIEW
with the Stars

How did that help the early church?

> ### Titus

At a time when the Jerusalem church was debating whether Gentiles could be true followers of Jesus without first becoming Jewish converts, Paul was able to trot me out and say, "Hey, look! Here's a Gentile believer whose faith in Jesus is undeniable." My faith really opened the door for other Gentiles to enter the church.

In what other ways were you effective in the development of the early church?

> ### Titus

I was a first-generation Christian—in other words, my faith in Jesus started with me. I didn't have the luxury of having parents or grandparents who passed down a legacy of faith to me. But I realized the importance of doing just that. Each generation is responsible for passing along the torch of the Gospel to those who are coming behind them. We just can't be content to sit with our faith and keep it to ourselves. We need to pass it on.

Is that something young people can do even now?

> ### Titus

Absolutely! There are few believers who are too young to begin thinking of those who are younger. Teens with a strong faith can have an incredible impact on their peers and on younger kids. In fact, kids often listen more closely to a teen share his or her faith than they will to an older adult. There are probably plenty of opportunities right now for teens to make a difference for Jesus in their church by working with younger kids. Take a look around and start passing that torch!

REVIEWS

ENCORE

For more of Paul's advice to a minister, read 1 and 2 Timothy. The letter to Titus is so much like 1 Timothy that both may have been written about the same time.

You know how when you start a new job sometimes they'll have a training video for you to watch. ("You flip the burgers three times before throwing them on the bun.") The book of Titus is like training video on parchment for pastors.

Titus was a pastor on the Island of Crete. Ever heard someone called a Cretan? It usually means they are stupid, vulgar, and insensitive. In other words, a total geekazoid. In his letter to Titus, Paul quoted a sixth-century B.C. Cretan poet and prophet named Epimenides, who said: "The people of Crete always tell lies. They are greedy and lazy like wild animals" (see 1:12), and the dude was talking about his OWN people! Paul told Titus that what the man said was true. Way back in that day (like 1000 B.C.), Crete was famous for its architects and engineers; Greeks traveled there to study the architecture. Later on, business moved elsewhere, and Crete became a hangout for pirates, thugs, and other scum-Cretans.

Why would Paul slam the people he says he's trying to help? Well, for one thing, the Cretans really *earned* their reputation and Paul was always a "tell it like it is" kind of guy. Paul also wanted Titus to know that he understood how hard the job of preaching to the Cretans really was. The church was having a tough time getting going in Crete, and Paul didn't want Titus to blame himself for things that weren't his fault. Thanks in part to Paul's encouragement, Titus eventually helped quite a few Cretans find Jesus and raise their cool factor way above the rest of the thugs.

Today, Crete, with its warm ocean breezes, sunbaked beaches and rich history is a pretty good place to take a vacation. The people are friendly, too. Makes you wonder what happened to all the nasty Cretans. If I didn't know better, I'd wonder if my little brother might be one.

Jordan Empathizer, Dean of Students,
Paul's school of problem congregations

Philemon

SCHEDULE OF SCENES

Jesus Is Born	Jesus Crucified Pentecost	Paul's Missionary Journeys Begin	Philemon Written	Temple Destroyed	Death of John
7/6 B.C.	A.D. 30	A.D. 46	A.D. 60	A.D. 70	A.D. 100

The tale of the runaway slave

Paul has a gift for being politically incorrect on social issues. Take slavery, for example. The subject of this letter is a slave named Onesimus to his Christian owner named Philemon. Paul's got a tough road to walk here. On one hand, *we* want him to take a stand against slavery. On the other hand, the people of Paul's day would have been shocked at how freely he associated with slaves. And they would have taken him to task for insisting that everyone deserves equal treatment, slave or free. After all, they would argue, how could any slave owner treat a slave like he's free? Would a man work your fields all day, every day, for nothing but room and board? And could you snatch a citizen out of his home and sell him for a profit?

The answer seems obvious. You can't treat slaves like they're free until you free them—which is exactly what Paul wants Christians to discover, and what he wants Philemon to do to Onesimus.

QUOTABLES

[Welcome him] no longer as a slave but more than a slave, a beloved brother (16, NRSV). Paul's advice to a slave owner on how to treat the runaway slave who has come back.

SNEAK PREVIEW

Ephesians
A message of freedom from behind bars.

BEHIND the SCENES
of Philemon

STARRING ROLES

Paul, traveling minister who starts churches throughout the Roman Empire, and who advises even churches he has not started—such as the one in Colossae (Colossians 1)

Philemon, a Christian slave owner, master of Onesimus, and one in whose home the Colossians meet for church services (verse 1)

Onesimus, runaway slave converted by Paul and sent back to his master (verse 10)

PLOT

Onesimus, a runaway slave, meets Paul and converts to Christianity. Paul convinces Onesimus to return to his slave owner, Philemon. Paul influences Philemon, a church leader, to help him see the heart of the issue with Onesimus. Paul writes a short but gripping letter for Onesimus to take to Philemon. In this letter, Paul asks Philemon to receive the slave in kindness. Paul also hints that Philemon should free Onesimus so he can help Paul.

STAGE DIRECTIONS

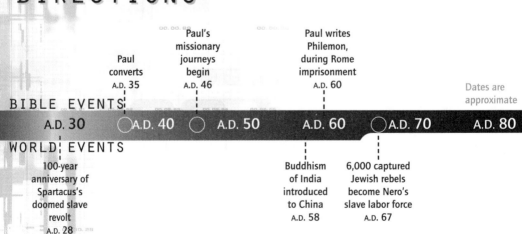

Paul's missionary journeys begin
A.D. 46

Paul converts
A.D. 35

Paul writes Philemon, during Rome imprisonment
A.D. 60

Dates are approximate

BIBLE EVENTS

A.D. 30   A.D. 40   A.D. 50   A.D. 60   A.D. 70   A.D. 80

WORLD EVENTS

100-year anniversary of Spartacus's doomed slave revolt
A.D. 28

Buddhism of India introduced to China
A.D. 58

6,000 captured Jewish rebels become Nero's slave labor force
A.D. 67

AUTHOR AND DATE

This letter is clearly from Paul. He's writing it from prison somewhere. Philemon lived in Colossae, in western Turkey.

It's uncertain when Paul wrote this letter. Some ancient manuscripts mention that he wrote from Rome during his two-year imprisonment, which started in about A.D. 60. Some Bible scholars doubt this. They argue that Rome, 1,000 miles from Colossae, is a long way off for a runaway slave with limited resources. They suggest Paul wrote from a closer jail, probably in nearby Ephesus.

ON LOCATION

Philemon and Onesimus live in Colossae, about a week-long trip east of Ephesus, Turkey (Colossians 4:9).

WHAT TO LOOK FOR

- **A masterpiece of tactful persuasion.** Paul doesn't come right out and ask Philemon to free Onesimus. But Philemon probably got the hint. Check out how Paul makes his case with Philemon:
  - Paul compliments Philemon on his growing faith in Jesus and his love for all of God's people—even slaves! (verse 5).
- Paul alludes to the power he has to free Onesimus if he wants (verses 13–14).
- Paul tells Philemon that he and Onesimus are a whole lot more than friends. And Philemon would not punish a visiting Paul as he would a runaway slave.
- Paul says he will pay back anything Onesimus may have taken to finance his escape. But he also reminds Philemon that he owes Paul his life (verses 18-19).
- This is not a private letter. It's to Philemon and the entire church. Others in the church would have heard Paul's request (a little added peer pressure? Probably!).
- When Paul gets out of jail, he plans to visit Philemon. This will be one awkward meeting if Onesimus is not free by then (verse 22).
- Paul is not alone in asking for kindness on behalf of the slave. Paul sends greetings from four associates, including Mark and Luke, implying that they support his request (verse 24).
- **A play on words.** Paul eases the tension this letter creates by making a play on words. The slave's name, Onesimus, means "useful." Paul acknowledges that Onesimus caused trouble for Philemon, the slave owner. But Paul argues that things are different now, and Onesimus was useless to Philemon, but he's useful to both of them (verse 11).

EXTREME SCENE
from Philemon

Philemon's Dilemma

Onesimus, a slave living in western Turkey, gets a chance to run away—and he takes it. During his flight to freedom, he runs into Paul and is converted to Christianity. Paul convinces him to return to his master, Philemon. Fortunately for Onesimus, Paul also teaches that slave owners should treat their slaves with respect. Paul send Onesimus home with this letter and asks Philemon to free Onesimus. The apostle promises to pay back anything Onesimus may have taken before leaving. Then Paul asks Philemon to welcome Onesimus as a friend, much like he'd welcome Paul.

DIRECTOR'S NOTES

Home Bible studies are nothing new. In fact, people met together in their houses to read Scripture and pray long before there were any churches. Church buildings as we know them today—places set aside specifically for Christian worship and Bible study—were not common until the third century. So, when you see the word *church* in the Bible, it's referring to a group of Christ's followers in a certain area. Philemon 2

INTERVIEW
with the Stars

The homecoming

Have you ever faced a problem that was so huge and so nasty that you felt like running away? *Behind the Bible's* next subject, Onesimus, faced a really tough situation. It was called slavery. And Onesimus decided to, literally, take the money and run from his master. But he didn't get very far before he learned that you can run, but you can't hide from God. Onesimus, tell us your story.

⋙ Onesimus

I belonged to a man named Philemon, who lived in Colossae. He was a believer; Paul had come to his house for church on several occasions. At that time, all their ramblings meant nothing to me. I was restless. I had had it with being considered just a piece of property, so I decided to rob my master and run. It was a dangerous, foolish thing to do, but I felt I had run out of options.

Then what happened?

⋙ Onesimus

I made it all the way to Rome where, guess what?! I ran right into the arms of Paul! Because of him, his great kindness to me, and his greater witness to the Lord Jesus Christ, I became a believer! Even though, technically, I was still considered a slave, I was freer than I had ever been in my life. It was the most remarkable thing! Because of my being a believer, though, Paul and I decided that I needed to return home to my master.

INTERVIEW
with the Stars

That couldn't have been an easy decision to make.

⋟ Onesimus

No, it wasn't. In the Roman Empire, the punishment for a runaway slave was at the very least a severe beating; in some cases, it was death on the cross. I had no idea what I was going back to; all I knew was that it was the right thing to do. Plus, Paul wrote a letter to Philemon and reintroduced me to my master as a fellow believer. Paul was certain I would receive a good welcome.

The Bible doesn't really tell us what happened when you went home, whether you ended up a leader in the church at Colossae or served as a slave for the remainder of your life.

⋟ Onesimus

True, but I think the point of my story is that I thought the solution to my problem was to run away. But it wasn't until I met Christ and *then* returned home that I was able to be in a position to truly be "useful," which is what my name means. It really doesn't matter what I did after I returned home. Having Christ in my life was the real difference-maker.

So what you're telling our readers is that if their approach to problem-solving is to run away, they can learn a lot from your experiences.

⋟ Onesimus

That's right. My escape was only temporary. But in the meantime, God reached down and changed my life totally. And He can do the same thing for you.

REVIEWS

This book is one of the earliest accounts of the civil rights struggle. Here we find Paul, who is already in jail for like the umpteenth time, writing a letter to Philemon. Paul met Onesimus, a Colossian slave who had run away from a guy named Philemon, converted him to Christianity, and sent him back, *but* with a letter asking for his safety and freedom. Paul even offered to pay the tab (back then, a lot of people became slaves to pay off bills). Smart move. See, Philemon *owed* Paul, so it was a good way for Paul to remind him that *Philemon* could easily find himself in the same position. It was still an act of faith for Onesimus to go back, even *with* the letter. Slaves were often punished or even killed for skipping town. Slavery was common in those days and talking about getting rid of it was a touchy subject, especially for a guy who spent most of his time in jail.

Paul does a great job of walking the line on this one. He never really talks about slavery being good or bad, just about how *all people* should treat each other. Instead of trying to start a revolution to fight the system, he works on changing the people inside the system.

Paul pulls off a good one here by rising above the subject to get to what's really important. He was really good at that, like in Ephesians where he says we all "have the same master in heaven" and that God "doesn't have any favorites" (see Ephesians 6:9). It took a thousand years for the Church to really come out against slavery in a big way, but Paul planted some ideas in the first century that helped to shape the movement permanently.

After Paul's death, the name Onesimus turns up again in a letter from a church leader named Ignatius to a *bishop*

ENCORE

For more on Paul's view of slavery, read 1 Corinthians 12:12–31; Galatians 3:23–4:7; Ephesians 6:5–9; Colossians 3:11–4:1; and Titus 2:9–10.

REVIEWS

named (you guessed it) Onesimus. A lot of folks aren't sure if this is the same guy, but he was bishop of Ephesus, and Onesimus the slave was from that neck of the woods. He even did some traveling with Tychicus, the dude who delivered the letters to the Ephesians and Colossians (Ephesians 6:21; Colossians 4:7–9). I like to think it's the same guy. I love happy endings. I think another important theme here is Paul's offer to pay the bill so that Philemon will forgive Onesimus and, hopefully, set him free. Can you think of anyone else who paid the price of other people's forgiveness and bought their freedom while suffering Himself?

Yeah, I thought you might have an answer to that one. Paul learned from the best, didn't he?

Joe Carpenter

Hebrews

SCHEDULE OF SCENES

Jesus Is Born	Jesus Crucified Pentecost	Paul's Missionary Journeys Begin	Hebrews Written	Temple Destroyed	Death of John
7/6 B.C.	A.D. 30	A.D. 46	A.D. 65	A.D. 70	A.D. 100

For believers ready to bag it

If you're thinking about dropping out of Christianity, read this book. Read this book once and you'll be convinced that it's written to Jewish Christians on the verge of returning to Judaism. It's obvious that's what's going on here...you're about to read the longest argument about Jesus Christ. One that would convince any fence-sitting Jewish person to drop over into Christianity. The author says that the old covenant, or agreement between God and Israel, has given way to the new agreement that Jeremiah predicted. God's law written on scrolls has been replaced by God's law written on the human heart—and animal sacrifices for sin have become obsolete because of the sacrificial death of God's Son.

One thing's for sure...this is a book for Jewish Christians. And, it's a book for any Christian facing things like temptation or frustration. Whatever the obstacle, the writer of Hebrews encourages Christians to keep their eyes on the finish line. Good advice for them. Great advice for us, too.

QUOTABLES

Jesus Christ is the same yesterday and today and forever (13:8, NRSV).

Faith is being sure of what we hope for and certain of what we do not see (11:1, NIV).

SNEAK PREVIEW

1 Chronicles
Follow a king's heart and you'll follow his kingdom.

BEHIND the SCENES
of Hebrews

STARRING ROLE

Jesus, God's Son, who establishes a new agreement between God and humanity—a covenant better than the one instituted by Moses and practiced in the temple (2:9)

PLOT

About a generation after Jesus' resurrection, some Jewish Christians are beginning to go back to their Jewish beliefs. To win back their loyalty, the writer of Hebrews writes an essay arguing that faith in Christ is better than Judaism. Basically, he makes three main points. (1) Jesus is superior to Old Testament heroes, including the prophets, Moses, and even the angels. (2) Jesus is superior to the high priest, who serves as a mediator between God and humanity. (3) Jesus is a better sacrifice than any animal offered on an altar.

The writer also adds that Jesus made the old covenant obsolete. The old covenant was based on rules in the Old Testament. The new agreement the writer talks about is based on laws God has placed in the heart.

STAGE DIRECTIONS

Unidentified
author
writes
Hebrews
A.D. 65

BIBLE EVENTS

Dates are approximate

A.D. **60**　　　A.D. **70**　　　A.D. **80**　　　A.D. **90**

WORLD EVENTS

Rome burns;
Christians
blamed,
persecuted
A.D. 64

Jews in
Israel
revolt
A.D. 66

Rome
destroys
Jerusalem
and temple
A.D. 70

Roman bishop,
Clement,
quotes Hebrews
A.D. 95

AUTHOR AND DATE

Guess what? You've got an interesting book here. Why? Because no one's really sure who exactly wrote this book. In the mid-second century, some Christian leaders attributed the book to Paul. That's pretty unlikely, since Paul usually identifies himself in his letters. And he writes in a lot simpler style. Scholars believe that this was probably written by someone who had never actually seen Jesus, but had heard a lot about Him.

So, who might have written this book? Here are two strong candidates: Barnabas and Apollos. In about A.D. 200, Tertullian (a theologian) quoted from Hebrews, which he identified as "an epistle to the Hebrews under the name of Barnabas." Barnabas was co-pastor with Paul at a church in Antioch, Syria. Later, Barnabas served as a missionary who preached throughout the Eastern Mediterranean. Apollos was a guy who knew a lot about Scripture (see Acts 18:24). And it would take a well-educated Jew to write Hebrews, which is among the most sophisticated writing in the New Testament and which is so intimately connected to the Jewish Scripture.

It's really tough to put an accurate date on when this book was written. It might have been written sometime in the A.D. 60s, as the second generation of Christians began to emerge as church leaders. The book's many references to the Jewish temple and sacrificial system suggest the writer completed it before A.D. 70—when Rome destroyed the temple and brought the whole sacrificial system to an end. Clement, a church leader in Rome, quoted several sections of the book in a letter he wrote in A.D. 95.

ON LOCATION

The message is aimed at Christians all over the Roman Empire, but especially to Jewish Christians. The writer sends greetings from believers in Italy, suggesting he lived there, perhaps in Rome (13:24). This possibility is strengthened by the fact that in A.D. 95, Clement, bishop of Rome, quoted from the book.

WHAT TO LOOK FOR

- **Old Testament quotes.** To convince Jewish Christians that the Christian faith is both God's idea and an outgrowth of Judaism, the writer quotes about forty passages of the Old Testament to support his arguments. He says that animal sacrifice isn't what pleased God. Animal sacrifice was simply a means to an end. Kind of a way to remind people that sin is wrong.
- **Jesus, the better way.** The writer compares Jesus to many people and practices revered in Judaism. And he writes that Jesus comes out as the winner every time. Jesus is better than angels, prophets, or even Moses. Angels worship Him (1:6). Prophets speak for God…Jesus is God. Moses told people about the future…Jesus is the future. High priests intercede for people on earth…Jesus intercedes in heaven. High priests have sinned…Jesus hasn't. Animals are sacrificed for one sin…Jesus was sacrificed for all sins. Jesus is way better than anything. No joke!

EXTREME SCENES
from Hebrews

Jesus and his dad (1:1–14)

It's always good to have a reminder of what you're leaving behind. That's what's going on here. The writer of this book tells Jewish believers that if they head back to their Jewish roots they'll be leaving a lot of essential stuff behind. Jesus is superior to anything their Jewish roots have taught them to rely on. And, better yet... Jesus is the Supreme High Priest. He's with God in heaven telling Him about our hurts, joys, and struggles. We don't have to go through an earthly priest... we have Jesus!

Sin...No problemo! (10:1–18)

Get the clash of sacrificial systems here? The old way of dealing with sin meant that you had to kill an animal for each sin. Basically, it went like this: When the Jews laid their hands on the head of an innocent sheep—symbolizing the atonement that the animal will make for their sin—and when the people saw the blood drain out of the animal, the life-and-death seriousness of sin became dramatically real. But the new covenant that God sets up through Jesus is different. Jesus is killed for ALL our sins. We don't need to go sacrifice an animal after each sin. We don't need a priest to help us get rid of our sins. We need Jesus.

DIRECTOR'S NOTES

Angels enjoyed tremendous popularity in the first century. Pagans, Jews, and Christians all placed a tremendous amount of importance on these heavenly beings. Some groups may even have gone so far as to worship angels. Others mistakenly believed that Jesus Himself was an angel, because of the miracles He performed. Hebrews 1:4

Ancient faith (11:1–40)

Faith is a tough word to define. Hebrews does its best to give us a definition we can use. Faith makes us sure of what we hope for and gives us proof of what we cannot see. And it was the faith of our ancestors that made them pleasing to God. To prove this, the writer of Hebrews mentions a lot of Old Testament heroes. Faith is more important to God than the Jewish rituals ever were. Before Israel had a system of laws and religious rituals, the faith of godly men and women gave God pleasure—people like Abel, Noah, Abraham, Sarah, Isaac, Jacob, and Moses.

INTERVIEW
with the Stars

The problem-solver

Behind the Bible has the privilege of talking today with a man who made a difference to his family, his friends, and ultimately his people, because he allowed God to work through him, using the skills and ability God had given him. Gideon, why don't you tell us a little bit of background about the situation the people of Israel were in?

⋙ Gideon

Sure. For years, we lived under the harsh rules of the Midianites. And I'm talking harsh. They were so cruel that many of us ran away and hid in the mountains. As soon as we planted crops, the Midianites would attack and leave us nothing to eat. I guess you could say it was our own fault because, as a people, we turned from God and wanted to live our own way.

And then what happened?

⋙ Gideon

Well, you could have knocked me over with a feather with what happened next. This angel came and told me that the Lord had chosen *me* to destroy our enemies. Me! Our family was the weakest in the entire tribe of Manasseh, and I was the youngest in my family! Who was I to lead the attack?

But God must have seen something in you?

⋙ Gideon

I suppose. I did have a knack for problem-solving. I told you about how they stole our food. Well, I came up with the idea of threshing our wheat in the winepress so the Midianites wouldn't see it. It was kinda like hiding a garden in a bathtub. But it worked!

INTERVIEW
with the Stars

And, because of your resourcefulness and creativity, you were chosen to lead the fight against the Midianites.

≥ Gideon

Well, I would have to give most, OK, *all* the credit to God. I did lead the rebellion, but it was God who gave me the plan. Following His directions, I went into battle with only three hundred men—each armed with a clay jar, a torch, and a trumpet—and we routed an army of over 120,000! (Believe me, the 300 men was all God's idea to prove exactly *who* was behind our victory!) It was an incredible victory. I had the ability to get things done, but without God in my life, I never would have been able to achieve the things I did.

It sounds like we need to keep ourselves open to the plans or events that God has for each one of us.

≥ Gideon

That's right. You may have unusual skills, or maybe, like myself, you are given an unusual opportunity to use those skills. As you open yourself to God's plan for you, you'll discover as I did that His plan will always include tasks that we cannot accomplish without His help. Making a difference isn't about what you can do; it's more about what God can do with you, in you, and through you!

Thanks, Gideon!

REVIEWS

ENCORE

The writer of Hebrews compares Jesus to the priesthood and sacrificial system of the Old Testament. To review some of the source material with which the writer worked, turn to Leviticus, especially chapters 1—9.

Every group of people has tags and labels they use to identify themselves as part of their group. If you see two long-haired guys give each other the "peace sign," they might be hippy-types. If you see people with their faces painted, wearing big jerseys with numbers on them and waving banners, they are probably football fans.

For the Jews, their biggest tags were the rituals and rules God had given them through Moses. The Law, as these rules were called, represented God's agreement with the Jews. If they followed the rules, they were given "most favored nation" status, and God would personally bless and protect them. Big *if*. The Jews, like most nations do, screwed up a bunch of times throughout history. They broke the Law, and sometimes, like when they had a king who turned his back on God, a lot of them ditched the Law completely. Through the prophet Jeremiah, God said that, since they didn't seem able to keep the old deal, the day would come when He would make a new agreement with the Jews (Jeremiah 31:31—33). Moses delivered the first agreement. Jesus delivered the new one and gave His life to earn forgiveness for those who had broken the old contract (Hebrews 9:15). The writer of Hebrews makes it clear that the new deal totally replaces the old one (8:13). So what if the Jews wanted to go back to the old agreement?

No way.

Least that's what the author of Hebrews says. He says that to ignore the new deal in favor of the old one is as bad as nailing Christ to the cross and insulting Him in public (6:6). He even says that it would be impossible to be brought back after doing so. Pretty tough words. Some

people take this literally to mean that a Christian who gives up his faith is lost forever. Others say that those who turn their backs on the new deal haven't experienced true faith in the first place. They aren't really rejecting anything because they don't even know the truth yet.

I think another way of seeing this may be that it is every person's choice to accept or deny Jesus for himself or herself. God is not about threats as much as He is about love and forgiveness. The Lord doesn't want people forced into believing and doing what is right. He wants them to do it because it is in their hearts. Anybody, and I mean anybody, who wants to come to God is welcome. All you have to do is follow Jesus' advice: "Ask, and it will be given you; search, and you will find; knock, and the door will be opened for you" (Matthew 7:7 NRSV).

Sam Aritan

James

Jesus Is Born — Jesus Crucified Pentecost — James Written — Temple Destroyed — Death of John

| 7/6 B.C. | A.D. 30 | A.D. 48 | A.D. 70 | A.D. 100 |

Talk is cheap

Imagine this world for a moment. It's a world where everyone says they're going to get to work, but they never really do. They talk about accomplishing things, but they rarely do. That's the world James is ticked with. It's the type of world he fears. It's the reason he writes this book. James has no patience with do-nothing Christians. When confronting them, sometimes he's diplomatic, and often he's not. James is tired of hearing Christians talk the talk. He wants to see some proof that the faith they're talking about is real. So James writes a short letter of instructions for Christian living. In it, he tells believers exactly what he expects of them.

What does he say? For starters, they should remain faithful even when others attack their beliefs. And when they see someone in need, they're supposed to lend a hand. And when they have an opportunity to slander someone, they need to keep their mouths shut. James comes off forceful. But he's talking to deadweight here. He hopes the momentum of his words will compel believers into action.

QUOTABLES

Resist the devil and he will flee from you. Draw near to God and He will draw near to you (4:7–8, NKJV).

Be quick to listen and slow to speak or to get angry (1:19).

Faith without deeds is useless (2:20 NIV). James teaches that true faith isn't kept inside; it's expressed through acts of kindness.

SNEAK PREVIEW

Philippians
Sometimes a thank you note to a friend is the greatest love letter of all.

BEHIND the SCENES
of James

STARRING ROLE

James, possibly the brother of Jesus and leader of the church in Jerusalem (1:1)

PLOT

Don't look for a plot here. This book doesn't even seem to address a particular problem. Instead, it's a collection of practical lessons about Christian living. Some of the lessons are: If you are poor, don't worry about it. If you are rich, worry like crazy—and give some money to the poor. Don't give in to temptation. Be slow to get angry. Don't treat rich people better than poor people. Do kind things for others. Watch your mouth. Run away from the devil and into the arms of God. Pray for people who need God's help.

STAGE DIRECTIONS

Paul starts churches on first missionary trip
A.D. 46

James leads church council in Jerusalem
A.D. 49

BIBLE EVENTS

Dates are approximate

A.D. 40 — A.D. 50 — A.D. 60 — A.D. 70

WORLD EVENTS

The Book of James written
A.D. 48

Jews rebel against Rome
A.D. 66

Rome destroys Jerusalem and temple
A.D. 70

AUTHOR AND DATE

The writer identifies himself as "James, a servant of God and of the Lord Jesus Christ" (1:1). But at least four men in the New Testament share this name, including an apostle. Since early Christian times the writer has been identified as the oldest of Jesus' four younger brothers (see Mark 6:3). James rose to become leader of the Jerusalem church. He also headed the first church council meeting (see Acts 15).

No one knows for certain when James wrote the letter. A Jewish historian named Josephus, who lived in the first century, said Jewish leaders stoned James to death before Rome destroyed Jerusalem in A.D. 70. So if the brother of Jesus wrote it, he must have written it before then. Some scholars say that the letter has a lot of Jewish tones in it. That leads some scholars to think that this letter was written when most of the church was still Jewish. If so, the letter could have been written in the A.D. 40s and might be the oldest literature in the New Testament.

ON LOCATION

James writes to "the twelve tribes scattered all over the world" (see 1:1). This may mean Jews who have become Christians. Or it can mean the entire Christian church, which James may be portraying as the New Israel.

WHAT TO LOOK FOR

- **Practical advice.** James has a ton of advice for people. All of it is about how believers should live. In fact, some scholars call it "Wisdom Literature" (a lot like the wisdom stuff you'd find in the Old Testament) because it has a lot of wise sayings in it. Check out some of his wise sayings in 1:26; 2–4; 4:11; and 5:1, 4.
- **Jewish perspective.** If you read carefully, you'll notice that the letter sounds like it's written by a Jew, for Jews. James addresses his letter to the twelve tribes, a common way of referring to Israel. He uses the Greek word for synagogue to describe the meeting place mentioned in 2:2. He uses the Hebrew title for God. And he speaks of the Jewish law with reverence. This is one guy who really knows his audience!

EXTREME SCENES from James

Get to work (2:14–26)

James has one objective...to move lazy believers into action. He's really concerned about Christians who have decided that knowing Jesus is all they need. James says, "Guys...what good is it to believe something if that belief doesn't affect your life?" Believers must help. They must provide for others. Faith without these outward expressions is no faith at all. James is bold, but he's not ignorant. He knows that some people will disagree with him. Some may argue that belief in God is enough. But James replies that even demons believe in God. Ohhhh. Cool (and true!) comeback!

DIRECTOR'S NOTES

You've heard of "hell on earth"? The Hinnom Valley, a deep ravine located south of Jerusalem, was the real thing. The Greek word translated "hell" literally means "Hinnom Valley." The ravine was actually an ancient garbage dump. All kinds of waste material and dead animals were taken to Hinnom Valley to be burned. Eventually, the place came to be used as a symbol of judgment and sorrow. James 3:6

Watch yer mouth! (3:1–12)

James gives one piece of advice that has become one of the most memorable pieces of advice throughout history. He challenges believers to watch their tongues. It can hurt. It can cause irreparable damage. Yeah, it's small, but so is a ship's rudder, and so is the spark that starts a forest fire. The tongue guides. It can start a fire...or it can heal a heart. And it's totally under our power.

INTERVIEW
with the Stars

A late bloomer

Can you imagine growing up and your big Brother is Jesus? Jesus, the One who never sinned, never had a wrong thought, never claimed the bathroom all to Himself, never fought over the last piece of cake. And you, the younger brother? What would it have been like? Can you imagine Mary saying, "Why can't you be more like your big Brother?" Talk about an intimidating comparison! *Behind the Bible's* next subject is James, Jesus' younger half-brother. James, give us some insight into what it was like.

⋙ James

First off, Mom never said, "Why can't you be more like your big Brother?" because I think she knew in her heart that no one could ever be like Jesus!

So you knew early on that Jesus was, shall we say, rather unique?

⋙ James

Absolutely. Even as a youngster, Jesus was different from the rest of us boys. I don't mean that He didn't play with us or stuff like that. It was more in the way He asked questions and responded to people that was different. Then, when He got older and started His ministry, well, you knew that He was not your run-of-the-mill preacher. There was definitely something different and special about Him.

Did you ever suspect, though, that your older Brother was the Messiah?

⋙ James

No, not at all, not while He was on earth. We heard all the talk and the things that other people were saying about Him. But I mean, come on. I admired my big Brother and all, and thought He did a lot of cool things. But the Messiah? My Savior? No, I had a hard time accepting that concept until after He had died.

INTERVIEW
with the Stars

What caused you to change your mind about Jesus?

⋗ James

After Jesus died and was raised from the dead, He paid a little visit to me. To say it was an incredible reunion is the understatement of the year! When I realized who Jesus truly *is*, then everything fell into place for me. All that He said, all that He did, the way He reached out to others, the way He reacted to the religious leaders of the day—it all made sense.

How did that realization impact your life?

⋗ James

Completely. Totally. Nothing was ever the same for me. In essence, I grew up. I may have been a later bloomer, but I made up for lost time. I became a leader of the Jerusalem church and helped shape the early church movement. Later, I wrote the book of James to help others, like me, be more like Jesus.

So I guess the good news is that it's never too late to respond in faith to Jesus.

⋗ James

Exactly. No matter how old or young you are; at what point in your education or development, just pick up my book and begin applying those lessons that I learned and passed along. It's written for people exactly like myself—believers who really want to make a difference for Jesus in their lives.

REVIEWS

ENCORE

For more wise sayings, read the Old Testament books of Proverbs and Ecclesiastes.

James was Jesus' little brother, but don't worry; he didn't get his name in the Bible just by having famous relatives. He had a lot of good things to say. I like the book of James because it covers things from a different angle than Paul did. Not that there was anything wrong with Paul—he's one of my favorites—it's just that sometimes you have to piece together parts of different letters to get the big picture. Paul focused on faith as the *only* way to salvation, but James states strongly that believing without *doing* something about it is worthless. A lot of experts, even famous ones like Martin Luther, have a hard time with such a major disagreement between two guys who were both really close to Jesus. Who's right? Stay with me here. *Both of them are right*. You just have to put the pieces together. Paul agreed that doing the right thing was important. He told the Ephesians "Do as God does, after all, you are his dear children. Let love be your guide.... Don't let it be said that any of you were immoral or indecent or greedy" (see Ephesians 5:1, 2, 3).

But James didn't argue that we're saved by doing works. He just said that real faith naturally expresses itself in kind acts, and if your faith is true, what you do will show it. Kinda like saying, "If you're gonna talk the talk you better walk the walk." Why are there *way* different spins on how Paul and James put things? A big part of it might been *who* the messages were being given to. James was preaching to a lot of people who talked one way and acted another (sounds like he was preaching at my high school), and Paul knew plenty of people who got so caught up in the rituals and laws of the faith that they thought they were getting saved just by *doing* things the way they were supposed to, without thinking much about *why*. Both extremes are wrong.

REVIEWS

It looks like Paul and James gave the lessons that were right for the different people they were trying to help. I don't see a problem here. We're saved by faith and, when we're saved, it shows in what we do. James *did* start a big hoo-ha by talking about *money*. In those days, a lot of Jews thought that rich people got that way because God was rewarding them. Jesus and His followers saw the truth in what Old Testament prophets like Amos said, who said that the rich often get rich by abusing the poor. James had these words for the rich: "While here on earth, you have thought only of filling your own stomachs and having a good time. But now you are like fat cattle on their way to be butchered. You have condemned and murdered innocent people, who couldn't even fight back" (see 5:5–6). He's not saying having fun is wrong (whew!), and he's not saying that the occasional extra cheese pizza is a bad thing, either. What he *is* saying is that enjoying all the cool stuff you buy and using all your time in the chase for more stuff without using any of your time and money to help other people is wrong. So, do you want a piece of my pizza?

Noah Proffit

1 Peter

Jesus Is Born	Jesus Crucified Pentecost	1 Peter Written	Temple Destroyed	Death of John
7/6 B.C.	A.D. 30	A.D. 64	A.D. 70	A.D. 100

How to smile when you're kicked in the teeth

Ever suffer? Maybe someone picked on you because you had braces. Maybe you had a bad hair day and the whole soccer team pointed and laughed at you. Ever suffer because you believe in Jesus? How did it feel? Like you were being kicked in the teeth?

Suffering is something almost every believer endures. That's the bad news. It gets a little tougher from there. There's a right way to suffer, then there's a better way to suffer. Peter writes this letter to help believers understand the best way to suffer. Peter gives several examples on how to suffer. Suffering believers should respect political authorities. They should live a godly life so they can silence stupid and ignorant people. Peter doesn't say that Christians should go looking for opportunities to be martyrs. But he does tell them that they should feel blessed when they suffer. Peter asks the believers to think of themselves not as victims, but as teachers with a unique opportunity to show others what Christians are really made of—and to follow in the footsteps of Jesus.

QUOTABLES

Do not repay evil for evil (3:9, NRSV).

Love covers over a multitude of sins (4:8, NIV). Apostle Peter says that love helps unite people, because it provides the motivation to forgive over and over.

Cast all your anxiety on him because he cares for you (5:7, NIV). Peter's advice to Christians being persecuted because of their religion.

SNEAK PREVIEW

> Jude
> Somebody thought they could water down God's grace. Not on my watch.

BEHIND the SCENES
of 1 Peter

STARRING ROLE

Peter, leader among the twelve original disciples of Jesus (1:1)

PLOT

Christians in five Roman provinces throughout western Turkey are facing serious persecution because of their belief in Jesus. Romans no longer consider Christianity as a branch of Judaism (a state-approved faith). So Roman authorities begin pushing Christians to accept the Roman gods. Refusing to give in meant death threats, attacks, and even execution.

Peter's aim with this letter is to inspire believers. He reminds them of Christ's sacrifice and what that means for them. They were bought with the price of God's Son. That's the kind of purchase that lasts forever. The apostle then urges Christians to live the righteous life to which God has called them. He says they should respectfully submit to those in authority and be prepared to gently defend the Christian faith.

STAGE DIRECTIONS

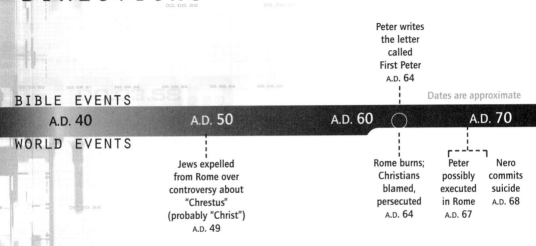

Peter writes
the letter
called
First Peter
A.D. 64

Dates are approximate

BIBLE EVENTS

| A.D. 40 | A.D. 50 | A.D. 60 | | A.D. 70 |

WORLD EVENTS

Jews expelled
from Rome over
controversy about
"Chrestus"
(probably "Christ")
A.D. 49

Rome burns;
Christians
blamed,
persecuted
A.D. 64

Peter
possibly
executed
in Rome
A.D. 67

Nero
commits
suicide
A.D. 68

AUTHOR AND DATE

The apostle Peter wrote this letter. However, it's written in a refined style that wouldn't have been common for a simple fisherman. Peter admits Silvanus helped him write this letter. Peter's words may have been polished by Silvanus, also known as Silas—a Christian who traveled with Paul throughout the Greek-speaking world (see Acts 15:22 for more info on Silvanus).

Peter may have written the letter during outbreaks of persecution in the early 60s. Or he might have written it later, after Nero blamed Christians for torching Rome in A.D. 64.

The A.D. 95 writings of Clement, a church leader in Rome, reflect an awareness of 1 Peter. And Christians writing in the second century, such as Polycarp, quote the book.

INSIDE SCOOP

The Roman Catholic Church considers Peter the first in a long line of church leaders, first called bishops of Rome and later called popes. They base this on what Jesus tells Peter: "I will call you Peter, which means 'a rock.' On this rock I will build my church. . . . I will give you the keys to the kingdom of heaven, and God in heaven will allow whatever you allow on earth" (Matthew 16:18–19).

ON LOCATION

Peter writes to Christians scattered throughout five Roman provinces in western Turkey. It's uncertain where Peter is writing from. He sends greetings from "Babylon" (5:13). This could refer to cities of that name in Iraq or Egypt. But it might be a code name for Jerusalem or Rome. Jews started calling Rome "Babylon" as early as A.D. 70, when Rome destroys Jerusalem. Perhaps they used the nickname even earlier. The Jews associate these two empires because each one is wealthy and evil, and because each one levels Jerusalem and destroys the temple.

WHAT TO LOOK FOR

- **Persecution.** The people Peter writes to are clearly facing persecution for their faith. They've lived what they believe, and, because the political climate is hostile towards believers, these believers are suffering badly. Peter's encouragement is to accept what's happening and still live for God.
- **Submission.** Peter urges suffering believers to submit to political rulers, to masters, to spouses, and to elders. To support his case, Peter appeals to the example of Jesus, who submitted to insults, beating, and death, yet without retaliating in any way.
- **Quotes from the Old Testament.** Peter is especially interested in taking the news of Jesus to his own people, the Jews. To do this, he quotes from Jewish Scripture, known to us today as the Old Testament.

EXTREME SCENE
from 1 Peter

⇒ Tough Obedience (4:12–19)

Christianity begins as a Jewish movement, led by Jews and embraced primarily by Jews. For this reason, Romans treat Christians with the same tolerance as Jews. As time passes, it becomes obvious to everyone that Christianity is more than just another of the many branches or denominations of Judaism. It's a new religion—and it really annoys some people. Romans don't like new religions, and they're convinced that Christianity is just another mysterious cult with secret meetings and possibly disgusting rituals. Communion services, where bread and wine represent the body and blood of Jesus, produce rumors of cannibalism. And the custom of greeting spiritual "brothers" and "sisters" with a kiss generates gossip about incest.

DIRECTOR'S NOTES

Gold is rarely found by itself. Usually it's mined with many other rocks and substances. So how did ancient miners separate the valuable from the worthless? They put everything into a large container and then set the container over a very hot flame. As the rocks heated, the impurities melted and separated from the gold. As the substance cooled, the impurities formed a crust that could be scraped off. The purifying process greatly increased the value of the gold. 1 Peter 1:7

INTERVIEW
with the Stars

Learning from mistakes

We *all* make mistakes; some mistakes are bigger and more critical than others are. But what happens after you make a mistake? Do you try to cover it up, or do you try to learn from it? Do you tend to quit, or do you keep going? *Behind the Bible* will interview a young man who made more than a few mistakes in following Jesus before he got it right. Let's welcome John Mark, or Mark as he is typically referred to. Why don't you tell us a bit about yourself?

⋟ John Mark

I probably was no older than most of your readers when I began hanging around Jesus and His disciples. Those guys were so cool; I just wanted to be with them. But I guess I wasn't really ready for full-fledged discipleship. When the going got tough, I lost it. Literally!

Tell us what you mean by that.

⋟ John Mark

I mentioned it in my Gospel (which I wrote with Peter's help). The night when Jesus was arrested, I got really scared. When the officials started looking for other followers, I took off so fast I literally ran right out of my clothes. It was totally humiliating.

INTERVIEW
with the Stars

Yet, you were chosen to go along with Paul and Barnabas on their first missionary tour.

⇒ John Mark

That's true, but you have to remember that Barnabas was my cousin. And I didn't do much better on my first trip out. It was hard going and I was homesick. Halfway out, I called it quits. The next time Barnabas and Paul were going out, my cousin wanted to give me another chance, but Paul said no way. It caused a split between the two. Barnabas went his own way, and thankfully, I did get that second (or is it third?) chance. Under his guidance and with God's grace, I finally grew up.

Did you ever fix things with Paul?

⇒ John Mark

Eventually. It took a lot of growing up on my part, but eventually Paul realized that I had become a real asset to the cause of Christ. He came to depend on me more and more later in his ministry. Thankfully, because God (and Barnabas!) never gave up on me I was able to make a difference for God.

It's also true, though, that you never gave up despite your mistakes.

⇒ John Mark

Well, no one is immune from making mistakes. But if you're going to follow Jesus, you need to grow through your failures. Believe me, I thought I never would be able to face Paul again after quitting on him. But with God's help and Barnabas's encouragement, I was able to keep going and grow through that experience. Growing in faith is going to take you through a lot of mistakes. The key is to keep getting up by God's grace.

REVIEWS

Peter spent so much time warning people to be meek—even to jerks—that some people think he was a wimp. WRONG! When Peter and John were busted and brought before the Jewish Council (which was kinda like Congress and the Supreme Court all rolled into one), he was ordered to stop preaching Jesus' message.

No dice.

He told them "We cannot keep quiet about what we have seen and heard"(Acts 4:20). Pretty tough words from one guy talking to seventy powerful lawmakers who could make his life miserable. Then, when he was arrested *again*, along with the other apostles, and he was facing a *death sentence, the council* (the same one that was planning to have Jesus executed) asked him why he was ignoring their orders. He kept a respectful tone, but he didn't flinch. He said—get this— "We don't obey people, we obey God." (see Acts 5:21) Did that take some guts or what? When it came to doing what the people in charge said to do, Peter gave right in on most things, but when it came down to a choice between doing what he was told vs. following Jesus, he stuck with Jesus and didn't back down from *anybody*.

Another thing we might have wrong about Peter is his view of women. A lot of his words are considered politically incorrect these days, but they might mean something entirely different than you might think. Peter said men should be "paying honor to the woman as the weaker sex" (1 Peter 3:7, New Revised Standard Version). He could have meant a lot of different things by that. Women were legally weaker than men in those days. In court, women were treated the same as children...no rights. Women were usually weaker physically, too, since the men did almost all the heavy lifting (and there was a lot of heavy lifting going on back then). Mentally, women may have been just as smart, but they usually weren't allowed to go to school, so their "mental muscles" didn't get as much of a chance to "work out." Weak and strong usually refer to power of one kind or another. Men definitely had most of the power back then, so Peter probably wasn't making a judgment about the relative worth of men vs. women. As a matter of fact, he reminds us that men and women are "heirs together of the grace of life" (3:7), which sounds pretty equal to me.

Idono U. Tehlme

➤ Second Peter is a sequel, warning against false teachers in the church.

➤ Some of the themes in 1 Peter seem drawn from Paul's letters to the Ephesians and the Colossians. For example, compare 1:1–3 with Ephesians 1:1–3; 3:1–7 with Ephesians 5:22–31; and 2:18 with Colossians 3:22.

2 Peter

SCHEDULE OF SCENES

Jesus Is Born	Jesus Crucified Pentecost	2 Peter Written	Temple Destroyed	Death of John
7/6 B.C.	A.D. 30	A.D. 65	A.D. 70	A.D. 100

Got Jesus?

For years people have been expecting Jesus to return. Many wait in anticipation, often laying awake at night and hoping that this night will be the one. The moment when Jesus comes to relieve their suffering and redeem their broken lives. Hey, guess what? This isn't a new theme. It's not a new hope. In the first century, believers weren't just looking for Jesus in the clouds, they were expecting Him any day. In fact, for about thirty years or more, apostles and other church leaders had been assuring believers that Jesus was coming back soon.

When He doesn't come back...and doesn't come back...and doesn't come back...people start to ask questions. They start to look for people who have the answers. Smooth-talking spiritual guides arrive on the scene. And, boy howdy...do they have answers! Peter, however, says that what they're full of is nonsense. Like the fraudulent Christians that Jude writes about, these smart-sounding teachers say it's okay for Christians to sin, since Christians have already been forgiven of sin. These teachers practice what they preach. Peter says they're immoral, greedy, and headed for trouble.

So, what's Peter's message? It's simple and direct: Don't give up the faith! Peter reminds them (and us!) that history is filled with examples of how God deals with sin. And as far as the Second Coming is concerned, Peter says that's in God's hands. The Day will come, and Christians should never lose hope of that.

QUOTABLES

The day of the Lord's return will surprise us like a thief (3:10). The second coming of Jesus will be perhaps as surprising as His first coming.

For the Lord one day is the same as a thousand years, and a thousand years is the same as one day (3:8). Peter begins to explain why Jesus has not yet returned.

SNEAK PREVIEW

1 Thessalonians
Forget waiting for the mother ship—Jesus is on the way!

BEHIND the SCENES
of 2 Peter

STARRING ROLE

Peter, leader among the twelve original disciples of Jesus (1:1)

PLOT

Fraudulent Christians teaching a new and distorted gospel. Believers begin listening to these liars. Peter has received word from heaven that he will die soon. So, he writes a short, final letter to warn believers not to get taken in by these false teachers. Peter assures believers that God will punish people who twist the gospel of Jesus Christ into a counterfeit, do-whatever-you-want type of religion. Instead of following these false teachers down the wrong path, Peter says, Christians should follow the example of Jesus and the directions given by the apostles and Paul.

STAGE DIRECTIONS

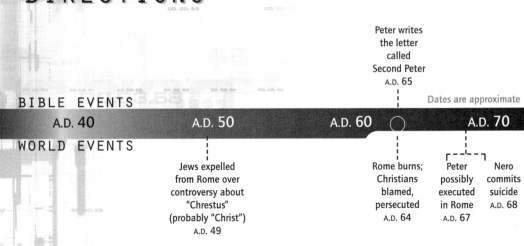

Peter writes
the letter
called
Second Peter
A.D. 65

BIBLE EVENTS — Dates are approximate

A.D. 40   A.D. 50   A.D. 60 ◯   A.D. 70

WORLD EVENTS

Jews expelled
from Rome over
controversy about
"Chrestus"
(probably "Christ")
A.D. 49

Rome burns;
Christians
blamed,
persecuted
A.D. 64

Peter
possibly
executed
in Rome
A.D. 67

Nero
commits
suicide
A.D. 68

AUTHOR AND DATE

The letter is from "Simon Peter, a servant and an apostle of Jesus Christ" (1:1). Scholars began debating whether or not Peter actually wrote this book as early as the second century. They say that it was possibly written by someone else in Peter's name.

Many scholars believe that Peter wrote this just before he died, since he says in the letter that Jesus told him that he's going to die soon (see 1:14). The Bible doesn't say anything about his death, but early Christian writers report that Peter was crucified upside down in Rome during Nero's persecution of Christians (A.D. 64–68). If the letter was written by someone other than Peter, scholars say it would have been written around A.D. 100 to 150.

INSIDE SCOOP

ON LOCATION

The letter doesn't identify where it was written, or to whom. Peter does say this is his second letter. He may be writing to the same people as he did in 1 Peter: churches in five Roman provinces throughout western Turkey.

WHAT TO LOOK FOR

- **Warnings about false teachers.** This is the primary motive behind the letter. As he's about to die, Peter sends an urgent message to the Christian community that has been invaded by heretical teachers (Read his message in 2:1, 3, 13–14).
- **The big delay.** After waiting several decades for Jesus to return, some believers are starting to wonder if He's ever coming back. Fraudulent teachers apparently capitalize on this impatience and start convincing people that Jesus is not returning. Peter goes to great lengths to explain why Jesus hasn't returned yet. He encourages believer to sit tight, live right, and wait patiently.

EXTREME SCENE from 2 Peter

Opportunists in the church (2:1–22)

Peter writes an open letter to all Christians revealing that he's going to die soon. So, this letter serves as his final words about the life of the believer. What you're reading are his deep desires: that Christians will continue growing in the faith (chapter 1), that they will reject false teachers (chapter 2), and that they will live in patient anticipation of the Second Coming (chapter 3).

Peter's really concerned with the false teachers that have made moves on believers. They were teaching that since Jesus had delayed so long, He obviously wasn't coming back. They're also teaching that there will be no Judgment Day and that Christians can live anyway they please, as long as they profess Jesus as Savior. This is really, really wrong. And Peter sets them straight on it.

DIRECTOR'S NOTES

You can't imagine how important water was to the people of the ancient Near East. Their entire economy depended on successful crops, which, in turn, depended on sufficient rainfall. During the summer months, rain was virtually nonexistent. People had to rely on well water to nourish their crops. Drought wasn't the only problem ancient farmers faced in the summer, though. Windstorms that produced violent and destructive whirlwinds were also an occupational hazard. 2 Peter 2:17

REVIEWS

ENCORE

⟩ Jude has interesting parallels to 2 Peter. Compare Jude 4–13, 16–18 with 2 Peter 2:1–17 and 3:1–3.

⟩ For other warnings about false teachers, review Colossians, 1 Timothy, and Titus.

Peter's second letter reads a lot like an episode of "Wanted," one of those shows that hunts down criminals at large.

If you've read much of Paul's writings, you might recognize a villain or two when you read Peter's. The fake Christian teachers that Peter writes about sound like some of the same fakes Paul ran across. Peter's advice for dealing with the religious frauds is on target with what Paul said as well.

Peter writes that these teachers profess to know Christ, but they live immoral lives and take advantage of others (2:13–14). Paul, writing the heresy-plagued church of Colossae, warns believers about the same kinds of things (Colossians 3:5).

Peter and Paul also teamed up on their standards for true teaching. They said any and all teachings about Christianity need to be measured against the original teachings of Jesus and the apostles. If new teachings don't measure up, they are false. "You must remember what the apostles told you our Lord and Savior has commanded us to do," Peter wrote (3:2). Teachings that contradict what Christ taught, Peter said, were nothing but "stupid nonsense" (2:18). This advice is just as good today as it was back then. Somebody is always trying to "cash in" on Jesus, for money or power or both. Keeping in touch with Him on a personal level and studying what He said and did is a great way to keep from getting fooled by these guys.

Most people agree that Peter and Paul knew what they were talking about when it came to heresy. There's some disagreement on something else, though. Even though the first verse of this letter says that it's from Peter, some people don't believe that Peter wrote it. They say it's a different style of language. Men like Origen (185–253) and Eusebius (265–340) wondered way back when whether Peter actually wrote the book. On the other hand, Bishop Clement of Rome refers to Peter's second letter.

Remember when Peter said in his first letter that he had help writing it? (1 Peter 5:12). That could account for the difference in style. Also, by the time Peter wrote this second letter, near the end of his life, some of Paul's letters would have been in circulation for ten years or more, and were becoming known as the real deal. Peter could have been influenced by his friend's style.

Peter D. Khopikat

1 John

SCHEDULE OF SCENES

Jesus Is Born — 7/6 B.C.

Jesus Crucified Pentecost — A.D. 30

Temple Destroyed — A.D. 70

1 John Written — A.D. 90

Death of John — A.D. 100

Battling warped teachings about Jesus

Before you read this book...answer this one question: What is truth? Take a minute or so to answer this. Whadya think? How would you answer that?

It's a tough question. Remember Jesus? He was asked that question all the time in one way or another. And, every time He was asked, He had an incredibly simple, easy-to-understand comeback to that all-important but supertough question. It's true...while Jesus walked the earth, understanding what was true seemed a little easier. But now, more than fifty years later, Christians started having trouble recognizing the truth. They didn't seem sure about who Jesus was and what exactly He taught.

What was the problem? Some Christians started adding to the Good News, trying to make it better. Guess what happened? They made it worse. For example, by the time the apostle John had become an old man, someone came up with the idea that Jesus was just a spirit who only looked human. A new religious movement started because of this belief, and churches split over the issue.

John steps into the battle for truth in this letter (okay, it was actually a sermon first) that points Christians back to the basics. He leads them back to Jesus' original teachings about what to believe, how to behave, and how to know they are true children of God. John also reminds the Christians that they have the added benefit of the Holy Spirit, who teaches from the inside out. John takes on truth in a time when the search for truth became more fun than actually finding it.

QUOTABLES

If we confess our sins, he is faithful and just to forgive us our sins, and to cleanse us from all unrighteousness (1:9, KJV).

SNEAK PREVIEW

Zechariah
Sometimes the way you keep house reflects the way you keep spirit.

BEHIND the SCENES
of 1 John

STARRING ROLES

Jesus, God's Son who has come to earth in human form to offer eternal life to everyone who believes in Him (1:3)

John, one of the twelve original disciples of Jesus, and probably the author of this letter along, with 2 and 3 John, the Gospel of John, and Revelation

PLOT

The church is in trouble. They split over a silly issue about whether Jesus was really human or just a spirit. These unorthodox Christians say that everything physical is flawed and evil, including the human body. They teach that God, on the other hand, is completely spiritual and good. They went on to argue that the Crucifixion plays no role in salvation, since the Son of God was not really killed. Salvation, they explain, comes from secret knowledge about how to transcend the body. This secret knowledge, apparently expressed in rituals and words, eventually gives the religious movement its name: Gnosticism, from *gnosis,* the Greek word for knowledge.

STAGE DIRECTIONS

| Jesus crucified A.D. 30 | First John written A.D. 90 | John writes Revelation from exile on Patmos island A.D. 95 |

BIBLE EVENTS

A.D. 30   A.D. 40   A.D. 50   A.D. 60   A.D. 70   A.D. 80   A.D. 90   A.D. 100

WORLD EVENTS

Dates are approximate

| Pilate begins 10-year rule as Judean governor A.D. 26 | Mount Vesuvius destroys Pompeii, Italy A.D. 79 | Emperor Domitian, persecutor of Christians, begins 15-year reign A.D. 81 | Paper invented in China A.D. 103 |

AUTHOR AND DATE

Whoever wrote this book doesn't identify himself. However, the themes and the style of writing (simple Greek) are similar to those of John's Gospel. Early Christian writers from at least the second century have attributed both books to the apostle John, a fisherman, and one of Jesus' closest disciples. John may also have been a first cousin of Jesus.

It's uncertain when the book was written. Christian leaders in the second century said John wrote it in Ephesus late in the first century, roughly A.D. 90 or maybe later.

ON LOCATION

John likely wrote during his old age, while living in Ephesus. The first documented use of the letter is in Ephesus.

INSIDE SCOOP

As Jesus hung on the cross, He entrusted His elderly mother to the care of an unnamed disciple He loved deeply. Since at least the second century, Christian writers have identified this disciple as John.

Jesus nicknamed John and his brother James the "sons of thunder," apparently because of their fiery temperaments. True to his nickname, John boldly calls professing Christians "liars" if they teach anything contrary to the original message about Jesus.

WHAT TO LOOK FOR

- **Antichrists.** John talks about people who are enemies of Christ and who come from the church. These former church members have left and formed their own congregation based on ideas blended from a variety of religions, and are trying to lure new members from the church.
- **Opposites.** Notice the contrasting figures of speech that are identical to those used in John's Gospel: truth vs. lies, love vs. hate, light vs. darkness, life vs. death.
- **A sermon.** First John reads more like a sermon or an essay than a letter. Many scholars suggest John wrote this message to deal with a regional problem, and that these words become a circular letter read aloud in many churches.

EXTREME SCENE
from 1 John

Jesus really had skin? (4:1–6)

Even though Jesus hadn't been gone that long, Christians are becoming increasingly confused about who He is and why He came. Some are starting to add to their beliefs with teachings from other religions and philosophies. They even went way outside the Christian beliefs to popular Greek philosophers who taught that divinity is a mysterious ideal that is both invisible and eternal—not physical and temporal—some Christians conclude that Jesus could not have been human. He was a spirit, they argue, who only looked human. This has serious effects on the church. It doesn't know what to believe. John does his best to set them straight.

DIRECTOR'S NOTES

Christ is not Jesus' last name. It's from the Greek translation of the Hebrew word for "Messiah" or "Anointed One." In Old Testament times, kings, priests, and prophets were all anointed, which means they had olive oil poured on their heads to show that they were specially chosen by God. The Jews of Jesus' day believed that the Messiah would become their king and free them from the control of the Roman Empire. Jesus, however, came as a spiritual leader who freed the world from the effects of sin. 1 John 5:1

REVIEWS

ENCORE

For more of John's writings dealing with similar religious issues, read 2 and 3 John, along with John's Gospel.

The early church leaders said John wrote these letters from Ephesus, during the final years of his life. This region, in what is now western Turkey, was a stew of different cultures and religions—an ideal location for mixing new batches of creatively blended religions, like those described in the Gospel and the letters bearing John's name. Maybe that was why John got so good at cutting to the chase. For him, the bottom line of Christianity was love, God's love shown to people, then people showing God's love to each other. John felt quite urgent about it.

"Children, this is the last hour," John wrote (2:18 NIV). That was about 17 million hours ago, give or take a few. Was his watch broken? There's another way of seeing it. Check it out.

"The last hour" is a phrase, like "the last days." It means more than the months or years just before the Second Coming. It also means "the age of the Messiah," which came into full swing with the death and resurrection of Jesus (for some of us "the last hour" is the time we finally start studying for a big test). This phrase is like one that John uses a whole bunch in his Gospel when he's talking about the Crucifixion. When Jesus realized it was nearly time for Him to fulfill the reason He came to earth—to die for *us*—He said "the time has come" (John 17:1 NIV).

"The last hour" can refer to events *immediately* before the Second Coming, but it also means the beginning of the final phase of God's long-term plan to save the world from sin. In 2:18, John is probably using the second meaning. Either way, it's getting closer every day.

Johnny Harbinger

2 John

Jesus Is Born	Jesus Crucified Pentecost		Temple Destroyed	2 John Written	Death of John
7/6 B.C.	A.D. 30		A.D. 70	A.D. 90	A.D. 100

Note to heretics: GET OUT!

If you checked out 1 John, you already know that the church was in trouble. They began adopting false teachings into the church. This book reads a lot like a P.S. to 1 John.

The apostle John boils down his five-chapter message of his first letter into a mere thirteen verses. In addition to repeating and abbreviating his warning against false teachers who argue that Jesus was not human, John adds that Christians should not show hospitality to these teachers. In Bible times, Christians aren't the only ones traveling around the land and preaching. So are fake-Christian evangelists, trying to spread the word that spiritual things are good and physical things are evil, and that because of this, Jesus was a spirit who only looked human. It was customary in early Christian days for believers to invite into their homes any traveling evangelists, and to later send them on their way with provisions for the trip. So, these evangelists aren't just making it into churches . . . they're in the homes of believers. The problem was really getting bad.

John warns church members not to support these people. He says if people don't preach the genuine story of Jesus, don't let them in. Period.

QUOTABLES

Love each other (1:5).

BEHIND the SCENES
of 2 John

STARRING ROLES

The church leader, identified in many translations as "the Elder," probably the apostle John, one of Jesus' twelve original disciples (verse 1)
A very special woman and her children, probably a figure of speech for the church and its members (verse 1)

PLOT

John had a soft spot in his heart for an unnamed church that he identifies only as "a very special woman and her children" (verse 1). So he writes a special letter to this congregation, repeating some of what he has said in 1 John. Then he adds a warning against showing hospitality to traveling evangelists who teach false doctrines. This letter is a little different from 1 John. First John doesn't have an introduction or conclusion...this book does.

AUTHOR AND DATE

The writing style, ideas, and testimony of Christian leaders in the second century indicate the writer was the apostle John. This close disciple of Jesus was also probably author of 1 and 3 John, along with the Gospel of John and Revelation.

No one's for sure when 2 John was written. Christian leaders in the second century said John wrote it in Ephesus late in the first century, roughly A.D. 90 or perhaps later.

INTERVIEW
with the Stars

A love transformation

Behind the Bible's next subject started out a fisherman. But under God's transforming love, he became a fisher of men. John, perhaps one of the most well-known disciples, was able to change the lives of many because God first changed his life. He probably was the youngest of the disciples. He lived the longest, and he contributed five books to the New Testament. But perhaps John's greatest contribution was the message he has passed down through the years. John, why don't you tell us about that?

⋛ John the Apostle

I'd be glad to. As you mentioned, my brother James and I were simple fishermen. But when Jesus came along and gave us the opportunity to join His team, it was a no-brainer. We dropped our nets and went with Jesus, looking for bigger fish. I spent three years with Jesus. I was there at the cross when He died. I was one of the first to see Him after the Resurrection. I soaked in all that Jesus said, all that He did, how He lived. If that wasn't enough, I was given a great privilege.

And that was?

⋛ John the Apostle

To be able to write about God's love. In all five of my books, you'll find this theme running through it: God's love. I experienced it firsthand; I was transformed by it; and my goal in writing about it was to convince my readers about the truth of Jesus and to help them experience, through Jesus, God's love for them.

INTERVIEW
with the Stars

Certainly, these words written by you have changed hundreds of thousands of lives over the centuries: *For God so loved the world that He gave His only begotten Son, that whoever believes in Him should not perish but have everlasting life* (John 3:16). What more could you say to our readers today?

⇒ John the Apostle

The message hasn't changed, but what *is* important is how it is received. Everyone who reads that verse needs to make it his or her own. Have you truly realized how far God's love went in sending Jesus to earth? Have you really believed that the gift was for you? Have you accepted forgiveness and eternal life from Him? How you answer those questions can make a huge difference in your life—just as it did in my life.

Thank you, John, for your time. The only thing we can add is to encourage those who find and experience God's love through Jesus, like John, to offer that difference-making message to others. It's love that lasts a lifetime—and beyond.

3 John

SCHEDULE OF SCENES

Jesus Is Born	Jesus Crucified Pentecost		Temple Destroyed	3 John Written	Death of John
7/6 B.C.	A.D. 30		A.D. 70	A.D. 91	A.D. 100

Be excellent to each other

Here's what you'd think. You'd think that in the beginning years of Christianity believers were really super-nice to each other. You'd think they sat around drinking tea and chatting about how much they loved each other. Well, guess what? It didn't quite happen that way. Evil people with false teachings and void of godly love had infiltrated the church. These evil people worshiped two things only: power and prestige.

So, what does John do? He writes a letter filled with quick advice for believers struggling with the issue. John's advice to believers is to keep doing what they know God wants them to do: Obey the truth, love others, and support those spreading the gospel, regardless of the risk.

This is a really personal letter. Unlike John's other letters this one's addressed to a specific person—Gaius. He congratulates Gaius for obeying the true teachings about Jesus, and especially for showing hospitality to Christian missionaries.

QUOTABLES

Follow the example of people who do kind deeds (11).

BEHIND the SCENES
of 3 John

STARRING ROLES

The apostle John, one of Jesus' twelve original disciples (verse 1)
Gaius, a Christian commended for showing kindness and hospitality to Christian travelers (verse 1)
Diotrephes, a dictatorial church leader who abuses his authority by excommunicating those who disagree with his policy of refusing to welcome Christian travelers (verse 9).

PLOT

In the early years of Christianity, the organization is loose; local churches are guided by letters and representatives sent from leaders scattered around the Roman Empire. In one church, a minister named Diotrephes has risen to power...and he likes it. He refuses to respect the authority of the apostle John, and even spreads rumors about him. When John writes to this church, Diotrephes refuses to read the letters in public. And when John sends representatives, Diotrephes refuses to welcome them. This guy's got a real attitude problem. John's out to encourage Gaius (a member of the church) and to promise that he'll meet with Diotrephes when he gets there.

AUTHOR AND DATE

The writing style, ideas, and testimony of Christian leaders in the second century indicate the writer was the apostle John, who also likely wrote 1 and 2 John, along with the Gospel of John and Revelation.
It's uncertain when 3 John was written. Christian leaders in the second century said John wrote it in Ephesus late in the first century, roughly A.D. 90 or perhaps later.

Jude

SCHEDULE OF SCENES

Jesus Is Born	Jesus Crucified Pentecost		Jude Written	Temple Destroyed	Death of John
7/6 B.C.	A.D. 30		A.D. 65	A.D. 70	A.D. 100

Put up yer dukes, buddy!

It's a classic tale. Christians (called "Followers of the Way" in the first century) often met with people who shortcutted their beliefs. They encountered people who said they had found an easier...shorter...better way to heaven. Almost like a loophole. What was it? Well, since Jesus had forgiven people of their sins, sin didn't matter anymore. Since they are forgiven, they can sin all they want. And God's grace is greater than their sins. So, sin was just no problemo. See? Classic. God has His way...creative shortcutter types create a way that *looks* like God's way, but it really isn't.

Hey, look, there's a place for creativity in the kingdom of God, but this is a bit much. Jude knows that professing Christians who are carriers of a light view of sin can infect and destroy an entire congregation.

Sin is serious business. As long as there are followers of the Shortcut, preaching the gospel of the Loophole, Jude says there needs to be knowledgeable Christians who can point to examples in Scripture. Jude encourages believers to put up their lives and defend their beliefs by the way they live.

QUOTABLES

To him who is able to keep you from falling and to present you before his glorious presence without fault and with great joy—to the only God our Savior be glory, majesty, power and authority, through Jesus Christ our Lord, before all ages, now and forevermore! Amen (24–25, New International Version). The benediction of Jude's letter.

SNEAK PREVIEW

2 Chronicles
From Solomon to Babylon. The spiritual path of a nation from kingdom to chaos.

BEHIND the SCENES
of Jude

STARRING ROLE

Jude, author of this letter, and possibly a brother of Jesus (verse 1)

PLOT

Jude writes a forceful letter warning believers about Christian imposters who have infiltrated the congregation and who are rising to positions of leadership. These people teach that immorality is okay. They're selfish, filthy-minded, and shameful. Jude shows that God punishes sin. He reminds them about Sodom and Gomorrah. And he strongly encourages true believers to take a stand for what they know is right.

AUTHOR AND DATE

The writer is "Jude, a servant of Jesus Christ, and brother of James." Many scholars believe Jude is also the brother of Jesus. They believe this because "Jude" is a form of the Hebrew name Judah, which is Judas in Greek. Jesus had brothers named Judas and James (Matthew 13:55). James rose to leadership within the Jerusalem, which may be why Jude identified himself as the brother of James.

It's not very easy to identify when this letter was written. It could have been written during the lifetime of Jesus' brothers. Paul addressed some of the same issues within about thirty years of the Crucifixion. Jude could have addressed his letter either to Jewish Christians or Gentile Christians. He makes a lot of references to Jewish Scriptures and legends that Jewish Christians would have found convincing.

Revelation

SCHEDULE OF SCENES

Jesus Is Born	Jesus Crucified / Pentecost	Paul's Missionary Journeys Begin	Temple Destroyed	Revelation Written	Death of John
7/6 B.C.	A.D. 30	A.D. 46	A.D. 70	A.D. 95	A.D. 100

The end?

This is one book of the Bible you want to stay away from. It's too bizarre. It's totally hard to understand. Its images will keep you awake, or give you nightmares. Okay, that's at least what some people believe about this book.

It's true—this one's a doozie. But that's no reason to avoid it. This book is often avoided because it carries with it undocumented fear. In other words, people are fearful of reading it, but they have no idea why. What you've got here is one misunderstood book. So, when you read Revelation, just what are you reading?

This closing book of the Bible is an encrypted message written especially for persecuted Christians near the end of the first century. Those believers have the key to interpret much of what John says. We have only part of their ancient insight into the dramatic symbols John uses. But this is more than enough to decode the main message: Satan Loses. God Wins. And, hey . . . if you know God, you win too! And for those who win with God, there's an unbelievable reward . . . Paradise. Heaven. Mansions. Eternity with God.

QUOTABLES

I am the Alpha and the Omega, the Beginning and the End (1:8, NKJV). Alpha and Omega are the first and last letters of the Greek alphabet.

God will wipe all tears from their eyes (7:17). Figurative language to describe the absence of sorrow in God's heavenly kingdom.

I saw a new heaven and a new earth (21:1, NKJV). In a vision, John sees God restore creation to the paradise it was before sin entered.

SNEAK PREVIEW

1, 2, 3 John
No matter what you look behind, love's there waiting.

BEHIND the SCENES
of Revelation

STARRING ROLES

John, author of the book, who describes his captivating visions of the future; possibly one of Jesus' twelve original disciples (1:1)

Jesus, Son of God, who returns to earth to judge all people and to take His followers to heaven (1:1)

PLOT

John has been exiled to a small and rocky island for refusing to worship the Roman emperor as god. While he's there, John experiences a long series of strange visions. Some visions are bizarre—even horrifying. Others are beautiful and deeply comforting. But all of them prove to John that his faith is real, and that no matter what Rome or any other power tries to do to God's church, the Lord and His people will prevail. John describes his visions in dramatic and disturbing detail. He speaks of international chaos, God's people martyred, world-shattering catastrophes, and cosmic upheavals. In the end, humanity and the world cease to exist. When everything's wiped out, God restores paradise. Human beings become spirit beings and enjoy God's new creation for the rest of eternity.

STAGE DIRECTIONS

BIBLE EVENTS

Paul and Peter executed in Rome
A.D. 67

John writes Revelation from exile on Patmos Island
A.D. 95

Dates are approximate

| A.D. 60 | A.D. 70 | A.D. 80 | A.D. 90 |

WORLD EVENTS

Rome burns; Nero blames Christians, launches persecution
A.D. 64

Rome destroys Jerusalem and temple
A.D. 70

Emperor Domitian assassinated, ending his persecution of Christians
A.D. 96

AUTHOR AND DATE

Here's a dilemma. The writer identifies himself as John, but which John is it? Christian writer Justin Martyr (about A.D. 100–165) is the first person on record to identify the author as the apostle John, one of the closest disciples of Jesus, and author of the Gospel of John and the three letters of John. About 100 years later, other Christians began to challenge this. Dionysius, a theologian from Alexandria, Egypt, said the writing style is not at all like the other works of the apostle John. However, the frequent references to the Old Testament and the style of the Greek that the writer used suggest he was a Jew from Israel. So, who knows?

John may have written this masterpiece of mystery during the Christian persecutions late in the reign of Nero, in the mid-60s. But most scholars date the book to the final years of Emperor Domitian, who was assassinated in A.D. 96. Late in his reign, Domitian forced his subjects to address him as "Lord and God." Those who refused were harshly punished. Many Christians were exiled or executed.

INSIDE
SCOOP

> Armageddon, the place where Revelation says the final battle between good and evil will take place, is a huge valley plain in northern Israel (16:16). Over the past 4,000 years there have been no less than 22 invasions into this valley. In John's time, Armageddon (Hebrew for "mountain of Megiddo") was already a name synonymous with war.

ON LOCATION

John writes from fifty miles offshore of western Turkey, on the rocky island of Patmos (a really small island...about ten miles long and five miles wide.) His book is addressed to churches in seven cities near the coast of western Turkey. The visions that John writes about involve the entire planet. He says the last battle between good and evil will take place in the Valley of Armageddon, known today as Megiddo, and that God will make a New Jerusalem. Since the book is apocalyptic and uses a lot of symbolism, scholars debate whether John had any of these actual sites in mind.

WHAT TO LOOK FOR

- **Apocalypse…A strange way of writing.** The unique style of writing in Revelation is called apocalyptic, from the Greek word *apocalypsis,* which means "reveal." That's where the book gets its name. This is a strange writing style. It's often very difficult to understand. Even though the promises are real, it kind of gets to them through strange visions and stuff that John sees. Why does John use this style? One reason is to prevent government authorities from deciphering the message. The Roman emperor wouldn't think it was too cool to hear that someone was going to destroy both him and his empire. There's a code in this book, too. And some of that code is revealed in this book. For example: stars are angels and lampstands are churches (1:20). The heavenly Jerusalem is the Church, the bride of Jesus (21:9–10; compare with Ephesians 5:25–32).

- **Numbers.** To secretly communicate his message, John uses all kinds of numbers. Here are some of the numbers he uses.
  - Seven. One of John's favorite numbers is seven, which he uses more than fifty times. He talks about seven churches, seven spirits, seven golden lampstands, seven stars, seven seals, seven trumpets—whew! Lots of sevens! Seven's an important number. It symbolizes completion; it was on the seventh day that God rested after finishing Creation. So when John writes these seven churches and uses the number seven, he and his readers may have understood that he was addressing the entire Christian church. In fact, the church today still looks to these letters for guidance.
  - 144,000. This number, which appears in Revelation 7:4, may be another one that symbolizes completeness. In Revelation it could mean "all God's people." John shows that this number comes from the twelve tribes of Israel: twelve times twelve, with multiplied thousands—suggesting the New Israel, which is the entire assembly of God's people.
  - 666. Known as the Mark of the Beast, 666 is likely a coded reference to Nero—Rome's most vicious persecutor of Christians. John tells readers that they need wisdom and understanding to figure this one out. Is that John hinting that this is Nero?
  - Hebrew and Greek letters have numeric equivalents. When the numbers that spell the Hebrew name of Nero Caesar are combined, the total is 666. Ohhhh. Freaky, huh?!

- **Connections to the Old Testament.** Revelation is full of allusions to the Old Testament. Nearly 300 of the approximately 400 verses have some connection to the Old Testament. Want some examples? Compare Revelation 4:1–8 with Ezekiel 1 and Isaiah 6:3, or, compare Revelation 8:7 with Exodus 9:22–26.

EXTREME SCENES from Revelation

→ John goes dreaming (4:1–5:14)

John's stuck on the tiny island of Patmos because he refused to worship the emperor as god. Believe it or not, that's good news. Other people were being killed for doing what John did. While he's there, John begins to have visions. First, he has visions about seven churches. Then, he has a vision where he's standing at God's throne. There are others there who are continually praising God. Suddenly, John sees God holding a scroll locked with seven seals. Among all the beings in the heavenly court, only Jesus can break the seals. As Jesus breaks each one, John experiences a new vision—including terrifying scenes of the four horsemen of the Apocalypse, who represent conquest, war, famine, and lethal disease. Silence falls as Jesus breaks the seventh seal. Suddenly, seven trumpets blast, one after another, each one heralding destruction, persecution, martyrdom, or God's punishment for humanity's evil.

DIRECTOR'S NOTES

The Roman emperor Domitian wasn't exactly what you would call a friend of Christianity. As far as he was concerned, Christianity was an illegal religion, and those who practiced it were asking for persecution. Tradition has it that the apostle John was sentenced to live on the island of Patmos for eighteen months because he refused to stop preaching about Jesus. Don't assume that island life on Patmos was easy, either. People sentenced to the small, rocky island (about thirty-five miles off the coast of what is now Turkey) were forced to work in mines and quarries. Revelation 1:9

→ A king and his horse (19:11–20:11)

The vision goes on, and things get even more terrifying. John sees two hideous monsters born of Satan. Some scholars believe this is supposed to be the Roman Empire, or perhaps humanity's evil. Others see in them the Antichrist, assisted by a satanic prophet who performs miracles that convince humanity to worship the Antichrist.

After seeing all this tragedy, John witnesses a glorious sight: a rider on a white horse, preparing to lead the army of heaven into battle against all the forces of evil. The rider wears a robe engraved with his title: KING OF KINGS AND LORD OF LORDS. The rider is Jesus Christ, coming as the warrior King that the Jews expected to see in their Messiah. A battle breaks out. Jesus wins. The two beasts and Satan are condemned to eternal torment.

⇒ You ready? (20:11–15)

The battle is over...things are about to get really good. Next, John sees the end of human history. He sees Judgment Day. He sees a white throne, and people standing before it being judged. For each person, the Book of Life is opened, and people are judged according to what they have done in life. The judge is Jesus.

⇒ Better than Christmas! (21:1–22:6)

When it's all over and the dust has settled, God's grand scheme is finally completed. Since history began, When Adam and Eve messed up bigtime and ruined God's creation with sin, God has been working to remove all the traces of sin. After all of these happenings listed in Revelation, John sees a new heaven and earth. God loudly proclaims that He's the Alpha and Omega...the Beginning and the End. And, with this, God and His people settle in for an eternity. Evil is gone. Beauty, tenderness, and joy fill the new heaven and earth. Humanity is finally back where it belongs.

DIRECTOR'S NOTES

Brimstone is another name for sulfur, a fast-burning, disgusting-smelling rock. Ancient armies sometimes used burning sulfur as ammunition in their catapults, launching it over city walls to set buildings on fire inside.
Revelation 14:10

Linen, which was handwoven from the fibers of the hemp plant, was considered to be the highest-quality fabric in the ancient world. For the most part, only people of great wealth or power wore linen. Priests and those who served in the temple were the exception. They, too, wore linen. Throughout the Bible, white linen symbolizes purity.
Revelation 19:8

⇒ The greatest promise ever (22:7-20)

To all of this, Jesus adds His closing comments. His words are simple."I am coming soon!" Jesus tells John. He invites the thirsty to come and drink. And, to Jesus' passionate plea John has an equally passionate response. Yes, Jesus...please come soon.

REVIEWS

ENCORE

➤ For other apocalyptic writings in the Bible, read Isaiah 24–27; Ezekiel 38–39; Daniel 7–12; Joel 2; Zechariah 9–14; Matthew 24; Mark 13; Luke 12.

OK, forget every scary movie you've ever seen and every Stephen King book you're ever read.

In Revelation, John talk about eternal punishment and describes hell. The whole tone of this book makes the hair on my arms stand up. Punishment for doing wrong is something most people seem to understand and accept. But eternal torture in a lake of burning sulfur is quite another thing—especially if the Judge delivering this sentence is God, whom the Bible describes as the essence of love (1 John 4:8).

The hard part of describing God's end-time punishment for sinners is that, as people, we only know the things of this world, so the Bible uses things from this world to describe what will take place in an entirely different dimension. John says Satan and his followers will be thrown into "a lake of burning sulphur" (Revelation 19:20) where they will suffer "in pain day and night forever and ever" (20:10, see also 20:15). Jesus confirmed that sinners are "in danger of the fires of hell" (Matthew 5:22), a place outside of the kingdom of God where people "cry and grit their teeth in pain" (Matthew 8:12). Jesus also describes this as a place of darkness (Matthew 8:12).

What exactly is that place of fire and darkness, which the Bible sometimes calls hell?

Y'know what? I don't even *want* to know. I figure that God, being all-knowing, can think up punishments I can't even imagine (and I can imagine some *scary* stuff). From beginning to end, the Bible is clear that people will suffer the consequences of their choices. God honors their decision to accept or reject Him, His love, and His rescue from sin and judgment. But exactly how those who reject Him will suffer remains in the hands of God.

Forget about *I Know What You Did Last Summer.* God knows what you did during your whole *life*. He even knows things you didn't do, but thought about. He knows what you have done in your heart. How this "scary movie" ends up is for each person to decide for themselves. I think I'd really, REALLY like to spend eternity in heaven. Anyone else?

Aliah Agag

30 Days with Jesus

1. John 1:1-51	11. Mark 8:1-38	21. Luke 18:1-43
2. Luke 2:1-52	12. Luke 10:1-42	22. John 9:1-41
3. Mark 1:1-11	13. Matthew 5:1-48	23. Luke 19:1-48
4. Luke 4:1-44	14. Matthew 6:1-34	24. Luke 20:1-47
5. John 3:1-36	15. Matthew 7:1–29	25. John 10:1-42
6. Luke 5:1-39	16. Luke 14:1-35	26. John 11:1-57
7. John 4:1-54	17. Luke 15:1-32	27. Mark 13:1-37
8. Luke 6:1-49	18. Luke 16:1-31	28. Luke 22:1-71
9. Luke 7:1-50	19. John 8:1-59	29. Matthew 27:1-66
10. Luke 8:1-56	20. Luke 17:1-37	30. Luke 24:1-53

60 Days with Paul

1. Romans 1:16-32	21. 1 Corinthians 15:1-28	41. Philippians 4:10-23
2. Romans 2:1-16	22. 2 Corinthians 1:3-14	42. Colossians 1:13-23
3. Romans 3:21-31	23. 2 Corinthians 1:15—2:11	43. Colossians 2:6-23
4. Romans 4:1-25	24. 2 Corinthians 4:1-18	44. Colossians 3:1-17
5. Romans 5:12-21	25. 2 Corinthians 5:1—6:2	45. Colossians 3:18—4:6
6. Romans 6:1-23	26. 2 Corinthians 6:14—7:1	46. 1 Thessalonians 1:1-10
7. Romans 7:1-25	27. 2 Corinthians 8:1-15	47. 1 Thessalonians 4:1-18
8. Romans 8:18-39	28. Galatians 2:11-21	48. 1 Thessalonians 5:1-28
9. Romans 10:1-21	29. Galatians 3:19—4:7	49. 2 Thessalonians 2:1-17
10. Romans 12:1-21	30. Galatians 5:1-26	50. 2 Thessalonians 3:1-15
11. Romans 13:1-14	31. Galatians 6:1-10	51. 1 Timothy 2:1-15
12. Romans 14:1—15:6	32. Ephesians 1:3-14	52. 1 Timothy 3:1-16
13. 1 Corinthians 1:10-31	33. Ephesians 1:15—2:10	53. 1 Timothy 4:1-12
14. 1 Corinthians 2:1-16	34. Ephesians 5:1-21	54. 1 Timothy 5:1-22
15. 1 Corinthians 3:1-23	35. Ephesians 5:22—6:9	55. 1 Timothy 6:3-21
16. 1 Corinthians 7:1-24	36. Ephesians 6:10-20	56. 2 Timothy 1:3-18
17. 1 Corinthians 7:25-40	37. Philippians 1:3-26	57. 2 Timothy 2:1—3:9
18. 1 Corinthians 9:19—10:13	38. Philippians 1:27—2:18	58. 2 Timothy 4:1-8
19. 1 Corinthians 12:1-31	39. Philippians 3:1-16	59. Titus 1:1—16
20. 1 Corinthians 13:1-13	40. Philippians 3:17—4:9	60. Titus 2:1—3:11

90 Day Overview of the Bible

1. Genesis 1:1—2:3
2. Genesis 3:1—3:24
3. Genesis 6:9—7:24
4. Genesis 8:1—9:17
5. Genesis 17:1-22
6. Genesis 22:1-19
7. Genesis 25:19-34
8. Genesis 27:1—28:9
9. Genesis 37:1-36
10. Genesis 41:1-57
11. Genesis 45:1-28
12. Exodus 1:8—2:15
13. Exodus 3:1—4:17
14. Exodus 5:1—6:13
15. Exodus 12:1-42
16. Exodus 13:17—14:31
17. Exodus 20:1-21
18. Numbers 13:1-33
19. Joshua 2:1-24
20. Joshua 6:1-27
21. Judges 16:4-31
22. 1 Samuel 1:1-28
23. 1 Samuel 3:1-21
24. 1 Samuel 10:1-27
25. 1 Samuel 16:1-13
26. 1 Samuel 17:1-58
27. 1 Samuel 24:1-22
28. 2 Samuel 11:1—12:25
29. 1 Kings 3:1-28
30. 1 Kings 17:8-24

31. 1 Kings 18:1-46
32. 2 Kings 2:1-18
33. 2 Kings 4:8-37
34. 2 Chronicles 35:20—36:23
35. Esther 2:1-23
36. Esther 6:1—8:8
37. Job 1:1—2:13; 42:1-17
38. Psalm 23
39. Psalm 51
40. Psalm 100
41. Psalm 121
42. Psalm 145
43. Proverbs 4:1-27
44. Ecclesiastes 11:9—12:14
45. Isaiah 53:1-12
46. Daniel 1:1-21
47. Daniel 3:1-30
48. Daniel 6:1-28
49. Jonah 1:1—4:11
50. Matthew 1:18—2:23
51. Matthew 5:1-16; 6:1—7:12
52. Matthew 14:13-36
53. Matthew 21:1-17
54. Matthew 26:47-75
55. Matthew 27:15-66
56. Matthew 28:1-20
57. Mark 1:1-20
58. Mark 4:1-20
59. Luke 1:26-56; 2:1-20
60. Luke 10:25-42; 14:25-35

61. Luke 15:1-32
62. Luke 22:1-23
63. Luke 24:13-53
64. John 1:1-18
65. John 3:1-21
66. John 4:1-42
67. John 8:1-11
68. John 11:1-44
69. John 14:1-31
70. Acts 1:1-11
71. Acts 2:1-47
72. Acts 8:26-40
73. Acts 9:1-31
74. Acts 11:1-18
75. Acts 16:11-40
76. Romans 3:1-31
77. Romans 8:1-39
78. Romans 12:1-21
79. 1 Corinthians 13:1-13
80. 1 Corinthians 15:1-58
81. Ephesians 2:1-22; 6:10-20
82. Philippians 3:1—4:9
83. Colossians 3:1—4:1
84. 1 Thessalonians 4:1-18
85. Hebrews 11:1-40
86. James 1:1-27
87. James 3:1-18
88. 1 Peter 1:3-25
89. 1 John 1:1—2:17
90. Revelation 21:1—22:21

365 Days Through the Whole Bible

Date	Reference
January 1	Genesis 1:1—3:24
January 2	Genesis 4:1—5:32
January 3	Genesis 6:1—8:22
January 4	Genesis 9:1—11:32
January 5	Genesis 12:1—14:24
January 6	Genesis 15:1—17:27
January 7	Genesis 18:1—20:18
January 8	Genesis 21:1—23:20
January 9	Genesis 24:1—28:9
January 10	Genesis 28:10—30:43
January 11	Genesis 31:1—36:43
January 12	Genesis 37:1—41:57
January 13	Genesis 42:1—45:28
January 14	Genesis 46:1—50:26
January 15	Exodus 1:1—4:31
January 16	Exodus 5:1—7:13
January 17	Exodus 7:14—12:30
January 18	Exodus 12:31—18:27
January 19	Exodus 19:1—24:18
January 20	Exodus 25:1—31:18
January 21	Exodus 32:1—34:35
January 22	Exodus 35:1—40:38
January 23	Leviticus 1:1—7:38
January 24	Leviticus 8:1—10:20
January 25	Leviticus 11:1—17:16
January 26	Leviticus 18:1—22:33
January 27	Leviticus 23:1—25:55
January 28	Leviticus 26:1—27:34
January 29	Numbers 1:1—4:49
January 30	Numbers 5:1—10:10
January 31	Numbers 10:11—14:45
February 1	Numbers 15:1—21:35
February 2	Numbers 22:1—25:18
February 3	Numbers 26:1—31:54

Date	Reference
February 4	Numbers 32:1—34:29
February 5	Numbers 35:1—36:13
February 6	Deuteronomy 1:1—5:33
February 7	Deuteronomy 6:1—11:32
February 8	Deuteronomy 12:1—16:17
February 9	Deuteronomy 16:18—20:20
February 10	Deuteronomy 21:1—26:19
February 11	Deuteronomy 27:1—30:20
February 12	Deuteronomy 31:1—34:12
February 13	Joshua 1:1—5:12
February 14	Joshua 5:13—8:35
February 15	Joshua 9:1—12:24
February 16	Joshua 13:1—19:51
February 17	Joshua 20:1—24:33
February 18	Judges 1:1—3:6
February 19	Judges 3:7—8:35
February 20	Judges 9:1—12:15
February 21	Judges 13:1—16:31
February 22	Judges 17:1—21:25
February 23	Ruth 1:1—4:22
February 24	1 Samuel 1:1—3:21
February 25	1 Samuel 4:1—7:17
February 26	1 Samuel 8:1—12:25
February 27	1 Samuel 13:1—15:35
February 28	1 Samuel 16:1—17:58
March 1	1 Samuel 18:1—20:42
March 2	1 Samuel 21:1—26:25
March 3	1 Samuel 27:1—31:13
March 4	2 Samuel 1:1—4:12
March 5	2 Samuel 5:1—7:29
March 6	2 Samuel 8:1—10:19
March 7	2 Samuel 11:1—12:31
March 8	2 Samuel 13:1—14:33
March 9	2 Samuel 15:1—20:26

Date	Reference
March 10	2 Samuel 21:1—24:25
March 11	1 Kings 1:1—4:34
March 12	1 Kings 5:1—8:66
March 13	1 Kings 9:1—11:43
March 14	1 Kings 12:1—16:34
March 15	1 Kings 17:1—19:21
March 16	1 Kings 20:1—22:53
March 17	2 Kings 1:1—8:15
March 18	2 Kings 8:16—10:36
March 19	2 Kings 11:1—13:25
March 20	2 Kings 14:1—17:41
March 21	2 Kings 18:1—21:26
March 22	2 Kings 22:1—25:30
March 23	1 Chronicles 1:1—9:44
March 24	1 Chronicles 10:1—12:40
March 25	1 Chronicles 13:1—17:27
March 26	1 Chronicles 18:1—21:30
March 27	1 Chronicles 22:1—27:34
March 28	1 Chronicles 28:1—29:30
March 29	2 Chronicles 1:1—5:1
March 30	2 Chronicles 5:2—9:31
March 31	2 Chronicles 10:1—14:1
April 1	2 Chronicles 14:2—16:14
April 2	2 Chronicles 17:1—21:3
April 3	2 Chronicles 21:4—24:27
April 4	2 Chronicles 25:1—28:27
April 5	2 Chronicles 29:1—32:33
April 6	2 Chronicles 33:1—35:27
April 7	2 Chronicles 36:1-23
April 8	Ezra 1:1—2:70
April 9	Ezra 3:1—6:22
April 10	Ezra 7:1—8:36
April 11	Ezra 9:1—10:44
April 12	Nehemiah 1:1—2:10
April 13	Nehemiah 2:11—3:32
April 14	Nehemiah 4:1—7:73
April 15	Nehemiah 8:1—10:39
April 16	Nehemiah 11:1—13:31
April 17	Esther 1:1—2:23

Date	Reference
April 18	Esther 3:1—4:17
April 19	Esther 5:1—10:3
April 20	Job 1:1—2:13
April 21	Job 3:1—14:22
April 22	Job 15:1—21:34
April 23	Job 22:1—31:40
April 24	Job 32:1—37:24
April 25	Job 38:1—41:34
April 26	Job 42:1–17
April 27	Psalms 1:1—4:8
April 28	Psalms 5:1—8:9
April 29	Psalms 9:1—12:8
April 30	Psalms 13:1—16:11
May 1	Psalms 17:1—20:9
May 2	Psalms 21:1—24:10
May 3	Psalms 25:1—28:9
May 4	Psalms 29:1—32:11
May 5	Psalms 33:1—36:12
May 6	Psalms 37:1—41:13
May 7	Psalms 42:1—45:17
May 8	Psalms 46:1—49:20
May 9	Psalms 50:1—53:6
May 10	Psalms 54:1—56:13
May 11	Psalms 57:1—59:17
May 12	Psalms 60:1—62:12
May 13	Psalms 63:1—65:13
May 14	Psalms 66:1—68:35
May 15	Psalms 69:1—72:20
May 16	Psalms 73:1—75:10
May 17	Psalms 76:1—78:72
May 18	Psalms 79:1—81:16
May 19	Psalms 82:1—84:12
May 20	Psalms 85:1—89:52
May 21	Psalms 90:1—92:15
May 22	Psalms 93:1—95:11
May 23	Psalms 96:1—98:9
May 24	Psalms 99:1—101:8
May 25	Psalms 102:1—104:35
May 26	Psalms 105:1—106:48

Date	Reference
May 27	Psalms 107:1—109:31
May 28	Psalms 110:1—112:10
May 29	Psalms 113:1—115:18
May 30	Psalms 116:1—118:29
May 31	Psalms 119:1-176
June 1	Psalms 120:1—124:8
June 2	Psalms 125:1—129:8
June 3	Psalms 130:1—134:3
June 4	Psalms 135:1—137:9
June 5	Psalms 138:1—140:13
June 6	Psalms 141:1—144:15
June 7	Psalms 145:1—150:6
June 8	Proverbs 1:1-33
June 9	Proverbs 2:1-22
June 10	Proverbs 3:1-35
June 11	Proverbs 4:1-27
June 12	Proverbs 5:1-23
June 13	Proverbs 6:1-35
June 14	Proverbs 7:1-27
June 15	Proverbs 8:1-36
June 16	Proverbs 9:1-18
June 17	Proverbs 10:1-32
June 18	Proverbs 11:1-31
June 19	Proverbs 12:1-28
June 20	Proverbs 13:1-25
June 21	Proverbs 14:1-35
June 22	Proverbs 15:1-33
June 23	Proverbs 16:1-33
June 24	Proverbs 17:1-28
June 25	Proverbs 18:1-24
June 26	Proverbs 19:1-29
June 27	Proverbs 20:1-30
June 28	Proverbs 21:1-31
June 29	Proverbs 22:1-29
June 30	Proverbs 23:1-35
July 1	Proverbs 24:1-34
July 2	Proverbs 25:1-28
July 3	Proverbs 26:1-28
July 4	Proverbs 27:1-27
July 5	Proverbs 28:1-28
July 6	Proverbs 29:1-27
July 7	Proverbs 30:1-33
July 8	Proverbs 31:1-31
July 9	Ecclesiastes 1:1—2:26
July 10	Ecclesiastes 3:1—5:20
July 11	Ecclesiastes 6:1—8:17
July 12	Ecclesiastes 9:1—12:14
July 13	Song of Songs 1:1—8:14
July 14	Isaiah 1:1—6:13
July 15	Isaiah 7:1—12:6
July 16	Isaiah 13:1—18:7
July 17	Isaiah 19:1—23:18
July 18	Isaiah 24:1—27:13
July 19	Isaiah 28:1—31:9
July 20	Isaiah 32:1—35:10
July 21	Isaiah 36:1—39:8
July 22	Isaiah 40:1—48:22
July 23	Isaiah 49:1—52:12
July 24	Isaiah 52:13—55:13
July 25	Isaiah 56:1—59:21
July 26	Isaiah 60:1—66:24
July 27	Jeremiah 1:1—6:30
July 28	Jeremiah 7:1—10:25
July 29	Jeremiah 11:1—15:21
July 30	Jeremiah 16:1—20:18
July 31	Jeremiah 21:1—24:10
August 1	Jeremiah 25:1—29:32
August 2	Jeremiah 30:1—33:26
August 3	Jeremiah 34:1—38:28
August 4	Jeremiah 39:1—45:5
August 5	Jeremiah 46:1—52:34
August 6	Lamentations 1:1—5:22
August 7	Ezekiel 1:1—3:27
August 8	Ezekiel 4:1—11:25
August 9	Ezekiel 12:1—17:24
August 10	Ezekiel 18:1—24:27

Date	Reference	Date	Reference
August 11	Ezekiel 25:1—32:32	September 18	Matthew 24:1—25:46
August 12	Ezekiel 33:1—39:29	September 19	Matthew 26:1—28:20
August 13	Ezekiel 40:1—48:35	September 20	Mark 1:1—3:35
August 14	Daniel 1:1—3:30	September 21	Mark 4:1—7:23
August 15	Daniel 4:1—6:28	September 22	Mark 7:24—9:1
August 16	Daniel 7:1—12:13	September 23	Mark 9:2—10:52
August 17	Hosea 1:1—3:5	September 24	Mark 11:1—12:44
August 18	Hosea 4:1—5:15	September 25	Mark 13:1-37
August 19	Hosea 6:1—10:15	September 26	Mark 14:1—16:20
August 20	Hosea 11:1—14:9	September 27	Luke 1:1—4:13
August 21	Joel 1:1—2:27	September 28	Luke 4:14—6:49
August 22	Joel 2:28—3:21	September 29	Luke 7:1—9:50
August 23	Amos 1:1—2:16	September 30	Luke 9:51—10:42
August 24	Amos 3:1—6:14	October 1	Luke 11:1-54
August 25	Amos 7:1—9:15	October 2	Luke 12:1-59
August 26	Obadiah 1-21	October 3	Luke 13:1—14:35
August 27	Jonah 1:1—2:10	October 4	Luke 15:1—16:31
August 28	Jonah 3:1—4:11	October 5	Luke 17:1—19:27
August 29	Micah 1:1—2:13	October 6	Luke 19:28—21:38
August 30	Micah 3:1—5:15	October 7	Luke 22:1-71
August 31	Micah 6:1—7:20	October 8	Luke 23:1-56
September 1	Nahum 1:1—3:19	October 9	Luke 24:1-53
September 2	Habakkuk 1:1—3:19	October 10	John 1:1—2:12
September 3	Zephaniah 1:1—3:20	October 11	John 2:13—3:36
September 4	Haggai 1:1—2:23	October 12	John 4:1-45
September 5	Zechariah 1:1—8:23	October 13	John 4:46—6:71
September 6	Zechariah 9:1—14:21	October 14	John 7:1—10:42
September 7	Malachi 1:1—4:6	October 15	John 11:1—12:50
September 8	Matthew 1:1—4:25	October 16	John 13:1—14:31
September 9	Matthew 5:1-48	October 17	John 15:1—17:26
September 10	Matthew 6:1-34	October 18	John 18:1—19:42
September 11	Matthew 7:1-29	October 19	John 20:1—21:25
September 12	Matthew 8:1—10:42	October 20	Acts 1:1—4:37
September 13	Matthew 11:1—13:52	October 21	Acts 5:1—7:60
September 14	Matthew 13:53—15:39	October 22	Acts 8:1—12:24
September 15	Matthew 16:1—18:35	October 23	Acts 12:25—15:35
September 16	Matthew 19:1—20:34	October 24	Acts 15:36—18:23
September 17	Matthew 21:1—23:39	October 25	Acts 18:24—21:16

Date	Reference	Date	Reference
October 26	Acts 21:17—28:31	November 29	2 Timothy 1:1—2:26
October 27	Romans 1:1—3:20	November 30	2 Timothy 3:1—4:22
October 28	Romans 3:21—5:21	December 1	Titus 1:1-16
October 29	Romans 6:1—8:39	December 2	Titus 2:1-15
October 30	Romans 9:1—11:36	December 3	Titus 3:1-15
October 31	Romans 12:1—16:27	December 4	Philemon 1-25
November 1	1 Corinthians 1:1—4:21	December 5	Hebrews 1:1—2:18
November 2	1 Corinthians 5:1—6:20	December 6	Hebrews 3:1—4:13
November 3	1 Corinthians 7:1-40	December 7	Hebrews 4:14—7:28
November 4	1 Corinthians 8:1—11:1	December 8	Hebrews 8:1—10:18
November 5	1 Corinthians 11:2—14:40	December 9	Hebrews 10:19—13:25
November 6	1 Corinthians 15:1—16:24	December 10	James 1:1-27
November 7	2 Corinthians 1:1—2:11	December 11	James 2:1—3:12
November 8	2 Corinthians 2:12—7:16	December 12	James 3:13—5:20
November 9	2 Corinthians 8:1—9:15	December 13	1 Peter 1:1—2:10
November 10	2 Corinthians 10:1—13:14	December 14	1 Peter 2:11—4:19
November 11	Galatians 1:1—2:21	December 15	1 Peter 5:1-14
November 12	Galatians 3:1—4:31	December 16	2 Peter 1:1-21
November 13	Galatians 5:1—6:18	December 17	2 Peter 2:1-22
November 14	Ephesians 1:1—3:21	December 18	2 Peter 3:1-18
November 15	Ephesians 4:1—6:24	December 19	1 John 1:1—2:27
November 16	Philippians 1:1-30	December 20	1 John 2:28—4:21
November 17	Philippians 2:1-30	December 21	1 John 5:1-21
November 18	Philippians 3:1—4:1	December 22	2 John 1—3 John 14
November 19	Philippians 4:2-23	December 23	Jude 1-25
November 20	Colossians 1:1—2:23	December 24	Revelation 1:1—3:22
November 21	Colossians 3:1—4:18	December 25	Revelation 4:1—5:14
November 22	1 Thessalonians 1:1—3:13	December 26	Revelation 6:1—8:5
November 23	1 Thessalonians 4:1—5:28	December 27	Revelation 8:6—11:19
November 24	2 Thessalonians 1:1—2:17	December 28	Revelation 12:1—14:20
November 25	2 Thessalonians 3:1-18	December 29	Revelation 15:1—16:21
November 26	1 Timothy 1:1-20	December 30	Revelation 17:1—20:15
November 27	1 Timothy 2:1—3:16	December 31	Revelation 21:1—22:21
November 28	1 Timothy 4:1—6:21		

Check out these other groovy products:

Extreme Teen Bible
—Paperback $19.99
—Hardcover $24.99
—Leather $39.99
  Slimey Limey Green
  Lava Orange
  Deep Purple
  Black

Extreme Word
—Paperback $19.99
—Hardcover $29.99
  Chromium
  Neutron Blue
—Leather $39.99
  Pitch Black . . . .

Extreme Answers to Extreme Questions $12.99

Extreme A-Z: Find it in the Bible $19.99

Journal $9.99

Extreme Faith $10.99

30 Days with Jesus $7.99

Extreme Encounters $9.99

Gospel of John $1.50

Extreme for Jesus Promise Book $12.99

Check it out! Get involved!
Make a difference!

Compassion International
God can use you to change the life of a child forever.
www.ci.org

Habitat for Humanity International
A Christian organization and welcomes volunteers from all faiths
who are committed to Habitat's goal of eliminating poverty housing.
www.habitat.org

National Right to Life Organization
Taking a stand...making a difference!
www.nrlc.org

National Center for Family Literacy
Promoting family literacy services across the United States.
www.famlit.org

Big Brothers Big Sisters of America
Making a big difference. One child at a time.
www.bbbsa.org